M
T€
=

Roman Italy, 338 BC–AD 200

Roman Italy, 338 BC–AD 200
A sourcebook

Kathryn Lomas
University of Newcastle upon Tyne

UCL
PRESS

First published in 1996 by UCL Press

UCL Press Limited
University College London
Gower Street
London WC1E 6BT

The name of University College London (UCL) is a registered
trade mark used by UCL Press with the consent of the owner.

British Library Cataloguing-in-Publication Data
A catalogue record for this book is available from the British Library.

Library of Congress Cataloging-in-Publication Data are available

ISBNs: 1-85728-180-2 HB
1-85728-181-0 PB

Typeset in Elegant Garamond.
Printed and bound by
Biddles Ltd, Guildford and King's Lynn, England.

Contents

CONTENTS

vi

CONTENTS

List of illustrations

Preface

Italy plays a vitally important part in the history of Rome. Italians formed an integral part of the Roman state, in a way that was not true of any of the other peoples conquered by Rome, and as such, had a unique and privileged position in the Roman world. The social and cultural history of Italy, one of the most densely urbanized regions in pre-modern European history, is also a subject of great complexity, which is essential for understanding how Rome itself developed. Until recently, there was comparatively little ongoing research on the history of Roman Italy, despite the wealth of literary and epigraphic data and the enormous (and ever-expanding) body of archaeological data. In the last ten years, however, this situation has changed radically, and there is now a large quantity of new research on Italy and its relations with Rome, using both traditional methodology and newly developed theoretical approaches.

This volume largely arises out of several years of attempting to teach courses on Roman Italy without the benefit of a user-friendly collection of sources to recommend to students, particularly those with no knowledge of ancient languages. Its main aim is to fill this gap, giving readers without a grasp of Greek and Latin access to source material on Roman Italy, but it also seeks to put these data in context and to provide an insight into the main issues and developments of the period 338 BC–AD 200.

I would like to thank the Leverhulme Trust for their generous financial support during the preparation of this volume, and Dr T. J. Cornell and Mr J. J. Paterson for their comments and assistance.

Abbreviations

RIL	*Rendiconti del Reale Istituto Lombardo di scienze e lettere*
SCO	*Studi Classici e Orientali*
SEG	*Supplementum Epigraphicum Graecum*
SHA	Scriptores Historiae Augustae
SIG	*Sylloge Inscrptionum Graecarum*
Smallwood	*Documents illustrating the principates of Gaius, Claudius and Nero* (Bristol, Bristol Classical Press)
Susini	G. Susini: *Fonti per la Storia Greca e Romana del Salento* (Bologna, 1962)
TAPA	*Transactions of the American Philological Association*

A note on terminology and nomenclature

Some of the most common Latin terms, such as titles of magistrates and officials, have been retained in the original language. Where necessary, the meanings of these are explained in the introductory text or commentary which accompanies each chapter, or are included in the glossary. Less frequent titles are translated. Latin and Greek names are presented in their original form (name + patronymic in Greek; *praenomen* + *nomen* + *cognomen* in Latin). The standard abbreviations for *praenomina* and voting tribes are used throughout, as are the abbreviations F., L. or Lib. and S. to indicate filiation, freed status, or servile status.

Introduction

The subject of Roman Italy is one of immense importance to our understanding of ancient history, and as such, has generated an enormous amount of new research in recent years. The ever increasing volume of archaeological data, and the wide range of sites from which it is obtained, constantly forces archaeologists and historians to revaluate their understanding of the subject, and new theoretical perspectives in fields as diverse as epigraphy, architectural history, iconography and urban geography have opened up radical new ways of approaching it.

Italy was at the very heart of the Roman empire, and enjoyed a unique relation with Rome itself. Unlike the vast majority of provincials, Italians were Roman citizens and Italy was thus an integral part of the Roman state after 90–89 BC. As such, it enjoyed a highly privileged position. Indeed, Rome's relations with Italy underpinned its domination of the Mediterranean and north-west Europe in many important respects. The means by which the Romans, inhabiting a city-state with the limited administrative resources available to the pre-industrial city, were able to overcome and rule vast tracts of territory and large populations were developed during the conquest of Italy and later adapted to non-Italian circumstances. The system of alliances and colonization which Rome evolved for maintaining control of Italy was the initial basis of relations with states outside Italy. Equally importantly, the Italian alliance also gave Rome access to enormous reserves of manpower and resources which enabled the conquest of the Mediterranean to take place. Without control of Italy, Rome would have simply remained one city-state among many.

One of the most notable features about ancient Italy remains its diversity, in both physical and human geography.[1] It embraces a vast range of climatic conditions, vegetation, natural resources and topography, from the alpine regions of the far north to the fertile plains of Latium and Campania and the arid mountains of Calabria. The Appennines, forming a ridge of high and inhospitable

1

terrain which stretches the length of the peninsula, inhibit communications between the Adriatic and Ionian coasts, and effectively divide Italy into two distinct halves. The cultural development of the Adriatic coast is characterized by close contacts with the Illyrian culture of the Dalmatian coast[2] which date back to the bronze age, if not earlier, and is very different from that of Ionian Italy. The rugged terrain also meant that the development of Appennine Italy was very different from that of the lower-lying areas. Economically, the peoples of the Appennines were reliant on a mixture of small-scale agriculture and pastoralism, and the upland valleys did not have the resources to support large concentrations of population.[3] Culturally and socially, the region remained impervious to outside influences for much longer than most other parts of Italy. As a result, the region was largely non-urbanized and developed its own indigenous forms of political and social organization.[4] When the process of urbanization finally took place in the first century BC, it was more closely related to political events than to spontaneous social or cultural factors, being largely a product of Roman determination to impose their own cultural norms and stamp out the last vestiges of resistance to their rule.[5]

In contrast, lowland Italy, and in particular the fertile plains of Campania, Latium and southern Etruria, was a rich and densely populated area, characterized by the early development of the city as the primary form of social and political organization and by a density of urban settlement which was virtually unequalled in western Europe until the eighteenth century. Unlike Greece, where the natural boundaries of the territory of each city-state tended to be fairly clear even in regions of dense urban settlement, Italy was topographically divided only by the Appennines. In these lower-lying regions, there were large areas where there were no clear natural boundaries, creating a built-in potential for territorial conflict and interstate wrangling. Given that many states of Latium, Etruria and Campania were rich in fertile territory and natural resources, as well as possessing few natural barriers to deter attackers, it is not surprising that warfare in these regions was more or less endemic, as cities competed for an ever greater share of land and wealth in order to support growing populations.

The diversity of Italy was equally marked in human terms. Although all but the Etruscans and the Greeks shared a common Italic origin, the inhabitants of Italy had developed into a large number of ethnically and culturally diverse groups, each with their own distinctive identity (Illus. 2). It is not possible to draw an accurate ethnic map of Italy before the fourth century BC as literary sources (mostly Greek) disagree profoundly even on which parts of the peninsula could be defined as Italy and even more so as to who lived where, with different authors frequently giving different names to the same groups or assigning them to different parts of the country.[6] For instance, the inhabitants of south-east Italy are variously named as the Messapi, Iapyges, Sallentini, Daunii, Peucetii and Apuli. It is equally difficult to equate any of these groups with the archaeological evidence for cultural boundaries. After the end of the fourth century, things become somewhat clearer, partly because of the rapid expansion of the Oscan-speaking peoples

2

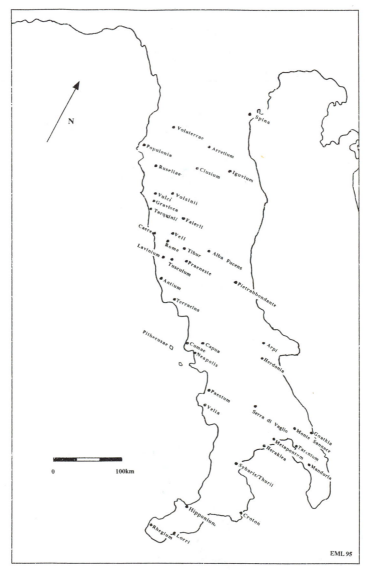

1. Pre-Roman Italy: major settlements

of the central Apennines *c*.430–400 BC, which placed most of central and southern Italy under Oscan domination. The indigenous populations were to a large
extent swamped by this and subsumed into a general Oscanized culture, just as
many of the smaller ethnic groups of southern Latium and northern Campania,
such as the Aurunci, Hirpini and Sidicini, were swallowed up by the expansion of
Rome.[7] The Messapic peoples of south-east Italy retained their Illyrian-derived
language and culture fairly intact, as did some (although not all) of the Greek

3

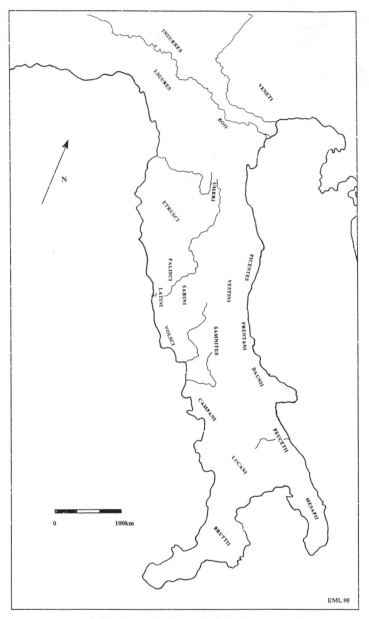

2. Pre-Roman Italy: principal ethnic groups

colonies, but southern Italy, and in particular the upland regions, was dominated by groups of Oscan origin – Lucanians and Bruttians in Calabria, Campani in Campania, Samnites in the central Appennine heartland and Vestini, Hirpini, Marrucini, Paeligni and Frentani in the northern Appennines and along the Adriatic coast. Apart from the Campani and some of the Lucanians, who ex-

4

panded into regions which were already substantially urbanized, all of these groups were characterized by a non-urban form of social and political structure which is described in more detail in Chapter 1.[8] Further north, the Sabines of the Tiber valley and the Umbrians seem also to have had very few urban settlements until a relatively late date (roughly the later first century BC) but, unlike the Samnites, both groups enjoyed good relations with Rome from the end of the fourth century and the delay in the phase of urbanization does not seem to have been caused by anything like the level of cultural resistance which took place in Samnium.

In Latium and Etruria, by contrast, cities had developed from the seventh century BC and both regions were densely urbanized.[9] Like most other ethnic groups, both comprised a number of independent states (traditionally 12 each, although in fact the numbers seem to have been somewhat larger) organized into leagues which operated a co-ordinated foreign policy and provided a framework within which conflicts and grievances could be solved. The Etruscans, whose origins are still unknown, enjoyed great wealth and power in the seventh and sixth centuries, represented in both their rich and highly Hellenized material culture and their political domination over much of Latium and Campania.[10] By the beginning of the fourth century, however, their power had waned. Control of territory south of the Tiber had been lost and the Latins, under the leadership of Rome, were inexorably extending their influence northwards at the expense of the southernmost Etruscan cities.

Inevitably, given the constraints of space, it is impossible to do more than give a brief description of the human and physical geography of ancient Italy, in providing some orientation as to the nature of the country and its ethnic composition. It is true to say, however, that in 338 BC Italy was still very diverse in its ethnic composition. Rome, which was eventually to prove such a powerful unifying force, was emerging as the major power of central Italy but had not yet achieved dominance outside Latium. Elsewhere, Capua was still a focal point for the Campanians, and Tarentum was indisputably the leading power of southern Italy.[11] The Samnites were a strong and expansionist people, and it may have been inevitable that conflict with Rome would arise as Roman power extended south into Campania, while the Etruscans remained a power to be reckoned with until the end of the fourth century. In southern Italy, the rise of Rome remained largely irrelevant until 286 BC. For the Greeks, the agenda was dominated by competition among themselves and with their Oscan and Messapian neighbours for domination and control of resources, and by events in Sicily and Greece.

Despite this diversity and the often bitter wars of conquest, there was also a very strong emotional and ideological bond between Italy and Rome. The differences between regions and ethnic groups, each of which had its own strong sense of identity, remained important, and there was a long gap between Roman conquest and the cultural Romanization of the peninsula, but the non-Roman cultures of Italy finally began to erode in the century following political unification.[12] By the reign of Augustus, the identification of Rome with Italy had become a powerful part of the governing ideology. As a counterpoise to the increasing influence on Antony of Hellenistic Greek culture, which was characterized in Augustan propaganda as pernicious and corrupting, Augustus constructed a whole programme of symbolism in public art and architecture[13] and in literature[14] which extolled the virtue of ancient Roman and Italian *mores* and equated the regime with this concept of Italian identity. There was, therefore, a strong and ever growing connection between Italian and Roman identities in the principate, although this must be balanced against the Hellenization of some aspects of elite culture and the growing influence of provincial elites during the second century AD.

Given the preponderance of sources from the late republic and principate and our reliance on material written from the Roman point of view, it is all too easy to forget that Rome did not exercise pan-Italian dominance until the early third century BC, and that the establishment of this dominance was by no means a foregone conclusion. Our image of Rome is of the huge metropolis and world power which it later became, but this is true only of imperial Rome. The imposing public buildings and monuments which are still extant date to the principate. Republican Rome was a much smaller and less well appointed city, which first began to acquire monumental and lavishly decorated buildings towards the end of the second century BC. Similarly, the notion that Rome and its manoeuvrings was the central issue of Italian history is not true until the conquest of the peninsula was completed in the early third century. Even during the Punic Wars, there is a distinct sense that the will of Rome was only one factor among many in determining the actions of other Italians, and it is really only with the reimposition of Roman authority after the defeat of Hannibal that Rome fully established domination over Italy. Paradoxically, it was this tightening of Rome's grip over the Italians, combined with widening differences in status between Romans and Italians and the increasingly obvious economic and political benefits of Roman citizenship, which led to the breakdown of relations between Rome and the Italian alliance, culminating in the Social War of 90–88 BC and the enfranchisement of the whole of Italy.

One of the difficulties of writing on any aspect of Roman history which spans both republic and principate is the disappearance of evidence which lends itself to narrative history after the civil wars. However, this dichotomy, enunciated by Millar[15], is not necessarily a major problem for the study of Roman Italy. It is indeed difficult to escape the constraints of narrative when dealing with the Roman conquest, but after this point the subject is best served by a thematic approach for both republic and principate. The principal issue for the history of Italy during the Punic Wars is the effectiveness of Rome's system of alliances and the points of weakness revealed by the stress of Hannibal's invasion, while the dominant issues of the second and first centuries BC are the causes of the breakdown of relations between Rome and the allies, and the beginnings of political integration between Italy and Rome in the aftermath of the Social War. Given that the settlement after the Social War also established the city as the primary form of social, political and economic organization throughout Italy, the history of Italy during the principate can best be approached by examining the principal aspects of civic life and the forms of contact between cities and Rome.

One major aspect of Roman Italy which is not covered separately in the following chapters is that of Romanization – the process of cultural, as opposed to political, integration with Rome – which is notoriously difficult both to define and to illustrate by extracts from literature. The problem lies in the fact that it is a long-term process which takes place at different rates, and manifests itself in different ways, according to its local context. As already mentioned, the Samnites were highly resistant to adopting Roman culture and forms of organization. They maintained their indigenous way of life until Rome crushed their revolt during the Social War and forcibly imposed Romanized, urbanized, structures of government. In the generation after this, the Oscan language fell out of use, traditional religious centres were abandoned, and as the Samnite nobility began to penetrate the ranks of the senatorial order at Rome, they transferred all their energies to creating a Romanized civic life.[16] In contrast, the Greek colonies on the Bay of Naples had good relations with Rome from the fourth century onwards and initially appeared to assimilate, but in the early empire, when familiarity with Greek culture had become a prerequisite for the cultured Roman noble, Greek language and culture made a reappearance at places such as Naples, trading on this interest in Hellenism.[17]

These two examples give some insight into how complex the processes of cultural assimilation can be. The mechanisms by which they took place are equally obscure, particularly below the level of the elite. Roman colonization, and the related insistence on cities as the favoured form of political life, was undoubtedly influential. The smaller Roman colonies were primarily military and strategic in purpose, but the larger ones, and all the later foundations, were an overt form of cultural reproduction. Those which were founded on open sites were laid out as ideal Romanized cities of the type which became commonplace all over the northern and western provinces. Typically, they had a square or rectangular shape and a gridiron street plan based on two main roads intersecting at right angles at the centre of the city, the point at which the forum was located, and a selection of typically Roman buildings, usually with a temple to the Roman cult of Jupiter Capitolinus prominent among them. Even where the terrain was notably steep, as at Cosa,[18] the regularity of the city layout could be a triumph of determination over topography. A Roman-style constitution and legal system was also routinely imposed.

Even in cities which were not colonies, the extent to which the physical structures evolved in the generation after the Social War to reflect increasing Romanization is noticeable. Urban plans were regularized, city walls were demolished and rebuilt in a uniformly Roman style, as stone structures with guard turrets at regular intervals,[19] and Roman public amenities – for instance theatres, amphitheatres, baths and monumentalized fora with special buildings for senate meetings, legal hearings and markets – were added.[20] The reasons for this are not yet fully understood, although they seem to lie in the competitive nature of elite society. Peer polity interaction – a model which explains simultaneous appearance of phenomena over a geographical area in terms of interstate competition[21] – suggests that cities may have been competing for status within regions by adopting perceived high-status symbols associated with the ruling power. Equally, the impetus may have come from realization among the elite that those who directed their munificence into appropriately Romanized channels could increase their chances of acceptance into the senatorial elite at Rome.[22]

These explanations are merely two possible approaches to the problem, neither of which is likely to address fully the complex dynamics of elite behaviour and cultural assimilation. The only thing that can be said for certain about Romanization is that the crucial period of transition within Italy occurred between the Social War and the death of Augustus – a period during which Latin became the dominant language of Italy and in which many aspects of regional culture became subsumed under a general veneer of *Romanitas*, reflecting an increasing level of assimilation between the elites of Rome and Italy. One point which must be stressed however, is that Romanization was by no means a one-way street. As the example of the Bay of Naples, quoted above, shows, there could be a very complex interplay between cultures, and there is powerful evidence that in some fields Italians were predominant in shaping Roman culture. This is particularly true in terms of the emergence of a Roman literature and intellectual tradition in the second and first centuries BC.[23] The most notable feature of the intellectual history of the late republic is that the vast majority of the prominent figures are not Roman but Italian.

Finally, a word must be added about the aims and scope of this volume and the criteria for selecting sources. The principal aim in selecting material is to present a collection of short texts and excerpts, including both literary and epigraphic sources, which will illustrate the major themes in the political, social, cultural and economic development of Roman Italy, and which will give insight into the forces which shaped Italian development during the period between the Roman conquest and the end of the second century AD. It is not, however, intended to provide a narrative history of the Roman conquest. Another major absentee from this volume is the city of Rome itself. The history and development of the city of Rome is an extensive topic in its own right, and the very size to which the city grew makes it anomalous in its social and economic development, even leaving aside the fact of its role as world power. Given that sources for subjects such as Roman politics and foreign policy are already easily available, and that a very small number of urban centres dominate existing literature on Roman cities – notably Pompeii, Ostia and Rome itself – this volume will focus on those aspects of Roman history which affect Italy and on giving access to sources relating to a wider range of sites. Inevitably, difficulties in presentation of non-literary material have dictated that emphasis is on inscriptions and literary sources, but the vast importance of archaeology to our understanding of ancient Italy cannot be overstated. Wherever possible, important archaeological evidence, and its relation to the literary sources, has been discussed in the introduction to each chapter, and the bibliography contains works analyzing the archaeology of Roman Italy.

The other limiting feature, the chronological reference points, must inevitably be arbitrary to some extent. The starting point – 338 BC – is the date at which Rome first established a coherent legal and administrative basis for controlling conquered territory, although the actual process of conquest had been going on for some considerable time before that. Conversely, AD 200 does not mark any particular event, but the third century AD was a time of rapid change and crisis throughout the empire which resulted in the undermining of Italy's pre-eminent position and the emergence of a very different society. The sources for Italy during this period of change and in late antiquity, while of great interest, lie outside the scope of this volume.

CHAPTER ONE

The rise of Rome: Italy 338–200 BC

This chapter aims to give a specifically Italian perspective by relating extracts to the relations between Rome and her allies in Italy, and to the operation of the system of alliances. It does not set out to provide a basic narrative of the Roman conquest of Italy and the Punic Wars, or a complete set of sources for the wars and diplomatic history of this period, as this material is already covered in numerous other works.

The 140 years covered are crucial in that they were the years in which Rome gained and consolidated control over Italy, which was the basis of the ultimate conquest of a world empire, and also the years in which the effectiveness of Roman domination of Italy was put to the test. In 338 BC, Rome was becoming established as the most powerful state of central Italy, controlling Latium and large parts of northern Campania and southern Etruria, but was not yet dominant elsewhere. The Latin war, which ended in 338, broke the power of the Latin league and allowed Rome to create a radical new system of treaties and alliances, reinforced with programmes of colonization, which is discussed in more detail in Chapter 2. The following years were a time of consolidation, in which Rome fought numerous campaigns to extend control over Campania and Etruria and to pacify and subdue existing allies who showed signs of restlessness, but in 327 BC, a much greater conflict began, which was to set Rome well on the way to control of the whole of peninsular Italy.

The Samnites, against whom Rome fought no less than five wars, all of them bitter and long drawn-out, were very unlike Romans in many respects.[1] They inhabited the central and southern Appennines, an inhospitable and mountainous region, living in dispersed communities rather than cities. Their language was Oscan, an Italic dialect common to the four Samnite peoples and to the Lucanians, Bruttians, Frentani, Paeligni and Vestini, all of whom originated in a rapid and large-scale expansion of the Samnite population in the fifth century BC

– a demographic explosion during which a large part of central and southern Italy came under Oscan rule. Apart from the Campanians, who migrated into an already urbanized territory, and small numbers of Lucanians and Bruttians, the majority of Oscan peoples were not urbanized, although they had many of the administrative and political features of a city-state. The Samnites, for instance, were a league of four distinct ethnic groups, each of which were subdivided into larger units called the *touto* and smaller ones called the *pagus*. At each level, there appear to have been mechanisms for assembling deliberative councils and electing magistrates – the *meddices* (sing. *meddix*) – who had similar responsibilities to the magistrates of a city, ranging from basic administrative tasks to decisions on peace and war, levy and command of armies and the administration of justice. Each community had its own fortified strong-point for defensive purposes, but most state activity centred on religious sanctuaries, the most important of which were large and elaborate complexes of buildings. This group of Oscan peoples developed their own distinct ethnic identities. The southernmost – Lucanians and Bruttians – were shaped, both in their culture and their political agenda, by their relations with the Greeks who controlled the coast,[2] and the Campanians were deeply influenced by both the Greeks and the Etruscans.[3] Nevertheless, there were strong resemblances in the ways in which they evolved, and there is a perceptible tendency for Oscan peoples to band together.

A conflict between Rome and the Samnites was to some extent inevitable, given that they were both vigorous and expansionist peoples whose territorial interests were leading them in the same direction. In 354 BC a treaty, for which evidence is very slight, was made between Rome and the Samnites which appears to have established the river Liris, which flows from Samnium into northern Campania, as the boundary between Roman and Samnite spheres of interest.[4] By 341, however, Rome was developing diplomatic connections well south of this, notably with Capua. A short war, resulting in the re-establishment of the treaty, may have been fought at this point, although sources are so poor and contradictory that the very existence of this first Samnite war has been called into question.[5] The serious hostilities began in 327 BC, when the inhabitants of Campania took exception to the foundation of a Roman colony at Fregellae and drove the colonists out. Rome initially declared war only on the Greek city of Naples, but anti-Roman feeling was rife throughout Campania and the Samnites had declared their interest in supporting Naples and the Campanians.[6] Livy, who is our main source, characterizes this from the start as the war which would decide who ruled Italy [No. 3]. This judgement is assisted by a large measure of hindsight, but it is certainly true that it was the Samnite wars which set Rome on the path to conquest of Italy. Both the second (327–303 BC) and third (301–295) Samnite wars were characterized by short periods of intense conflict punctuated by long interludes of skirmishing and diplomatic manoeuvring, during which both sides tried to build up blocks of allied territory which would limit and outflank the other.[7] Rome had the additional problem of the Etruscans, who were not Roman allies but who were bound to neutrality by a series of fixed-term

12

truces which they regularly broke in order to support the Samnites[8]. The result, however, was that in addition to gaining control of Samnium and adding a great deal more territory to the Roman *ager publicus*, Rome also acquired a network of allies as far afield as Umbria and Apulia, initially formed to outflank the Samnites. Some of the confiscated land was used for an extensive programme of colonization which underpinned Rome's grip on central and southern Italy, and the new allies greatly increased Rome's manpower.[9]

The final element in the conquest of Italy was the Pyrrhic war (281–270 BC), during which Rome defeated the Greeks of Italy, led by Tarentum and assisted by Pyrrhus, the king of Epirus and the leading general of his day, and also put down further risings by the Samnites and Etruscans.[10] Although Rome showed relatively little interest in the Greeks once they had been subjugated and brought into alliance [No. 11], the Samnites were harshly punished. The Samnite league may have been broken up into its four component parts at this date, more Samnite territory was annexed, and a colony was established at Beneventum. The Caudini, who controlled a strategically sensitive area on the borders of Campania were forced to abandon their indigenous way of life and form themselves into cities on lines dictated by Rome.[11]

The history of the Samnites is vital to the understanding of Rome's relationship with Italy before 89 BC. Of all Italian peoples, they were the ones who came closest to preventing Roman domination. Like the Romans, they were vigorously expansionist, with a wide network of alliances and diplomatic contacts which gave them domination of the central and southern Appennines, as well as access to the economically and strategically vital region of Campania. They also had a profound sense of their own political and cultural identity, fostered by the geographical impenetrability of Samnium, which made them extremely resistant both to conquest and to cultural assimilation. Except where imposed by Rome, urbanization did not take place in Samnium until after the Social War, and Oscan language and culture also persisted until the late republic. They remained only grudgingly allied to Rome and the history of the Roman republic is punctuated by signs of Samnite disaffection – during Hannibal's invasion, most of the secessions from Rome occurred amongst the Oscan-speaking peoples of Samnium, Lucania and Campania, but the final flare-up of Samnite independence occurred in 90 BC. The most persistent of the Social War rebels were the Samnites and some of the Campanians.[12] After this, however, the independent identity of Samnium finally began to disappear. The war, and the subsequent proscriptions of Sulla, took a great toll of the Samnite nobility, while the imposition of Roman law and a Romanized urban framework on Italy as a result of enfranchisement finally undermined non-Roman cultures, political structures and social systems in Samnium as in other regions. By the Augustan period, the Oscan language was no longer spoken and the Samnites had been absorbed into municipal Italy.

The later third century was an equally crucial period in Roman history, as this was the point at which the Roman alliance received its first real test, and also the point at which it is possible for historians to look in detail at how the alliance worked in practice, what strains affected it, and why parts of it broke down.

As the period 338–270 is dominated by the Samnites, so the period 264–200 is dominated by conflict with Carthage. The First Punic War (264–240 BC) was the catalyst which led Rome to extend her power outside Italy for the first time, and which brought the first non-Italian region – Sicily – under Roman control, initially using a modified system of alliances and clientship, but later as the first Roman province. The war was fought almost entirely in Sicily, or at sea, and had little impact on Italy, other than that generated by Rome's military levies [Nos 14–15]. The Second Punic War (218–200 BC) was a completely different case. Although the initial *casus belli* was a dispute over Rome's growing interests in Spain and an attack by Carthage on one of Rome's Spanish allies, Hannibal's spectacular march across the Alps ensured that the main campaigns of the war were fought in Italy. Although the conflict eventually spread to much of the Mediterranean, embracing Spain, Sicily, North Africa and Macedon, the crucial issue was the outcome of the war in Italy. Livy's history of the war is the only extended account available to us of the Roman alliance in operation, and allows a unique insight into how Rome's control of Italy worked in practice, and at a time of great pressure. It also allows examination of the tensions already inherent in the alliance, through analysis of the patterns of secession from Rome and grievances of disaffected allies. Defeats for Rome at the battles of Trebia (217), Trasimene (217) and Cannae (216) undermined any claims to be able to defend the allies from Hannibal and triggered a wave of defections from the alliance. A central core of Latins and loyal Italians remained, and eventually Rome regained the vast majority of secessionist states, either by conquest or voluntary change of sides. By 203 BC, Hannibal had been forced back into Bruttium, where he retained some support to the last, but was then recalled to Africa to assist in the defence of Carthage from Scipio's invading army.

The main points of interest about the Punic Wars for the study of Roman Italy concern the workings of Rome's alliance with the Italians. The war placed a severe strain on this in several respects. For the states which were loyal to Rome throughout, there was a drain on military manpower, needed both to supplement Roman forces and to defend individual states from Hannibal.[13] The emergence of another power in Italy, explicitly posing as an alternative to Rome, also exposed the weaknesses of the alliance and highlighted the factors which might break it up. Areas such as Samnium, Campania and the Hellenized south of Italy were always likely to be vulnerable, having a long history of resistance to Rome and a powerful sense of regional, non-Latin, identity. Samnium and the regions to the south of it were also fairly recent additions to Rome's network of alliances, and thus less committed to Rome. The very distance of some of these states from Rome made them much easier to detach, either by force or by persuasion, and the tenuousness of Rome's claim to be able to protect allies was graphically underlined during 215–212. The Bruttian city of Petelia was openly told by the senate that Rome was unable to assist with the defence of the besieged city and that it must look after itself [No. 29]. In contrast, the Latin colonies can be seen to be the core of Rome's control of Italy. None of these made any overt moves towards defecting, but the extravagant expressions of horror by the consuls of 209 when 12 colonies refused any further military assistance and the heavy punishment visited on these from 204 onwards [Nos 34 and 37] illustrate how vital these states were to Rome, and the extent to which they were seen by the senate as such.[14]

The extent to which Rome's strength lay in domination of Italy was fully appreciated by Hannibal. Both Polybios and Livy stress that on crossing the Alps, he immediately implemented policies designed to drive a wedge between Rome and the allies. Allied prisoners were well treated, released for minimal ransom and treated to a discourse on Hannibal as liberator of Italy from the clutches of Rome, while Roman captives were held in harsher conditions [No. 21]. Initially this had little effect, although there were large-scale secessions after the battle of Cannae exposed Roman weakness and removed any possibility of Roman protection from much of southern Italy. The most striking thing about Hannibal's tactic is not that he misjudged the nature of the relationship between Rome and the Italians, as some commentators have suggested, but that his whole approach is formed by contemporary Greek conventions. The slogan "the freedom of the Greeks" was one which was widely used in the Hellenistic world to justify many military and diplomatic manoeuvrings and numerous dynasts in Greece and Asia Minor justified their policies by claiming to be liberating the Greeks from foreign control. Carthage was substantially Hellenized by this date, and Hannibal's liberation rhetoric is not a sign that he genuinely regarded the Italians as oppressed by Rome but that he was couching his appeal to them in the diplomatic conventions of the Greek world.[15]

The factors that could be important in driving a city to revolt obviously vary widely according to individual circumstance, but some of the instances treated in detail by Livy give some insight into the process. In his description of the defection of Capua [Nos 26–28], and those of the Greek cities of Locri, Croton and Tarentum, the important features highlighted are a strong network of local contacts and alliances, independent of Rome, and a high level of internal political conflict and instability.[16] Not surprisingly, given the date at which Livy was writing, political patterns are described in terms of late republican Rome, contrasting the sound pro-Roman *optimates* with the demagogic and unreliable anti-Roman *populares*. Clearly this is anachronistic and in many cases the factional politics described do not fit this model, but this need not detract from the more general point that there was a fierce and often violent level of political disagreement in many Italian states which polarized around the issue of support for Rome or for Hannibal. One thing that is clear is that the global issue of whether to remain loyal to Rome or to support Hannibal was not necessarily the central point for some cities, but was merely the issue around which local considerations and internal political divisions crystallized. At Capua, Pacuvius Calavius, a man with close kinship ties with the Roman nobility, used it as an opportunity to bring himself and his faction to power and to secure treaty terms more advantageous than those granted by Rome [Nos 26–28]. At Croton, the long-standing animosities between the Greeks and their Bruttian neighbours were exploited by Hannibal to persuade the city to secede to him,[17] and there are clear indications that the secession was also connected with events in Locri, further along the Calabrian coast, raising the possibility of connections between the two states [Nos 30–32]. The evidence seems to point to a very clever exploitation by Hannibal of local factors, both in interstate contacts or conflicts and in domestic politics.

The aftermath of the war ushered in a period of profound change, during which Rome's acquisition of an overseas empire, and the economic upheavals brought about by agrarian developments, the stresses of large-scale warfare and the upsurge of trade and urbanization, fundamentally altered the nature of both Rome and Italy. It also tilted the balance of power within Italy decisively, and overtly, in favour of Rome. Fierce reprisals were meted out to allies which had rebelled. Treaties were reimposed as cities were reconquered, sometimes with added penalties. In Campania, anti-Roman leaders were killed, imprisoned or exiled and much territory was confiscated. An example was made of Capua, the most powerful of the secessionist states [Nos 35, 62]. The aristocracy were massacred and only the common people were allowed to remain. All the land and buildings became the property of the Roman state and Capua ceased to exist as a political entity, being administered directly from Rome. A large-scale programme of colonization was instituted, to create a network of cities guarding the coast against further invasion and to pacify and Romanize turbulent regions. Many areas of Italy were placed under the supervision of Roman commissioners. Even states which had not revolted but whose loyalty was thought to be compromised were punished, such as the 12 Latin colonies which withdrew their contributions to the Roman army in 209 [No. 34]. As will be discussed in more detail in Chapter 4, the overall result of the Punic Wars was to establish Roman dominance in the Mediterranean and to create an unchallengeable and overt hegemony in Italy which ultimately contained the seeds of its own destruction.

The Samnites

1. Livy 9.13.7

The Samnites, who at that time lived in villages in the mountains, ravaged the places on the plain and along the coast, whose cultivators they despised as softer and, as often happens, similar to their place of origin, just as they themselves were rough mountain men.

The Samnite Wars

2. Livy 8.22.1–2 (328 BC)

The following year, during which P. Plautius Proculus and P. Cornelius Scapula were consuls, was not distinguished by any events, either in the field or at home, except that a colony was sent to Fregellae – to land which had belonged to Signia, then to the Volsci.

3. Livy 8.22.7–23.10

This city [Naples], committed many acts of hostility against the Romans living in the *Ager Campanus* and *Ager Falernus*, partly relying on their own strength, partly on Samnite infidelity to their alliance with Rome, and partly on the plague which was reported to be attacking the city of Fregellae. Therefore, when L. Cornelius Lentulus and Q. Publilius Philo (for the second time) were consuls, fetials were sent to Palaepolis to seek redress, and when they brought back from the Greeks, a people stronger in words than in deeds, a fierce reply, the People, on the authority of the Senate, ordered war to be made . . . The senate was assured by both consuls that there was very little hope of peace with the Samnites: Publilius reported that 2,000 Nolan troops and 4,000 Samnites had been taken into Palaepolis, more by Nolan force than willingness on the part of the Greeks; Cornelius reported that the Samnite magistrates had announced a levy and that the whole of Samnium had risen in revolt, and the neighbouring peoples, Privernum, Fundi and Formiae, were being sounded out without any ambiguity. Having decided, on account of these reports, to send envoys to the Samnites prior to declaring war on them, the Samnites sent back a fierce response. Furthermore, they accused the Romans of harming them, and did not neglect to clear up those charges brought against themselves: the Greeks were not receiving any official advice or assistance from them, nor had Fundi or Formiae been suborned; indeed, they had enough strength of their own, if they wished to fight. Nevertheless, they were not able to hide the annoyance of the Samnite state that Fregellae, which they had captured and razed, should be restored by the Roman people, and a colony set up in Samnite territory which the colonists themselves called Fregellae; this insult and injury to them, if it was not undone by the perpetrators themselves, they would drive out themselves, with all force. When the Roman envoy called upon them to debate the issue with common allies and friends, the Samnites replied "Why do we speak ambiguously? Romans, our quarrels will not be decided by the words of envoys or the arbitration of any man, but by Mars, on the Campanian plain on which we will meet, and by arms and common strife. Then let us draw up camp against camp, between Capua and Suessula, and decide whether Samnite or Roman will rule Italy."

[327 BC. War with Naples and the Samnites. In this passage Livy refers to Naples as Palaepolis, explaining that at this date Naples consisted of two physically discrete settlements, Palaepolis and Neapolis, which were only unified after the end of this war in 326 BC.]

4. Livy 8.25.3 (326 BC)

For the Lucanians and the Apulians, peoples who had not had any contact with the Roman People until then, placed themselves under their protection and promised arms and men for war, and were therefore received into a treaty of friendship.

5. Livy 9.26.1–5 (314 BC)

In the same year, Luceria went over to the Samnites, having betrayed its Roman garrison to the enemy. The betrayers did not go unpunished for long: there was a Roman army not far away which captured the city, which was located on a plain, at the first assault. The Lucerians and the Samnites were killed; anger was such that in Rome, when the senate was debating the sending of colonists to Luceria, there were many who advocated destroying the city. Apart from hatred, which was strong against people who had been captured twice, the distance made them shrink from sending citizens so far from home amongst such hostile peoples. However, the view that colonists should be sent won. 2,500 were sent.

6. Livy 9.29.1–2 (312 BC)

When the war with the Samnites was drawing to a close, but the Roman senators had not yet laid aside their anxiety about it, rumour of a war with the Etruscans grew up. At that time there was no other people (apart from Gallic revolts) whose arms were more terrifying, as much for their numbers of men as for the closeness of their territory.

7. Livy 9.45.1–4

In the consulship of P. Sulpicius Saverrio and P. Sempronius Sophus, the Samnites sent envoys to Rome to ask for peace, either seeking to end or to delay the war. . . . In that year, the Roman army marched through Samnium and since it was peaceful and supplies [for the army] were given willingly, their old treaty was restored to the Samnites.

[304 BC. End of the second Samnite War. The treaty referred to is probably one signed in 354 BC, the main purpose of which was to demarcate territory by establishing the river Liris as the boundary between Roman and Samnite spheres of influence.]

8. Livy 10.12.1–2 (299 BC)

The debate of the senate was short; all unanimously supported making a treaty with the Lucanians and taking issue with the Samnites. They replied kindly to the Lucanians and a treaty was made; The fetials were sent to order the Samnites to leave allied territory and remove their army from the lands of the Lucanians; they were met by messengers for the Samnites who said that if they appeared before the Samnite assembly, they would not get away unharmed. After this had been heard at Rome, the senate advised a war against the Samnites and the people commanded it.

9. Livy, *Periochae* 11

Assisted by [Fabius Maximus'] advice and help, his son [Fabius Gurges] the consul triumphed, having defeated the Samnites; C. Pontius, the Samnite general was executed after being led in triumph. . . . The Samnites sued for peace and the treaty with them was renewed for the fourth time.

[295 BC. End of the third Samnite War.]

The Pyrrhic War

10. Livy, *Periochae* 12 (280 BC)

The Samnites revolted. Several battles were fought against them and the Lucanians, Bruttians and Etruscans, by a number of generals. Pyrrhus, king of Epirus, came to Italy to bring assistance to the Tarentines. When a Campanian legion, with Decius Vibellius as its commander, was sent to the Rhegines as a garrison, he killed the Rhegines and occupied Rhegium.

11. Livy, *Periochae* 15 (270 BC)

The Tarentines, having been conquered, were given peace and freedom. The Campanian legion which had occupied Rhegium was besieged and, having been forced to surrender, was executed. . . . Colonies were founded at Ariminum in Picenum and Beneventum in Samnium. At this time, the Roman people first

19

began to use silver [coinage]. The Umbrians and Sallentines were beaten and their surrender was accepted.

12. *Inscriptiones Italiae* 13.3.79

Appius Claudius C. F. Caecus, censor, consul twice, dictator, interrex three times, praetor twice, curule aedile twice, quaestor, military tribune three times. He captured a number of towns from the Samnites, and defeated an army of Sabines and Etruscans. He prevented peace being made with King Pyrrhus. During his censorship, he paved the Via Appia and built an aqueduct for Rome . . .

[3rd century BC. Restored in the Augustan period. Arretium. Inscription honouring Appius Claudius Caecus.]

Treaty with Carthage

13. Polybios 3.24.3 (348 BC)

There is to be friendship on these terms between the Romans and their allies, and the Carthaginians and Uticans and their allies . . . And if the Carthaginians capture any city in Latium which is not subject to the Romans, they may keep the property and captives but must give up the city. If a Carthaginian captures anyone who is a member of a city with a written treaty with Rome, but not an ally, he may not bring him into any Roman harbour. If he does, a Roman can touch him and free him . . .

First Punic War

14. Polybios 1.20.7 (264 BC)

When they [the Romans] first attempted to send their army across to Messana, not only did they lack any decked ships, but they had no warships of any kind, not even a single ship; borrowing pentekontors and triremes from the Tarentines and Locrians, and also from the Velians and Neapolitans, they transported their troops across in them, at considerable risk.

15. Polybios 1.20.9–11

. . . for the first time they began to build ships, 100 quinqueremes and 20 triremes. As the shipwrights were entirely inexperienced in building quinqueremes, since none of the communities of Italy used such ships at that date, the enterprise caused much difficulty to the Romans . . .

[264 BC. Transport of a Roman force to Messana to defend it against the Carthaginians. Polybios stresses the reliance of Rome on allied naval resources in the early stages of the First Punic War. Traditionally, only two squadrons of Roman warships were maintained under the command of the *duoviri navales*. By 264 BC, the office of *duovir navalis* had fallen into abeyance and the Greeks were the nearest source of sea power, but none of them had any quinqueremes.]

Roman manpower

16. Polybios 2.24

I must make it clear from the facts how large the resources were that Hannibal dared to attack, and how great was the power which he boldly confronted; despite this, he came close enough to his aim to inflict major disasters on the Romans. At any rate, I must proceed to describe the levy and the number of troops available to them at that time. Each consul commanded four legions of Roman citizens, composed of 5,200 infantry and 300 cavalry each. The allied troops in each consular army totalled 30,000 infantry and 2,000 cavalry. The Sabines and Etruscans, who had temporarily come to Rome's aid, had 4,000 cavalry and more than 50,000 infantry. The Romans gathered these troops and stationed them on the border of Etruria, commanded by a praetor. The levy of the Umbrians and Sarsinates, who lived in the Apennines, totalled around 20,000, and there were 20,000 Veneti and Cenomani. [. . .] The lists of men able to fight that were sent back were as follows: Latins, 80,000 infantry and 5,000 cavalry; Samnites, 70,000 infantry and 7,000 cavalry; Iapygians and Messapians, 50,000 infantry and 16,000 cavalry; Lucanians, 30,000 infantry and 3,000 cavalry; Marsi, Marrucini, Frentani and Vestini, 20,000 infantry and 4,000 cavalry.

[225 BC. Total survey of Italian manpower carried out in response to a threatened Gallic invasion. cf. no. 52.]

17. Livy 22.11.7–8

The consul was ordered to set out for Ostia immediately and man the ships which were at Rome or at Ostia with soldiers or allied marines, and to follow the enemy fleet and defend the Italian coast. A great force of men was conscripted in Rome; even freedmen, who had children and were of military age, were sworn in.

[217 BC. Emergency levy to make good the losses suffered at the battle of Trasimene.]

18. Livy 22.36.1–4 (216 BC)

The army was increased; how big a force was added to the infantry and to the cavalry I cannot say for certain, as authors differ both on the number and type of forces. Some say 10,000 new troops were conscripted as reinforcements, others that four new legions were raised, to make [a total of] eight; some say that the

21

number of infantry and cavalry in a legion was increased by 1,000 infantry and 100 cavalry, so that it was composed of 5,000 infantry and 300 cavalry, and that allies gave double the number of cavalry but the same number of infantry, and that at the time of the battle of Cannae, there were 87,200 men under arms.

19. Livy 22.32.4–9

When, impeded by winter, the war had ground to a halt at Gereonium, Neapolitan envoys came to Rome. They brought 40 gold dishes of great weight into the senate house with them and delivered a speech which said: that they realized that the treasury of the Roman people was drained by war and, since it was being fought as much for the cities and lands of the allies as for the power of Rome, the leader and protector of Italy, the Neapolitans had decided that it was right that they should assist the Roman people with that gold which had been left by their ancestors to enrich them and adorn their temples. If they had believed their own persons had value, they would have given themselves just as willingly.

[216 BC. The implication of this passage is that Naples, although an ally, was not obliged to make regular contributions of either money or manpower to Rome but was offering the gold as a favour. In this case, the senate accepted one of the pieces of plate, but a similar offer from Paestum (22.36.9) was declined, possibly because Paestum, as a Latin ally, was already committed to a substantial military levy.]

Hannibal and the allies

20. Livy 21.5.1

From the day on which he was appointed general, Hannibal, as if he were ordered to take Italy as his *provincia* and make war on Rome [. . .] decided to make war on Saguntum.

[219 BC. Appointment of Hannibal to lead the Carthaginian forces in Spain. The word *provincia* is used here in its Roman sense of a sphere of command rather than a block of territory.]

21. Polybios 3.77.4–7

Hannibal, while wintering in Cisalpine Gaul, kept the Romans whom he had captured in battle imprisoned, giving them just enough to eat; but he continued to show great leniency to those from the allies and later called a meeting of them and spoke to them, stating that he had not come to wage war on them but on the Romans on their behalf, and so if they were sensible, they would enter into friendship with him, since he had come principally to restore the freedom of the peoples of Italy and also to assist them to regain the cities and territories which had been taken from them by the Romans. Having spoken in this manner, he sent them all to their homes without ransom, his intention in doing this being to win over the peoples of Italy to his side and also to turn their loyalties against Rome . . .

[218–17 BC. Both Livy (22.58) and Polybios agree that undermining the Roman alliance in Italy was central to Hannibal's strategy. His lack of success in promoting revolt before the crushing Roman defeat at Cannae in 216 has led to this being perceived as a major misunderstanding of Roman–Italian relations. However, the analysis of the alliance as the source of Rome's strength is perfectly correct.]

22. Livy 22.13.1–3

Hannibal crossed from the territory of the Hirpini into Samnium, ravaged the territory of Beneventum and captured the city of Telesia, in order to provoke the Roman general by his actions so that, angered by such undeserved disasters of the allies, he could be drawn into an equal conflict. Amongst the many Italian allies who had been captured at Trasimene and released by Hannibal were three Campanian knights who had been induced on many occasions by gifts and promises to recommend Hannibal to their people. These now declared that if Hannibal moved the army into Campania, he would have the possibility of taking Capua . . .

[217 BC. Beginnings of defection from Rome in Campania. Hannibal's indecision at this point lost him the initiative and he came close to being trapped by Fabius, the Roman general, before retreating into Apulia for the winter.]

Reasons for revolt

23. Livy 21.25.1–3

Meanwhile in Italy, nothing more than the report of the legates from Massilia that Hannibal had crossed the Ebro had reached Rome, when the Boii incited the Insubres to revolt as if he had already crossed the Alps, not just because of their long-standing anger against the Roman people but because they could hardly endure the foundation of the colonies of Placentia and Cremona, near the river Po, on Gallic territory.

[218 BC. Defection of the Gauls of northern Italy.]

24. Livy 21.45.2

While the enemy were occupied with this work, the Carthaginians sent Maharbal with a squadron of Numidian cavalry, 500 horse, to ravage the land of the Roman allies; he ordered that the Gauls should be spared as far as possible and their leaders should be urged to secede.

[218 BC. Build-up to the battle of Ticinus. The strategy partly paid off as 2,000 Gallic troops deserted from Rome after the battle and joined Hannibal.[18]]

25. Livy 23.1.1–2 (216 BC)

After the battle of Cannae and the capture and looting of the camps, Hannibal rapidly moved from Apulia into Samnium, driven into the territory of the Hirpini by the promises of Statius Trebius that he would hand over Compsa to him. Trebius was a native of Compsa and a nobleman amongst his own people; but the faction of the Mopsii, a family made powerful by Roman gratitude, had suppressed him. When news of the battle of Cannae was heard and Trebius talked of the arrival of Hannibal, the supporters of the Mopsii left the city, and the town was handed over to the Carthaginians without a struggle, and a garrison was accepted.

26. Livy 23.2.1–4

From here, he directed his route towards Capua, wealthy and luxurious and long favoured by fortune, but greatly corrupted, more than anything by the licence of the people who exercised unlimited freedom. Pacuvius Calavius, a nobleman and a man of the popular party, who had gained power by certain evil stratagems, had made the senate subject to both himself and the people. By chance, this man held the highest magistracy in that year when the bad events at Trasimene happened, and knowing that the people had long hated the senate he thought that they would dare to commit a great crime in the hope of political change, such that if Hannibal came to that place with his victorious army, Capua would be handed over to the Carthaginians, the senators having been killed; he was a wicked man but not lost to extreme evil, since he preferred to control a state which was unharmed rather than overturned, and since he believed that no state could be intact without a public council, he made a plan which both preserved the senate and made it subservient to himself and the people.

[216 BC. Secession of Capua.[19]]

27. Livy 23.4.6–8

... after the disaster at Cannae, they despised the power of Rome, which they used to respect. The only thing which delayed their immediate defection was the ancient right of *conubium*, which linked many powerful and distinguished families with the Romans and, which was a stronger link, 300 horsemen, the most noble of the Campanians, who had been serving amongst others in the Roman army, had been chosen by the Romans and sent to garrison the cities of Sicily.

[216 BC. Secession of Capua.]

28. Livy 23.7.1–2

Envoys went to Hannibal and peace was made on these conditions: that no Carthaginian general or magistrate should have jurisdiction over any Campanian citizen and no Campanian citizen should be forced to serve in the army or perform another duty against his will; that Capua was to have its own laws and magistrates; that 300 of the Roman prisoners held by the Carthaginians should be given to the Campanians, whom they themselves had chosen, with whom they would arrange an exchange for the Campanian cavalry who were serving in Sicily.

[216 BC. Terms agreed between Carthage and Capua.]

29. Livy 23.20.4–8 (216 BC)

At this time, the people of Petelia, the only ones amongst the Bruttians to remain in friendship with Rome, were attacked not just by the Carthaginians who held the surrounding countryside, but also by the rest of the Bruttians from whom they were alienated by their decision. When they were unable to resist this evil, the Petelians sent envoys to Rome to ask for a garrison. The tears and entreaties of these – for they wept in the entrance to the senate house, having been instructed to look after themselves – moved the senate and the people to great pity; having been consulted again by M. Aemilius, the praetor, the senators were forced to admit, after looking at all the resources of the empire, that no protection could now be given to distant allies, and they told them to return home and, maintaining their fidelity to the end, should consider only themselves, as fortune should determine.

30. Livy 24.1.1, 13

Returning to Bruttium from Campania, Hanno made moves against the Greek cities, with the assistance and guidance of the Bruttians; the Greeks remained more willingly in the Roman alliance because the Bruttians, whom they hated and feared, had taken the side of the Carthaginians. . . . By order of Hannibal, the Locrians were given peace and freedom to live under their own laws, the city should be open to the Carthaginians, the harbour remained under control of the Locrians, and the alliance stood under the obligation that the Carthaginians should help the Locrians, and the Locrians the Carthaginians, in peace and war.

[215 BC. Operations in Calabria.]

31. Livy 24.2.1–8

Thus the Carthaginians left the Straits, to the anger of the Bruttians, because they had left intact Rhegium and Locri, cities which they had intended to sack. And so, having levied and armed 15,000 of their young men, they set off on their own to fight against Croton, also a coastal Greek city, believing that they would gain greater wealth if they held a city on the sea, with a good harbour and strong walls. They were anxious because they dared not ask for Carthaginian help in case they seemed not to have acted like allies and, if the Carthaginians again were the brokers of peace rather than helpers in war, they would fight in vain for the freedom of Croton, as previously of Locri. And so it seemed best to send envoys to Hannibal to be assured by him that once captured, Croton would be Bruttian property. Hannibal replied that the person who was there present should be consulted, and referred them back to Hanno, but Hanno gave no assurances; for he did not want a famous and wealthy city to be sacked and hoped that, when attacked by the Bruttians, while the Carthaginians neither supported not assisted the attack, they would defect more readily. At Croton, there was unity neither of opinion nor will amongst the people. For a single disease had infected all the cities of Italy, that the people and the *optimates* were in disagreement, the senate favouring Rome and the people dragging policy towards the Carthaginians.

[215 BC. Assault on Croton.]

32. Livy 24.3.11–15

At last, the Bruttians, seeing that the acropolis could not be taken with their strength, were forced by necessity to ask Hanno for help. He tried to persuade the Crotoniates to surrender on condition that they allowed a colony of Bruttians to be founded, thus restoring the level of population of the city, which was deserted and devastated by earlier wars, but no one apart from Aristomachus was convinced. The rest affirmed that they would rather die than be turned towards foreign rites, customs, laws, and soon even language, by an admixture of Bruttians. Aristomachus defected to Hanno alone, having not prevailed in persuading them to surrender, nor succeeded in betraying the acropolis as he had betrayed the city. Shortly afterwards, Locrian envoys entered the acropolis with the permission of Hanno, and persuaded the Crotoniates to allow themselves to be moved to Locri and not to put themselves to the ultimate test; permission to do this had already been sent by Hannibal *via* these same envoys. And so Croton was abandoned and the Crotoniates were conducted to the sea, onto ships; the entire population left for Locri.

[215 BC. Surrender of Croton. Aristomachus was the leader of the pro-Carthaginian faction mentioned in No. 31.]

33. Livy 24.45.1–5

Dasius Altinius of Arpi came to the camp secretly at night, with three slaves, promising that if he were rewarded, he would betray Arpi. The matter having been referred for discussion by Fabius, it seemed to the others that he should be flogged and executed for desertion as a common enemy with a divided mind, who had gone over to Hannibal and dragged Arpi into revolt after the disaster at Cannae, as if fortune should determine loyalty; then, because Roman fortunes, against his hopes and expectations, seemed to be reviving, he was promising to repeat betrayal by new treachery, an unfaithful ally and worthless enemy . . .

[213 BC. Reversion of Arpi to alliance with Rome.]

34. Livy 27.9.7

At that time, there were 30 Latin colonies; 12 of these, when representatives of all of them were at Rome, informed the consuls that they no longer had the resources to provide men or money. They were Ardea, Nepete, Sutrium, Alba, Carseoli, Sora, Suessa, Circeii, Setia, Cales, Narnia and Interamna. Having been struck by this new blow, the consuls, wishing to deter them from this horrific decision and thinking that they could do so by castigation and reproof rather than by a gentler approach, said that they had dared to say that which the consuls themselves could not bring themselves to repeat in the senate; for this was not just dereliction of military duties but open defection from the Roman people.

[209 BC. Despite Livy's interpretation this was not an actual act of revolt, but the exhaustion and distancing from Rome by this group of Latin colonies deeply shocked the senate. The angry reaction and the harsh punishment meted out in 205 [No. 37], when Rome was under less acute pressure and thus able to take action, illustrates just how central the Latins were to Roman control, both psychologically and practically.]

Treatment of secessionist allies

35. Livy 26.16.5–8

Returning to Capua from Cales, he [Fulvius Flaccus] accepted the surrender of Atella and Calatia; there, too, those who had influenced public policy were executed. A total of seventy leading senators were killed, and approximately 300 Campanian nobles were imprisoned, while others were sent under guard to cities of the Latin allies and died in various ways: the rest of the citizens of Capua were sold as slaves. There was a discussion about the city and the remaining land, some being of the opinion that a city so powerful, so close and so inimical must be destroyed. Presented by others, practicality triumphed; on account of the land, which everyone considered to be the most fertile of any in Italy, the city was saved as a home for farmers. To populate the city, the inhabitants of the territory, freedmen and traders and craftsmen were allowed to stay: All the land and buildings became property of the Roman people.

[211 BC. As well as confiscation of land and exile or execution of the ruling elite, Capua suffered loss of its civic institutions and was ruled for a time directly from Rome. For more on the post-war status of Capua see No. 62.]

36. Plutarch, *Life of Fabius Maximus* 22

Apart from the Bruttians, many Tarentines were slaughtered, 30,000 were sold as slaves, the city was sacked by the Roman army and the *aerarium* was enriched by 3,000 talents.

[209 BC. Sack of Tarentum. The ultimate fate of the city is unclear, but it probably became a Roman ally again, although with considerable loss of territory. Livy[20] says that there was a proposal to inflict the same loss of civic status as Capua, but that this was rejected by the Senate. It remained under the jurisdiction of a Roman commissioner for at least twenty years [Nos 73–4]. In 123 BC, a Gracchan colony was founded in the *Ager Tarentinus* although the original Greek city continued as a separate entity until 89 BC.]

37. Livy 29.15.2–5

Having aroused their interest, they laid before the senate the case of the 12 Latin colonies which had refused to give troops in the consulship of Q. Fabius and Q. Fulvius and had now had exemption from military service for nearly six years as if for honour or good service, while good and obedient allies, from loyalty and obedience to the Roman people, were drained by continual levies every year. Because of this speech, not only was the memory of an almost forgotten matter revived in the senate, but also anger. And so, before any other business, it was decreed that the consuls should summon the magistrates and ten leading men of Nepete, Sutrium, Ardea, Cales, Alba, Carseoli, Sora, Suessa, Setia, Circeii, Narnia and Interamna – for these were the colonies in question – to Rome; they were to demand from them that however many troops each colony had given to Rome while the enemy was in Italy, they should give double that number of infantry and 120 cavalry; if any could not fulfil that quota of cavalry, they were allowed to give three infantrymen for each horseman; both infantry and cavalry were to be chosen from amongst the wealthiest men and sent wherever outside Italy reinforcements were needed. If any colony refused, the magistrates and envoys of that colony were to be detained, and no senatorial hearing was to be granted, if they asked for one, before these orders had been carried out. A tax was also levied on these colonies of one *as* in every thousand, and collected annually, and a census was to be taken in these colonies according to the formula used by the Roman censors.

[204 BC. Despite Livy's interpretation [No. 34], these Latin cities did not revolt against Rome, but actively refused to take an active part in the war from 209 onwards.]

38. Livy 29.19.6–8

The senate should openly reply to the Locrians that neither the senate nor the Roman people had wanted the deeds they complained had been done; they were to be called good men and friends; their wives and children and goods which had been taken would be restored: the money taken from the treasury of Proserpina would be recovered and double this money replaced in the treasury, and rites of expiation would be carried out after consultation with the college of priests who would say what rites should be performed, to which god and with what victims, since the sacred treasury had been disturbed, opened and raided: all the soldiers who were at Locri would be sent to Sicily: four cohorts of Latin allies would replace the garrison at Locri.

[204 BC. Peace settlement between Rome and Locri. The fraught circumstances surrounding this are described at length in Livy 29.16–19. After the exiled pro-Roman party at Locri had managed to regain control of the city in 209 BC, a Roman commissioner, Q. Pleminius, was put in charge of the city but committed a number of acts of misgovernment, including allowing the Roman garrison to terrorize the citizens and plundering the treasury of the sanctuary of Proserpina. The Locrians complained to the senate, Pleminius was arrested and a peace settlement which restored self-government was made. This was an attempt to undermine Scipio, who had appointed Pleminius, and the Locrians were encouraged to press charges against Scipio himself.[21] The declaration that the Locrians were "viros bonosque et amicos" echoes a widely used Greek formula. It also points to the fact that they would have the privileged status of *amici populi romani*.]

39. Livy 29.36.10–12

At the same time in the other part of Italy, M. Cornelius, the consul, continued to hold Etruria not so much through fear of force as of the law; almost all of it had turned to Mago in the hope of change. He was empowered to hold these commissions of inquiry without restriction, by decree of the senate; many Etruscan noblemen who had either gone in person or sent envoys to Mago regarding the secession of their people, had appeared and been condemned, and later others who had been driven into exile by their consciences were condemned *in absentia* . . .

[203 BC. Suppression of unrest in Etruria.]

CHAPTER TWO

Mechanisms of Roman control: treaties, alliances and colonies

The conquest of Italy left Rome with a particularly pressing logistical problem. The administrative machinery of a city-state was entirely insufficient to govern the vast new amount of territory which now came under Roman control, and indeed had become so at a relatively early stage in Rome's wars of conquest. A way had to be found to administer this without stretching the components of the Roman state to breaking point. The way in which this was done was by building up a complex mosaic of *ad hoc* alliances with conquered peoples and colonies established by Rome.

Very quickly, the territory acquired by Rome became too large and too far-flung to allow for direct rule and incorporation into the *Ager Romanus*. The solution was to make alliances with defeated enemies which allowed them to maintain some degree of local autonomy, thus relieving Rome of the administrative burden. Only a small number of the most recalcitrant opponents were sacked and had their civic structures dismantled. The defeat of the Latin states and the dissolution of the Latin League provided the springboard for the formalization of this into a structure for the government of Italy.

The terms of the settlement of 338 BC included a number of innovative features. One was the creation of the notion of *civitas sine suffragio* – a form of limited Roman citizenship consisting of civil rights but not the right to vote, thus disbarring holders from participation in the political process.[1] Like Latinity, the extension of full or modified Roman citizenship to other Italian communities was, in the fourth and third centuries BC, a means of Roman control and exploitation of Italian manpower and resources. The earliest *municipia*, as communities of full or partial Roman citizens were known, were viewed by Rome in terms of *munera* – obligations – which largely consisted of backing Rome up militarily and giving Rome access to Italian manpower.[2] *Civitas sine suffragio* became prized in the second century BC as a route to full citizenship, but it was originally imposed as a punishment and was greatly feared and resented [No. 61]. The second innovation was the breaking of the connection between Latinity as a legal status and Latinity as an ethnic origin. Henceforth, it was possible to be a Latin by virtue of being granted a package of legal rights and obligations by Rome, or coming from a community which had such rights, without being born in Latium or descended from Latin parents. The third principal feature of the settlement was the dissolution of the Latin League and its replacement with a number of bilateral treaties, tying each individual Latin state to Rome on a one-to-one basis and breaking up the decision-making bodies of the League, which had provided a forum for multilateral decisions. Each state now had a relationship only with Rome, not with other former members of the League, effectively breaking up the communal identity of the Latin states and replacing it with Roman domination – in Greek terms, a hegemonial alliance.

As Roman power expanded after 338 BC, conquered Italians were organized into the three categories described above, each with a different legal status and relationship to Rome – Roman citizens (with or without the vote), Latins, or allies. By doing this, Rome was able to extend control by building up a network of alliances, voluntary or imposed, and thus sidestepped the need to make alternative administrative arrangements – since the vast majority of communities continued to be self-governing – and the highly contentious task of imposing change and limiting autonomy. This arms-length approach allowed Rome to gain kudos from apparent magnanimity and maintain the convenient fiction of being merely first amongst equals in the emerging power block. The extent to which loss of self-determination and the demolition of collective identity was regarded with horror is illustrated by the protests of some communities faced with incorporation as *cives sine suffragio* [No. 61] and the infliction of this as the ultimate punishment on the Capuans in 211 BC [No. 62].

The smallest category, but with increasingly the highest status, were Roman citizens. The core of this group were, obviously, the people of the city of Rome itself who were Romans by virtue of birth and ethnic origin. Unlike most Greek states, however, the Romans had a relatively open, but also highly legalistic, attitude to citizenship. The bottom line was that citizenship and Latinity were not defined in terms of ethnic or kinship groups but were a specified status in Roman law, which could be conferred or withdrawn by act of the state.[3] The extent to which this happened in practice was therefore dependent on circumstance and senatorial policy at any given time. Thus grants of citizenship were not unusual during the wars of conquest in Italy, but became much more restricted during the second century BC, in response to Rome's obvious dominance in the Mediterranean and the growing desire to restrict access to what had become an economically and politically advantageous status.[4] After this period of retrenchment and corresponding growth in demand for an extension of citizenship amongst other Italian communities, the social war provoked a reversal of policy and the extension of full Roman citizenship to all Italians, although access to non-Italians remained limited. This was a source of great incomprehension and frustration to the Greek elite of the eastern empire. The notion that even manumitted slaves in

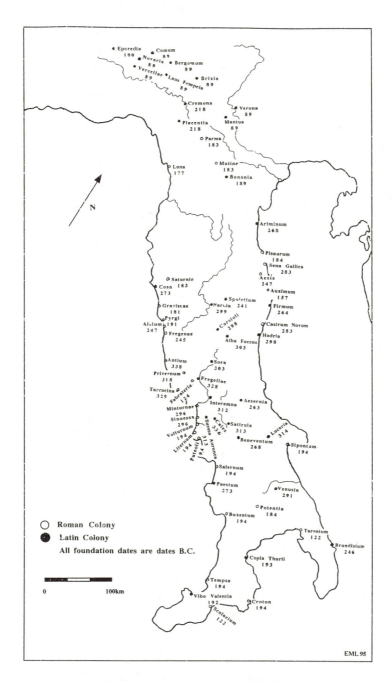

Roman colonization in Italy: 338–89BC

(Map labels)

Eporedia 100
Comum 89
Novaria 89
Bergomum 89
Vercellae 89
Laus Pompeia 89
Brixia 89
Cremona 218
Verona 89
Placentia 218
Mantua 89
Parma 183
Luna 177
Mutina 183
Bononia 189
Ariminum 268
Pisaurum 184
Sena Gallica 283
Aesis 247
Saturnie
Cosa 273 183
Auximum 157
Spoletium
Graviscae 181
Narnia 241
Firmum 264
Pyrgi
Carsioli 298
Castrum Novum 283
Alsium 191 247
Fregenae 245
Hadria 298
Alba Fucens 303
Antium 338
Sora 303
Privernum 318
Fregellae 328
Tarracina 329
Fabrateria 124
Interamna 312
Aesernia 263
Minturnae 296
Sinuessa 296
Cales 334
Saticula 313
Luceria 314
Volturnum 194
Suessa Aurunca 313
Beneventum 268
Liternum 194
Puteoli 194
Sipontum 194
Salernum 194
Paestum 273
Venusia 291
Buxentum 194
Potentia 184
Tarentum 122
Brundisium 246
Copia Thurii 193
Tempsa 194
Vibo Valentia 192
Croton 194
Scolacium 122

N

○ Roman Colony
● Latin Colony
All foundation dates are dates B.C.

0   100km

EML 95

3. Roman colonization in Italy: 338–89BC

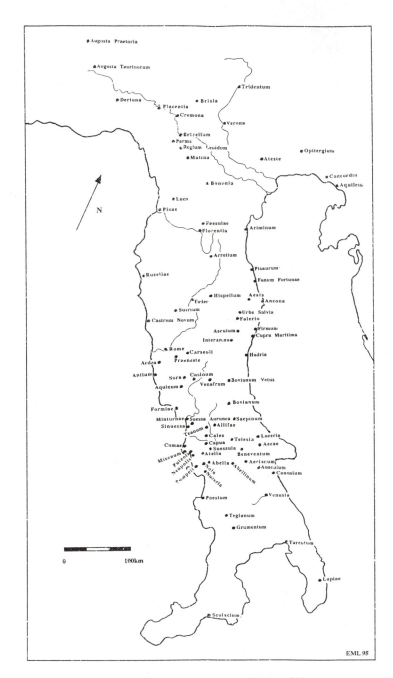

Augusta Praetoria

Augusta Taurinorum

Tridentum

Dertona   Placentia   Brixia
            Cremona   Verona

Brixellum
Parma
Regium Lepidum   Opitergium
Mutina   Ateste

Bononia   Concordia
            Aquileia

Luca

Pisae   N

Faesulae
Florentia   Ariminum

Arretium

Ruselae   Pisaurum
            Fanum Fortunae

Hispellum   Aesis
Tuder   Ancona
Sutrium   Urbs Salvia
Castrum Novum   Falerio
            Firmum
Asculum   Cupra Maritima
Interamnae
Rome   Carseoli   Hadria
Ardea   Praeneste
Antium   Sora   Casinum
            Bovianum Vetus
Aquinum   Venafrum
            Bovianum
Formiae
Minturnae Suessa Aurunca Saepinum
Sinuessa   Allifae
Teanum   Cales   Luceria
Cumae   Capua   Telesia   Aecae
Misenum   Suessula
Puteoli   Atella   Beneventum
Neapolis   Aeclanum
Pompeii   Abella   Aeculanum
            Nola   Abellinum   Canusium
            Nuceria
            Paestum   Venusia

Tegianum
Grumentum

Tarentum

0   100km

Lupiae

Scolacium

EML 95

4. Roman colonization in Italy: 89BC–AD300

34

Rome and Italy could gain the civil rights of a Roman citizen, and male descendants could have full political rights, including the right to stand for office, while members of the provincial elites were excluded, was something which Dionysios of Halicarnassus found puzzling and rather distasteful.[5] However, the fact that attitudes to Roman citizenship changed considerably over the period 338–90 BC must not be forgotten. The vast majority of our sources were written after the second century BC, a period during which the status of Roman citizenship underwent a profound change. The acquisition of an empire and the economic benefits which came with it, as well as the growing disparity of power and status between Romans and non-Romans, caused Roman citizenship to become a much sought after commodity, just at the time when the senate began to place increasingly severe restrictions on it, and on the ways in which it could be obtained. During the fourth and third centuries, however, this was not the case. *Civitas sine suffragio* was imposed in 338 as a punishment, and the threat of it was certainly felt as such. Autonomy within the framework of an alliance with Rome was much more valued at this date. Roman citizenship, particularly *civitas sine suffragio* which carried civil but no political rights, was seen as a gross intrusion into the civic life of another state, and as such, was fiercely opposed.

There were a number of means by which citizenship could be obtained.[6] Individuals or small groups could be enfranchised for services rendered to Rome. In 340 BC, Campanian aristocrats who had remained loyal to Rome during the Latin war were given Roman citizenship [No. 40]. A later instance was the enfranchisement by Marius of a contingent of Umbrian troops from Camerinum who had shown conspicuous gallantry at the battle of Vercellae in 101 BC [No. 46], a controversial move, since one view was that it infringed the terms of the treaty between Rome and Camerinum.[7] During the second and first centuries, the niceties of enfranchisement of allies, the circumstances in which they could take place, and the legal relationship between enfranchisement and a pre-existing treaty, were hotly debated and became a legal minefield. Several of Cicero's speeches relate to contested claims of citizenship and one, the *Pro Balbo*, summarizes in detail the issues raised by the grant of citizenship to Balbus, otherwise a native of the allied city of Gades [Nos 45–51]. The basic principle was that Roman citizenship was not exclusive, and that under Roman law, it was perfectly possible to hold it concurrently with citizenship of one's native city.[8] Indeed this was the principle underlying the municipalization of Italy. Cicero makes it clear that most Italians felt themselves to belong simultaneously to Rome and to their home city, and that local patriotism, often keenly felt, was no bar to an equally profound sense of Roman identity [No. 174].

By the second century BC there were several other ways, in addition to a direct grant, for an individual to gain citizenship, some of which are discussed in more detail in Chapter 5. Briefly, they involved migration to Rome itself or a Roman colony and the establishment of right of residence, or later, the holding of a senior magistracy in a city with Latin status. However, much the most common and largest-scale way of disseminating Roman citizenship was through colonization programmes and grants of citizenship *en bloc* to whole communities. As already noted, the enforcement of Roman citizenship on an entire pre-existing state was often a punishment – a means of destroying autonomous existence, as at Capua in 211 BC. Most colonies were, however, not founded on existing cities until the Gracchan colonization programme of 133–120 BC, and the large-scale veteran settlements of the first century BC and the early empire. The majority, although not all, were new settlements, founded *ab initio* by Rome. Their inhabitants were given the status of Roman citizens, and their civic organization, usually laid out in a colonial charter, mirrored that of Rome, being based on a local senate and a cursus of annual magistracies headed by a board of two *duoviri*.[9] Typically, a citizen colony was small in size, often comprising no more than 300 settlers and their families. Settlements were often made on land confiscated from defeated enemies and the purpose of this type of colony was frequently overtly strategic. Citizen colonies tended to be placed in strategically vulnerable locations or on newly conquered territory to provide a core Roman presence and act as an informal garrison. This ethos is most openly expressed in connection with the *coloniae maritimae* which were, as the name suggests, citizen colonies founded at strategic points along the coast to act as coastal defences.[10] Unlike other colonies, which had to supply troops on request to the Roman army, these were exempt except in cases of emergency, or occasionally, when the exemption was withdrawn as a punishment. Instead, they were expected to defend the coast against pirates and control formerly threatening coastal cities such as Antium, which was defeated by Rome in 338 BC after a fierce struggle. A sizeable group of new foundations, which was made in 194–3 BC[11] to guard southern Italy against a possible second invasion by Hannibal, illustrates this function, and also the difficulties posed by using colonists to settle, and implicitly guard, out-of-the-way places. A tour of inspection of some of these colonies by a Roman magistrate in 187[12] revealed that many of the colonists had lost interest in living in these isolated and inhospitable locations and had left, necessitating the enrolment of a second batch of colonists.

Like Roman citizenship, Latin status was not an ethnic identity but a collection of legal rights which could be conferred by the state. Also like citizenship, it was primarily disseminated by means of colonization or grants to communities. It was possible to receive an individual grant of Latin status but this was comparatively rare before the first century AD. Essentially, it was a collection of legal rights, including those of trade and intermarriage with Roman citizens and the right to restricted participation in the Roman political process, subject to certain residence requirements at Rome, and military obligations.[13] The impact was to forge a closer social and economic link between Rome and the Latins than was the case with the rest of Italy, and also to make the Latins the core of Rome's fighting strength. Particularly at the elite level of society, legal protection for trade and commercial contracts facilitated economic interaction, and the recognition of the legitimacy of offspring from intermarriages helped maintain kinship links between Rome and the Latin communities. Like citizen colonies, Latin communities also had to provide troops when required by the Roman levy, but since these were not citizens, they fought in their own local units, not as part of the Roman legions. Livy's references to levies during the second century almost always give figures of troops as a breakdown into specified numbers of Romans, Latins and Italian allies, possibly mirroring the way in which the senate expressed the levy.[14] They also differed from citizen colonies in that whereas these were part of the Roman state and thus had limited autonomy, Latin colonies were self-governing. They each had a colonial charter establishing their administrative structures, which were usually based around a senate and a board of four annually elected *quattuorviri*.

Latin colonies also differed in other ways. They were usually much larger than citizen colonies. A Latin colony might consist of 2,000–5,000 settlers and their families, and larger examples are known from northern Italy.[15] This discrepancy in size and location indicates a difference in function. While some Latin colonies were founded on existing settlements, many were placed on new sites in areas with a low level of urbanization, or were in areas suffering from demographic decline. The primary purposes seem to be to urbanize regions such as Samnium and the far north of Italy on suitably Romanized lines, and to regenerate failing cities. In 273 BC, for instance, two Latin colonies were sent out, to Paestum in Lucania and to Cosa in Etruria.[16] Paestum was a city with a long and notable history – a Greek colony which had been overrun by the Lucanians in 410 BC and become Oscanized, then fallen under Roman control during the Pyrrhic war of 281–70 BC.[17] While it was not obviously in serious decline in terms of population, the colony may have been intended to dilute the Oscan and Greek population and pacify a turbulent area. Cosa, on the other hand, was a new settlement – a prototypical Roman colony with a regular street plan and Roman public buildings dominating a stretch of good farmland and a harbour on the coast of Etruria.[18] Whatever the political and strategic purposes behind colonization, it also had the effect of disseminating Romanized social units and forms of urbanization as well as settling concentrations of Roman or Romanized people in all parts of Italy and in considerable numbers.

The other Italian states remained independent and relations with Rome were governed by individually negotiated treaties. These were bilateral agreements, which created a web of alliances with Rome very firmly at the centre. Rome gradually undermined multilateral league structures in Italy by insisting on dealing individually with the constituent members. Networks of informal contacts and formal alliances between groups of Italians did, of course, exist, and sometimes caused complex clashes of interests, as the needs of one treaty cut across the demands of another.[19] Rome, however, maintained the initiative by virtue of being the one common point of contact between all the other members of the alliance.

The terms of the treaties which underpinned this structure are very poorly documented. Texts of a number of treaties between Rome and various allies have survived, but all of these are of later date than the conquest of Italy (mostly second century BC) and all relate to alliances in the eastern Mediterranean, not to Italy.[20] The only direct evidence relating to Italy is Dionysios of Halicarnassus' text of the *foedus Cassianum* of 493 BC [No. 44]. This is usually cited by both modern scholars and ancient writers such as Cicero as a sort of proto-treaty on which all others were based. It establishes peace between the Romans, the Latins, and the Hernicians and lays down a small number of stipulations. It explicitly says that it is meant to be permanent, that each signatory shall assist the others with armed force if attacked, and that laws relating to sales and contracts between the signatories shall be upheld.

The accuracy of this text is obviously very open to question. Cicero[21] says that a copy of the *foedus Cassianum* was still extant in his own day, and could be consulted, but there is no certain evidence that Dionysios actually did consult this, or that the very archaic Latin in which it would have been written was comprehensible to Romans (or Greeks) of the first century BC. Comparison with later texts of treaties reveals a surprising degree of consistency, but this may be as much a reflection of treaties of Dionysios' own day as of historical accuracy. Nevertheless, the terms of the *foedus Cassianum* and the second century treaties do not seem implausible as the basis for Roman expansion. All are relatively vague, stipulating only that peace and friendship should exist between Rome and the other signatories, and that in the event of either party being attacked, the other shall provide military assistance. In the case of war with a third party by either signatory, the other was required to maintain benevolent neutrality by denying safe passage or provision of food and supplies to the enemy and supplying these things for the ally.[22]

Needless to say, as Rome's power grew, the defensive nature of these alliances came to be honoured more in the breach than the observance. Levies of troops from allies and from Latin colonies became an annual event as Rome's wide-ranging interests and obligations made annual campaigns, and eventually a standing army, a necessity. The principle that if one of Rome's allies was threatened, Rome could call on the whole alliance for support, was also rapidly established. The growing disparity between the power of Rome and that of any other individual ally from the fourth century onwards ensured that from being, in theory, an alliance between equals, it rapidly evolved into a hegemonial structure dominated by Rome. At the same time, the notion that only the *bellum iustum*, the "just" or defensive war, could be sanctioned by religious custom, began to disappear, and by the second century, when Rome was expanding into both the east and west Mediterranean, the allies were being increasingly called upon to support overt wars of conquest.[23]

The central duty of a Roman ally was to support Rome in time of war. In other respects allies were, in theory, self-determining independent states, although during the second century BC, Rome began to interfere increasingly in their internal affairs, and to consolidate the growing differences in status between Roman citizens and Italians. The practical mechanisms by which Rome actually put the terms of the treaties into practice is obscure. A small number of references to a *formula togatorum* in connection with troops has been variously interpreted[24] but evidence for troop levies is obscure. Polybios records a levy in 225 BC at which allies were required to submit a record of their full fighting strength, but this was during a state of emergency and was clearly not usual [Nos 16, 52]. He also provides a detailed description of a Roman levy, but this is now regarded as idealized and anachronistic and not a true representation of the procedures in use in his own day. In his books covering the second century BC, Livy frequently makes reference to a system whereby the senate allotted troops to each commander at the beginning of the year, specifying maximum numbers of infantry and cavalry levied from Roman citizens, Latins, and allies but rarely any restriction on where they were to come from.[25] The portioning out of numbers amongst the allies seems to have been left to the individual general in most cases. The few cases where there is senatorial intervention over the obligations of a particular state are usually where there are unusual circumstances, for instance the doubling of the obligations of some Latin colonies in 204 as a punishment [No. 37]. Overall, the lack of a central administration for Italy seems to have resulted in the creation of a rather *ad hoc* structure for regulating allied behaviour and enforcing their military obligations.

This is consistent with the very *ad hoc* way in which the Roman alliance evolved generally. As far as we know, the terms of treaties were very non-specific, and the notion of treaties which can be classified into a coherent hierarchy is probably untrue. Some states undoubtedly obtained more favourable terms than others, depending largely on the circumstances in which the treaty was made. Cities which became Roman allies voluntarily, or which chose to negotiate peace rather than fighting a war to the bitter end could expect better terms than those which were inveterate enemies of Rome. However, the idea that treaties could be classified into two formally defined types, the *foedus aequum* and the *foedus iniquum*, is no longer tenable.[26] There is no evidence at all for the *foedus iniquum*, and the term *foedus aequum* seems to be used principally by Cicero[27] to indicate a treaty of unusually favourable nature, not as a technical description.

Not all Roman foreign policy relied on treaties, but exceptions were short-lived and tended to result in negotiation of a treaty eventually. For instance, wars with Etruscan states in the fourth century tended to be concluded by *indutiae* [No. 57], truces of fixed length, usually of at least one year, and in one case, as long as 100 years. These were merely cessations of hostilities and did not set up any formal relationship with Rome, possibly an indication of lack of Roman interest in the region. Eventually, however, most Etruscan cities became allies.[28] Similarly, some agreements with the Samnites were made by *sponsio* [No. 56], a formal and binding oath sworn by both parties. Again, however, these were interim measures which were eventually replaced by a treaty.

Certainly, the system of alliances and colonization proved to be a highly effective means of controlling Italy without the need to invest resources in developing and imposing a centralized form of government. Its other great strength was that it was a relatively open system, allowing for changes of status and role according to need, and it was this loss of openness, particularly in terms of access to Roman citizenship, which contributed to the eventual breakdown of the alliance structure towards the end of the second century. Even in the ancient world, the Roman willingness to create new citizens, and their colonization programme, were identified as major sources of their strength [Nos 58, 63].

The Latin War and the basis of Roman control

40. Livy 8.11.13–16

Latium and Capua had their territory confiscated. The Latin territory, with the addition of the lands of Privernum and Falernus (which had belonged to the Campanian people), as far as the river Volturnus, was divided amongst the Roman people. Two *iugera* per person in Latium, supplemented by three-quarters of a *iugerum* from Privernate land, were given, or three *iugera* on the *ager Falernus*, with a fourth *iugerum* added because of its remoteness. The people of Laurentum and the Campanian cavalry were exempt from the punishment of the Latins, because they had not revolted. The treaty with Laurentum was ordered to be renewed, and it has been renewed every year since then, on the tenth day after the Latin festival. The Campanian cavalry were given Roman citizenship, and as a monument a bronze tablet was put up in the temple of Castor at Rome. The people of Campania were also ordered to pay an annual tax – there being 1600 of them – of 450 denarii.

[340 BC. First settlement of the Latin and Campanian revolt. The Campanian cavalry referred to are the cavalry class of Capua, and therefore a high-status group in both the social and the economic sense. In this passage, the people of Campania are probably not the Campani as a whole but the people of Capua.]

41. Livy 8.14

The leaders of the senate praised [Camillus'] proposals on this matter, but, since each case was different, his advice could be most easily carried out if the consuls would refer each individual people by name to the Roman people, as each seemed to deserve. The Lanuvians were given citizenship and their sacred places were given back to them, on condition that the grove of Juno Sospita should be common to the citizens of Lanuvium and the people of Rome. The people of Aricia, Nomentum and Pedum were granted citizenship on the same basis as the Lanuvians. The Tusculans retained their existing citizenship, and the crime of rebellion was levelled at a few instigators, without harming the state. The people of Velitrae, long-time Roman citizens, were severely punished because they had often rebelled: their walls were demolished and the senate was removed and ordered to live on the other side of the Tiber, on the condition that if anyone was caught across the Tiber, the ransom would be 1,000 pounds in bronze, nor could the person who had captured him release him from chains before the ransom was paid. Colonists were sent out to the senatorial lands, and having been enrolled, Velitrae regained its old appearance of populousness. A new colony was sent to Antium, on the condition that the people of Antium were allowed to enrol themselves as colonists if they wanted to; their warships were impounded and the Antiates were forbidden to go to sea, and they were given citizenship. The people of Tibur and Praeneste had territory confiscated, not only because of the recent allegation of rebellion along with the rest of the Latins, but because they had once joined in arms with the Gauls, a savage people, out of distaste at Roman power. The rest of the Latin peoples were denied rights of trade, intermarriage and common assembly between themselves. The Campanians (in honour of their cavalry, because they had not rebelled with the Latins) and the people of Fundi and Formiae (because they had always allowed a safe passage through their territory) were given citizenship without the vote. It was decided to give the people of Cumae and Suessula the same rights and terms as the people of Capua.

[338 BC. Settlement at the end of the Latin war, involving close incorporation of large parts of Latium and northern Campania into the Roman state, either with or without voting rights. Livy makes it clear that each Latin and Campanian city was dealt with individually, and that rights such as trade and intermarriage, which had been held communally, were now removed. They were replaced by bilateral agreements with Rome. For the peace settlement with Capua of 340 BC, see No. 40.]

42. Ulpian Digest 19.4–5

Purchase can take place between Roman citizens and Latin colonists and Junian Latins, and those foreigners to whom trading rights have been given. . . . *Commercium* is the right to buy and sell between themselves.

Roman colonization

43. Velleius Paterculus, *Roman History* 1.14.1–15.5

. . . and to insert at this point what colonies were founded on the instructions of the senate after the date at which Rome was captured by the Gauls; for the names of military colonies reveal their purpose and their founder. It will seem not untimely if, at this point, I weave in at the same time the extensions of citizenship and the growth of the Roman Name through the sharing of laws.

Seven years after the Gauls captured the city, a colony was founded at Sutri, and the following year at Setia, and after a nine-year interval, at Nepete. Thirty-two years after this, the people of Aricia received citizenship. 360 years ago, during the consulship of Sp. Postumius and Veturius Calvinus, *civitas sine suffragio* was given to Campania and part of Samnium, and a colony was founded at Cales in the same year. After a three-year interval, the people of Fundi and Formiae received citizenship, in the same year in which Alexandria was founded. Following this, in the consulship of Sp. Postumius and Publilius Philo, the people of Acerrae were given citizenship by the censors. And after three years a colony was founded at Terracina, after four years another at Luceria and then after a three-year interval at Suessa Aurunca and Saticula, and another two years later at Interamna. Then this work [of founding colonies] was abandoned for ten years:

after this, colonies were founded at Sora and Alba, and two years later at Carseoli. But in the fifth consulship of Q. Fabius and the fourth of Decius Mus, the year in which Pyrrhus began his reign, colonies were sent to Sinuessa and Minturnae, and after four years, to Venusia: After two years, while M' Curius and Cornelius Rufinus were consuls, the Sabines were given *civitas sine suffragio*: this took place almost 320 years ago. 300 years ago, Cosa and Paestum were founded, in the consulship of Fabius Dorso and Claudius Canina, and after five years, in the consulship of Sempronius Sophus and the son of Appius Claudius Caecus, colonists were sent to Ariminum and Beneventum, and the right of suffrage was given to the Sabines. At the beginning of the First Punic War, Firmum and Castrum were occupied by colonists, a year later Aesernia, and 17 years later Aefulum and Alsium, and two years later, Fregenae. Brundisium was founded in the following year, in the consulship of Torquatus and Sempronius, and Spoletium three years afterwards, in the year in which the Floralia began. Two years later, Valentia was founded, and just before Hannibal's arrival in Italy, Cremona and Placentia.

After this, the Romans had no time for founding colonies, neither while Hannibal lingered in Italy, nor during the years immediately after his departure, since while the war lasted, they had to acquire soldiers rather than discharge them, and after the war, their strength needed to be restored rather than dispersed. However, during the consulship of Manlius Vulso and Fulvius Nobilior, a colony was sent to Bononia, almost 217 years ago, after four years, others to Pisaurum and Potentia, after three years to Aquileia and Gravisca and after four years to Luca. At the same time, although some people are doubtful about this, colonists were sent to Puteoli, Salernum and Buxentum, and also to Auximum in Picenum, about 185 years ago, about three years before Cassius the censor began building a theatre.

Roman treaties and their terms

44. Dionysios of Halicarnassus 6.95

These were the terms of the treaty: "Let there be peace between Rome and all the cities of the Latins for as long as the sky and the earth shall remain in their places. And let them not make war on each other, or bring in other enemies or grant right of passage to the enemies of either. Let them help each other, when at war, with all their strength, and let the spoils and plunder from wars fought in common be divided into equal shares for each of them. Let disputes about private contracts be decided within ten days and in the state where the contract was made. And do not let anything be added or subtracted from this treaty except by consent of Rome and all the Latins." These terms were agreed by the Romans and the Latins and ratified by oaths and sacrifices.

[493 BC. *Foedus Cassianum* (Cassian treaty). This treaty provided the basis for all Roman treaties in Italy, and for many outside Italy, although terms tended to become more elaborately defined in the second century BC. The basics are that of a defensive alliance, with both parties assisting each other in times of war or maintaining a benevolent neutrality, and having equal status in the partnership.]

Treaties and the law

45. Cicero, *Pro Balbo* 19

The case of Cornelius originates, gentlemen, from that law which L. Gellius and Cn. Cornelius passed, according to a decision of the senate; we can see that it was enacted by that law that those who had citizenship awarded to them individually by Cn. Pompeius, with the agreement of his advisers, should be Roman citizens. Pompeius, here present, says that it was conferred on L. Cornelius, public records show this, and the prosecutor confirms it, but denies that anyone from a people bound by treaty can be accepted into citizenship unless that people has formally agreed to this.

[The *Pro Balbo* addressed the issue of the status and responsibilities of allies and citizens, in relation to L. Cornelius Balbus, a supporter of Pompey. Balbus was a native of Gades, in Spain, and had been among a group of allies who had been enfranchised by Pompey, in his case for service in the Roman army during the revolt of Sertorius (79–72 BC). His family must have been included, as his father, brother and nephew also adopted Roman nomenclature.[29] The grants were ratified by the Lex Gellia Cornelia (72 BC), and the legality of Pompey's actions is not in question. The basis of the case is whether viritane grants of citizenship could be made as a unilateral act by Rome, without the prior consent of the allied community to which the individual belonged.]

46. Cicero, *Pro Balbo* 46

[Marius] gave citizenship to M. Annius Appius of Iguvium, the most courageous and virtuous of men, and also to two whole cohorts from Camerinum, when he knew that Camerinum had the most sacred and most equitable of all treaties with Rome.

[101 BC. The grant of citizenship to the troops from Camerinum is one of the major examples of group enfranchisement for services to Rome, justified by Marius on the grounds that expediency on campaign overrode some of the finer points of law.[30] The comment that this infringed the treaty between Camerinum and Rome has caused much debate. It was clearly favourable in nature, but the exact problem with enfranchising citizens of Camerinum is obscure. Sherwin-White[31] argues that the *foedus aequum* was a technical name for a type of treaty which guaranteed a greater degree of autonomy and exemption from military demands, but this is debatable. The evidence for this type of treaty, which comes principally from Cicero, is usually in the form *foedus aequissimum*, which seems to be a typically Ciceronian hyperbole for an extremely favourable treaty rather than a technical description. Similar references occur in respect of Naples, which negotiated exceptionally favourable terms while Rome was under pressure during the Second Samnite war.[32]]

47. Cicero, *Pro Balbo* 24

For it is a serious matter for the Roman people that they cannot make use of allies of excellent merit, who wish to share our dangers along with their own; in fact, it is an injury and an insult to those allies with whom we are presently concerned, and those states bound to us by treaty, to exclude our closest and most faithful allies from the rewards and honours which are open to tributary states, to enemies, and often even to slaves.

48. Cicero, *Pro Balbo* 27–8

. . . but he [the prosecutor] is ignorant about changes of citizenship, which is, gentlemen, based not only on the laws of state, but also on the wish of the private individual. For under our laws, nobody can change his citizenship against his will, or, if he wishes to change, he cannot do so unless he is accepted by that city whose citizen he wishes to become. . . . None of our citizens are allowed, under civil law, to be a citizen of two states; he who accepts citizenship of another city cannot be a citizen of this one [i.e. Rome]. Nor is it only by such an acceptance, which we can see in the case of the misfortunes of the eminent men Q. Maximus, C. Laenas, Q. Philippus, [exiled] to Nuceria, C. Cato [exiled to] Tarraco, Q. Caepio, and R. Rutilius, [exiled to] Smyrna, who all became citizens of these cities, and could not have left the citizenship [of Rome] before they had changed residence by changing citizenship, but also by the "right of return" [*postliminium*] that a change of citizenship can be made.

[The examples cited were all eminent political exiles of the second century who retired to allied cities, mostly outside Italy, and took local citizenship, thereby ceasing to be Roman citizens. The term *postliminium* refers to the right of exiles and prisoners of war, who automatically forfeited citizenship and civil rights as a result of extended absence from Rome and residence outside Roman territory, to resume citizenship and civil rights on their return.]

49. Cicero, *Pro Balbo* 31

How admirable and divinely-inspired is the law developed from the beginning by our ancestors in the name of Rome, that none of us can be the citizen of more than one city (since different cities necessarily have different laws), that no one should change citizenship against his will, or remain as a citizen against his will. This is the strongest foundation of our freedom, that everyone has the power to retain or renounce his own citizenship. It has, without any doubt, been fundamental to our power and the expansion of the reputation of the Roman people, that the first founder of this city, Romulus, taught us by the treaty with the Sabines that the citizen body should be enlarged even by admitting enemies. On his authority and by his example, our ancestors never stopped granting citizenship. And so many peoples from Latium, such as the Tusculans and Lanuvians, and whole peoples from other tribes, such as the Sabines, Volsci and Hernici, were enrolled as citizens; members of these states would not have been forced to change their citizenship, if they were unwilling, nor would it have been seen as a violation of their treaty if any of them had gained Roman citizenship as a gift of the Roman people.

50. Cicero, *Pro Balbo* 35

. . . why is it not allowed by this treaty to admit a man from Gades into our citizenship? For there is nothing else in this treaty other than "There shall be sacred and eternal peace". What has this to do with citizenship? The following is also added, which is not found in all treaties: "They must amicably defend the majesty of the Roman people." It has this force, that they [the Gaditanians] are the subordinate party in this treaty.

51. Cicero, *Pro Balbo* 41

I submit that many years ago, the citizens of Gades publicly made L. Cornelius [Balbus] their guest-friend at Rome. I can produce the token of friendship [*tessera hospitalis*].

[The *hospes publicus* [guest-friend] fulfilled a similar role to that of the *proxenos* in the Greek world. He undertook to represent the interests of his native city in that in which he was resident, and to look after any of his fellow citizens there. The *tessera hospitalis* was a token which was divided, one half being retained by each party, to symbolize the agreement. For the concessions and favours won for Gades by Balbus in his capacity as *hospes publicus*, see *Pro Balb*. 43.]

Military levies and how they worked

52. Polybios 2.23

There was extreme and widespread alarm in Rome, as it was believed that they were in immediate and severe danger; indeed, this was natural, since the fear which had been generated by the ancient invasion was still in their minds. So nobody considered anything else, and they occupied themselves levying and enrolling their own army and ordered those of their allies to be prepared. All of their allies were ordered to present a list of men of military age, since they wanted to know what their entire forces came to.

[225 BC. The threat of a Gallic invasion was always likely to cause fear in Rome since the sack of the city by the Gauls in 386 BC, and on this occasion they seem to have contemplated a levy of the entire Roman and allied military strength. cf. No. 16.]

53. Polybios 6.12

In preparing for war and the overall conduct of campaigns, [the consuls'] power is virtually unconfined; they have the authority to demand whatever they choose from the allies, to appoint tribunes, to levy troops, and to choose those who are most fit for service.

54. Polybios 6.21.4

At the same time, the consuls sent their instructions to the cities of the allies in Italy which they wish to contribute troops, saying how many they want, and the day and the place at which they must be present. The magistrates despatch them, having chosen them in the manner described, sworn them in and appointed a commander and a treasurer.

55. Polybios 6.26.5–6

The allies having gathered at the same place as the Romans, their organization and command are overseen by officers of the consuls called *praefecti sociorum*, who are 12 in number. . . . the number of allied infantry is usually equal to that of the Romans, and the cavalry are three times the number.

Alternatives to treaties

56. Livy 9.41.20

On the next day, and those following, the Umbrian peoples surrendered; Ocriculum was accepted into friendship by *sponsio*.

[308 BC. Capitulation of the Umbrians during the second Samnite war. The interesting thing about the Ocriculans is that they joined the Roman power bloc by *sponsio*, a formal agreement, usually negotiated in the field by a general and then ratified by the senate, rather than by a treaty.]

57. Livy 9.41.5–7

The other consul, Decius, was also successful in war. By fear, he forced the people of Tarquinii into supplying corn to his army and seeking a truce for 40 years. He also took some strong points belonging to Volsinii by force; he razed some of these, so that they could not shelter the enemy; and by waging war on the surrounding area, he made himself so feared that all the Etruscans asked the consul for a treaty. They did not obtain their request from him; they were given a truce for a year. The pay for the Roman army in that year was paid by the enemy, and two tunics per soldier were demanded from them; this was the price of the truce.

[308 BC. Negotiation of a truce by Tarquinii. The refusal to grant a treaty may be a sign that Rome was still preoccupied by the Samnites at this time, and was seeking to gain time without having to make a permanent commitment in Etruria. Decius is the consul for 308, P. Decius Mus.]

Ancient views of Roman alliances

58. *SIG* 543

. . . the Romans, who, when they free their slaves, admit them to citizenship and grant them a share in their magistracies, and in this manner, they have not only increased the size of their own country, but have also been able to send colonies to nearly 70 places.

[217 BC. Letter of Philip V of Macedon to the city of Larissa]

59. Livy 35.16.5

. . . in what way are the people of Smyrna and Lampsacus more Greek than those of Naples, Rhegium and Tarentum, from whom you take tribute, and from whom you demand ships, according to your treaty . . .

[193 BC. Debate between the envoys of Rome and King Antiochus relating to Roman claims to be upholding the freedom of the Greeks of Asia. These claims are contrasted with Roman demands made on Greek allies in Italy under the terms of their treaties.]

60. Livy 28.34.7

It was an old Roman custom, where they were not linked by treaty or the friendship of equal laws, not to make use of the authority of a conqueror over a defeated enemy until everything belonging to men and gods had been surrendered, hostages taken, arms confiscated and garrisons placed.

[206 BC. Roman practice of demanding unconditional surrender in cases where no prior connection by treaty or *amicitia* existed.]

61. Livy 9.45

And after the treaty with the Samnites had been ratified at Rome, when the fetials had come to demand reparations, [the Aequi] had repeatedly said that they were trying, by threat of war, to intimidate them into becoming Roman citizens; how little this was to be wished for was demonstrated by the Hernici, since those who had been allowed to had opted for their own laws rather than Roman citizenship: those who had not been allowed to choose were to have citizenship forced upon them as a punishment.

[304 BC. War with the Aequi.]

62. Livy 26.16

All land and buildings became public property of the Roman people. It was decided that Capua should remain a city only as a place of habitation; It was to have no political structure, no senate, no assembly of the people, no magistrates; for it seemed that the people, without any political body to control them or military organization, and sharing no common interest, would not be capable of any type of communal activity. A praetor would be sent each year from Rome to administer justice. The settlement of Capuan affairs was admirable in all respects: most of the guilty were swiftly and harshly punished; most of the free citizens were scattered and had no hope of return; buildings and fortifications which had committed no crime were spared the futile savagery of fire and demolition; and apart from profiting from the city's preservation, Rome was able to appear before her allies in the persona of a merciful conqueror . . .

[211 BC. Settlement after the recapture of Capua from Hannibal.]

63. Cicero, *De Lege Agraria* 2.73

Is every place of such a type that it does not matter to the state whether a colony is founded there or not, or are there some places which require a colony and some which obviously do not? In this, as in other matters of state, the care of our ancestors is worth remembering, who sited colonies in such suitable places to keep away danger that they seemed not just cities in Italy but also bastions of the empire.

CHAPTER THREE

The decline of the alliance:
Italy in the second century BC

Although the defeat of Hannibal had secured Rome's position as the dominant power in Italy and had shown the strengths of the carefully constructed system of alliances on which it was based, the aftermath was not a period of consolidation but of instability. The second century BC was a time of transition, in which great wealth and the status of a world power, conferred by the conquest of Spain and much of the Greek East, was matched by internal tensions and growing dissatisfaction with Roman rule in Italy. The imbalance between the status of Rome and that of her allies became increasingly obvious, and increasingly resented; wars in the East and in Spain were a drain on both Roman and allied manpower, and the increasing degree of urbanization was matched by a corresponding decline in small-scale subsistence farming; within Rome, political tensions manifested themselves in challenges to the authority of the senate and the growth of bitter factional politics. It was on the back of this last development that agrarian reform, and with it the question of Italian status and the extension of Roman citizenship, became a central problem.

The immediate post-war period was inevitably one of recovery and reconstruction, but also of continuing tension. Although Hannibal and the remains of his army were recalled to Carthage in 203 BC, and a peace treaty was finally signed in 200,[1] Rome was still heavily committed to war in Spain (from 197) and Macedon (from 200), with a consequent drain on economic and military resources. In Italy, there was considerable unrest and economic disruption, and also a deep unease about the possibility of a renewed outbreak of war. Hannibal fled from Carthage in 195 BC, and took refuge at the Seleucid court, under the protection of King Antiochus.[2] Although there is little sign that his machinations were ever likely to come to anything, Rome was, until his death in 183 BC, plagued by periodic scares over the possibility of his return. Closer to home, there were numerous campaigns in northern Italy against the Ligurians and various Gallic tribes.

The pacification of southern Italy was a long, slow business. Settlements with some of the allies who had revolted had already been reached,[3] but there were many loose ends to tie up. Some allies were still under provisional military governorship. Tarentum was originally to be deprived of its autonomy, but this seems not to have happened. It continued to be closely supervised, however. It was still under military control in 197 BC and was strategically sensitive, being one of the principal routes of communication with Greece and Macedon. The importance of the region, and Roman uneasiness about its loyalty and security, is illustrated by the fact that control of Tarentum and Apulia continued to be a praetorian province as late as 186 BC.[4] Nor was this alarmism on the part of Rome. Livy makes reference to intermittent but widespread brigandage in parts of the south, notably Apulia, throughout the 190s and 180s [Nos 73–4], which required a number of judicial interventions and the condemnation of several thousand people. The so-called Bacchanalian conspiracy of 186 BC, to which Rome reacted with a swift and savage programme of repression throughout Italy, was the best documented example in a long period of outbreaks of unrest [Nos. 70–73].

Security considerations were also integral to the programme of Roman colonization of the 190s. Citizen colonies were founded in 197 and 194, with a deduction of new colonists in 186 for those which seemed to be failing to flourish [Nos 64–6]. The location of these, at Liternum, Volturnum, Puteoli, Buxentum, Croton, Tempsa and Sipontum, indicates a concern with the security of the coast of Campania, Bruttium and Apulia. Two further foundations, both Latin colonies, on territory taken from Thurii and Vibo, were rather larger and may have been intended to settle discharged troops and provide a rather more substantial Roman presence.

In the 180s a larger-scale programme of colonization took place in northern Italy, urbanizing at a stroke a region which was relatively newly conquered and providing a system of defence against possible Gallic incursions. Colonies at Bononia, Parma, Mutina and Aquileia were of a more substantial size than the citizen colonies of southern Italy,[5] perhaps a sign that they were meant to serve as a basis for urbanization and local administration, not just act as garrisons.

The economic history of the second century BC is extremely difficult territory for the historian, although light is being shed by the results of archaeological surveys and excavation. The traditional view, based on literary sources, is that the devastation wrought by Hannibal, the scorched earth policy of Fabius Maximus, and the economic drain of nearly 50 years of continuous warfare brought the agrarian structure of Italy to the point of collapse. A vicious circle ensued[6] in which a declining rural population and the recruitment of a large percentage of Italy's peasant farmers into the army for long terms of service left many small farms abandoned and lying fallow; land speculators, many of them from the Roman elite, bought up land using wealth generated by overseas conquests, or simply misappropriated it; estates of increasing size were formed, dedicated to stock-raising and cash crops; access to a supply of cheap slaves, generated by Rome's wars overseas, allowed landowners to drive out tenant farmers and run their estates more cheaply using slave labour. The end result of this dismal scenario was chronic agrarian depression and an increase in urban poverty, as the dispossessed flocked to the cities, typified by the devastation that Tiberius Gracchus was said to have witnessed in Etruria [No. 102] – a landscape filled with slaves and sheep – while the Italian peasantry declined into poverty.

Needless to say, the problem was not that simple. Estimates of the damage done by Hannibal, and the length of time it took to recover, vary widely. Damaged olive groves take up to twenty years to recover, but other crops become viable much more quickly, and there seems strong reason to doubt that the recovery of Italian agriculture could not have been accomplished within a few years.[7] The depopulation question is rather more difficult to address, thanks to lack of reliable statistics. There were certainly problems, due both to high casualties during the war and the continued need for military manpower after it, and there is no doubt that terms of service were becoming longer as a citizen militia designed for fighting local and seasonal campaigns struggled to cope with the demands of distant and long-term warfare. However, the level of colonization, particularly in northern Italy, suggests that there was still a considerable level of surplus population.[8] What was involved was not so much depopulation in the absolute sense as a redistribution of population from the rebellious areas of southern Italy to the newly colonized north, and from rural to urban areas.

It must also be borne in mind that migration by purely personal initiative was not easy[9] and that when it took place, it was not necessarily for economic reasons. One factor which raised concern amongst the Latins, and also among the Samnites and Paeligni [No. 80], was the extent to which their citizens were exercising the *ius migrationis*, which gave Latins the right to move to Rome and become Roman citizens. This became an increasingly fraught issue, as Rome became more restrictive of citizen rights and allies more inclined to demand them. However, it is clear as early as 177, and becomes clearer from 123 onwards, that Rome's preoccupation with ejecting non-citizens from the city was generated by political, not economic, factors. This is not to deny that there were profound changes in the agrarian economy of Italy, which will be discussed further in the relevant chapter, but they cannot be entirely assimilated to a model of wholesale decline and decay. The Gracchan crisis was at least as much bound up with the political issues of land tenure, citizen rights and factional tensions, if not more so, as with a decline in the agrarian economy.

In a different sphere, economic changes profoundly affected the nature of Italian society in the second century. The conquest of an overseas empire brought with it immense wealth and trading opportunities. The scale of this can be judged by the fact that the booty collected in 187 BC from campaigns in Macedon enabled the senate to remit direct taxation for all Roman citizens for several years, and the final sum secured by Aemilius Paullus allowed this remission to be made permanent in 167 [No. 86]. Trading interests outside Italy were established by the third century, and involved Latins and Italians as well as Romans. The 500 Italians imprisoned by Carthage for supplying her rebel mercenaries and the

Italian merchants harassed by Queen Teuta in Illyria in 230 provide evidence of this [No. 89]. However, the scale of operations increased dramatically after the end of the second Punic war, and in particular, with the grant in 167 of the status of a free port to Delos,[10] already the centre of the slave trade. Delos provides our best source of evidence, with many surviving inscriptions set up by, or in honour of, Italians, but the phenomenon was not confined to the island. Italians appear in inscriptions all over the Mediterranean, from the Dalmatian coast to Egypt and Asia Minor.[11] The tendency for Greek inscriptions to describe all Italians as *Rhomaioi* – Romans – makes it difficult to identify the origins of most of these people, with the exception of those from the Greek-speaking areas of southern Italy, who identify themselves in the Greek manner, by their ethnic origin as well as their name. Analysis of regional derivations of gentilicial names, however, suggests that a very large number of the *negotiatores* were Oscans, from Samnium, Lucania and Campania [Nos 93–6]. One possibility is that they were initially people who were political exiles or who had fled from the war, and Roman punishment of those who had revolted, but it is difficult to account for both the numbers and the persistence of the phenomenon solely in these terms.[12]

The primary activities of these people were almost certainly trade, banking and tax farming, but they also appear in other contexts. Italian youths enrolled as ephebes at Athens and Delos, an early example of the development of a Greek tour as a final stage in the Roman noble's education,[13] and Italians competed in athletic and artistic festivals in the second and early first centuries BC.[14] The business dealings and social connections of entire families can be traced over several generations through inscriptions from Delos, implying a stability of population, and some individuals made considerable investments in the development of the island, notably the building of the Agora of the Italians and the Sanctuary of the Foreign Gods. Other factors indicate a certain amount of fluidity, particularly in terms of nationality. Philostratos, son of Philostratos, for instance, was a banker and merchant who is attested, together with his sons and slaves, in a substantial group of inscriptions, originates as Philostratos of Ascalon, in Syria, but acquired Neapolitan citizenship at some stage, and is named as Philostratos of Naples in later inscriptions. However, there was still a strong element of segregation. Italian religious cults and associated *collegia*, such as those of the *Compitales* and *Mercuriales*, were exported, and many cities in the East had a *conventus civium Romanorum* – an assembly of Roman citizens, which provided a focus for the activities of Romans and possibly also for Italians.[15] The massacre of Italians in Asia by Mithridates in 88 BC indicates that Italian communities were both highly visible and deeply disliked.

As far as Italy is concerned, the impact of the influx of wealth can be seen in the lavish building programmes mounted both by cities and by individuals. Rome acquired its first marble temple, dedicated to Jupiter Stator, in 146 BC[16] and put such a large amount of money into public works in Rome and Italy that the contracts are described as too numerous to count [No. 87]. The increasing presence of conspicuous consumption in both public and private life was cause for comment and for sumptuary legislation. Outside Rome, the effects are seen in the enormous amount of building activity in the cities of Campania, often with a distinctly Hellenizing flavour, and in Roman-generated projects such as road building.

By 133 BC, however, two themes of second century history converge to cause a political crisis – namely the status of the allies and the problem of land ownership. Relations between Rome and her allies were in a state of steady decline throughout most of the second century BC. The imbalance of power between Rome and the rest of Italy was becoming increasingly obvious, and there is a perceptible tendency for Rome to interfere more in the affairs of allied states. The commissions to suppress public disorder, and in particular the Bacchanalian conspiracy, in which the senate suppressed the cult of Bacchus even in allied territory, were a powerful assertion of Rome's right to interfere with allied autonomy on the pretext of maintaining security and public order. Individual magistrates became more willing to impose on allied communities, and also more willing to bend the law to serve Rome's interests.

Both citizenship and Latin status were more restricted in definition and awards were more tightly controlled by Rome. Communities of *cives sine suffragio* were gradually upgraded to full citizenship but further grants were not made, thus crystallizing the divisions between citizens and non-citizens. The grey area represented by native populations who were absorbed into colonies was clarified by the ruling that the Ferentinates were illegal in their attempt to join a citizen colony and to become citizens, and a loophole which allowed allies to become citizens by selling themselves into slavery to a citizen and then arranging manumission was closed. The *Lex Sempronia Repetundarum* (123 BC) enshrined the right of Roman officials to conduct judicial investigations in allied territory, and offers grants of citizenship and/or military exemption as a reward to informers, something which is elaborated in a fragment of an extortion law of *c.*100 BC from Tarentum. The changing rights and definitions of Latin and allied status have been discussed elsewhere, and the growing demand for citizenship is the subject of the next chapter, but by the last quarter of the second century, allied discontent with their status and with Roman treatment was becoming a powerful factor in Roman politics.

The emergence of both the land and the citizenship questions occurred in the legislation of Tiberius Gracchus in 133 BC, and as a result, his tribunate marks a watershed in the history of Roman Italy. The Gracchan land reforms had their roots in the agrarian problems outlined above, but they also had a strong political dimension. Gracchus was not concerned with agrarian reform *per se* but with the distribution of the *ager publicus*. This was land which had been confiscated from defeated enemies during the conquest of Italy and by the second century BC amounted to a considerable proportion of Italian land.[17] Some of it was used for the foundation of colonies, and the rest was publicly owned and – in theory – was let out by the censors in return for rent. In fact, this system had substantially fallen into abeyance. In many areas, the existing tenants of the land may have remained on it. Rents were not regularly collected, boundaries with private land were not securely established, and the regulations defining the maximum holdings per person were no longer enforced, allowing individuals to amass very large estates.

Gracchus' law provided for the enforcement of an upper limit of 500 *iugera* per person, with a subsidiary allowance for 250 *iugera* for children, up to 1,000 *iugera* altogether. In choosing these limits, Gracchus claimed to be merely enforcing the terms of the *Lex Licinia Sextia* of 367 BC, but this is unlikely as the limits are unusually high by the standards of fourth century estates. It is possible that figures for the laws of 367 are in fact an anachronistic reflection of the terms of the *Lex Sempronia*. The land freed by these regulations would be distributed to the landless poor and decreed inalienable. The scheme would thus, at a stroke, have solved the problems of urban poverty and shortage of military manpower, and incidentally given Gracchus a *clientela* of unprecedented size. At any rate, the reforms were hugely unpopular in the Senate, and Gracchus only managed to have them passed by taking them direct to the people, using his tribunician powers, and packing the three-man land commission set up to implement them with his relatives. His attempt to be re-elected for a second term as tribune failed and he was killed in the ensuing riot.

The reforms pose an enormous historical problem in that we do not know exactly who stood to lose land by this law, and who stood to benefit.[18] Of our two principal sources, Appian takes the view that Italians were being driven off the land by land-hungry Romans, and stood to gain because the *Lex Sempronia* would allow them to participate in the distribution, while Plutarch takes a much more Romano-centric view, implying that the land distribution only applied to Roman citizens. It may be possible, however, to dispose of this difficulty, since Plutarch, writing in the second century AD, appears to be totally unaware that there was a legal difference between Romans and Italians. On balance, it is likely that at least some members of the Italian elite stood to lose land under the law, as well as Roman landowners. Certainly the activities of the land commission which was set up to implement the law caused a great amount of complaint among allied communities. The intended beneficiaries of the law are similarly obscure. Both sources make reference to large amounts of rural support for Gracchus and to large crowds who came to Rome to attend the assembly, but it is by no means certain that these were allies, as Appian implies. They could equally have been citizens living outside Rome. Instances of viritane assignments of land to allies suggest that there was no legal bar to allies being assigned *ager publicus*.[19] However, there is also a small amount of evidence that Tiberius Gracchus may have promised to extend citizenship to non-citizens who received land [No. 123].[20]

What is certain is that whatever the intention, the activities of the land commissioners fell hardest upon the allies. Appian underlines the difficulties faced in tracing ownership of land and establishing boundaries between *ager publicus* and *ager privatus*, and hints that many allied landowners found themselves dispossessed or relocated to marginal land. Of the surviving Gracchan boundary markers, we have some which explicitly record the confirmation of an existing tenant. A longer and more informative inscription from Lucania refers to the ejection of herdsmen to make room for farmers, and the building of Forum Popilii.[21] This may represent the ejection of herdsmen who had usurped public land in favour of Gracchan colonists, but it may equally represent the removal of indigenous pastoralists. In either case, it provides an example of interference with land use by Rome. Traces of Roman centuriation in the Vallo di Diano in Lucania also attest to the presence of Gracchan colonists.[22] There seems to be a distinct lack of political will in the senate to sort out these problems.

Gracchus' younger brother, Gaius, was no more successful in his reforms, although he did manage to create some sweeping judicial changes which gave control of the law courts to the equestrian order. His proposals to grant citizenship to the Latins and Latin status to the rest of Italy, ostensibly to buy off Italian opposition to land distribution, failed [Nos 126–8]. As far as land is concerned, he reverted to the idea of distribution by colonization, founding colonies at Scolacium, Tarentum and Carthage, the first to be founded outside Italy. There may also have been a colony at Capua, but there is no corroborating evidence, and the only datable deduction there is that of 59 BC.[23] Significantly, Gracchus had mass support in Italy as a whole, to the extent that the senate had to eject all non-citizens from Rome during the law's passage, and seems to have planned to include allies in his land schemes [Nos 115, 129].

The Gracchan land laws, whatever their original intention, seem to have had the effect of alienating both the Roman senate and large numbers of Italians, and after the death of Gaius Gracchus they were largely undone. A further tribunician law revoked the concept of inalienability, allowing participants in the distribution to sell their land, and finally, the *Lex Thoria* gave up on the whole problem by decreeing that the land commission should be disbanded and landowners should be confirmed in their existing holdings, subject to payment of rent. The extant but fragmentary text of a *Lex Agraria* of 111 BC is probably the *Lex Thoria*, although damage to the text and lack of information about Roman landholding makes it a very problematic document.[24]

In summary, the second century BC was a period of intense change, characterized by the tensions between the emergence of Rome as a world power and the breakdown of relations with the rest of Italy, and between agrarian problems and an economic boom on the proceeds of empire. Roman encroachment of allied autonomy led to increasing bitterness, and exclusion of allies and Latins from the full economic benefits of imperial expansion exacerbated the problem. The Gracchan land reforms, which in their application favoured the rights of Romans over those of allies, took place at a time when the demand for the extension of Roman citizenship was becoming a major political issue and, in effect, set the scene for the Social War and the enfranchisement of Italy.

Colonization

64. Livy 32.29.3 (197 BC)

C. Atinius, a tribune of the plebs, proposed that five colonies should be founded on the coast of Italy, two at the mouths of the rivers Volturnus and Liternus, one at Puteoli and one at Castrum Salerni: this place is next to Buxentum; 300 families were to be sent to each colony. The three commissioners for founding these, who were to hold office for three years, were M. Servilius Geminus, Q. Minucius Thermus and Ti. Sempronius Longus.

65. Livy 34.45.1–5 (194 BC)

In that year, colonies of Roman citizens were founded at Puteoli, Volturnum and Liternum, with 300 men each. At the same time, colonies of Roman citizens were founded at Salernum and Buxentum. They were established by the commissioners Ti. Sempronius Longus, who was then consul, M. Servilius and Q. Minucius Thermus. The land which had belonged to the Campanians was divided. At the same time, Sipontum was founded as a colony of Roman citizens, on land which had belonged to Arpi, by other commissioners, D. Junius Brutus, M. Baebius Tamphilus, M. Helvius. Colonies of Roman citizens were also sent to Tempsa and Croton. The territory of Tempsa had been captured from the Bruttii, who had ejected the Greeks; Croton was still occupied by Greeks. They were established by the commissioners Cn. Octavius, L. Aemilius Paulus and C. Laetorius for Croton and L. Cornelius Merula, Q. [. . .] and C. Salonianus at Tempsa.

66. Livy 39.45.5–9 (183 BC)

The senate were debating whether to found a colony at Aquileia, but could not decide whether to send a colony of Latins or Roman citizens. In the end, the senators decided that a Latin colony should be founded. P. Scipio Nasica, C. Flaminius and L. Manlius Acidinus were appointed as commissioners.

In the same year, Mutina and Parma, colonies of Roman citizens, were founded. 2,000 men were settled on land which had most recently belonged to the Boii, but previously to the Etruscans; eight *iugera* each were allotted at Parma and five at Mutina. The commissioners for the foundation were M. Aemilius Lepidus, T. Aebutius Parrus and L. Quinctius Crispinus. A colony of Roman citizens was also founded at Saturnia, in the *ager Caletranus*.

67. Livy 39.23.3–4

At the end of the year, because Sp. Postumius, the consul, had reported that in the course of his journeys along both coasts of Italy in connection with the commission of enquiry, he had found the colonies of Sipontum on the upper sea and

Buxentum on the lower sea abandoned, L. Scribonius Libo, M. Tuccius and Cn. Baebius Tamphilus were made commissioners for enrolling new colonists by T. Maenius, the urban praetor, acting on the authority of the Senate.

[183 BC. The reason for much of this colonization was to provide a system of defence for the Italian coast, particularly against the possibility of a seaborne invasion from the eastern Mediterranean. These coastal colonies had only 300 settlers, but there was a programme of much larger colonies in northern Italy. The commission referred to was the inquiry into Bacchanalian activities [Nos 70–2]. Contrary to Livy's suggestion that the colonies failed, archaeological evidence from Buxentum indicates a city which formed the centre of local political and economic networks.[25]]

Unrest in Italy

68. Livy 39.8.1–9.2; 14.3–10; 17.1–18.8

The inquiry into clandestine conspiracies was allotted to both consuls. A Greek of low status came to Etruria, who had none of those arts which the Greeks, a most learned people, brought to us in large quantities for the cultivation of both mind and body, but was a small-time priest and fortune-teller. Nor was he the sort who had an open religion, and by openly disclosing his belief and practice led minds into errors, but was a priest of secret and nocturnal ceremonies. There were initiations, which were at first passed on only to a few people, but then became generally known among men and women. The delights of wine and feasts were added to the ceremonies, in order to attract the minds of more people. When wine had inflamed minds, and night, and the mixture of male and female, age and youth, had extinguished all boundaries of modesty, all types of corruption began to take place, since everyone had pleasure ready to hand, whatever the inclination of his nature. There was not just one form of vice, the promiscuous defiling of freeborn men and women, but false witnesses, fraudulent signatures and wills and evidence, all of it coming from the same workshop. There were also poisonings and clandestine murders, so that sometimes the bodies were not even found for burial. Many things were done by artifice, and many more by violence. The violence was hidden because among the ululations and the noise of cymbals and drums, no voice could be heard screaming during the debauchery and murder.

The stain of the evil entered Rome from Etruria, like the infection of a disease. At first, the greater size of the city, with greater tolerance of such wickedness, concealed it. At last, traces of it came to the consul, Postumius, in this way . . .

[186 BC. The Bacchanalian conspiracy. This account includes stock features of Roman response to initiatory religion. The charges of debauchery and murder or cannibalism as part of the rite were also made against Christianity. Rome was particularly nervous of cults which practised their rites in secret, creating closed

groups within society. Livy includes details of P. Aebutius, whose stepfather alleg-
edly tried to corrupt him through Bacchic initiation to prevent him disclosing the
mismanagement of Aebutius estate, but who was saved by the decision of a
courtesan, Hispala, to reveal the plot to the consuls. The cult of Bacchus was
highly suspect because of its foreignness and secretive nature. Its origin is
obscure, but Dionysiac cults were common in the Greek cities of southern Italy,
attested by numerous Dionysos figurines. The prominence of these at Tarentum
has caused speculation that the cult may have originated there, being transmitted
to Campania and Etruria before reaching Rome. The suppression of the cult was
due not to its foreign origins, but to the lack of senatorial control over it.[26]]

69. Livy 39.13.7–9

Then Hispala explained the origins of the rites. At first it was a women's rite, to
which it was the custom that no man should be admitted. Three days each year
were earmarked, on which initiations into the rites were held during the day. It
was the custom to appoint the matrons in turn as priestesses. Annia Paculla, a
Campanian, had changed everything during her term as priestess, as if by a warn-
ing of the gods. For she had been the first to initiate men, her own sons Minnius
and Herennius Cerrinius. She had made the rites nocturnal, instead of by day,
and instead of three days a year, she held initiations on five days per month.

[The identification of a Campanian, Annia Paculla, as the source of the corrupting influence within the cult is consistent with Livy's portrayal of the Capuans,
who are described as corrupt and disloyal, and are subject to severe criticism for
their decision to defect to Hannibal in 215 BC. The ringleaders are eventually
identified as the Romans Gaius and Marcus Atinius, the Faliscan L. Opicernius
and Minnius Cerrinius, one of the sons of Paculla.[27]]

70. Livy 39.14.7–8

They [the senate] delegated the inquiry into the devotees of Bacchus and their
nocturnal rites to the consuls as extra-ordinary duties; they instructed them to
ensure that the witnesses Aebutius and Faecennia were not harmed and to
encourage other witnesses by rewards; the priests of these rites, whether they were
men or women, should be tracked down, not just in Rome but in all the *fora* and
conciliabula, so that they were in the power of the consuls; meanwhile, it should
be proclaimed in the city of Rome, and edicts should be sent through the whole of
Italy, that no one who was a Bacchic initiate should assemble or meet to perform
the rites, or to carry out any other sacred business. Above all, an inquiry should be
made into those who had met or conspired, in order to commit indecency or
crime. This was decreed by the Senate.

71. Livy 39.18.7–19.2

Then the consuls were given the job of suppressing the Bacchic cult, first in Rome, then in the whole of Italy, apart from where an ancient altar or image had been consecrated. Then, for the future, it was decreed that there should be no Bacchic cult in Rome or in Italy. If anyone considered these rites to be traditional or necessary, or felt unable to omit them without sin and atonement, he should bring the case before the *praetor urbanus*, who would consult the senate. If he were permitted, provided there were no less than 100 people present in the senate, he could celebrate the rite, so long as not more than five people were present at the ceremony, and as long as there was no communal treasury, no master of the rites, and no priest.

19. Then another *senatusconsultum*, related to this one, was passed, having been proposed by Q. Marcius, the consul, that the whole matter of those who had assisted the consuls as informers should be referred to the senate, when Sp. Postumius had returned to Rome after completing the inquiry. They voted to send Minnius Cerrinius the Campanian to Ardea in chains, and to warn the magistrates of Ardea in advance to guard him carefully, not only so that he should not escape but also so that he should not attempt to kill himself.

72. *CIL* 1².581

The consuls Q. Marcius Q. F. and Sp. Postumius L. F. consulted the senate on the Nones of October [7th], in the temple of Bellona. M. Claudius M. F., L. Valerius P. F. and Q. Minucius C. F. witnessed the recording of the decree. Concerning the Bacchic rites, they decreed that the following letter should be sent to those who are allied to Rome by treaty:

No one may decide to keep a cult place of Bacchus. If anyone says that they need to keep a cult place of Bacchus, they must come to the *praetor urbanus* at Rome, and when it has heard their petition, our Senate will decide on these things, provided that at least 100 senators are present when the matter is discussed. No man, neither Roman citizen, nor Latin, nor any ally, may attend a meeting of Bacchanalian women, unless they have applied in advance to the *praetor urbanus* and obtained his permission with the agreement of the senate, as long as no fewer than 100 senators are present when the matter is debated. This was agreed.

No man shall be a priest. No man or woman shall be a master; nor shall anyone decide to keep a common fund; nor shall anyone decide to make either a man or a woman a master or vice-master; nor shall anyone wish in future to make oaths, vows, pledges or promises between themselves nor to exchange assurances between themselves. No one may perform ceremonies in secret, and no one may perform ceremonies in public or private or outside the city boundaries unless they have applied in advance to the *praetor urbanus* and obtained his permission with the agreement of the senate, as long as no fewer than 100 senators are present when the matter is debated. This was agreed.

No one may hold a ceremony in a group larger than five men and women alto-gether, and not more that three men and two women may attend it, except with the permission of the *praetor urbanus* and the agreement of the senate as recorded above.

These instructions must be proclaimed at a public assembly for no fewer that three successive market days, and so that you are aware of the decision of the sen-ate, the decision was as follows:

They decided that if there is anyone who acts against the decree recorded above, they will be prosecuted on a capital offence. And they decided that it was right and proper that you should inscribe this on a bronze tablet and order it to be set up where it can be most easily read; and that within ten days after receiving this document, you must ensure that any Bacchic cult places which exist are destroyed, as recorded above, except if they contain anything holy. In the *Ager Teuranus*.

[186 BC. Found at Tiriolo, Calabria. Bronze tablet containing a letter from the senate, and the accompanying text of the *senatusconsultum de bacchanalibus*,[28] which was circulated among the allies. It outlaws the cult of Bacchus, except in very restricted circumstances and under direct senatorial supervision, through-out Italy. It represents both a change in Rome's attitudes towards foreign cults, which had previously been very open, particularly to Greek influences, and the first major attempt to enforce a senatorial ruling of this type over allied states. As such it, and the *quaestiones* which were set up to enforce it, represent a serious encroachment on allied autonomy.]

73. Livy 39.39.8 (185 BC)

That year, there was serious slave unrest in Apulia. L. Postumius held Tarentum as his province. He conducted a severe inquiry into a conspiracy of shepherds, who had made the roads and public pasturage unsafe by their brigandage. He condemned approximately 7,000 men, of whom many escaped, but many suf-fered capital punishment.

74. Livy 39.41.5–7

After the election of censors, the consuls and praetors left for their provinces, apart from Q. Naevius, who was detained for not less than four months before he could set out for Sardinia by the investigations into poisonings, the greater part of which took place outside Rome, in the *municipia* and *conciliabula*, because this seemed more convenient. If Valerius Antias is to be believed, he condemned more than 2,000 people. And L. Postumius, the praetor to whom the province of Tarentum had fallen, put down large-scale conspiracies of herdsmen, and fol-lowed up the rest of the Bacchanalian investigation with great thoroughness. Many who had not appeared when summoned or who had jumped bail were hiding in that part of Italy; in some cases, he pronounced these men guilty, and in others, he arrested them and sent them to the senate, in Rome. All of them were imprisoned by P. Cornelius.

[184 BC. Suppression of rural unrest and the final stages of the Bacchanalian inquiry. The "conspiracies of shepherds" in Apulia indicate slave revolts or brigandage, a major problem in pastoral areas of Italy. Given that this is not the only Roman commissioner sent to Tarentum, there may still have been some unrest among the allies in this region. The *quaestio de bacchanalibus* set a precedent for increasing Roman interference with allied autonomy, particularly when it could be justified on the pretext of maintaining public order.]

War in northern Italy

75. Livy 40.18.4

The Histrians were added [to the list of provinces allotted] because the Tarentines and Brundisians had reported that the coastal land was being raided by pirates, and by ships from across the sea. The Massilians made the same complaint about Ligurian ships.

[181 BC. Piracy was endemic in the Mediterranean at this date [Nos 88–9], but this was part of a larger campaign against the Ligurians, who threatened colonies in northern Italy and threatened to invade Italy.]

76. Livy 40.26.1–3 (181 BC)

At Rome, Baebius' letter [reporting that Aemilius Paullus was besieged by the Ligurians] caused great trepidation, which was all the greater after a few days because when Marcellus arrived in Rome, having handed his army over to Fabius, he removed the hope that the army which was in Gaul could be led against the Ligurians, because it was making war on the Histrians, who were preventing the foundation of the colony at Aquileia. Fabius was on his way there, and could not turn back, now that war had broken out. . . . Authority was granted to [the consuls] to enlist emergency troops on the spot wherever they went, and take them with them. The praetors Q. Petelius and Q. Fabius were ordered that Q. Petelius was to enrol two emergency legions of Roman citizens and should swear in everyone under 50 years of age, and Fabius should levy 15,000 infantry and 800 cavalry from the Latin allies.

77. Livy 40.28.6–7

More than 15,000 of the Ligurians were killed on that day, and 2,300 were captured. Three days after this, the whole of the Ligurian Ingauni surrendered, having given hostages. The steersmen and sailors who had been on the pirate ships were hunted down and were all held under guard. Thirty-two ships of this kind were captured off the Ligurian coast by C. Matienus, the *duumvir*.

[181 BC. Rome held an emergency levy after Aemilius Paullus found himself besieged by the Ligurians and war broke out with the Histrians. However, Aemilius fought his way out of camp and won a victory over the Ingauni, after which they surrendered.]

Changes in allied status

78. Livy 38.36.5–7

The Campanians, since the censors forced them to be assessed at Rome under a *senatusconsultum* which had been passed the previous year (for before that, it had been uncertain where they should be registered), asked that they should be allowed to take Roman citizens as wives, and for those who had already done so, that they could remain married to them, and that children born before this day should be legitimate and able to inherit. Both things were granted. Concerning the municipalities of Formiae, Fundi and Arpinum, C. Valerius Tappo, a tribune of the people, proposed that the right to vote – for previously they had citizenship without the vote – should be given to them. When four tribunes vetoed this proposal because it was not made on the recommendation of the senate, they were informed that it was the right of the people, not the senate, to grant the right to vote to whomever they wished, and they gave up. The measure was passed, so long as the people of Fundi and Formiae should vote in the tribe Aemilia, and the Arpinates in the Cornelia.

[188 BC. The position of the Campanians who were placed under direct rule by Rome after their recapture in 211 BC was gradually regularized, allowing them to be registered by the censors and have rights of intermarriage with citizens. In effect, this converted them to full citizens, despite the fact that Capua still did not exist as an autonomous community. Livy also refers to the process of upgrading *cives sine suffragio* to full citizenship.]

79. Livy 34.42.5–6 (195–4 BC)

In that year the Ferentinates attempted to obtain a new right, namely that Latins who had enrolled in a Roman colony should become Roman citizens: colonists of this status had been enrolled at Puteoli, Buxentum and Salernum and, when they tried to become Roman citizens by this means, the Senate adjudged that they were not Roman citizens.

80. Livy 41.8.6–12 (177 BC)

The senate was persuaded by delegation from the Latin allies, who had exhausted both the censors and the consuls of the previous year, and were at last brought before the senate. The gist of their complaints was that many of their own citizens had migrated to Rome and been included in the Roman census; if this were permitted, in only a few more five-year intervals, deserted towns and deserted farms would not be able to provide any soldiers. The Samnites and Paeligni also complained that 4,000 families had moved from their territory to Fregellae, and neither of them gave fewer troops during the levy. Also, two types of fraud had been used to gain individual changes of citizenship. The law gave Latin allies who left their children in their own city, the right to become Roman citizens. By abusing this law, some were injuring allies and some were injuring Roman citizens. So as not to leave their children behind, they would give their sons as slave to any Roman at all, on condition that they should be manumitted, and become freedman citizens; and those who had no children to leave adopted some, in order to become Roman citizens. Later, giving up pretence of legality, without regard to the law, and without reference to children, they transferred to Roman citizenship by migration and inclusion in a census. So that this should not go on, the delegates requested that the senate should order allies to return to their cities; secondly, that a law should be made that no one should acquire or relinquish a son for the purposes of changing citizenship; finally, that if anyone had become a Roman citizen, this should be revoked. These things were granted by the Senate.

81. Livy 41.9.9–12

Then C. Claudius initiated a law about the allies, with the approval of the Senate, and announced that all those Latin allies, or their forebears, who had been registered as Latins in the censorship of M. Claudius and T. Quinctius or after, should return to their own cities before the Kalends [1st] of November. An inquiry into those who had not returned was delegated to L. Mummius, the praetor. To this law and consular edict, a ruling of the senate was added, that any dictator, consul, *interrex*, censor or praetor who was now in office, or would be in the future, before whom a slave was brought to be freed and to have his freedom ratified, should require an oath that whoever was performing the manumission was not doing so in order to bring about a change of citizenship. They decreed that if this oath was not sworn, the manumission could not take place.

[177 BC. The censorship referred to took place in 189 BC.]

82. Livy 41.13.6–8

C. Claudius, the consul, arrived in the city; when he had reported to the senate on affairs in Histria and Liguria and their successful outcome, his request for a triumph was passed. He triumphed over two peoples simultaneously during his year of office. In this triumph, he carried 307,000 *denarii* and 85,072 *victoriati*. Soldiers received 15 *denarii* each, centurions received double, and the cavalry three times as much. Allies received half of the allowance given to citizens. And so they followed the triumphal chariot in silence, so that their anger was obvious.

[170 BC. The treatment of the allies contrasts with that in 180 BC, when Fulvius Flaccus distributed a donative to Latins at the same rate as to citizens.[29] This incident is only one example of the increasing discrimination against allies by Rome in many spheres of activity.]

Maltreatment of allies

83. Cicero, *De officiis* 1.33

Injustices often arise through malpractice, or rather too clever and fraudulent an interpretation of the law. . . . Not even one of our own people is to be approved of, if it is true that Q. Fabius Labeo, or someone else (for I have nothing on this except hearsay), having been sent by the senate to arbitrate a boundary dispute between Naples and Nola, spoke to both sides separately on his arrival, saying that they should not act greedily, and not seek expansion, but seek to make a concession rather than an acquisition. When both sides had agreed separately to this, there was a certain amount of land left between the boundaries. And so he set the boundaries of the cities as each had individually agreed; that which was left between them, he adjudged to belong to the Roman people.

[The exact date is unknown, but Q. Fabius Labeo was consul in 183 BC, so it can be attributed to the first half of the second century. It was not uncommon for allies to appeal to Rome for arbitration of disputes.]

84. Livy 42.1.6–12

Before the magistrates set out for their provinces, the Senate decided that the consul L. Postumius should go to Campania to establish the boundaries of *ager publicus* and private land, since private citizens, by gradually moving their boundaries outwards, were occupying a great part of the *ager publicus*. Postumius, who was angry at the Praenestines because when he had gone there as a private citizen to make a sacrifice in the temple of Fortuna no signs of respect had been given either publicly or privately by them, sent a letter to Praeneste before he set out from Rome, saying that the magistrates should come out to meet him, that quarters should be prepared at public expense where he could be entertained, and pack animals should be ready for him when he left. Before his consulship, no one had ever put any burdens or expense on the allies in any circumstance. Magistrates were given mules and tents and other military equipment so that they should not demand this of allies. They had private arrangements for hospitality; they kindly and companionably cultivated these, and they opened their own houses in Rome to guests, with whom they themselves were accustomed to stay. Envoys who were sent anywhere unexpectedly could demand one pack animal from each town through which their journey took them. Roman magistrates did not make any other impositions on allies. Even if justified, the anger of the consul should not have been displayed while he was in office, and the silence of the Praenestines, either from modesty or fear, established as a precedent the right of magistrates to make these demands, which grew more burdensome by the day.

[173 BC. As Livy indicates, the behaviour of L.Postumius in mistreating the Praenestines is an early example of the increasing tendency of Rome and its magistrates to treat the allies as subordinates and to increase impositions on them, both in terms of collective demands and the behaviour of private individuals.]

Increasing wealth and the benefits of empire

85. Polybios 6.57.5

For when a state has survived many great dangers, but then gains unchallenged supremacy, it is clear that as a result of habitual prosperity, life-styles will become more extravagant and men will become more ambitious for office and for other objects.

86. Cicero, *De officiis* 2.76

When he got hold of the entire wealth of Macedon, which was very large, Aemilius Paullus brought so much money into the treasury that the spoils of only one general abolished direct tax forever.

[The *tributum*, or direct tax, was abolished for Roman citizens in 167 BC, as a result of the huge influx of wealth after the conquest of Macedon.[30]]

87. Polybios 6.17.3–4

So huge a number of contracts that one can hardly count them are given out by the censors throughout the whole of Italy, for the building and repair of public amenities . . .

[Polybios, in commenting on the control exercised by the senate over public life, stresses the enormous amount of money that was being poured into public works in the second century. Although literary sources emphasize building in Rome itself, there is evidence that the same phenomenon occurred elsewhere, with a particular upsurge in civic development and building programmes in Campania.[31]]

Trade and finance: Italians in the East

88. Polybios 1.83.7–8 (239 BC)

When they [the Carthaginians] captured traders sailing from Italy to Libya with supplies for the enemy, they took them to Carthage, and there were nearly 500 of them in prison there, much to the annoyance of the Romans.

89. Polybios 2.8.1–3

For a long time, they [the Illyrians] had had the practice of harassing ships sailing from Italy, and now, while they were at Phoenice, a few of them left the fleet and robbed, or killed, many Italian merchants.

[230/29 BC. Both of these passages of Polybios indicate that Italians were engaged in trade with other parts of the Mediterranean in the third century, but the volume increased greatly between 200 and 88 BC.]

90. Livy 35.7.2

For there was another problem, because the city was struggling under interest payments, and because, although greed was restricted by many laws curbing usury, a way of evading these had come into being, by transferring their transactions to allies who did not have these laws. Debtors were thus being ruined by these unregulated interest rates. In looking for a way of checking this practice, it was decided to set the last Feralia festival as a time limit, so that after that day, any allies who were owed money by Roman citizens should disclose this, and that regarding money lent from that day the rights of creditors should be determined by whatever laws the debtor chose. Then, after the magnitude of the debt created by these fraudulent agreements had been revealed by these declarations, M. Sempronius, a tribune of the people, brought a proposal before the people on the authority of the senate, which was carried, that the same laws about lending money which applied to Roman citizens should be applied to the Latins and allies.

[193 BC. The use of Italian agents by Romans to circumvent legal limits on rates of interest is an early example of Italian involvement in trade and finance which became an important feature of the development of the eastern provinces.]

91. *SEG* 3.378

. . . The consul shall send letters to all peoples who are friends and allies of Rome in which he shall command them to ensure that citizens of Rome and her Latin allies from Italy can conduct their business which is necessary in safety among the eastern cities and islands, and can sail safely on the sea in their ships . . .

[c.100 BC. Extract from a Greek inscription from Delphi, which records a decree, made in response to a deputation from Rhodes to Rome, that all states should exclude pirates from their harbours in order to allow Romans and Latins to trade in safety.]

92. Livy 38.44.4

Taking the opportunity when Flaminius happened to be away through illness, the senate passed a decree on the motion of Aemilius, that the Ambraciotes should have all their property returned to them; that they should be free and should use their own laws; that they should collect what harbour duties they wished, on land and sea; provided that the Romans and Latin allies were exempt.

[187 BC. Rome's order to Ambracia to allow Romans and Latins unrestricted commercial access, by exempting them from *portoria*, indicates both the privileged status of the Latins *vis-à-vis* other allies and the expanding commercial interests of Italians.]

93. *Insc. Del.* 4.1645

To Theophrastos, son of Herakleitos, of the deme Acharnai, previously overseer of Delos, who laid out the agora and built piers around the harbour, dedicated by the Athenians living on Delos and by the Romans and the other foreign traders and owners of ships resident on Delos, in honour of his virtue, goodwill and benefactions.

[126/5 BC. Delos. Statue set up in honour of Theophrastos, who was involved in laying out the agora and harbour of the island.]

94. *CIL* 3.2.14203

M. Granius M. L. Her, Diodotos slave of C. and Cn. Seius, Apollonius slave of Q. Laelius, Prepon slave of M. Alleius, Nicandrus slave of M. Rasennus, dedicated this to Jove Liber.

[Second century BC (?). Delos. Bilingual inscription in Latin and Greek recording a dedication by a group of slaves and freedmen to Jupiter Liber/Zeus Eleutherios. Although the names of the dedicants are all Greek, their owners all have Oscan *nomina*.]

95. *CIL* 3.2.14203

M. Pactumeius M. F., M. Tuscennius L. F. Nobilior, D. Folvius D. F., C. Gessius D. L., P. Granius P. L., L. Arellius A. L., *Magistri* of Mercury and Maia.

[Second century BC. Delos. Bilingual inscription in Latin and Greek listing the *magistri* of the college of Mercury and Maia. Like many of the Italians in the Aegean, they are of predominantly Oscan origin. Colleges of Mercury are well-attested from Italy. Other colleges found on Delos are those of the *Hermaistai*, *Apollonastai* and *Poseidoniastai*, dedicated to Hermes, Apollo and Poseidon, respectively.]

96. *Insc. Del.* 4.1725

The merchants and the men who do business in the square agora of Apollo, Artemis and Leto [set up this statue] of Maraios Gerillanus, Mar. F. the Roman, and banker on Delos, because of his generosity to them. Made by Agasias, son of Menophilos, of Ephesos.

[Early first century BC. Inscription on statue from Delos. The name of the dedicant, Marius Gerillanus, M. F., is distinctively Oscan, even down to the Oscan spelling Maraheis, despite the Greek custom of referring to all Italians as *Rhomaioi* (Romans).]

97. *Insc. Del.* 4.1724

To Philostratos, son of Philostratos, of Naples, who was merchant at Ascalon and banker on Delos, set up by P., C. and Cn. Egnatius, sons of Q. Egnatius, Romans, in honour of their benefactor. Dedicated to Apollo. Made by Lysippos, son of Lysippos, from Heraklea.

[98–7 BC. Delos. Greek inscription from a dedication to Apollo in the Syrian sanctuary. Other inscriptions from Delos refer to Philostratos, who was from Ascalon in Syria, but took Neapolitan citizenship, after which he is usually referred to as Philostratos of Naples. His name appears on the dedicatory inscription on the portico of the Agora of the Italians, on an *exedra* in the agora itself and on a number of other fragments. He played a prominent role in the trade and finances of Delos, and was active there from *c*.140 BC until *c*.98–7.]

Economic background to the land reforms

98. Plutarch, *Life of Ti. Gracchus* 8

When the Romans annexed land from their neighbours as the result of wars, they customarily sold part by auction. The rest was made common land, and was distributed amongst the poorest and neediest of the citizens, who were allowed to cultivate it on payment of a small rent to the public treasury. When the rich began to outbid the poor and drive them out by offering higher rents, a law was passed which forbade an individual to hold more than 500 *iugera* [*c*.310 acres] of land. This constrained the greed of the rich for a while, and helped the poor, enabling them to remain on the land which they had rented, so that each could occupy the allotment which had been granted to them. After a while, the rich in each area contrived to transfer many of these allotments to themselves, by using fictitious names, and eventually, they overtly took possession of most of the land under their own names. When they found themselves forced off the land, the poor became increasingly unwilling to volunteer for military service, or to raise a family. Thus there was a rapid decline of free peasant farmers throughout Italy, their place being taken by gangs of foreign slaves, used by the rich to cultivate the estates from which the free citizens had been driven off. . . .

[The earlier law referred to is the *Lex Licinia Sextia* of 367–6 BC. The maximum size of allotment looks suspiciously large for the fourth century, and is probably an anachronism based on the limits set by the *Lex Sempronia* of 133.]

99. Appian, *Civil wars* 1.7–8

As they conquered the Italians in war, the Romans seized a portion of their lands and built cities there, or enrolled colonists of their own to occupy existing ones. These had the function of garrisons. The cultivated part of land acquired in war was assigned immediately to colonists, or sold, or leased out. Since there was no opportunity to allot the part which was devastated by war (usually the larger part), they proclaimed that meanwhile, anyone who was willing to work it may do so for a toll of the annual yield – one tenth of the grain and one fifth of the fruit. Those who kept flocks were required to pay in stock, both larger and smaller livestock. These things were done in order to multiply the Italian people, which was considered to be the most hard-working of all peoples, so that they might have many allies at home. In fact, the opposite happened. For the rich, gaining possession of most of the undistributed land, and gaining boldness through time to believe that it would not be taken away, absorbed adjacent strips of land and neighbouring farms, partly by purchase and partly by force, and came to cultivate large tracts of land instead of single farms, using slaves as labourers and herdsmen, in case free workers should be taken from farming into the army. At the same time, ownership of slaves brought great wealth through their many offspring, who increased because they were not enlisted into the army. Thus powerful men became very rich and a race of slaves multiplied throughout the country, while the Italian people declined in numbers and strength, being afflicted by poverty, taxes and military service.

Earlier land legislation

100. Appian, *Civil wars* 1.8

For these reasons [i.e. depopulation and the growth of slave-run estates], the [Roman] people became anxious that they would no longer have enough Italian allies and that the state itself would be endangered by such a huge number of slaves. As they could not see a solution, it being difficult and unjust to deprive men of possessions they had held for so long, including their own trees and houses, a law was passed, with difficulty and at the insistence of the tribunes, that nobody should hold more than 500 *iugera* of this land [*ager publicus*], or pasture more than 100 cattle or 500 sheep on it. To ensure that the law was observed, it was provided that a certain number of freedmen should be employed on the land, to watch and report what was happening. Having included all this in the law, they took an oath over and above the law, and fixed penalties for breaking it, and it was believed that the rest of the land would soon be divided among the poor, in small units. But little heed was paid to the law and oaths. The few men who seemed to respect them fraudulently transferred land to their relatives, but most men ignored it entirely.

101. Plutarch, *Life of Ti. Gracchus* 8

. . . Scipio's friend C. Laelius tried to reform this abuse [of the Licinio-Sextian laws], but when he was opposed by estate-owners, he became afraid of the conflict that his reforms seemed likely to cause, and he abandoned the attempt. . . . . Tiberius, on the other hand, went to the root of the problem as soon as he had been elected tribune. He was encouraged in his plans, as most writers report, by Diophanes the orator and Blossius the philosopher. Diophanes was an exile from Mytilene, but Blossius was a native Italian from Cumae . . .

Motivations for reform

102. Plutarch, *Life of Ti. Gracchus* 8

Others maintain that Tiberius was influenced by his jealousy of one Sp. Postumius. This man was the same age as Tiberius and a rival as an orator. When Tiberius returned from his campaign against Numantia and found that his rival had outstripped him in fame and influence and attracted general admiration, it seems that he resolved to outdo him by introducing a challenging political programme which would arouse great expectations among the people. His brother Gaius, however, has written in a political pamphlet that while Tiberius was travelling through Etruria to Numantia, he saw how the countryside had been deserted by its inhabitants, and how those who farmed the land or herded the flocks were barbarian slaves introduced from abroad. It was this experience that inspired the policy which later brought so many misfortunes on the two brothers. But it was above all the people themselves who did most to arouse Tiberius' energy and ambition by inscribing slogans and appeals on porticoes, monuments and the walls of houses, calling upon him to recover public land for the poor.

The Terms of the Land Law, 133 BC

103. Plutarch, *Life of Ti. Gracchus* 9

. . . The men who deserved to be punished for breaking the law, and who should have been fined as well as forced to surrender their land, which they had been illegally enjoying, were only required to give up their unjust acquisitions – for which they were compensated – and to allow ownership to pass to the citizens who most needed the land.

104. Plutarch, *Life of Ti. Gracchus* 10

These tactics angered Tiberius and he withdrew his conciliatory law and introduced one which was more pleasing to the people and harsher to the landowners. It demanded that they should vacate the land which they had acquired against earlier laws, but this time it offered no compensation.

105. Velleius Paterculus 2.2.2

. . . in the consulship of P. Mucius Scaevola and L. Calpurnius, 160 years ago, Tiberius Gracchus split away from the nobles and promised citizenship to the whole of Italy, and at the same time by proposing an agrarian law which everyone immediately desired [to see passed], he mixed up the highest and the lowest, and brought the state into extreme danger.

[This passage provides some evidence that Tiberius Gracchus pre-empted his brother in proposing to extend citizenship to the Italians as part of his land reform programme.[32]]

The Land Commission

106. Plutarch, *Life of Ti. Gracchus* 13

After this, Tiberius' land law was passed and three men were appointed to survey and distribute public land. These were Tiberius himself, his father-in-law, Appius Claudius, and his brother, Gaius Gracchus, who was not in Rome at this point, but was serving with Scipio in a campaign against the Numantines.

107. Appian, *Civil wars* 1.13

The first commissioners appointed to carry this [the land law] out were Gracchus, the creator of the law, his brother, who had the same name, and Appius Claudius, the father-in-law of Tiberius Gracchus, because the people were afraid that if Gracchus and his family did not take the lead, the law would not be put into execution. Gracchus gained great popularity because of the law, and was escorted home by the crowd as if he were the founder not just of one city or people but of all the peoples of Italy. After this, those who were victorious went back to their land, which they had left in order to take part in [the vote], but the defeated stayed behind, talking and saying that when Gracchus became a private citizen again, he would regret that he had insulted the sacred and inviolable office of tribune and sown the seeds of civil war in Italy.

108. Plutarch, *Life of Ti. Gracchus* 14

Soon after this, King Attalus Philometor died, and Eudemos of Pergamum brought his will to Rome, in which the Roman People were named as his heirs. Tiberius immediately made a bid for popularity by introducing a law by which Attalus' money should be distributed amongst citizens who had received grants of public land, as soon as it arrived in Rome, in order to help them stock and cultivate their farms.

[Attalus Philometor was King of Pergamum (*c.*138–133 BC), who bequeathed his private fortune, including part of the kingdom of Pergamum, to the Roman people. Both Plutarch and Appian make it clear that the land law and its implementation were concentrated in the hands of Gracchus and his immediate family, and that it created both immense short-term popularity and the potential for a very large Gracchan *clientela*. Appian stresses the importance of rural supporters of Gracchus, who helped to carry the law in 133, but whose absence was instrumental in his downfall later that year.]

109. Appian, *Civil wars* 1.14

It was now summer, and the election of tribunes was about to take place. As polling day drew near, it was very apparent that the rich had strongly supported the election of those most hostile to Gracchus. He, afraid that something bad would happen if he were not re-elected as tribune for the next year, called on the people in the fields to attend the election. As they were engaged with the harvest, and with little time remaining before election day, he turned for support to the people of the city and went round them individually, asking them to elect him as tribune, on account of the danger he was in on their behalf. When the voting took place and the first two tribes both voted for Gracchus, the rich proposed that it was illegal for the same man to hold the office for two terms. Rubrius, the tribune who had been chosen by lot to preside over the assembly, was doubtful, but Mummius, who had been elected tribune in place of Octavius, encouraged him to hand over the electoral assembly to him. Octavius did so, but the rest of the tribunes argued that the presidency must be decided by lot. When Rubrius, who had been chosen by this method, resigned, the whole process should be taken again. Since there was much contention on the issue, and since he was coming off worst, Gracchus adjourned the election until the next day.

[Election of the tribunes for 132 BC. Gracchus attempted to stand for a second time but the mass support of the rural voters which he had relied on in the previous year was not forthcoming, and he was opposed in the *comitium*. Gracchus and his supporters occupied the Capitol and the *comitium*. When fighting broke out, the elections were abandoned and a state of emergency declared. A group of senators led by Scipio Nasica broke up the riot, during the course of which Gracchus was killed.]

110. Appian, *Civil wars* 1.18

After Gracchus had been killed and Appius Claudius had died, Fulvius Flaccus and Papirius Carbo were appointed to distribute the land, together with the younger Gracchus, and since those who were in possession of the land would not give details of their estates, a proposal was made that informers could provide evidence against them. Immediately a large number of embarrassing legal cases arose. For where a plot of land had been bought or had been divided amongst allies, the whole area had to be surveyed because of the measurement of this one plot, to find out how it had been sold or divided. Many people did not have contracts or title deeds. Where these could be found, they were often ambiguous. When they had been surveyed again, some people were forced to give up their orchards and buildings in exchange for open ground. Others were moved from farmed to uncultivated land, to marshes and to wetlands.

111. *CIL* 1.643

M. Fulvius M. F. Flaccus, C. Sempronius Ti. F. Gracchus, C. Papirius C. F. Carbo, commission for adjudicating and assigning lands. Estate allowed to existing occupier, at no charge.

[123 BC. Aeclanum. Assessment of the Gracchan commission in favour of existing owner.]

112. *CIL* 1.719

M. Terentius M. F. Varro Lucullus, *propraetor*, superintended the re-establishment, by decree of the Senate, of boundary stones in the places where P. Licinius, Appius Claudius and C. Gracchus placed them.

[82–1 BC. Found between Pisanum and Fanum (Umbria). Renewal of Gracchan boundary stones, by decree of the Senate.]

113. *CIL* 1.638

[P. Popilius, C. F.], consul. I built the road from Rhegium to Capua and placed all the bridges, milestones and signposts on it. From this place, it is 51 miles to

Nuceria, 84 to Capua, 74 to Muranum, 123 to Consentia, 180 to Valentia, 231 to the Straits [of Messina] at the Statue, 237 to Rhegium. The total number of miles from Capua to Rhegium is 321. Also, as praetor in Sicily, I overcame runaway slaves belonging to Italians and returned 917 of them [to their owners]. Also, I was the first to force herdsmen to give up *ager publicus* to farmers. I built a forum and public buildings in this place.

[132 BC. Forum Popilii (Polla), Lucania. Inscription marking the implementation of the Gracchan laws and the foundation of Forum Popilii. There is controversy over the identity of the consul as the stone is damaged. It may have been set up by P. Popilius Laenas or by one of the Annii.[33]]

Further reforms: 132–122 BC

114. Appian, *Civil wars* 1.19

The Italians who protested about the disturbances and particularly of the lawsuits against them, chose Cornelius Scipio, who destroyed Carthage, to defend them against these injustices. As he had received enthusiastic support from them in war, he was unwilling to ignore the request and so brought the matter before the senate, and although he did not criticize Gracchus' law, out of respect for the people, he outlined its problems and suggested that these cases should not be judged by the commissioners, since they did not have the trust of the litigants, but sent to other courts. As this seemed reasonable, they accepted his judgment; Tuditanus, the consul, was appointed to judge the cases. Having begun the task and seen the extent of its problems, he undertook a campaign against the Illyrians, so as not to have to make the judgments, and since no one else brought the cases to trial, the land commissioners did nothing. The people felt hatred and indignation towards Scipio because he, on whose behalf they had on many occasions opposed the powerful and thus incurred their displeasure, and twice elected consul contrary to the law, now supported the Italians against themselves. Scipio's enemies, having seen this, announced that he had decided to abolish Gracchus' law entirely.

[The belief that the land laws were to be repealed caused widespread alarm, partly alleviated by the death of Scipio, and ushered in a period of further turbulence due to continued political instability and dissatisfaction with the activities of the land commissioners [No. 110].]

115. Appian, *Civil wars* 1.27

The civil strife of the younger Gracchus ended. Soon, a law was passed to allow landholders to sell the land, about which they had quarrelled. For this had been forbidden by the law of the first Gracchus. And immediately, the rich began to buy up the allotments of the poor, or to find cause to seize them. The situation of the poor declined, until the tribune Spurius Thorius introduced a law that the land distributions should stop, but that land should belong to those holding it, and rent should be paid by them to the people, and that the money collected should be distributed. This was a help to the poor, but did not help to increase the population. By these means, the Gracchan law, which was a good and useful one if it could have been put into operation, was overturned, and a short while later the rent was abolished by another tribune, and the people lost everything.

The legislation of C. Gracchus, 123 BC

116. Plutarch, *Life of C. Gracchus* 5

Gracchus now proposed a number of laws, which he hoped would please the people, as well as undermining authority of the senate. Of these, one concerned the *ager publicus*, which he proposed to divide among the poor citizens.

117. Plutarch, *Life of C. Gracchus* 9

This showed clearly that the senate did not object to Gracchus' measures them-selves, but was determined to humiliate and crush him. For instance, when Gracchus brought forward a proposal to found two colonies, to be made up of the most loyal citizens, they accused him of attempting to curry favour with the people; but when Livius proposed to found 12 colonies and to send 3,000 of the poorest citizens to each, they heartily approved the measure. Also, when Gracchus distributed *ager publicus* amongst the citizens who had the greatest need, provided that every man should pay a small amount of rent to the public treasury, they protested fiercely and accused him of wooing the people; when Livius proposed to remove even the token contribution from the tenants, they supported him readily.

118. Appian, *Civil wars* 1.23

The senate also instructed another tribune, Livius Drusus, to use his veto against Gracchus' laws, but not to give the people his reasons. A tribune did not have to give his reasons for a veto. They awarded him the foundation of 12 colonies, as an act of kindness to the people. The people were pleased by this, and disdained the laws of Gracchus.

119. Velleius Paterculus 1.15.4–5

During the consulship of Cassius Longinus and Sextius Calvinus, who defeated the Sallues at the waters which are called Aquae Sextiae, Fabrateria was founded, about 153 years ago. In the following year, Scolacium Minervium, Tarentum Neptunia and Carthage in Africa, the first colony outside Italy as I have already mentioned, were founded.

[124 BC. The last three of these formed part of the Gracchan programme of colonization.]

120. Gasperini (1971), *3° Misc. Greca e Romana*

A. Titinius A. F. gave a small shrine to Diana as a well-deserved gift.

[Tarentum. Second or early first century BC. Bilingual dedication to Diana/Athena in Greek and Latin. Titinius may be one of the Gracchan colonists of 122 BC.]

Legal reforms

121. *CIL* $1^2.583$

With reference to the holding of an investigation for evidence: with reference to the person to be summoned under this law, the praetor shall cause the court to be set up on the earliest possible day and shall assign to the man who brought the summons as many days as he thinks necessary for investigation of the evidence, to the best of his ability, provided nothing is done contrary to this law; nor, after this law is passed. . . . he shall ask for evidence to be collected in Italy in the towns, *fora* and *conciliabula* which are usually administered by *praefecti*, or outside Italy in the towns, *fora* and *conciliabula* usually administered by *praefecti* . . .

On the Granting of Citizenship: If anyone who is not a Roman citizen summons another person . . . . before the praetor responsible for undertaking such an inquiry under this law, and this person is condemned in such a court under this law, then the person who brought the summons and by whose doing, beyond all other non-citizens, it is proved that the accused was condemned . . . shall be made a Roman citizen by this law, if he wishes, together with the sons born to him, and the sons of his sons shall be full Roman citizens, and whichever tribe the person summoned by him under this law voted in, these men shall vote in the same tribe and be assessed by the censor; and these men shall be exempt from military service and all money and allowances of this type shall be considered earned.

[Two extracts from a law (123 BC) which has been variously identified as a *Lex Acilia*, passed by the tribune Acilius Glabrio as part of C. Gracchus' programme, or a *Lex Sempronia*, proposed by Gracchus himself. It was designed to curb extortion and to remove the extortion court from the control of the senate to that of the Equites. The law exists only in a series of 11 fragments, of which these are the two which most directly concern the Italians.]

122. *Fragmentum Tarentinum* (*ZPhE* 45 [1982], 127–38)

If someone who is not a Roman citizen has reported someone to the praetor who is conducting the investigation, in accordance with this law, and that person is found guilty by this investigation, then the person who reported him and by whose particular efforts he has been convicted, if he does not hold the post of dictator, praetor or aedile in his own city and if he does not wish to become a Roman citizen, according to this law, then he, and his sons and grandsons born of his sons, will be immune in every respect in their own cities, including payment of tribute, and have the right to appeal to Roman magistrates or pro-magistrates on the same basis as Roman citizens, and they will be considered absolved of all obligations to military or public service and all military payments and allowances.

If he, or his sons or the sons of his sons, summon someone else in a legal case, or if they are summoned by someone else in legal proceedings, then the case may be tried at Rome if they wish, and in front of any magistrate before whom Roman citizens may lawfully appear in such a case. No magistrate or pro-magistrate may instigate the diminution or extension of the judicial procedure in the case of such a man. The magistrate to whom he is referred shall not act in any way in his case other than that which is laid down by law. If any decision is made in this instance which is against this law and is without his consent, the judgement may be legally restrained in respect of this magistrate, provided that it results from the magistrate's deceit.

If a Roman citizen has reported someone else's name, in accordance with this law, and this person is convicted by judicial inquiry, then the man by whose particular efforts he was convicted, together with his sons and their sons, can lawfully vote in the tribe of the convicted man, for those of them who wish to do so, and also be registered in that tribe at the census. And a call to military or public service, and military pay and allowances to them, shall be regarded as fulfilled. In the case of a summons to public or military service, now or in the future, under this law, no magistrate or pro-magistrate can force him in his community to do this against his will, nor order him to do so, nor proceed against him against the right of appeal, nor register him as a soldier, nor administer the military oath, nor demand an oath of allegiance, nor order him to be asked to do this, nor lead him into battle, nor ask anyone else to do this, except in the case of a Gallic or Italian revolt . . .

The *praetor peregrinus* is responsible for copies of this law being given to delegates of the allies, to all Latin communities, and to foreign peoples and client kings if they wish. And he shall administer the reading of this law in public assembly and in the senate six months before and six months after this publication.

The *quaestor* of the *aerarium* will be responsible for the posting in the forum, at eye-level, of a bronze tablet inscribed with this law, in engraved lettering. When this has been posted, the magistrates will be responsible for checking that it has not been taken down or defaced by those who drafted it and were present at the inscribing or anyone who handled it for any other reason.

The *praetor* responsible will ensure that a list is published, in the forum on a white tablet, of the informers during his year of office, from each ally, people or city in the state. In connection with this list, when judgment had been passed in accordance with this law, he shall be responsible for recording the decision of the jurors in the case concerning whoever may be acquitted under this law, or found guilty under this law.

If someone has been found guilty under this law, and it has been proposed that one of those by whose efforts he was brought to justice should be rewarded [concerning that matter with regard to those who reported him], each juror shall cast a vote in court, openly and individually, and the praetor shall honour the man who is seen to have a majority of the votes of the jurors with a reward as detailed above, and he will see to it that the name of the man rewarded in this fashion is inscribed on a bronze tablet and fixed to the base of the Rostra.

The magistrate or pro-magistrate and the jurors enrolled under this law shall swear by Jupiter and the Penates that they will do the things demanded by this law and they will not act contrary to it deliberately nor interfere in such a way that the law will be undermined or diminished. Anyone who has not sworn to this law cannot be a candidate for a magistracy or receive *imperium*, nor act nor speak in the senate, nor can any censor select him for, or admit him to, the senate.

Anyone who has sworn this under this law is responsible for the recording of his name with the *quaestor* of the *aerarium*, and this *quaestor* shall receive these names, and administer the recording of the names of those who have taken the oath before him under this law in the public records.

For those who are required to take the oath under this law, the *praetor peregrinus* will publicly summon them to take the oath when he has announced the deadline for taking the oath under this law on three market days in succession. After this, the names of those who have sworn [the oath] under this law will be inscribed on a tablet and published in the forum. When cases are brought . . . the *praetor* responsible by this law will ensure that the whole tablet is read out.

Nobody shall deliberately commit any fraud against this law, nor decide anything so that the things required by this law are diminished or undermined. If anyone acts contrary to this law, the praetor shall fine each person [. . .] *sesterces* for each offence.

If anything of a ritual nature has been done incorrectly, nothing shall be done under this law. The tribunes of the people of the year in which they are bound by this law, or in which they swear to this law, shall enact nothing under this law.

[110–100 BC. Tarentum. Fragmentary bronze tablet containing a heavily restored text of a Roman law concerning extortion and maladministration, and openly inviting delation as a means of controlling official corruption. The rewards offered for non-citizens seem to offer an alternative to those offered under the *Lex Sempronia* (123–2 BC, but probably superseded by 111), which limited its rewards to an offer of citizenship for the successful informant and his descendants in the male line.]

CHAPTER FOUR

The social and civil wars, 90 BC–AD 14

The first decade of the first century BC brought the tension between Rome and the Italians to a head, leading to years of disruption in Italy. The revolt of the Italian allies and the ensuing enfranchisement of Italy led to a major reorganization of governmental structures in Italy, but was also a prelude to a protracted period of civil war, deriving mainly from political tensions within the Roman elite, but with a profound effect on the whole of Italy. The roots of the Social War, however, lie in the history of the second century BC.

As already mentioned in the previous chapter, the later part of the second century is characterized by a growing imbalance between the status of the allies and the power of Rome, and by increasing Roman interference with the allies, both in terms of policy and in the actions of individual members of the elite. At the same time as the material benefits of imperial conquest were becoming evident, Rome was becoming visibly more reluctant to share these benefits by admitting Italians to citizenship, or even treating them with a reasonable measure of equality. These tensions are perceptible throughout the century, manifesting themselves in such ways as Roman attempts to restrict the use of *ius migrationis*, preferential terms of military service for Roman citizens as compared to Latins and allies, restrictions on assumption of citizenship by joining a colony, and by increasing Roman interference with allied autonomy, mostly using the pretext of maintaining public order, as in the case of the Bacchanalian commission. However, the emergence of a coherent demand for enfranchisement and the question of Italian status as an important issue in Roman politics did not happen until towards the end of the century. Indeed, the strength of the demand for citizenship, and the date at which the "Italian question" became important, are open to debate. The chronology of some of the measures concerning allied status in the 120s is deeply uncertain, which means that it is difficult to attribute causes, effects and motives. Interpretation also has to come to grips with the fact that allied (and Roman) perceptions changed during the 40 years between the agrarian legislation of Tiberius Gracchus and the outbreak of war. Although most of the signals put out by the allies during the 120s indicate a wish for closer links with Rome, albeit not necessarily in the form of citizenship, the actual revolt was a separatist one, powerfully symbolized by the designation of Corfinium (renamed Italica) as the capital of a new Italian federation – almost an "anti-Rome".

The issues raised by depopulation of allied cities and mass migration of Latins and Italians to Rome are a useful illustration of the ambiguities presented by the evidence. As already noted in Chapter 3, this was an issue which had been an intermittent problem for most of the second century. Steps had been taken by the senate to send home migrants who had drifted to Rome in 187 BC, and again in 177 and 173 [Nos 80–81]. On each occasion, commissions were set up to establish who had rights of residence in Rome and who should be sent back to their native city. However, this was not simply a case of Rome becoming restrictive over the number of Italians allowed to live there, and thus enjoy limited political rights. In 187 and 177, the expulsions (which amounted to 12,000 Latins in 187, according to Livy[1]) were at the behest of the allies themselves, rather than part of a Roman initiative. In both cases where Latins were expelled from Rome, and in the case of the expulsion of Samnite and Paelignian settlers from the Latin colony of Fregellae, the reason given by Livy is the same. All communities affected feared depopulation and consequent inability to meet their military obligations to Rome. It is probably this argument that eventually prompted the senate to act, although the implication of Livy's account of 177 BC is that it was actually very reluctant to become involved, and gave in mainly as a result of a long campaign of political lobbying by the Latins. On this particular occasion, the expulsions were backed up by some restrictions on the Latin right of *ius migrationis*, which made fictitious enslavement and manumission of an ally by a citizen, undertaken solely for the purpose of gaining citizenship, illegal, as well as restricting adoptions between Romans and Latins, and stipulated that a Latin migrating to Rome must leave his sons in his home city.

The ultimate fate of the *ius migrationis* is unclear. Salmon[2] argues that the restrictions of 177 amounted to a *de facto* abolition, but Brunt[3] indicates, correctly, that these limitations did not affect the fundamental right, and suggests that if *ius migrationis* was abolished entirely, this must have taken place after 168 BC, when Livy's history comes to an end, on the grounds that restrictions on allies and their activities are a topic which he routinely covers. Having said this, there is no actual evidence that the *ius migrationis* was ever abolished as such, but it was certainly diminished. The continued anxieties that surface periodically in connection with migration to Rome rather suggest that it was not formally abolished, but there seems to be a definite change of emphasis by 126, when another commission to eject Latins and allies was set up by the tribune Junius Pennus.[4] In this case, it was definitely a Roman rather than allied initiative. The chronology of this measure, and its relation to other events of 126–5 is obscure and will be discussed in further detail below. It is notable, though, that both in 126 and in 122, when the senate became concerned at the number of Italians who came to Rome to agitate on behalf of C. Gracchus' legislation, the issue is not illegal assumption of citizenship, but the involvement of Italians in the political process.

There is one further problem connected with access of Latins to Roman citizenship. At some date in the second century BC the holders of the most senior magistracies in Latin cities (the local equivalents of the consulship) acquired the right to become Roman citizens *ex officio* [No. 136]. The date of this measure, and therefore its relation to changes in the law covering *ius migrationis*, is unknown. Tibiletti[5] connects it with the revolt of Fregellae in 125, and the clauses of the *Lex Sempronia Repetundarum* (123–2 BC) and the *Fragmentum Tarentinum* (111–10 BC) [Nos 121–2] which refer to the extension of this privilege to informants and prosecutors under the *repetundae* laws, suggest that it was established by the late 120s.[6] What it strongly suggests is a shift in emphasis in favour of the Italian elite, in that while mass migrations were increasingly restricted, opportunities to gain citizenship were opened up by the enfranchisement of office-holders and their descendants. This would indeed fit into the pattern of the mid-120s as an attempt by the senate to buy off certain groups of Italians – in this case the social group whose interests were most closely allied to those of the Roman elite – by offering limited concessions in return for their support on other issues. Fulvius Flaccus adopted much the same approach in offering concessions on citizenship to persuade the Italians to drop their opposition to the land commission.

Another issue which was symptomatic of the growing tensions and inequalities between Rome and the allies was the treatment of allies on military service. The chief duty of allies was to provide military assistance to Rome, and a large part of the military burden of the second century conquests fell on them. For much of the second century BC, Rome was levying troops at the rate of *c.*40,000 legionaries *per annum*, and a roughly equal number of allies.[7] There was unease even in Rome, with riots at the annual levy and complaints to the tribunes on several occasions in the 160s and 150s. Both length and location of service were the subject of grievances. Those troops serving in the East could expect lucrative rewards, but this was not true for those serving in the western provinces. The Latins complained about the length of service and size of the levy as early as 209 BC.[8] As a result, the senate punished the 12 dissenting colonies in 205 BC by doubling their troop quotas.[9] In particular, terms of service for the allies also declined, and differences between their treatment and that of Roman citizens became marked. The *Lex Porcia* of 195 BC banned capital punishment for Roman citizens on active service, and this was extended to corporal punishment in 184 BC.[10] Both were still possible for Latins and allies, and were used on occasions. For instance, Turpilius, a Latin, was flogged and executed in Africa during the Jugurthine war.[11] Plutarch, however, says he was innocent of the charge but was set up by Marius. There was also an increasing tendency to divide land and spoils unequally between Romans and allies. At the triumph over the Ligurians in 170 BC, allies received donatives worth only half those of Romans [No. 82].

On top of these tensions over the allied role in the conquest of the empire, and their rewards for it, came the impact of the Gracchan land reforms. As discussed in Chapter 3, there are immense problems in using the literary sources for the Gracchan land law to decide whether Italians were due to benefit under the terms of the law. What does seem clear from the single surviving account [No. 110] of the activities of the land commission is that whatever the intention in theory, in practice many Italians suffered and feelings against the commission were running high by the mid-120s. This provides the background to the emergence of the question of Italian enfranchisement as a major political issue.

Tiberius Gracchus himself may have raised the question, although the evidence for this is not conclusive. Velleius Paterculus [No. 123] states that he offered to enfranchise the Italians at the same time as he promulgated his land law. Modern analysis has suggested that citizenship was a prerequisite of holding *ager publicus*, and that if Gracchus wished to include Italians in the land distribution, he would have to grant citizenship at the same time. However, there are other instances of non-citizens receiving land grants of this type without any apparent legal problem. It is entirely possible that Tiberius Gracchus did make a proposal to extend the franchise, but its relation, if any, to his land law remains obscure, and without much corroborating evidence, it is difficult to judge the nature of his proposals.

Italian enfranchisement as a political question emerges much more seriously with the legislation of Fulvius Flaccus in 125 BC. According to Appian [No. 124], his proposal to extend Roman citizenship to all Italians who wanted it, and the *ius provocationis* to those who did not, was directly linked to the activities of the land commission. His motive was to offer citizenship in return for the Italians dropping their opposition to the land commission. This appears to have had strong support in Italy, but was blocked by the senate, who sent him to command an army overseas before the legislation was complete. Superficially, this appears to relate closely to two other events, the revolt of Fregellae in 125 BC and the establishment of another citizenship commission by the tribune Junius Pennus in 126, and to indicate that there was a growing demand for citizenship among the allies and hardening opposition to this in the senate.

In fact, there are major chronological problems with this.[12] The Junian measure was passed before Flaccus proposed his citizenship law, and its context is the ongoing Roman anxiety about migration to Rome (as demonstrated by similar measures in 187, 177 and 173) as much as agitation for citizenship. It may also have been partly in response to a famous case, which came to light in 130/129 BC, in which it was discovered that M. Peperna, the consul for 130 BC, had not been a citizen [No. 137]. He himself was dead by this time, but his father appeared on a list of migrant citizens whose return was requested by their cities. Badian similarly attacks Brunt's idea that there was already a considerable demand for citizenship building up among the Latins by 126, attributing earlier waves of migration to Rome to a desire for material benefits, not change of legal status.[13] Overall, the impression is that 126–5 is a watershed, marking the beginning of serious allied agitation for Roman citizenship *per se*. Certainly, the revolt of Fregellae shortly after the failure of Flaccus' bill suggests that the issue now aroused strong feelings, presumably exacerbated by the fact that the revolt was ruthlessly crushed and Fregellae itself sacked. The connection of Italian enfranchisement with popular politics also persisted. In 123 BC, during the tribunate of C. Gracchus, a third citizenship proposal was put forward. Like Flaccus' bill, it was not a straightforward extension of citizenship, which may indicate both that there was no possibility of getting such a bill passed, and that the demand for full citizenship was not universal in Italy. Instead, it offered full citizenship to all Latins in Italy, and Latin status – which included important civil rights and limited routes to Roman citizenship – to the rest of the allies. Accounts of Gracchus' behaviour during his tribunate [No. 129] make it clear that he was actively cultivating Italians and seeking to build up an Italian *clientela* by his involvement in public works throughout Italy, and the mass support from Italians who came to Rome during the abortive attempt to pass the bill caused a serious threat to public order.

After the failure of Gracchus' proposed legislation, Roman interest in the Italian question seems to have declined somewhat, although the demand for citizenship did not go away. Allied grievances at their status continued to smoulder, with occasional outbreaks of acrimony. However, little specific information is available. Saturninus included some Italians in his agrarian schemes of 103 and 100 BC, and the activities of the Gracchan land commission were wound up by the *Lex Thoria* in 111 BC [No. 115]. Marius, himself of Italian origin, enfranchised a cohort of troops from Camerinum for bravery at the battle of Vercellae, but the legality of this act was hotly debated [Nos 46, 139]. In the end a very limited power to confer citizenship was granted to Marius, but this only extended to enfranchising three individuals in each of the colonies he founded.

The event which sparked the final decline in relations between Rome and the Italians was the *Lex Licinia Mucia* of 95 BC [Nos 141–2]. A *quaestio* was set up to identify and eject Italians who had illegally assumed Roman citizenship, and its operation apparently involved processing large numbers of cases and dealing with numerous members of the Italian elite. Unlike earlier commissions, the concern here seems to have been with legal status throughout Italy, not simply with ejecting illegal immigrants from Rome. Assuming that the senate did not legislate for minor or non-existent phenomena, the implication is that usurpation of the citizenship had been taking place on a mass scale and in high places.[14]

In 91 BC, the issue came to a head. One of the tribunes for the year, Livius Drusus, had a reputation as a champion of the senate and a supporter of the notion of restoring the powers removed from it by Gaius Gracchus, but he also had close ties of friendship with members of the Italian nobility, notably Popaedius Silo who was one of the most vocal supporters of Italian enfranchisement. As part of his legislative programme, he announced his intention to enfranchise the Italians at the end of his year of office. The delay between the announcement and the schedule for completion has never been satisfactorily explained, but is clearly connected with the controversial nature of Drusus' programme and the need to gain the support from other interest groups to force it through.[15] However, the programme proved too controversial. One of his measures, possibly an agrarian bill, even alienated some Italian communities in Etruria and Umbria, and opposition amongst senators and equites began to harden. A number of plots to provoke a revolt came to light in Italy, and Popaedius attempted to force the issue by marching on Rome with a large armed contingent, although he ultimately allowed himself to be dissuaded from attacking Rome. In the increasingly restless atmosphere, Drusus was assassinated, and a coalition of Italian states, under the leadership of Pontius Telesinus and Popaedius Silo, declared their independence from Rome.

One of the major issues concerning the Social War is the way in which many of Rome's allies moved away from their initial demands for citizenship, and thus integration with the Roman state, to a desire for complete separation from Rome. Patterns of migration during the second century, and the legislation proposed by the Gracchi and Fulvius Flaccus strongly suggest that at least some Romans perceived a growing demand for integration, strongest in the Latin communities but also present elsewhere, which generated a sporadic but highly charged political debate. By 90 BC, however, this had changed considerably. What emerged in the fall-out from Livius Drusus' abortive legislation was an anti-Roman coalition centred on the Samnite and Marsic heartlands of the central Appennines, a part of Italy which had proved extremely resistant to Roman conquest and to cultural assimilation. The initiative had been seized in the years leading up to the crisis of 91/90 by a group of Oscan aristocrats, notably the Marsian Popaedius Silo, who assumed leadership of the growing number of disaffected Italian states and maintained links with sympathetic politicians in Rome, exerting increasing pressure for change. The failure of Drusus marked a crisis point which tipped the balance away from further pressure for citizenship and towards the formation of a breakaway state.[16]

In this, however, the ethnicity of the Italic rebels is significant. The vast majority of the states which revolted were Oscan in origin – Samnites, Marsi, Paeligni or Campanians – the group which had formed the core of resistance to Rome in Italy during the fourth and third centuries, and which had proved remarkably resistant to Romanization, at least in the Appennines. Divisions within Italy are apparent in 91, when the Etruscans and Umbrians gave priority to questions of land distribution rather than citizenship [No. 147]. Support for the revolt in this region did not take root until the middle of 90 BC, several months after the outbreak of war, and petered out rapidly. The Greek states of the south also appear largely uninvolved, and Naples and Heraklea made active efforts to avoid being incorporated, saying that they would prefer to remain allies rather than become Roman citizens [No.160]. Given that Greek notions of citizenship, and even of isopolity, were rather different from Roman ones, it is possible that the whole issue of enfranchisement was perceived as having little relevance in this region.[17]

The notion of an independent state based around a federation of Oscan cities had a clear resonance, harking back to the great days of the Samnite League in the fourth century. One of the first acts of the rebel leaders was the establishment of a

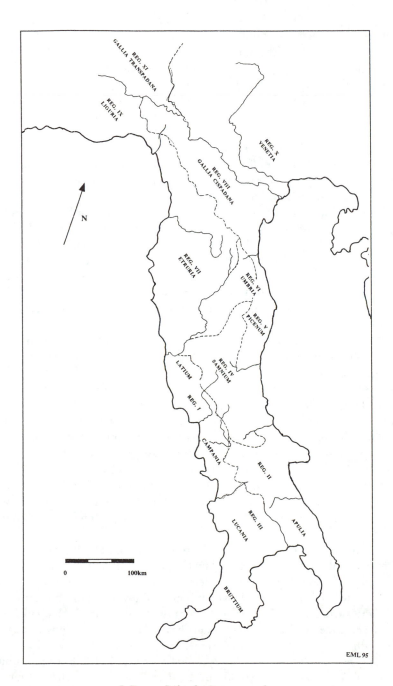

REG. XI
GALLIA TRANSPADANA

REG. IX
LIGURIA

REG. X
VENETIA

REG. VIII
GALLIA CISPADANA

N

REG. VII
ETRURIA

REG. VI
UMBRIA

REG. V
PICENUM

REG. IV
SAMNIUM

LATIUM

REG. I

CAMPANIA

REG. II

LUCANIA

REG. III

APULIA

BRUTTIUM

0   100km

EML 95

5. *Roman Italy: the Augustan regions*

league of cities independent of Rome. Details of its organization are obscure, but it may have resembled the Roman alliance in some respects. Its capital, at Corfinium in the territory of the Paeligni, was renamed Italica [Nos 155, 157]. Just in case the significance was lost on anyone, the league also began to issue its own coinage bearing suitably symbolic emblems. The Roman wolf was replaced by the Italian bull, and the head of Roma, an anthropomorphism of the state, by that of Italia. Other symbols include an oath-taking ceremony, and an Italian warrior trampling a Roman standard. Examples of both Oscan and Latin legends are found.[18] Diodorus notes that a forum and senate house were built at Italica, indicating a clear intent to create a monumental and imposing capital, although it is doubtful if any of these buildings were completed.[19]

The war between Rome and the new league was short but bloody and left a lasting legacy of bitterness in some areas. The initial strategy of the rebel forces was to capture key centres still held by Rome.[20] An incursion into Picenum by Pompeius Strabo was defeated and Peperna's attempt to raise the siege of Alba Fucens went so disastrously wrong that he was demoted in favour of Marius. Overall, however, the war in Picenum remained evenly balanced, with Rome maintaining a firm grip on Firmum Picenum and the rebels controlling Ausculum.

In Campania, L. Julius Caesar failed to protect the border with Samnium and was forced back into the *Ager Falernus*. Nola fell to the rebels, and control of part of the coast enabled attacks on Roman ships importing corn from Sicily. These advances were matched by similar successes in Apulia, where there was a similar pattern of pro- and anti-Roman factions struggling for domination in most cities. Marius scored some notable successes in Umbria, but by and large, the Italian forces held the upper hand. There was a considerable amount of internal bickering and paranoia at Rome, with allegations of suspect loyalty and betrayal levelled at some of the associates of Livius Drusus. The close ties between Roman and Italian individuals was also a problem. An encounter between the forces of Marius and Popaedius ended with a spontaneous strike by both armies when troops on both sides recognized friends amongst the opposing forces and refused to fight.

A rebellion broke out in Etruria and Umbria part of the way through the year, but this was substantially neutralized by the passage of the *Lex Julia de Civitatis* by Sex. Julius Caesar shortly after his election as consul for the year. This granted citizenship to those parts of Italy which remained loyal, but did not provide for rebels who surrendered. The recognition of the basic principle that citizenship had to be extended had already been made by the *Lex Calpurnia* (possibly datable to early 90) which allowed enfranchisement in reward for bravery in battle [Nos 158–63]. The terms of the *Lex Julia* seem to have been fairly effective in limiting the spread of the revolt, but could not, by their terms of reference, attract any Italians already in revolt. However, by the end of 90 BC, the allied advance had reached its maximum point. Early in 89, a combined effort by the Marsi and Picenes to raise the Roman siege of Ausculum came to grief, and the Italian force was heavily defeated. Sulla also had some notable successes in Campania, capturing Pompeii and Stabiae, and driving the Italian forces back to Nola after heavy losses. In the north, the Marsi and Vestini were comprehensively defeated, and Ausculum was captured and sacked by Pompeius Strabo. Both peoples surrendered, along with the Paeligni, at the beginning of 88 BC and the Italic capital was moved south to Aesernia. Sulla completed the subjugation of Campania, with the exception of Nola, and set about reducing the heartlands of Samnium, while a second Roman force conquered Lucania. By the end of 88, the war was effectively over. A few pockets of resistance remained, including Nola and the league capital at Aesernia, but an alliance with Mithridates against Rome proved abortive. The final (and bloody) suppression of the last of the revolt was undertaken by Sulla, then Cinna, during the period 88–82 BC. The extension of citizenship to rebels who surrendered was granted by the *Lex Plautia Papiria*, passed early in 89, and this seems to have undermined the resolve of some Italian communities, although others fought to the bitter end, often at the cost of being sacked by the victorious Roman forces. The grudging nature of Rome's acceptance of the need to enfranchise the Italians is reflected in the initial proposal that the new citizens should be placed in a limited number of new voting tribes, thus limiting their political influence severely. The mechanisms of enfranchisement, and particularly the voting arrangements, for the new citizens became a political football at Rome during the 80s BC, with some politicians, notably Cinna, courting the Italians by promising reforms to ensure them a fairer degree of influence. Even when Cinna gained power, however, he was extremely slow to honour his promises, and there is little evidence that the Italians had much political influence in the years after the war.

The reorganization of Italy was a long and haphazard business. The *Lex Julia* and the *Lex Plautia Papiria* had set up a rudimentary mechanism for absorbing the new citizens and creating a suitable means of governing them, but the process of municipalization was very long. These laws provided for a formal extension of the citizenship to any Italians who registered themselves in their city of habitual residence during a specified registration period. Enfranchisement was then undertaken city by city, with all Latin and Italian states required to formally lay down their own laws and government in favour of Roman law and a municipal (or colonial) charter which set up the mechanisms of administration. This neat theory was not, needless to say, reflected in practice. The disruption caused by the war, and by the ensuing civil war between Marius and Sulla, the Sullan proscriptions and his large-scale programme of colonization, all exacerbated the already substantial administrative problems. Further legislation was passed by Pompey to register the substantial number of Italians who had not yet done so, and both Caesar and Augustus undertook substantial programmes of administrative reform in Italy. Claims of false registration and other irregularities surfaced in the courts, typified by the case of Licinius Archias, successfully defended by Cicero on a charge of falsely claiming citizenship. The case turned on a grant of citizenship by Heraklea, which became a *municipium* under the *Lex Julia*, but which had no records of this as the record office had been destroyed during the civil war.[21]

Surviving pieces of municipal charters, such as that of Tarentum, and the digest of municipal laws and regulations on the Table of Heraklea [Nos 323–4], give some flavour of the sort of administrative arrangements made by Rome. Regulations are laid down for the conduct of public life, with fines for misdemeanours by magistrates, which could be channelled to a number of public ends, notably the holding of games. There were also regulations designed to prevent the elite leaving Tarentum permanently, presumably in favour of migration to Rome, in the form of a requirement to maintain a house of specified (and substantial) size in the city. Other sections concerned the duties of the magistrates and the arrangements for elections. The structure of municipal government was by no means as straightforward as the conventional division between *coloniae*, governed by boards of two *duoviri* and *municipia*, governed by four *quattuorviri*, would suggest. The difference between these two types of constitution and the chronology of their introduction is still only partially understood. Various interpretations have been put forward, including differences according to status, with *municipia* having quattuorviral constitutions and *coloniae* duoviral ones, and according to chronology, assigning *quattuorviri* to early charters and suggesting that they were phased out in favour of *duoviri* under later legislation.[22] However, none of these can satisfactorily explain the numerous anomalies. The question is also greatly complicated by the fact that the century after the Social War was also one of large-scale colonization, a process which cut across the post-war municipalization. In fact, there is reason to believe that instead of standardizing administrative arrangements, many charters simply adapted existing structures of government and attached Roman titles to indigenous offices. The Greek offices of *demarchos* and *archon* were retained at Naples until the second century AD, but this is an extreme example and probably owes much to the privileged position of Greek culture in Roman Italy.[23] Other examples include the boards of three aediles which governed Arpinum, Formiae and several other cities in the Liris valley, and the praetor who is recorded as the chief magistrate of Cumae, and who may well be an Oscan *meddix* with a new Romanized title [Nos 325–6]. Unlike the Hellenized administration of Naples, most of these peculiarities are a feature of the Sullan period and disappear after the reforms of Caesar and Augustus.

The other phenomenon which had a direct and immediate impact on Italian communities was the Sullan programme of colonization. This was designed to secure the loyalty of cities which had held out until the later stages of the social war or supported Marius during the civil wars by settling a substantial core of Sullan veterans in them, often on land confiscated from men killed in the proscriptions or known as opponents of the regime. This was a widespread phenomenon, affecting numerous cities throughout Italy. Unlike many earlier colonies, most of these were not new settlements but additions of colonists to existing ones. The effects can be seen strikingly at Pompeii, where a group of 2,000–3,000 colonists were added to a city with a population of only 10,000–12,000, thus creating a substantial new element in the citizen body. The fall-out from this can be seen both in the epigraphy, from which the names of the pre-war Oscan elite soon disappear, and in Cicero's references to political strife there resulting from an attempt by the colonists to disbar the indigenous population from full political rights.[24]

Despite this high level of instability in municipal life after the war, and the generally unsettled conditions of most of the first century, those elements of the Italian elite which had survived and were on good terms with Rome prospered. Although only a few Italians – Cicero and Marius being notable examples – gained full access to a political career at Rome, the contacts between Rome and the Italian elite were increasing. Cicero's letters highlight the wide-ranging network of municipal contacts which he maintained and the extent to which he took pride in promoting the interests of the individuals and the cities of which he was patron. A number of his speeches, notably the *Pro Roscio Amerino*, *Pro Sulla*, *Pro Cluentio* and *Pro Plancio*, focus on high-profile cases concerning prominent men of municipal origin [Nos 166, 177–8]. The development of a social network based aound luxury villas outside Rome also strengthened ties between Roman and Italian elites in specific regions. This was particularly true of the coast of southern Latium and the area around the Bay of Naples, where there was a period of intensive villa-building, by both the indigenous and Roman nobility. Nevertheless, the tension between local loyalties and Roman patriotism was a live issue for Cicero and his contemporaries. Cicero makes a strong case for every Italian having two citizenships, emotionally as well as legally, and upholds strong local loyalties within a higher loyalty to Rome as a positive virtue [Nos 174, 416]. He expresses some impatience with those who fail to see beyond their immediate locality, both directly and in recording criticism of his grandfather, who refused a career at Rome in favour of one at Arpinum [No. 176]

The contacts between Italy and the eastern Mediterranean, which had generated such high levels of wealth and Greek cultural influences in the second century initially persisted but were brought to an abrupt halt by the Mithridatic war. Mithridates, the king of Pontus, and a considerable number of other Greeks, had a hatred of Romans, and by extension, all Italians. During his rapid conquest of much of the region, culminating in the capture of Athens in 88 BC, he systematically slaughtered all the Italians in the cities he conquered. This caused a sudden hiatus in trade with the east, but with the defeat of Mithridates and the reorganization of much of the east into provinces, Italians, along with Romans, became prominent once again in the mercantile and financial affairs of the eastern empire.

The renewal of civil war in the mid first century caused further disruption to the economy and society of Italy. Many of the pivotal battles of the war between Caesar and Pompey were fought outside Italy, but the enfranchisement of Italy and the Marian army reforms meant that Italians were now the backbone of the legions, and any war, let alone a civil one, was inevitably a drain on manpower and resources. In addition, the pattern found in the Hannibalic war and the war between Marius and Sulla persisted. Individual cities tended to declare for one side or the other, creating a mosaic of conflicting loyalties across Italy and thus a proliferation of the war into a number of local conflicts. During the wars between Octavian and Antony, Italy became much more central. As a major part of Octavian's province, under the treaty of Brundisium, it was central both in terms of resources and in terms of ideology. Some of Antony's supporters fought bitterly to retain a foothold there, and this last phase of civil war was marked once again by war and factionalism throughout Italy, as well as savage proscriptions which decimated the Roman and Italian elites.

The victory of Caesar brought a brief respite, and also another attempt to create a rational administrative structure for Italy. Unfortunately, the Caesarian municipal reform, implemented posthumously by Antony, is very poorly documented and little is known about its contents. The Latin Table of Heraklea was once believed to be part of a *Lex Julia Municipalis*, but is now thought to be a digest of passages from several laws.[25] Augustus did not undertake a programme of grassroots municipal reform, but he passed several measures affecting the government of Italy, notably the division of the country into 11 administrative regions, replacing the old ethnic groupings with new artificial divisions [No. 179].

The other notable feature of the civil war period is the extensive Roman colonization which took place. Sulla, Caesar and Augustus were all faced with the problem of how to pacify cities of uncertain loyalty and what to do with the enormously increased number of men under arms once hostilities had ceased. Loyal veterans expected to be rewarded, and the risk involved in disappointing them was large. The solution to both problems was to establish colonies of discharged veterans in suitable cities, thus ensuring a core of loyal supporters within Italian communities, boosting declining populations and redistributing lands confiscated from enemies to supporters.

To sum up, the period of civil war between 90 and 30 BC created profound changes within Italy. The very basis of relations between Rome and other Italians underwent a revolution. All Italians were now Roman citizens, with full civil and political rights. The Italian elite were beginning to integrate with the elite of Rome, and both were faced with the need to come to terms with the changed political circumstances of the principate. The civil wars had exposed the deep divisions between, and even within, Italian communities and had resulted in widespread disruption to economy, social structures and demographic patterns which were to take a considerable time to repair.

Enfranchisement and the Gracchan Land Law

123. Velleius Paterculus 2.2.2

. . . and he [Tiberius Gracchus] promised citizenship to the whole of Italy, and at the same time, he promulgated his agrarian law.

[Tiberius Gracchus' involvement in the question of citizenship is hotly debated. Velleius implies that he promised to extend the franchise when the agrarian bill was introduced. This is supported by Cicero[26] but not mentioned by Plutarch or Appian. The suggestion that any allies who received allotments of *ager publicus* under the *Lex Sempronia* must have been enfranchised in order to hold the land legally is unlikely, since there are precedents for grants of land to non-citizens, both as viritane allotments and as colonial settlements.[27]]

124. Appian, *Civil wars* 1.21

After this [the threat by Scipio Nasica to abolish Tiberius Gracchus' land laws], the possessors of land delayed the division of it for a very long time, for various reasons. There were proposals that all the allies, who had put up strong resistance to the land distributions, should be enrolled as Roman citizens, so that they would stop arguing about land out of gratitude for a greater concession. The Italians were ready to accept this, preferring citizenship to land. Fulvius Flaccus tried as hard as possible to have this passed, being both consul and land commissioner. However, the senate was angry at the idea of making its subjects equal citizens with themselves.

Thus the attempt was given up, and the people, who had long hoped for land, became disillusioned. While they were in this state, C. Gracchus, the younger brother of Gracchus the law-giver, who had been quiet for a while after his brother's death but who had gained favour with the people over the land question, stood as tribune. Because he was treated with contempt in the senate, he announced his candidacy for the tribunate.

[The enfranchisement of the Italians became a central problem in Roman politics in the 120 BC, and is explicitly connected by Appian with the land question. It would have given Italians the right to participate in the land scheme (if indeed they were formally excluded), although Appian does not highlight this aspect. Rejection of Flaccus' proposals was followed by the revolt of Fregellae in 125 BC.]

Gaius Gracchus and the extension of citizenship

125. Plutarch, *Life of C. Gracchus* 3

After this, his [Gracchus'] enemies made further charges and accusations against him; they accused him of inciting the Italian allies to revolt, and with having participated in the plot at Fregellae, which had just, at that time, been denounced at Rome. Gracchus was again able to clear himself entirely, and when he had proved his innocence, he began immediately to campaign for election as tribune. Without exception, all the most noble men in Rome joined together against him, but such a large number of people flooded into Rome from parts of Italy in support of his candidature, that many could find nowhere to stay; and as the Campus Martius was too small to accommodate them, they climbed up to attics and rooftops to show their support for him.

[The charge of inciting an Italian revolt was also levelled at Gracchus' associate, Fulvius Flaccus.[28]]

126. Plutarch, *Life of C. Gracchus* 5

Another [of Gracchus' laws] was concerned with the allies, and extended to Italians the voting rights which were already held by Roman citizens.

127. Plutarch, *Life of C. Gracchus* 8

. . . Gracchus drew up a group of new laws to rally the people to his cause. He proposed that new colonies should be founded at Tarentum and at Capua, and that the rights and privileges of Roman citizens should be granted to the Latins.

128. Plutarch, *Life of C. Gracchus* 10

And when Gracchus proposed to extend equal voting rights to the Latins, the aristocrats expressed great offence, but they passed a law of Livius which established that no Latin should be beaten with sticks, even while on military service.

129. Appian, *Civil wars* 1.23

Gracchus built major roads throughout Italy, placing many contractors and craftsmen under an obligation to him, so that they were prepared to do what he commanded, and he proposed many colonies. He called on all the Latins to demand citizenship, since the senate was unable to oppose this with any fairness, for people who were related to them. To the other allies, who did not have the right to vote in Roman elections, he proposed to give this right, so as to have their support in passing his laws. The senate was very anxious about this, and ordered the consuls to proclaim that nobody who did not have the vote could stay in the city or come within 40 *stadia* of it during the voting on these laws.

[Plutarch presents the action of the senate in 123–2 BC as anti-Gracchan rather than anti-populist or anti-Italian, contrasting opposition for Gracchan proposals with support for very similar proposals by an anti-Gracchan tribune, Livius Drusus. Appian, in contrast, stresses senatorial opposition to enfranchisement as such, and does not mention Drusus' legislation. He also draws attention to Gracchus' growing group of clients, both Roman and Italian. Both sources indicate a distinction in treatment between Latins, who were to have full citizenship, and Italians, who were to have the limited voting rights, restricted to a single tribe, currently enjoyed by Latins.[29]]

130. Plutarch, *Life of C. Gracchus* 12

Then Gracchus introduced the rest of his proposed measures, so as to have them ratified by a vote of the people. But when a great crowd from all parts of Italy began to gather in Rome to support him, the senate prevailed on Fannius, who was then consul, to expel everyone who was not Roman by birth from the city. Then a strange and unusual announcement was made that any ally or friend of Rome was forbidden to enter the city during this time. Gracchus replied by issuing another edict in which he denounced the consul for this measure and promised to support the allies if they refused to leave the city. Despite this, he failed to keep his promise.

Trade and finance:
Romans and Italians in the provinces

131. Sallust, *Jugurthine War* 27

Then Jugurtha had Adherbal tortured to death, then carried out an indiscriminate massacre of all the Numidians and the [Italian] traders.

[112 BC. Italian *negotiatores* in Cirta advised Adherbal, the pretender to the Numidian throne, to surrender the city to Jugurtha, who was besieging it, believing that Rome would assert diplomatic pressure to protect it because of their presence. In fact, the Senate did not respond.]

132. Appian, *Mithridatic War*, 4.22–3

Meanwhile, Mithridates built a large fleet of ships for an attack on Rhodes, and secretly wrote to all his governors and magistrates of cities that on the thirteenth day after that date, they should attack all the Romans and Italians in their cities, and their wives and children and freedmen of Italian origin, kill them, leave their bodies unburied, and divide their belongings with Mithridates. He threatened to punish anyone who buried the dead or hid living persons, and announced rewards for informers and anyone who killed people who were hiding. Slaves who killed or handed over their masters were offered freedom by him, and debtors who did likewise to their creditors were offered the remission of half of their debt. Mithridates sent these secret orders to all the cities at the same time. When the day came, massacres occurred throughout Asia, of the most varied kinds, including these:

The Ephesians tore the fugitives who had fled to the sanctuary of Artemis and were clinging to the statues of the goddess away from them and killed them. The Pergamenes shot those who had fled to the sanctuary of Aesculapius with arrows, without pulling them away from the statues to which they clung. The Adramyttines chased into the sea after those who tried to escape by swimming, killed them and drowned their children. . . . This was the dreadful fate of the Romans and Italians in Asia – men, women, children, freedmen and slaves, everyone who was of Italian origin. In this way, it was made very obvious that it was just as much hatred of Rome as fear of Mithridates that drove the Asians to commit these atrocities.

[The massacre of Italians in 88 BC, said to have amounted to the slaughter of 80,000 people,[30] substantially reduced the number of Italians in the East, but did not end their influence. Cicero's experiences in Cilicia show that Italians and Romans continued to have large-scale trading, banking and tax-farming interests in the eastern provinces.]

133. Cicero, *Letters to Atticus* 5.21 (50 BC)

I have sent Q. Volusius, the son-in-law of your friend Tiberius and a man not only reliable but scrupulous, to Cyprus for a few days, so that the small number of Roman citizens who do business there cannot deny that they had their lawsuits tried; for Cypriots cannot be summonsed outside the island.

134. Cicero, *Letters to Atticus* 5.21

Your friend Brutus is an associate of the creditors of the people of Salamis, on Cyprus, M. Scaptius and P. Matinius; these people were recommended to me by him. I do not know Matinius, but Scaptius came to me in camp. Because of Brutus, I promised that I would ensure that the Salaminians paid him the money. He thanked me. Then he asked me to appoint him as a *Praefectus*. I said that I never give these appointments to *negotiatores*. . . . Our friend Appius had given this Scaptius some squadrons of cavalry with which to coerce the Salaminians and had made him a *Praefectus*. He was harassing the Salaminians, so I ordered the cavalry to leave Cyprus. Scaptius was not pleased. What else happened? So as to keep my promise, when the Salaminians, and Scaptius, came to me at Tarsus I ordered them to pay him the money. Much was said about the debt and about Scaptius' damaging behaviour. I refused to listen. . . . Meanwhile, although I had said in my governor's edict that I would observe an annual rate of interest of 1 per cent, Scaptius was asking 4 per cent under the terms of his credit note. "What are you saying?" I asked. "Are you suggesting I act against my own edict?" However, he submitted a senatorial decision taken during the consulship of Lentulus and Philippus (56 BC) that "the governor of Cilicia should give judgement in accordance with the credit note". Initially, I was horrified, for the city would be

94

ruined. Then I discovered that there were two *senatusconsulta* passed in the same year about the same debt. When the Salaminians wanted to take out a loan at Rome, they were unable to because the *Lex Gabinia* did not allow it. Then Brutus' friends agreed to lend the money at 4 per cent interest, thanks to the influence of Brutus, as long as they were protected by a *senatusconsultum*.

[This is an example of the abusive financial transactions perpetrated in the provinces by Italians and Romans. Although this gives the impression that the debt is owed to Scaptius, a later letter[31] makes it clear that Brutus was the creditor and that Scaptius and Matinius were merely agents. Despite protests, Cicero stuck to his ruling[32] that the maximum sum payable under the *Lex Gabinia* and his own edict was 106 talents (1 per cent interest) rather than the 200 talents (4 per cent interest) demanded by Scaptius.]

Restrictions on allies

135. Cicero, *De officiis* 3.47

The people who want to ban foreigners from the city and would exclude them from its boundaries as Pennus did in our fathers' time, and as Papius has done recently are also wicked. It may not be right to allow someone to behave as a citizen who is not a citizen; a law about this was brought forward by our wisest consuls, Crassus and Scaevola; but it is still inhuman to ban foreigners from enjoying the advantages of the city.

[A commission was set up by the tribune L. Junius Pennus in 126 BC to examine the right of allies in Rome to be there, and to eject those who were there illegally and attempting to acquire citizenship by *migratio*. This is usually interpreted as a response to an influx of Italians into Rome to support Fulvius Flaccus' abortive proposal to extend the citizenship, but cf. Keaveney and Badian[33] for the view that there was no widespread wish for citizenship until after 126.]

136. Asconius 3C

Cn. Pompeius Strabo, the father of Pompeius Magnus, established colonies across the Po. He did so, not by settling new colonists, but by giving Latin rights to the existing inhabitants, who remained where they were: that is to say that they have the same rights as other Latin colonies, namely that men from there could obtain Roman citizenship by holding a magistracy in their own city.

[Grant of Latin rights to the inhabitants of Gallia Transpadana, 89 BC. This is one of the few passages to provide solid evidence for the right of magistrates in Latin communities to take Roman citizenship, a right which eventually replaced the *ius migrationis*.]

137. Valerius Maximus 3.4.5

The disgrace of M. Peperna took place not long after his consulship, in as much as he was a consul before he was a Roman citizen . . . he who had triumphed in life was condemned, in death, under the *Lex Papia*: for his father, . . . was forced to return to his original home. Thus the name of M. Peperna was darkened by a false consulship . . .

[The case of M. Peperna became something of a *cause célèbre* when it was discovered after his death that his family were not actually Roman citizens, despite his having held the consulship. The matter came to light when the name of Peperna's father appeared on a list of people resident in Rome whose return was requested by their native cities.]

138. Valerius Maximus 9.5.1

. . . M. Fulvius Flaccus, who was consul along with his colleague M. Plautius Hypsaeus, proposed laws, which were most damaging to the state, to give citizenship to Italy and the right of *provocatio* to those people who did not want to change their citizenship; when he was forced, with difficulty, to enter the senate house, he was urged by a mixture of threats and appeals to stop what he was doing, but he refused to answer this.

[Optional Roman citizenship for Italians, with an alternative of *ius provocationis*, was proposed by Flaccus in 126 BC. The failure of Flaccus' law was widely believed to be the cause of the revolt of Fregellae in the following year, and the influx of Italians into Rome to support him may have been the reason for the citizenship commission set up in 126.]

139. Valerius Maximus 5.2.8

Two cohorts of the Camertes who had held the force of the Cimbri in the front line with exceptional courage were given Roman citizenship by Marius. This was against the terms of the treaty of the Camertes with Rome.

140. Cicero, *Pro Balbo* 48

And so, when citizenship came under the severest scrutiny a few years after this gift of citizenship by the *Lex Licinia Mucia*, was anyone of those from an allied state who had been given citizenship brought before the courts? T. Matrinius of Spoletium, from a most important and distinguished Latin colony, was the only one of those to whom C. Marius had given citizenship who pleaded a case. When he was prosecuting him, L. Antistius, a most eloquent man, did not say that the citizens of Spoletium had not given consent to this (for it seemed to him that communities usually consented to things concerning their own law but not to things concerning ours), but, since the colonies specified by the *Lex Appuleia*, a law which Saturninus had passed on behalf of C. Marius so that he could make three individual colonists Roman citizens, had not been founded, he argued that this favour should not retain its force, since the law itself had been invalidated.

141. Cicero, *Pro Balbo* 54

Even under the *Lex Servilia*, that most severe of laws, our leading men, the most wise and serious of our citizens, allowed, by the will of the people, a way for citizenship to remain open to the Latins, that is, to people bound to us by treaty; this was not infringed by the *Lex Licinia Mucia*.

142. Asconius 67C (=Cicero, *Pro Cornelio*)

With regard to the *Lex Licinia Mucia*, concerning the reduction of the number of citizens, it seems to me to be entirely agreed that it was not only ineffective but seriously harmful to Rome, although it was passed by the two consuls who were the wisest of all we have known. . . . At a time when the peoples of Italy were inspired by an inordinate desire for Roman citizenship, and because of this many of them were passing themselves off as Roman citizens, it seemed necessary to pass a law to restore everyone to his correct legal citizenship in his own city. But the leaders of the Italians were so alienated by this law that it may have been the main cause of the Italian war which broke out three years afterwards.

[The *Lex Licinia Mucia* (95 BC) set up a commission to scrutinize claims to Roman citizenship and to expel from Rome any resident Italians and Latins who could not justify their presence. The *Lex Appuleia* (100 BC) provided for the foundation of Latin colonies in several provinces, each of which was to include a group of three citizens who were to be offered full Roman citizenship. All Saturninus' measures of 100 BC were invalidated following his death in a riot later in the year, thus undermining the legality of grants of citizenship already made by this law. However, Asconius' comments firmly link the outbreak of war to the outrage caused by this legislation.]

143. Pliny, *Natural history* 25.52

Drusus was the most famous popular tribune of all, a man whom the people stood up and cheered above everyone. The optimates blamed him for the Marsic war.

144. Seneca, *De brevitate vitae* 6.1–2

Surrounded by an enormous crowd from all over Italy, he [Livius Drusus] had proposed new laws and Gracchan-style iniquity. Unable to see any way out for his proposals, which he had failed to carry, and which he was no longer able to give up once he had started on them, he is said to have cursed bitterly the turbulent life he had led ever since he was a child . . .

[91 BC. This identifies the programme pursued by Livius Drusus as the successor to Gaius Gracchus' reforms. Like Gracchus, he had mass support from Italians.[34]]

145. *De viris illustribus* 66

As tribune, he [Livius Drusus] gave citizenship to the Latins, land to the people, membership of the senate to the equites, and the law-courts to the senate.

146. Plutarch, *Life of the younger Cato* 2

Rome's allies were trying to gain Roman citizenship. One Popaedius Silo, a military man of the highest status, was a friend of Drusus and spent many days at his house.

147. Appian, *Civil wars* 1.35–6

After this, the tribune Livius Drusus, a man of the most distinguished family, promised, at the request of the Italians, to propose yet again a law to enfranchise them. The Roman citizenship was what the Italians wanted more than anything, for at one stroke, they would become masters instead of subjects. So as to put the Roman people into a frame of mind to accept this, Drusus tried to win them over with many colonies in Italy and Sicily, which had been promised long before but never carried out. He also tried to unite the senate and the equites, who were in serious disagreement over the law-courts, by a common law. Since he could not openly transfer the courts to the senate, he worked out the following compromise: he proposed to add to the senate, which was then hardly 300 in number because of internal problems, an equal number of men selected from the equites on grounds of ability and good birth, so that in future, the courts would be chosen from this entire body of 600 members. He also proposed that members of this new body should be open to prosecution if they took bribes, a charge which had virtually vanished because of the common practice of bribery. This was his compromise suggestion, but it rebounded on him. . . . And so it happened that the senators and equites were in agreement over their hatred of Drusus, although they were in opposition to each other. Only the people were happy about their colonies. As for the Italians – and it was for their good more than anything that Drusus was following these policies – they were anxious about the colonial law, worried that Roman *ager publicus*, that part of it which had not been distributed and which they were continuing to farm, either in open defiance of the law or secretly, would immediately be taken away from them, and they also thought that they would have a lot of trouble about their own lands as well. The Etruscans and

Umbrians, who shared the anxieties of the Italians, were seemingly brought to Rome by the consuls to overthrow Drusus, which was their true aim, although the pretext was that they intended to denounce him. Their opposition was open and vocal, and they waited in readiness for the moment of decision.

148. Livy, *Epitome* 70–71

When it could no longer tolerate the despotic manner in which the equestrian order managed the law courts, the Senate began to struggle with all its might to transfer the courts to itself, with the support of the tribune Livius Drusus, who stirred up the people with promises of generous rewards in order to build up his power. . . . In order to gain greater strength to uphold the cause of the senate, which he had promised to defend, M. Livius Drusus tried to win over the allies and the Italians by holding out the hope of Roman citizenship. Having passed agrarian and corn laws by violence, with their assistance, he also passed a judicial law which stipulated that the courts should be shared equally between the senate and the equites. But when, at last, it proved impossible to give the allies the citizenship that had been promised, the Italians were furious and began to make ready to revolt against Rome.

149. Diodorus Siculus 37.13

The leader of the Marsi, Popaedius, began a great and unexpected enterprise. He gathered 10,000 men from those who feared the inquiry and led them to Rome, with weapons hidden under their clothing. He planned to encircle the senate with armed men and demand citizenship, or if this was not granted, he would destroy the rule of Rome by fire and sword.

[91 BC. Popaedius was dissuaded from this before he reached Rome, by the intervention of one C. Domitius, whose exact identity is uncertain.]

150. Diodorus Siculus 37.11

I swear by Jupiter Capitolinus and Roman Vesta and by Mars, the Sun and the Earth, the benefactress of animals and things that grow, and also by the demi-god founders of Rome and the heroes who have helped to extend the rule of Rome, that the enemy and friend of Drusus shall be my enemy and friend, and I shall not spare my life, nor my parents nor my children nor my soul if it seems right to Drusus and those who swear this oath. And if I become a citizen by Drusus' law, I shall consider Rome to be my home country and Drusus my greatest benefactor. And I will exact this oath from as many of my fellow countrymen as I am able. May all good come to me if I keep this oath, and the reverse if I break it.

[91 BC. Text of the so-called "Oath of Philippus", a formal oath supposedly sworn by Italian supporters of Drusus, the implication of which is that his citizenship bill would give him a huge *clientela* and therefore great political power. In point of fact, it was widely publicised by Drusus' enemy L. Philippus, and is more likely to have been concocted to discredit Drusus.]

151. *De viris illustribus* 66

The people were content with their land grants but the dispossessed were angry, the equites chosen as senators were pleased, but those passed over were annoyed, the senate was happy with its renewed control over the courts, but did not like having to accept equites into its number. Because of this, Drusus was anxious and repeatedly put off the demands of the Latins who were lobbying strongly for the citizenship, which they had been promised, when he suddenly fainted in public. . . . Public prayers for his recovery were offered in all parts of Italy, and when the Latins were planning to assassinate the consul at the Latin festival on Mount Albanus, Drusus warned him to be on his guard.

152. Asconius 68–69C

I think you may remember that these Livian laws are the ones which the tribune M. Livius Drusus passed that year. He began by supporting the senatorial cause and passing laws in favour of the optimates, but later he became so wild and extreme that he lost all sense of moderation. So his enemy, the consul Philippus, persuaded the senate to agree to invalidate all his laws by a single decree. It was declared that they had been passed in contravention of the auspices and the people were not bound by them.

[Drusus' legislation was later annulled.[35]]

153. Asconius 22C

A short time before this, when the Italian war had begun because the nobility was hated for refusing citizenship to the allies, the tribune Q. Varius passed a law to set up a commission of enquiry into those men through whose advice and assistance the allies had taken up arms against the Roman people.[36]

The Social War

154. Justin 38.4.13

So that I do not dwell only on ancient examples, at that time when the whole of Italy had risen up in the Marsic War [i.e. the Social War], they [the Italians] were not now seeking freedom, but partnership in power, and Roman citizenship.

155. Diodorus 37.2.4

The Italians took Corfinium, which was very large and noteworthy and had only just been completed, as their capital. They provided it with everything intended to strengthen a large city and government, with a capacious forum and senate house, and provided it abundantly with everything for a war, including a large supply of money and copious provisions. They also set up a common senate of 500 members there, from which those best suited to govern the state and competent to consider the common safety would be those who took the lead. They entrusted the conduct of the war to these, although it was the senators who held the ultimate authority. The senators decreed that two consuls and 12 praetors should be chosen each year.

156. Livy, *Epitome* 72

The Italian peoples revolted against Rome; the Picenes, Vestini, Marsi, Paeligni, Marrucini, Samnites and Lucanians. The war started in Picenum. Q. Servilius, the proconsul, was murdered in the city of Ausculum along with all other Roman citizens in the city.

[The immediate cause of the outbreak of war was the murder of the proconsul Q. Servilius Caepio at Ausculum in 91 BC.]

157. Velleius Paterculus 2.15.1.–17.1

In the consulship of L. Caesar and P. Rutilius, the whole of Italy took up arms against the Romans. The revolt began with the Ausculans, who had killed the praetor Servilius and his deputy Fonteius; then it was taken up by the Marsi, then made its way into all areas of Italy. The fate of the Italians was as cruel as their case was just, for they were demanding citizenship in the state whose power they were defending by armed force: every year and in each war, they were providing a double force of men, both infantry and cavalry, and yet they were not admitted to citizen rights in the state which had reached such a high position through their efforts that it could look down on men of the same origins and blood as foreigners and allies.

The war wiped out more than 300,000 of the young men of Italy. In this war, the most noted commanders on the Roman side were Cn. Pompeius, father of Pompey the Great; C. Marius, who has already been mentioned; L. Sulla, who had held the praetorship the previous year; and Q. Metellus, son of Metellus Numidicus . . .

On the Italian side, the most famous leaders were Popaedius Silo, Herius Asinius, Insteius Cato, C. Pontidius, Pontius Telesinus, M. Egnatius and Papius Mutilus; nor should I deprive my own family of glory through too much modesty, especially when I am only telling the truth; much credit is due to the memory of Minatius Magius of Aeclanum, my great-grandfather and grandson of Decius Magius, a leader of the Campanians and a man of great renown and loyalty. Such faithfulness was shown towards the Romans in this war by Minatius that he took Herculaneum himself, together with Titus Didius, with a legion which he himself had enrolled among the Hirpini, besieged Pompeii with L. Sulla and occupied Compsa. . . .

The Italian war was so bitter and full of such vicissitudes that in two successive years two Roman consuls, Rutilius, then after that Porcius Cato, were killed by the enemy; the armies of the Roman people were defeated in many places, and the Romans were forced to adopt military dress, and to retain this dress for a long time. The Italians selected Corfinium as their capital, and named it Italica. Then gradually the strength of the Roman people was increased by admitting to citizenship those people who had not taken arms or who had been quick to lay them down again, and Pompeius, Sulla and Marius restored the faltering power of the Roman people.

Apart from the remnants of rebellion which remained at Nola, the Italian war was to a large extent ended, and the Romans, who were themselves exhausted, agreed to grant citizenship to the conquered and humiliated [Italians] rather than giving it to them as a whole at the time when their own strength was undamaged.

158. Appian, *Civil wars* 1.49

While these things were happening on the Adriatic side of Italy, the people of Etruria and Umbria, and other neighbouring peoples on the other side of Rome heard about them, and were all moved to revolt. Afraid that they would be surrounded by the war and unable to protect themselves, the senate garrisoned the coast from Cumae to Rome with freedmen, who were levied for the army for the first time, because of the scarcity of troops. They also decreed that the Italians who had remained faithful to their alliance should be admitted to citizenship, which almost all wished for above everything. When the news reached Etruria, the Etruscans accepted citizenship gladly. By granting this favour, the senate made the faithful more so, won over the waverers, and softened and undermined those at war with Rome by hopes of a similar concession. The Romans did not enrol these new citizens in the 35 existing tribes, in case they should outvote the existing citizens in elections, but enrolled them in ten new tribes, which voted last of all. It was frequently the case that their votes were pointless, as a majority was found from the 35 tribes who voted first. Either this was not noticed initially, or the Italians were too pleased even with this. But later, when it came to be understood, it caused another political crisis.

[The sources are ambiguous about the enrolment of new citizens. Appian's view that ten new tribes were created is at odds with other sources, which say that they were enrolled in eight or ten of the existing tribes.[37] What is certain is that they were differentiated from the existing citizens and were only admitted to a minority of the tribes. The result, as Appian points out, was to restrict the power of the Italian vote in any election.[38]]

159. Appian, *Civil wars* 1.38–39

When the Italians heard about the murder of Drusus and the exile of the victims of the *Lex Varia*, they thought it unbearable that this should befall men who were working on behalf of their interests. They decided on outright secession and full-scale war, since they saw no other way remaining to them to gain citizenship. They held secret discussions between themselves, formed a united front and exchanged hostages with one another as a token of good faith. For a long time the Romans remained ignorant of this because of their absorption with trials and political strife in Rome. When they did find out, they dispatched men who knew particular cities well, to discover unobtrusively what was happening. One saw a youth being taken as a hostage from Asculum to another city, and passed this news to Servilius, who was proconsul in that area. At that time, it seems, certain magistrates were ruling some parts of Italy as proconsuls. The emperor Hadrian revived this practice much later on, but it did not outlast him by long. Servilius hastened to Asculum, where a festival was in progress, and delivered a threatening speech to the throng, who assumed that the plot had been uncovered and killed him. They also murdered Fonteius, his legate (this is what they call men of senatorial rank who accompany provincial governors as assistants) and followed these killings by not sparing any of the other Romans there, who were set upon and killed by the crowd, which then looted their belongings.

The uprising having begun, all the neighbouring peoples joined in: Marsi, Paeligni, Vestini and Marrucini. They were followed by Picenes, Ferentini, Hirpini, Pompeians, Venusians, Iapyges, Lucanians and Samnites, peoples who had been enemies of Rome previously, and by all the other peoples between the river Liris (which I think is now the Liternus) and the end of Adriatic gulf, both coastal and inland. Apart from garrisons, they levied a communal army of 100,000 infantry and cavalry. The Romans sent an equal number of troops to face them, made up of Roman citizens and allies who were still loyal.

160. Cicero, *Pro Balbo* 21

In the time of our ancestors, C. Furius passed a law about wills, Q. Voconius one on inheritance by women, and there have been innumerable other measures on questions of civil law; of these, the Latins have adopted those statutes that they wished; finally, there was the *Lex Julia*, by which citizenship was granted to the allies and Latins, but those states which had not given a formal agreement should not hold the citizenship. Because of this, there was a great disagreement amongst the citizens of Heraklea and Naples, where the greater part of the citizens preferred the freedom conferred by their treaty to our citizenship. Lastly, the force of that law and its terms is that states give agreement as a result of our grant, not of their own legal processes.

[Cicero argues that consent to allow an individual to accept Roman citizenship is implied by the grant of citizenship itself and does not require a special agreement with the allied state concerned. The *Lex Furia* of 183 BC and the *Lex Voconia* of 169 both restricted the right to bequeath property outside the group of immediate male heirs.[39] The *Lex Julia* (90 BC) was the law which enfranchised the Italian allies at the time of the Social War. Naples and Heraklea were anomalous in that they were Greek colonies and had notably favourable treaties, whose privileges would be lost on becoming Roman citizens. Both eventually accepted citizenship.[40]]

161. *CIL* 1[2].709

Cn. Pompeius, Sex. F., commander in chief, granted Roman citizenship to the Spanish cavalry as a reward for bravery in the Roman camp at Ausculum on 17th November, in accordance with the *Lex Julia*. On the general's staff were : [names of 60 staff officers].

The Salluitan squadron: [names of 30 Spanish cavalrymen, including C. Cornelius, son of Nesille and P. Fabius, son of Enasagin, whose Roman names indicate some degree of assimilation]

Cn. Pompeius, Sex. F., general, presented the Salluitan squadron in camp with a helmet horn and plate, a necklace, a bracelet, chest plates and a double ration of grain, as a reward for bravery.

[90 BC. Latin inscription recording grants of citizenship to Pompeius Spanish cavalry, some of whom already have Romanized names. Block grants of citizenship to units of soldiers became a regular feature of discharge settlements for provincial auxiliaries under the empire. The *Lex Julia* specifically allowed commanders to confer citizenship in the field, but mechanisms for enfranchising individuals were not put into place until the passage of the *Lex Plautia Papiria*.]

162. Velleius Paterculus 2.27.1–2

On the Kalends [1st] of November, during the consulship of Carbo and Marius, 109 years ago, Pontius Telesinus, a Samnite leader, who was brave in spirit and in deeds and hated to the core the very name of Rome, collected approximately 40,000 of the bravest and steadiest young men who still persisted in bearing arms, and fought a battle against Sulla close to the Colline gate, which was so critical as to place both Sulla and Rome in the gravest danger.

163. Cicero, *Pro Archia* 4.7

Under the law of Silvanus and Carbo, Roman citizenship was granted to "everyone whose names are listed in the census rolls of the allied cities, if they are permanently resident in Italy at the time when this law was passed and if they register with a praetor within 60 days".

The civil wars

164. Appian, *Civil wars* 1.95–103

After crushing Italy by war, fire and murder, Sulla's generals visited the cities and placed garrisons at places which were suspect. . . .

There were also many massacres, exiles and confiscations amongst the Italians who had followed Carbo, Norbanus, Marius or their officers. Throughout the whole of Italy, harsh judgements were made against them by the courts on various charges – for holding military command, for serving in the army, for giving money, for giving other services, or even for giving advice against Sulla. Hospitality, friendship or borrowing or lending money were all equally considered crimes. Sometimes, a person would be arrested for doing a favour for a suspect, or simply for accompanying him on a journey. These accusations were particularly prevalent against the wealthy. When accusations against individuals were exhausted, Sulla took his revenge against entire cities. He punished some by destroying their citadels, or their walls, or by imposing communal fines and crushing them under weighty payments. He founded colonies of his soldiers at many of them so as to hold Italy under garrison, confiscating their territory and houses and dividing them amongst his troops, and by this means he made them [the veterans] loyal to him even after his death. . . .

By these means, he ensured that he had 10,000 men among the plebeians always ready to obey his orders. So as to provide the same kind of protection throughout Italy, he distributed a large amount of land in the various cities to the 23 legions that had served under him, . . .

165. Velleius Paterculus 2.20

Cinna was no more restrained than Marius or Sulla. Though the citizenship had been given to Italy in such a way that the new citizens were to be distributed among eight tribes, the idea being that their power and force of numbers should not swamp the position of the old citizens and that the beneficiaries should not have more power than their benefactors, Cinna promised to distribute the Italians among all the tribes.

166. Cicero, *Pro Cluentio* 24–25

Not only immediate relatives but the whole of Larinum was moved by hatred of Oppianicus and pity for this youth [M. Aurius, murdered by Oppianicus]. And so when Aurius, who had previously denounced him, began to pursue him with outcry and threats, he fled from Larinum and took refuge in the camp of Q. Metellus, a most distinguished man. After this flight, which bears witness both to his guilt and his bad conscience, he never dared expose himself to the law, or to his enemies if he was unarmed, but he took advantage of the victory of violence under L. Sulla to descend on Larinum with an armed force, to general terror. He deposed the *quattuorviri* chosen by the citizens; he said that he and three others had been appointed by Sulla and that he had been ordered by him to oversee the proscription and execution of that Aurius who had threatened to denounce him on a capital charge, and another Aurius, his son Lucius, and Sextus Vibius, whom he was said to have used as go-between in bribing the informant. And so they were most cruelly killed, and everyone else was gripped by no small fear of proscription and death.

[The Cluentius case was a convoluted tale of political strife and murder within a number of interrelated families at Larinum. It provides a vivid insight into the machinations of a municipal elite of the first century BC and exposes the fissures within civic society wrought by Sulla. Oppianicus' power lies in the fact that as a supporter of Sulla, he is able to call on his connivance in assuming power at Larinum, and is able to use the Sullan proscriptions to settle personal scores.]

167. Cicero, *Letters to Atticus* 1.19

The tribune Flavius is assiduously pushing his agrarian law, with Pompey's support, although the only thing popular about it was its supporter. I was well received by an assembly when I proposed to delete from the bill all clauses which encroached on public rights, to exempt land that was *ager publicus* in the consulship of P. Mucius and L. Calpurnius (i.e. 133 BC), to confirm the holdings of Sullan veterans and to allow the people of Volaterra and Arretium to keep possession of their lands which had been confiscated but not distributed by Sulla. The sole clause which I did not reject was that land should be bought with the funds gained from the new foreign revenues over the next five years. The senate opposed the entire agrarian plan, suspecting that Pompey was aiming to gain new powers. Pompey was set on getting the law passed. With the complete support of the applicants for land, I supported the confirmation of holdings for all private citizens by supporting purchase of land, as I thought that if it was assiduously carried out, the dregs of the city could be drained and deserted parts of Italy repopulated; as you understand, our strength lies in the wealthy landowners, but at the same time I satisfied Pompey and the Roman people, which I also wished to do.

[The agrarian bills of 63–60 BC, which are the subjects of three speeches and extensive correspondence by Cicero, were part of a package designed to use revenue from Pompey's conquest of the East to pay for a land distribution scheme and to tidy up some of the anomalies left by Sullan colonization and the programmes of land reform from 133 onwards. Cicero had very mixed feelings on the subject, in particular the proposal to distribute the core of the remaining *ager publicus* around Capua.]

168. Suetonius, *Life of Julius Caesar* 38

He paid 24,000 sesterces booty each to all soldiers in his veteran legions, in addition to the 2,000 each which he had paid them at the beginning of the civil war. He also assigned them lands, but not adjacent to each other, so as to avoid dispossessing former owners.

[Unlike Sulla, Caesar seems to have drawn a clear distinction between rewarding troops and punishing communities.]

169. Suetonius, *Life of Augustus* 13.10

After the victory, they divided government between them. Antony took on the reorganization of the East, while Octavian himself was to lead the veterans back to Italy and gather together municipal lands for them, but he did not win thanks from either the veterans or the landowners, since one group complained that they were being evicted, while the other had hopes of better rewards.

[The establishment of the second triumvirate after Philippi. Control of Italy and the colonization programme enabled Augustus to gain much good will amongst the troops, and to gain a decisive propaganda advantage by portraying himself as a true Roman, representing the interests of Rome and Italy against the corrupt and Hellenized influence of Antony.]

170. Suetonius, *Life of Augustus* 12

Augustus expressed dismay at this temporary departure from the popular party by inflicting a heavier fine on the people of Nursia than they were able to pay, and then banishing them from their own city. They had given offence to him by setting up a memorial to their citizens who had been killed at Mutina . . .

171. Suetonius, *Life of Augustus* 17

[Augustus] also exempted the people of Bononia, who had been clients of the Antonii from ancient times, from taking the oath [to him] along with the rest of Italy.

[32 BC. Many Italian cities adopted hereditary patrons to defend their interests at Rome, and this relationship with the Antonii was the grounds for excepting Bononia from the oath of loyalty.]

172. Appian, *Civil wars* 4.3 (43 BC)

To encourage the army with hope of plunder, they [Antony, Lepidus and Octavian] promised 18 cities of Italy as colonies, as well as other gifts – cities which were exceptional in wealth, and in the splendour of their villas and houses

– which were to be divided up, along with their land, houses and everything else, as if they had been captured in war from an enemy. The most famous of these were Capua, Rhegium, Venusia, Beneventum, Nuceria, Ariminum and Vibo. In this way, the most beautiful parts of Italy were assigned to soldiers.

173. Appian, *Civil wars* 5.12

The job of assigning soldiers to their colonies and dividing land was one of the utmost difficulty. The soldiers demanded the cities which had been chosen for them as rewards for bravery and the cities demanded that the whole of Italy should share the burden, or that lots should be cast with the other cities; they asked that the recipients should pay for the value of the land, but there was no money. They came to Rome by turns, young people and old, women and children, to the forum and the temples, lamenting and saying that they had not done anything wrong for which they should be driven away from their land and hearths like people vanquished in war.

[41 BC. The Octavian colonization programme was based around a group of 18 cities which were assigned as spoils of war. Although the *Res Gestae* [No. 186] contains the boast that all colonial lands were paid for, this is undermined by other sources.]

Elite mobility and integration in the first century BC

174. Cicero, *De legibus* 2.5

Atticus: But what was that which you said a short while ago, that this place, by which I understand you to mean Arpinum, was your ancestral fatherland? So you have two home cities? Or is there a single common homeland? Unless, perhaps, the home city of the wise Cato was not Rome, but Tusculum?

Cicero: By Hercules, I believe that he and all men from the *municipia* have two homelands, one by birth and one by citizenship, so that Cato, who was born at Tusculum, received citizenship among the Roman people; since he was a Tusculan by birth and a Roman by citizenship, he had one homeland by place of birth and another by law. . . . But that which is the common citizenship must stand first in our affection in the name of the state; for it is our duty to die for this and to give ourselves completely, to consecrate ourselves and offer up everything we have. But that into which we were born is not less sweet to us than that into which we were adopted. And so I will never deny that this [i.e. Arpinum] is my homeland, although the other [i.e. Rome] is greater, and includes this one within it.

175. Cicero, *Letters to Atticus* 8.13.2

People from both the city and the *municipia* talk to me; they do not think of anything other than their fields, their little villas and their money.

176. Cicero, *De legibus* 3.36

. . . when this matter was reported to him, M. Scaurus the consul said "I wish, M. Cicero, that you had preferred to turn your mind and energies to our great republic, rather than to your *municipium*." . . .

[The M. Cicero concerned is the grandfather of the orator. It illustrates the growing importance of municipal elites at Rome even before the Social War, and the importance placed on their role by Cicero himself.]

177. Cicero, *Pro Plancio* 19–21

But let us come to the origin and source of this question of ancestry. You are from the ancient *municipium* of Tusculum, from which there are more consular families, amongst whom are the Juventii, than all other *municipia* put together; he is from the *praefectura* of Atina, neither as ancient, nor as distinguished, nor as close to Rome. What electoral significance do you wish to attribute to this factor? Firstly, do you think that the people of Atina or of Tusculum are greater supporters of their compatriots? The former (for I can know this easily as I am a close neighbour) were delighted when they saw the father of that excellent and distinguished man Cn. Saturninus become aedile, then praetor, because he was the first to bring curule office not just to his family but also to his *praefectura*; the latter, I have never understood to be overjoyed at honours to their citizens (I believe this is because the city is full of ex-consuls; I know that it is not due to ill-will). It is the case with me, and with my city. Need I mention myself, or my brother? I can almost say that our honours have been acclaimed by the very fields and the hills. But when do you see a Tusculan glorifying M. Cato, a leader in every virtue, or Ti. Coruncanius, his compatriot, or all the Fulvii? No one says a word. But whenever you meet someone from Arpinum, even if you do not want to you will have to listen to something, possibly even about me, but certainly about C. Marius. Firstly, therefore, [Plancius] had the ardent support of his compatriots: you had only as much as from people satiated with honours. Secondly, your fellow citizens, who are very distinguished men, are few in number, compared with those of Atina. Plancius' *praefectura* is full of very valiant men, such that nowhere else in the whole of Italy can be said to be more so. You can see crowds of them here now, gentlemen, wearing mourning in supplication. Did so many Roman knights, and so many tribunes of the *aerarium* (or the people, excluded from the court but all present at the election) not add strength and status to his candidature? For they did not bring him the Terentine tribe, of which I shall speak elsewhere, but they brought him status and made him the focus of everyone's gaze, and brought him solid, vigorous and persistent support; for local interests generate great outbursts of feeling in our *municipia*.

178. Cicero, *Pro Cluentio* 197–8

They did not send the decree of praise [for Cluentius] in writing, but wished that most honourable men, whom we all know, should be present in large numbers to praise him in person. There are present most noble men of Ferentinum, and Marrucini of equal distinction: you see Roman knights, most honourable men, from Teanum Apulum and Luceria, praising him: honourable testimonials have been sent from Bovianum and the whole of Samnium, and men of great distinction and highest rank have come with them. As for those who have estates in the territory of Larinum, or business interests, or herds of animals, all honourable men of great distinction, it is difficult to find words for their anxiety and concern.

[Support for Cluentius from the nobility of Apulia and from cities in Latium, Samnium and elsewhere. This illustrates the extent to which Roman and Italian economic interests were becoming entwined by the middle of the first century, and the importance of lobbying by regional interests in the judicial and political processes of the Ciceronian period.]

CHAPTER FIVE

Italy and the emperor

An assertion which has been made in recent years[1] is that Italy ceases to have a history under the empire. This is entirely true in the sense of a linear narrative history. There are simply no issues centred on Italy around which we can construct one. The sort of broad historical themes which could underpin such a narrative are concentrated elsewhere – high politics is increasingly centred not just on Rome but on the imperial court and most military and diplomatic activity now takes place at the periphery of the empire, in the frontier provinces and the outlying client kingdoms.

It is, however, manifestly not true of social and economic history or the history of cultural development, areas for which imperial Italy has an abundance of historical and archaeological evidence. But even here, there is a perceptible change of emphasis. As the various provinces become increasingly integrated into the empire, Italy becomes much less dominant as the main focus of attention. Macroeconomic systems are much more important as a means of understanding an economy governed by empire-wide taxation and trade, supply and demand. In social terms, provincial families enter the Roman elite in increasing numbers, creating a unified Graeco-Roman nobility by the end of the second century AD.

Just as importantly, Italy itself has no central authority, equivalent to a provincial governor and his staff, to provide a focus of control and mould its identity. Before the third century AD, it was merely an agglomeration of self-governing cities, supervised directly from Rome. It had no governor, no direct taxation and no military presence other than the praetorians and urban cohorts outside Rome and the fleets based at Misenum and Ravenna. In theory, Italy was under the authority of the senate and the consuls, even during the principate. Individuals or communities could appeal to the emperor, but his duties did not include routine administrative decisions, as stressed by Nero [No. 194]. In practice, many decisions did tend to be passed to the emperor, but in most cases, any imperial involvement was not proactive.

To some extent, these factors make it infuriatingly difficult to create any coherent impression of the history of Italy during the early empire. However, one angle which is vital to our understanding is the relationship between Italy and the emperor. Inevitably, the mere fact of a single governing figure, who was an individualized embodiment of power and control in a way that the senate was not, must have changed the perceptions of the people of Italy. Nevertheless, the ways in which the emperor interacted with Italy and *vice versa* is plagued not so much by lack of evidence, as by the discrete nature of the evidence available. There are a wealth of snippets in the literary record, as well as inscriptions, coins and physical structures, but working these into a coherent whole is extremely difficult.

One of the most immediate effects of the civil war was that it broke the stranglehold of the senatorial order on political power and introduced a substantial number of new *gentes* into the political elite, many of them of Italian rather than Roman origin. This was in part the effect of the mass slaughter of the period, during which many leading Roman families had died out or been impoverished and so lost status. It was also, however, a direct effect of Augustan rule. Many of Augustus' closest supporters were of non-Roman origins – men such as Maecenas, who was an Etruscan nobleman, Agrippa, and the Sabine Salvidienus Rufus, ridiculed by his aristocratic rivals as "the mule-driver", a pointed reference to the origins of his family's wealth.[2] After he established his authority many of these became leading men in the state and influential advisers. In this respect Augustan policy maintained a delicate balance. The Roman senatorial elite could not by any means be excluded from the inner circle of power; Augustus needed them to legitimize his regime and support the notion that he was simply the leading senator – the "first amongst equals". However, he also needed to balance them by introducing new elements which owed loyalty and advancement principally to himself. By choosing to promote men of the Italian nobility, he could do this without obvious controversy and ill-feeling. There were strong historical contacts between the Italian and Roman aristocracy, and even before the civil wars Italians had begun to be absorbed into the Roman elite, albeit grudgingly.[3] The process was not confined to Augustus, however, but gathered pace rapidly. By the middle of the first century AD, it was possible for Claudius to propose admitting the Gallic nobility to the senate, and after the death of Nero in AD 68, the highest office of state came to be dominated by outsiders. The Flavians were Sabines from Reate, while Trajan and Hadrian were provincial senators from Spain. The culmination of the process, towards the end of the second century AD, was that the Roman senate came to be dominated not by Romans, or even Italians, but by the elite families of the provinces.

Inevitably the extent of the emperor's engagement with Italy varied according to the events and circumstances of each reign and also the individual temperament and preoccupations of each emperor. Augustus was notable for the extent of his interest. His natural family, the Octavii, were of municipal origin[4] although his adoption by Caesar had brought him into the highest level of the Roman aristocracy, but his concern with Italy was much deeper and more complex. As *triumvir*, he was assigned the western provinces and Italy while Antony gained control of the more lucrative territories in the east, but he managed to turn this to his advantage by establishing an Italian identity as central to a new ideology of government. During his rise to power he promoted old-fashioned Italian and Roman virtues and played on the fear of the foreigner and oriental, disseminating the rumour that Antony intended to establish himself as sole ruler, governing from Alexandria in association with Cleopatra.

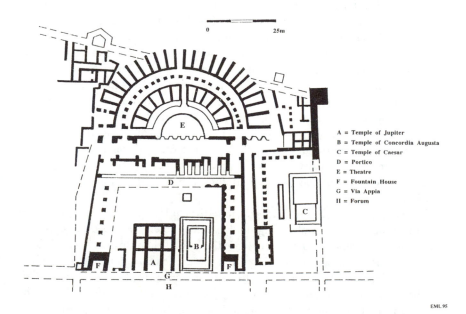

A = Temple of Jupiter
B = Temple of Concordia Augusta
C = Temple of Caesar
D = Portico
E = Theatre
F = Fountain House
G = Via Appia
H = Forum

EML 95

6. Minturnae: theatre and temples

Even after his rule was established he continued to promote this view, instituting an ideological programme which was reflected in literature and the arts as well as in more practical measures.[5] Much of the rebuilding in Rome itself took place not simply to beautify the city, as Augustus asserts in the *Res Gestae* [No. 214], but to embody his personal view of what Rome stood for.[6] The Hellenistic artistic and architectural conventions of the late republic were abandoned in favour of an archaic Italic style, favoured for some temples, or a classicizing Hellenism drawn from fifth century Athenian models, as embodied on the Ara Pacis. Iconographic references to the Aeneas legend and to the gods (notably Apollo) with which Augustus associated himself abounded in both art and literature, and vast architectural complexes such as the forum of Augustus were built to embody the new Italic ideology. Outside Rome, the same trend is also visible although not as marked. Suetonius' assertion that Augustus supplied his colonies with a full set of public buildings – in effect creating a series of "Rome clones" – is not borne out by the epigraphic or archaeological evidence,[7] although there are some spectacular examples of Augustan building, for instance at Minturnae.[8] His vision of an ordered society based on traditional lines was the source of a number of pieces of legislation which did extend to the whole of Italy, such as his modification of the laws on matrimony and adultery, and the *Lex Julia Theatralis*, which was inspired by the sight of a senator at Puteoli unable to find a seat in a crowded theatre, and which turned games and festivals into a visual representation of social hierarchy [No. 207].

Despite this intense engagement with Italy, both in fact and as an ideological tool, Augustus made very little attempt to bring it under any sort of administrative control. His division of the country into 11 artificial administrative regions was a symbolic ordering of space and an attempt to cut across and break up ethnic and local loyalties, but otherwise Italy was largely left to administer itself. Dio's famous debate [No. 180] in which Maecenas urges Augustus to turn Italy into a province with its own governor, administrative structure and army is more a reflection of an issue current in his own day rather than an indication that Augustus seriously considered this. His main administrative concern was the city of Rome, where unrest could have much more profound consequences. Great care was taken to safeguard the corn supply, and to organize the *vici*, the subdivisions of the city, in such a way as to maintain a firm grip on public order [Nos 182, 192].

The extent to which any emperor actually could pursue a conscious and coherent policy towards Italy is highly debatable. There have been attempts to argue that some emperors tried to regulate the Italian economy,[9] but it is difficult to see these interventions as anything other than specific responses to individual problems. Claudius offered privileges to anyone prepared to fit out grain ships for trade between Italy and the east [No. 208], but this is clearly motivated more by concern for the food supply of the city of Rome, and particularly the grain dole, than anything else. Domitian is said to have restricted the growing of vines throughout the empire after a particularly poor grain harvest [No. 201] but there are strong arguments against this being a serious attempt to regulate the economy in favour of the growing of grain. In particular, the decree must be set against the fact that most large-scale wine production took place on large estates, mostly owned by the senatorial class, and thus the measure can be seen as principally a means of regulating the activities of senators, not the economy as a whole. Trajan also passed a land law emphasizing the special place of Italy in the empire [No. 202], but this was also a measure which was primarily concerned with regulating senatorial behaviour and preventing a drainage of both economic resources and senatorial loyalty from Italy. The two exceptions to this rule are Augustus and Trajan, who both had specific ideas about the role of Italy in the empire and set about putting these into action.

By the second century AD, problems of depopulation, economic mismanagement and declining decurial orders were prompting increasing imperial supervision of municipal affairs. The office of *Curator Rei Publicae* was instituted at the beginning of the second century AD, coming into its own under Trajan. The incumbents were usually local notables or municipal patrons who were given responsibility for overseeing municipal finance and government in one or more cities. They were chosen for their existing contacts and connections with the cities they oversaw, and their role seems to have been to monitor public affairs and report any problems. Later, Marcus Aurelius introduced *iuridici*, praetorian officials, first attested in 163 AD, whose function was to supervise civil cases, and whose sphere extended to one or more of the Augustan *regiones* of Italy. In addition to starting this trend towards central supervision, Trajan took a close interest in Italy and instituted several major programmes of benefactions designed to rejuvenate it.[10] Nevertheless, after Augustus the main impression is of a remarkably hands-off approach. Some emperors were more concerned with the wellbeing of Italy than others, but when most become actively involved in Italy, it tends to be in response to very specific circumstances.

The chief of these is public order. Inevitably, this was a very sensitive area, and there are numerous examples of imperial interference if situations were seen to threaten peace and stability. Tiberius was notably concerned with security [No. 192] and took steps to place more troops at strategic points in Italy. He also kept a strict eye on notoriously turbulent groups such as actors and enforced punitive measures when the population of Pollentia became disorderly during the funeral of a prominent citizen, impounding the body until the relatives agreed to provide suitably lavish games. An even better documented example [No. 194] is the riot at the games in Pompeii in AD 59, in which a considerable number of Pompeians and Nucerians were killed. Nero took an extremely dim view of this and banned the games at Pompeii for ten years.

Imperial edicts gave wide-ranging, but not unlimited, powers to impose decisions on Italy and the empire. All *collegia* were banned by Julius Caesar unless they could prove ancient origin, as a means of restricting the activities of the political clubs which were frequently behind outbreaks of civil disorder in Rome. Augustus confirmed this, forcing all *collegia* in Italy to secure senatorial patrons and imperial sanction before they could exist legally. All emperors possessed, and many used, the power to eject unwelcome or subversive groups of people from Rome, and this ban was frequently extended to the rest of Italy. Examples include the banning of certain religious groups, such as Jews and devotees of some Egyptian cults [No. 302]. The more distant corners of Italy were also used as places of exile for people who had fallen foul of the regime. Agrippa Postumus was sent to Tarentum, and Julia spent the last part of her life at Rhegium after being allowed to leave Pandateria.[11] Imperial power was not unlimited, however. Tiberius made efforts to divert a bequest given to the city of Trebia to the socially useful purpose of road building, but was unable to alter the terms of the legacy [No. 358].

Despite these powers, however, the impression given is that imperial involvement in Italy took place on a very *ad hoc* basis and in reaction to circumstances. Where emperors can be found intervening in municipal affairs, this is very rarely spontaneous. All Roman citizens possessed the right of appeal to the emperor, and many interventions were clearly the result of such an appeal by either an individual or a community for assistance in solving a dispute or a problem. Where there was spontaneous action from the centre, the reason was often a threat to order or security, as discussed above, or something which touched on the emperor's private estates. These estates were, in themselves, no small administrative burden. Tacitus remarks approvingly [No. 204] that under Tiberius, the imperial *patrimonium* was still small and so draws an implied contrast between this and the later extent of the estates. Bequests and confiscations from convicted or murdered opponents swelled the imperial holdings considerably, and also contributed to the development of these estates as a large number of discrete holdings scattered all over Italy. Changes of the imperial dynasty also had this effect, bringing new land into the estates. By the late second century, approximately 30 per cent of land in Italy was under imperial control in one form or another. Not all estates owned by emperors and their relatives can be located, so the overall figure depends largely on a combination of ancient estimates and inferences from archaeological evidence. Nevertheless, a considerable number of imperial villas and estates have been identified with reasonable certainty, either from literary sources, or from funerary inscriptions of imperial slaves and freedmen found there [Nos 205–6].

An example of how the emperor could be forced to intervene in clashes between municipal interests and those of his estates is the letter recorded in an inscription from the city gate of Saepinum [No. 269]. This was written to the magistrates of the city by a high-ranking member of the imperial bureaucracy to impose a settlement on a dispute between the city magistrates and the herdsmen who drove their sheep through Saepinum during the twice-yearly movement of flocks. The point is that this is not an example of gratuitous interference but that the involvement of the emperor's staff indicates that the sheep whose passage was being stopped by the Saepinates were imperial property, presumably in transit between summer and winter grazing on imperial estates.[12]

Given that the cities of Italy were in theory self-governing, the relationship between city and emperor was often as much based on benefaction and patronage as on more formal administrative devices. The favoured status of Italy in general was reflected in the numerous tax exemptions granted by various emperors. Italians, as Roman citizens, were exempt from direct taxation in any case,[13] and there was a trend towards repealing indirect ones as well. The ½ per cent inheritance tax was abolished by Gaius, and there were numerous remissions of the *vehiculatio*, which paid for the imperial post, and the *aurum coronarium* payable to the emperor on a variety of festivals and anniversaries [Nos 189–91]. Cancellation of debts and tax arrears also became increasingly common in the second century.

Modifications to the taxation system were universal in nature, but most other imperial benefactions were selective and local. Occasions varied, as did the generosity of individual emperors, but there seems to have been a consensus that the emperor was expected to help out in times of natural disaster. Titus was noted for his generosity anyway [Nos 219–20], but his reign coincided with a series of destructive natural events, most notably the eruption of Vesuvius, which elicited imperial funds for repair of damage and relief for the victims.

Other patterns of imperial benefaction are more difficult to pin down. Colonial settlements could stimulate new programmes of public buildings, but this was not universal, and was not necessarily paid for by the emperor. According to Suetonius, Augustus equipped his colonies with public amenities, but this is not entirely borne out by archaeological and epigraphic evidence.[14] Although public building is attested in a proportion of Augustan colonies, it was not all paid for by him. The most likely projects to attract imperial finance seem to have been those which were beyond the scope of an individual *municipium*, either because of their cost or because they were not confined to the territory of a single state. This type of project, particularly road building, also carried a large amount of publicity and status value, of the sort which was now routinely monopolized by the emperor. The Via Traiana is the most notable example, creating a new route from Rome to Brundisium to facilitate Trajan's Parthian campaign, but also involving some rebuilding in the cities along its route to accommodate its passage and often to provide inscribed monumental arches to mark its construction. Apart from roads, aqueducts were sometimes built from imperial funds, but even in colonies of imperial veterans, the majority of public building was undertaken at the expense of the city or members of the elite, not by the emperor. The level of benefactions also varied considerably according to the temperament and circumstances of individual emperors. Augustus, Titus, Trajan and Hadrian were all benefactors on a substantial scale, but other emperors, in particular Vespasian and Tiberius were noted for their financial circumspection and were rather less liberal in this respect.

It was commonplace for Italian cities to make gestures of loyalty to the emperor in the form of honorific inscriptions and statues, but it is difficult to assess the significance of these in representing a degree of actual contact with the emperor. Some of them expressly say that they are in recognition of imperial benefactions, but others seem to be a more generic expression of loyalty. The conferment of honorary magistracies on emperors is a documented phenomenon, but there is only one example where this can be linked to actual benefactions [No. 234]. Hadrian was chosen as *archon* by Athens and *demarchos* by Naples, both cities with which he had close associations. In this case, these are part of a coherent exchange of honours and benefactions based on Hadrian's interest in, and support for, Greek culture. It also demonstrates the fact that chances of a community gaining a meaningful degree of patronage from the emperor were greatly increased by proximity to a well-frequented imperial villa such as those at Baiae. It was not uncommon for members of the imperial family to become patrons of cities, but after the Augustan period, this did not noticeably generate large-scale benefactions for these cities.

Overall, imperial benefactions in Italy seem more limited than one might suppose, with the exception of large construction projects such as road building, canal building or harbour construction, or in the context of colonization. It is notable, too, that this type of project was concerned not just with the needs of a single city but with the more general infrastructure of Italy. It is also noticeable that the needs of the city of Rome took precedence over patronage in Italy. The vast amount of imperial expenditure on building took place in Rome itself, and many Italian projects, such as harbour building at Ostia and Puteoli and the increase of arable land generated by Claudius' draining of the Fucine lake, were directly connected with the welfare, and more specifically the food supply, of Rome.

Just how difficult it can be to interpret imperial initiatives in Italy is illustrated by the case of the *alimenta* scheme set up by Trajan. Trajan is particularly noted as having a strong interest in the welfare of Italy. He expressed concern over the declining population of many Italian cities and instituted a number of measures designed to tackle some of the administrative problems. One of the most important changes was the *alimenta*, a scheme set up by Nerva but vastly elaborated by Trajan, to provide financial support for the raising of children in Italy [Nos 221–3]. Some of the details of the scheme's operation, as recorded on a long inscription from Veleia, are obscure, but in essence it was an investment and mortgage scheme, in which imperial funds provided capital for local landowners in each of the participating cities. Each loan represented a small amount of the overall value of the secured property, thus minimizing defaults, and the interest payable on the loan was set at 5 per cent. This interest was distributed at a fixed rate to pay for the raising of a specified number of local children. Other schemes funded entirely by private benefactions from local notables are also known [No. 378]. The number of children, size of payments, number of payments made and gender balance of the group of beneficiaries all varied from city to city. The distribution of these alimentary funds was very patchy, with a high concentration (identified either from direct epigraphic evidence or the presence of the *curator alimentarum* who administered the funds) in Latium and Campania. The traditional interpretation of the *alimenta* has been as a form of primitive poor relief, indicating a serious problem of depopulation and concentrating on raising the birthrate by subsidizing poor children. More recently[15], it has been pointed out that the only direct evidence for the scheme as poor relief comes from a much later Christian source [No. 221], and that the concentration of schemes in some of the wealthiest areas of Italy suggests that it should be seen not as evidence of urban decline but in the context of elite benefaction and civic patronage. Although Trajan's intention was certainly to increase the birthrate in Italy, the scheme is not necessarily aimed at the poorest in society. Indeed the existence of inscriptions set up by beneficiaries of the alimentary schemes at some cities indicates that they belonged to a social and economic group able to pay for such things – significantly, since inscriptions demanded an outlay which put them beyond the reach of the very poor.

Overall, the evidence for relations between Italy and the emperor indicate that although the establishment of the principate enabled the Italian elite to gain access to power to a much greater extent than previously, and temporarily raised Italy to a central role in Augustan ideology, imperial concerns were generally fairly limited. Supervision of the imperial estates, adjudication of appeals, maintenance of public order and disaster relief were the main fields of interest. Taxation was increasingly remitted, and an administrative structure for Italy began to develop under Trajan, expanding throughout the second century but by no means complete until the third. The emperor's role in public benefactions and civic patronage was relatively small, and usually focused on projects which were too large for a single city, or which were connected either with the interests of the city of Rome or with a colony. Much imperial activity was dependent on the individual emperor, Augustus and Trajan being the two who had the most active Italian policies. Despite this, the mere fact of the existence of a single figure embodying the Roman state may have helped to unify Italy and identify it with Rome. The imperial cult and the numerous statues and inscriptions in honour of the emperor brought the ruler and symbol of Roman power into every city in Italy.

The organization of Italy

179. Pliny, *Natural history* 3.46

I will now list a circuit of Italy, and its cities. In doing this, it is necessary to follow the authority of the deified Augustus, and to adopt the division, which he created, of the whole of Italy into 11 regions, but to take them in the order imposed by the coastline; it is not possible, in a brief account, to keep neighbouring areas together, and in dealing with inland areas, I will be following his alphabetical arrangement, adopting the catalogue of colonies which he set out in that list.

180. Dio 52.22.6

Do not be surprised that I also advise you to divide Italy into these administrative districts. It is large and heavily populated and so cannot be well governed by magistrates in the city [Rome]; for a governor should always be present in the area he governs, and no tasks should be given to the magistrates of the city which they cannot fulfil.

[29 BC. Extract from Dio's reconstruction of a speech given by Maecenas, in which he presents proposals for reorganizing the administration of the empire and the role of the senators and equites. The key issue here is that he recommended that only an area within a 100-mile radius of Rome should remain under direct control of Roman magistrates. The rest, along with the provinces, should be carved up into administrative districts, each with its own governor and garrison. Needless to say, this was not accepted by Augustus, but it reflects an awareness in the third century AD that the lack of any coherent administrative system and military support for Italy was anomalous.]

181. Tacitus, *Annals* 13.4

The senate will maintain its traditional role. The people of Italy and the public provinces will, by applying to the consul, come before its tribunals.

[AD 55. Speech of Nero to the senate on his accession, confirming its authority over Italy and the senatorial provinces.]

182. Suetonius, *Life of Augustus* 30.10

He divided the city into *regiones* and *vici*, and instituted annual magistracies selected by lot to control the *regiones*, and magistrates chosen by the people of the *vici* to control the *vici*. He organized night watchmen to warn against fire; to control flooding, he widened and dredged the Tiber, which had been full of rubbish and narrowed by projecting houses. In order to make the approach to the city easier, he paid for the repaving of the Via Flaminia as far as Ariminum, and warned other men who had celebrated triumphs to repair other roads with their prize money.

183. SHA, *Life of Hadrian* 22.10

He appointed four men of consular rank as judges for the whole of Italy. These *iuridici* were first appointed by Hadrian, but given greater scope and a different status by Marcus Aurelius.

184. SHA, *Life of Antoninus* 3.1

[Antoninus] was chosen by Hadrian as one of the four consulars under whose jurisdiction Italy was placed, to administer the part of Italy in which he had most of his estates.

Imperial colonization

185. Augustus, *Res Gestae* 3.3

Around 500,000 Roman citizens were under oath to me. Of these, I settled more than 300,000 in colonies or sent them back home, their service having been completed, and I assigned lands to all of these, or gave money as a reward for military service.

[The "citizens under oath" were Augustus' veterans. For colonization, cf. Nos 172–3, 186–7.]

186. Augustus, *Res Gestae* 10.2

I paid cash to *municipia* for the lands which I distributed to soldiers in my 4th consulship, and later, in the consulship of M. Crassus and C. Lentulus Augur; that sum which I paid for lands in Italy was about 600,000,000 sesterces, and about 260,000,000 for lands in the provinces. I was the first and only one of any who had founded colonies in Italy or the provinces to have done this, in the memory of our time.

187. Augustus, *Res Gestae* 28

I founded colonies of troops in Africa, Sicily, Macedonia, both parts of Spain, Achaea, Asia, Syria, Gallia Narbonensis and Pisidia. In addition, Italy has 28 colonies, heavily populated during my lifetime, which were founded by my authority.

188. Suetonius, *Life of Augustus* 46

After organizing the city of Rome and its citizens in this manner, he founded and populated 28 colonies in Italy, and in many places, provided them with public works and revenues, and even gave them rights and status equal to that of Rome by inventing a type of vote by which the decurions of the colonies could vote for magistrates at Rome in their own colonies, and send these, under seal, to Rome to be opened on the day of the election. And so that nowhere should be lacking in groups of honest men or of multitudes of offspring, he allowed men from any city to seek equestrian military rank on the basis of public recommendation.

Taxation and remissions

189. Augustus, *Res Gestae* 21.3

As consul for the fifth time, I remitted 35,000 pounds of *aurum coronarium* contributed to my triumphs by the *municipia* and *coloniae* of Italy.

[Remission of the *aurum coronarium* (gold offered by cities on the occasion of a triumph or other state occasion, originally to make triumphal crowns) became a regular form of imperial munificence, practised by Hadrian and Antoninus amongst others.[16]]

190. BMC Imp. 3.21, 119–211

Remission of the *vehiculatio* in Italy.

[Legend on coin of Nerva, commemorating the remission of the *vehiculatio*, the levy made on cities in Italy to pay for the imperial post and courier service.]

191. SHA, *Life of Hadrian* 7.6

Hadrian cancelled an incalculable sum of money owed to the treasury by private debtors in Roman and in Italy, and also huge sums of arrears in the provinces, and he burned the records of debt in the forum of the deified Trajan, to reinforce the overall sense of security. He ordered that the property of condemned people should not go to his private treasury, but that the whole amount should go to the state treasury. He gave an increased payment to the boys and girls to whom Trajan had also given support payments.

[The practice of debt and tax remission by emperors became increasingly common.[17]]

Law and order

192. Suetonius, *Life of Tiberius* 37

He [Tiberius] gave a high priority to securing safety from robbers and brigands and outbreaks of lawlessness. He distributed garrisons of troops throughout Italy, closer together than previously. At Rome, he built a camp to hold the praetorian cohorts, which before that time, had been dispersed in scattered lodgings. He suppressed any unrest amongst the people with great severity, and took great care that such things should not arise. When there was a death in the theatre because of a quarrel, he exiled the leaders of the factions and the actors who were the cause of the trouble, nor could any pleading by the people ever persuade him to recall them. When the people of Pollentia would not let the corpse of a *primuspilus* out of the forum until they had extorted money by force from his heirs for gladiatorial games, he sent a cohort from the city, and another from the kingdom of Cottius, concealing the reason for the transfer; he sent them into the city by different gates, suddenly revealing their weapons and sounding their trumpets, and threw the greater part of the people and decurions into prison for life.

193. Tacitus, *Annals* 13.48

During this consulship, the people of Puteoli sent delegations to the senate which were divided between the decurions and the people; the first group complained of violence by the mob, and the second of embezzlement by magistrates and other leading men. There had been riots, in which stones were thrown and fires threatened, and C. Cassius was appointed to prevent armed strife and find a remedy. But because the city could not put up with his severity, the job was handed over to the Scribonii brothers, on his own request; they were given a cohort of praetorian guards, fear of whom – and a small number of executions – restored harmony.

[AD 58. Problems of civic riots in Puteoli. The men detailed to sort out the problem are C. Cassius Longinus, succeeded by P. Sulpicius Scribonius Proculus and Sulpicius Scribonius Rufus.]

194. Tacitus, *Annals* 14.17

Around this time, there was on outbreak of serious violence between the people of two Roman cities, Nuceria and Pompeii. It arose from a trivial incident at the gladiatorial games given by Livineius Regulus, whose expulsion from the senate I have already mentioned. Insults, characteristic of these disorderly towns, were exchanged, then stones, and finally swords were drawn, and the people of Pompeii, where the games were being held, proved the stronger. So, many injured and maimed Nucerians were taken to Rome, and many bereavements were suffered by both parents and children. The emperor instructed the senate to investigate this incident, and the senate passed it on to the consuls. When the matter was referred back to the senate, it prohibited Pompeii from holding public gatherings for ten years, and *collegia* which had been illegally set up were dissolved; Livineius and others who had instigated the disorder were exiled.

[AD 59. This riot at Pompeii illustrates the process of appeal to senatorial or imperial authority by aggrieved parties, and the strong measures which could be taken to suppress disorder. The passage of the *Annals* which deals with Livineius and his demotion is lost.]

Italians in high places

195. Tacitus, *Annals* 3.55

Once, rich and noble families were destroyed by their habit of magnificence. For at that time, to court, and be courted by, the people, the allies and monarchs was permitted. . . . Later, when there was terror of death and a great reputation meant execution, the rest turned to greater prudence. At the same time, the new men admitted to the senate from the *municipia* and *coloniae*, and from the provinces, brought domestic frugality, and although many became rich in their old age, by good luck or industry, their outlook remained as it had been before.

[AD 22. Tiberian letter to the senate about public extravagance and sumptuary laws. Tacitus goes on to ascribe the change in the conduct of public life to the emergence of emperors of non-Roman origin, such as Vespasian.]

196. Suetonius, *Life of Vespasian* 1–2

T. Flavius Petro, a citizen of Reate, and during the civil war a centurion or veteran of Pompey's army, fled from the battle lines at Pharsalia and returned home, where he worked as a debt collector, having at last obtained a pardon and discharge. His son, whose *cognomen* was Sabinus, had no military experience – although some say that he was a *primuspilus*, and others that he was discharged because of sickness while in command of a cohort. He was the tax-collector for the *quadragesima* in Asia. There remain in place statues set up by cities under this inscription: *Kalos Telonesanti* (to the honest tax-collector). Later, he was a banker among the Helvetii, and died there, survived by his wife, Vespasia Polla, and two children, of whom the elder, Sabinus, went on to become *praefectus* of Rome, and the younger, Vespasianus, to become emperor. Polla came from an honourable family from Nursia, and was the daughter of Vespasius Pollio, three times military tribune and *praefectus castrum*; her brother became a senator of praetorian rank. There is a place called Vespasiae on top of a mountain at the sixth milestone from Nursia on the road to Spoletium, where there are many monuments to the Vespasii and many indications of the status and antiquity of the family. Nor will I deny that some say that Petro's father was from Transpadana and was a contractor of the casual labourers who come every year from Umbria to the Sabine area to work the fields, but that he settled in Reate and married there. However, I have found no evidence for this, in spite of making inquiries.

Vespasian was born in Sabine territory, in a village outside Reate named Falacrina, on the evening of the 15th day before the Kalends of December, in the consulship of Q. Sulpicius Camerinus and Cn. Poppaeus Sabinus, five years before the death of Augustus; he was brought up by his paternal grandmother Tertulla, on her estates at Cosa.

197. Tacitus, *Annals* 11.24

"I do not forget that the Julii came from Alba, the Coruncanii from Camerium, and the Porcii from Tusculum, and lest I seem to look only to antiquity, that Etruscans, Lucanians, and the whole of Italy, have been admitted to the senate, and finally that Italy itself has been extended to the Alps . . ."

[AD 48. Claudius' speech in defence of his proposal to admit Gallic nobles to the senate.]

198. Suetonius, *Life of Vespasian* 9

He reformed the two highest orders, which were drained by a number of murders and degraded by long-standing neglect, and added to them, reviewing both the senate and the equestrian order, demoting the unworthy and enrolling the most distinguished of Italians and provincials.

Emperors and the economy

199. Suetonius, *Life of Augustus* 42.25

[Augustus] writes that when the *annona* had at last improved, he had the idea of abolishing the public grain distributions for good, because reliance on them caused the cultivation of the land to decline.

200. Suetonius, *Life of Claudius* 20

He undertook public works which were large-scale and necessary rather than numerous, but principally included these: an aqueduct started by Gaius, also the outflow for the Fucine Lake and the harbour at Ostia, although he knew that the first of these had been denied to the Marsians by Augustus, despite their assiduous requests, and that the latter had often been planned by the deified Julius but abandoned because of the difficulties involved.

[The public works listed concern the water and food supply (imported via Ostia) of Rome. The draining of the Fucine lake may have been an attempt to maximize the amount of arable land within easy reach of Rome.]

201. Suetonius, *Life of Domitian* 7

On one occasion, when there was a very abundant yield of wine and a very poor one of wheat, considering that the fields were neglected for too great a concentration on vines, he [Domitian] passed an edict that nobody was to plant any new vines in Italy, and that vineyards in the provinces should be cut down, or that no more than half should be left standing; however, he did not persist in pursuing this measure.

[This is one of the few instances of an attempt at central economic planning, and has been interpreted as evidence of an agrarian crisis in first century AD Italy, involving the abandonment of cereal farming by villa owners in favour of viticulture, which was both potentially more profitable and more socially acceptable.[18] However, it is more likely that there were other motives behind this. The grain supply for the city of Rome was a problem for all emperors, as shortages which affected the corn dole were prone to cause unrest. Domitian's edict seems to be an extreme response to a particularly poor harvest, and possibly a hint to some landowners who were over zealous in their enthusiasm for wine-growing. Significantly, Suetonius himself says that the matter was not pursued in practice. Recent field surveys in the Abruzzi and northern Campania[19] show little sign of the decline in rural population and changes in land use which would be expected if there was indeed a serious agrarian problem.]

202. Pliny, *Letters* 6.19

Do you know that the price of land around Rome has gone up? The cause of this sudden rise has stirred up much debate. At the last *comitium*, the senate passed a most honourable decree "the candidates for any office cannot give any celebration or gift, or deposit sums of money". The first two of these practices went on as freely as they were unconcealed, the third, although secret, was known to go on.

Our Homullus, vigilantly using this consensus, instead of addressing the motion, proposed that the consuls should inform the emperor of this universal wish and ask him to intervene to prevent this abuse, as he has others. He did so; for he applied the law against bribery to limit the disgraceful and infamous expenditure of candidates; they now have to invest one third of their wealth in land, as he thought it wrong, as it was, that those who sought office treated Rome and Italy not as their homeland but as an inn or boarding-house for travellers. Therefore the candidates are running about; they struggle to buy up whatever they hear is for sale, and so bring more onto the market. And so, if you are fed up of your Italian estates, by Hercules, now is the time for selling up and buying in the provinces – these same candidates are selling there in order to buy here.

Imperial estates

203. Suetonius, *Life of Augustus* 72

During his holidays, he often frequented the coast or islands of Campania, or the cities close to Rome – Lanuvium, Praeneste or Tibur, where he often sat in judgement in the portico of the Temple of Hercules.

[The imperial villas in the vicinity of Rome and at Baiae on the Bay of Naples became important residences, regularly frequented by most emperors, and preferred by some to Rome.]

204. Tacitus, *Annals* 4.6

The estates of Tiberius in Italy were few, his slaves were modest and his household had few freedmen.

[Tacitus cites the modest size of the imperial *patrimonium* at this date with approval. The implied contrast is with the much larger estates of his own day.]

205. Gasperini (1971), *3° Misc. Greca e Romana*

Dis Manib(us) Ursilla, slave of the emperor, who lived 40 years, lies here. This was set up by Ulpius Fortunatus, for a deserving mother.

[Second century AD. Tarentum. The existence of imperial estates (in this case, probably Trajanic) in the *ager Tarentinus* is indicated by the epitaphs of a number of imperial slaves.]

206. *ILS* 1643

[D. M.] Ti. Claudius Daus, freedman of the emperor, clerk of accounts of the imperial *patrimonium*. He lived 59 years. Servilia Aphro to a most dear husband.

[First century AD. Capena. Epitaph of an imperial freedman, probably of Claudius or Nero, who had worked in the accounts department of the estates owned by the emperor.]

Imperial edicts

207. Suetonius, *Life of Augustus* 44

He regulated the confused and disorderly manner of watching these games, moved by the dishonour of a senator who, on attending a crowded and very famous games at Puteoli, was not offered a seat by anyone. Therefore, a senatorial decree was passed that at any public performance, wherever it was held, the front row must be reserved for the senatorial order, and at Rome envoys from free or allied peoples were forbidden to sit in the *orchestra*, because he found out that even freedmen were sent as envoys. Soldiers were separated from civilians. Married men of plebeian status were assigned special seats, as were under-age boys, who were seated near their tutors, and no one was allowed to wear a dark cloak except in the back rows. Women were not even allowed to watch gladiatorial shows except from the back rows, whereas before they had sat with everyone else. The Vestal Virgins were excepted, and given a special place in the theatre opposite the praetor's box. Women were banned from all athletic festivals . . .

208. Suetonius, *Life of Claudius* 19

To the merchants, he offered certain wealth by underwriting any losses which might happen because of storms, and offered major rewards to those who built merchant ships, defined according to their circumstances: for a citizen, exemption from the *Lex Papia Poppaea*; for a Latin, rights of citizenship; for a woman, the status of a mother of four children. These measures are still in force today.

[The grain supply for the city of Rome was a constant problem, and bread riots at times of shortage were not infrequent. Claudius' measures were designed to make investment in merchant shipping attractive, and to encourage winter sailings. The *Lex Papia Poppaea* was the final piece of Augustan legislation regulating marriage, and laid down a system of financial and legal penalties for adults who did not marry or who were childless, and of corresponding rewards for those with large numbers of children. Under this law, a woman with four or more children gained legal independence, and could act for herself in financial and legal transactions without the necessity of a guardian.]

209. Suetonius. *Life of Claudius* 23

He [Claudius] ruled that . . . and that anyone who was banished from a province by its magistrates, should also be banned from the city of Rome and from Italy.

210. Suetonius, *Life of Claudius* 25.3

He [Claudius] passed an edict that travellers should not pass through the cities of Italy except on foot or in a sedan chair or in a litter. He stationed one cohort each at Puteoli and Ostia to guard against the occurrence of fires.

211. Josephus, *Jewish antiquities* 19.91

It is my wish that magistrates of the cities and colonies and *municipia*, both inside and outside Italy, and kings and rulers through their own ambassadors, have this edict inscribed and set up for no less than 30 days, in a place where it can readily be read from the ground.

[AD 41. Clause of a letter of Claudius on Jewish rights, specifying that copies of the document must be displayed legibly throughout the empire.]

Benefactions and imperial patronage

212. SHA, *Life of Hadrian* 10.2

. . . he went to Campania and gave assistance to all its cities by benefactions and largesses, securing all the leading men to his friendship.

213. Augustus, *Res Gestae* 20.5

During my seventh consulship, I rebuilt the Via Flaminia as far as Ariminum and also rebuilt all the bridges except the Mulvian and Minucian.[20]

214. Suetonius. *Life of Augustus* 28.25

He was aware that the city was not adorned in accordance with her imperial position, and was open to damage by flooding and fire, and he used to swear that he had left the city clothed in marble, which used to be of sun-dried brick.

215. *ILS* 147

Tiberius Claudius Ti. F. Nero, *pontifex*, consul twice, *imperator* twice, holding tribunician power for the fifth year, and Nero Claudius Drusus Germanicus, Ti. F., augur, consul, *imperator* . . . built the walls, gates and towers at their own expense.

[2 BC–AD 4. Saepinum. Payment for building or repairs to the city walls of Saepinum by Tiberius and Drusus.]

216. Suetonius, *Life of Tiberius* 40

Having travelled through Campania, where he dedicated the Capitolium at Capua and the temple of Augustus at Nola, which he had given as the reason for his journey, he went to Capri. . . . He was immediately recalled by the assiduous pleas of the people because of the disaster in which over 20,000 people had been killed at Fidenae when the amphitheatre collapsed during a gladiatorial show.

[Although he offered assistance in this case, Tiberius was not noted for his munificence, and made a point of trying to curb excessive extravagance in both public and private life.[21]]

217. Suetonius, *Life of Nero* 31.3

He also began a pool extending from Misenum to Lake Avernus, roofed and enclosed by colonnades, into which he planned to divert all the hot-water springs of Baiae; he also planned a canal from Avernus to Ostia, so that the journey could be made by ship but not at sea, which was to be 160 miles long and wide enough for quinqueremes to pass each other. In order to undertake these schemes, prisoners from everywhere were to be transported to Italy, and even people convicted of capital crimes would be condemned to nothing except this work.

218. Suetonius, *Life of Vespasian* 17

Vespasian was most generous to all ranks of men; he topped up the census for senators, supported impoverished ex-consuls with an annual pension of 500,000 sesterces, and restored to better circumstances many cities throughout the world which had suffered from earthquakes or fires, and particularly favoured artists and men of ability.

219. *IG* 729 (=*CIL* 10.1481)

Imperator Titus Caesar Vespasianus Augustus, son of the deified Vespasian, *Pontifex Maximus*, holder of the tribunician power ten times, holder of 15 triumphs, consul eight times, censor, *Pater Patriae* . . . restored that which was destroyed by the earthquake.

[AD 81. Naples. Bilingual inscription in Latin and Greek, recording the restorations paid for by Titus after a major earthquake.]

220. Suetonius, *Life of Titus* 8.3–4

Some dreadful and unexpected things happened during Titus' reign, such as the eruption of mount Vesuvius in Campania, and a fire at Rome which burned for three days and as many nights and, at the same time, an epidemic of an extent which had not been known before. In these great disasters, he showed not just the concern of a ruler but also a parental affection, passing edicts of condolence and assisting as far as his means allowed. He chose curators for the restoration of Campania by lot from among the number of ex-consuls; the estate of those killed in the eruption of Vesuvius and with no surviving heirs were contributed to the rebuilding of the damaged cities.

221. *Epitome de Caesaribus* 12.4

[Nerva] decreed that daughters and sons of impoverished parents in the cities of Italy should be fed at public expense.

[This passage, from an anonymous source writing at some date after AD 395 provides the only available evidence for alimentary schemes which pre-date Trajan, and for an explicit link with poverty. This interpretation may be an anachronism, stemming from the concern of fourth century Christian emperors for alleviating poverty and discouraging infant exposure.[22]]

222. *CIL* 11.1147

Payments on estates to the sum of 1,044,000 sesterces, in order that through the generosity of Imperator Caesar Nerva Trajanus Augustus Germanicus Dacicus, best and greatest of emperors, boys and girls may receive support: 245 legitimate boys, at 16 sesterces each per month, totalling 47,040 sesterces; 34 legitimate girls at 12 sesterces each, totalling 4896 sesterces; illegitimate boys, 1144 sesterces [per year]; illegitimate girls, 1120 sesterces [per year]; total, 52,200 sesterces, equalling 5 per cent interest on the capital mentioned above.

C. Volusius Memor and Volumnia Alce, acting through their freedman, Volumnius Diadumenos, registered the Quintia-Aurelia farm and the hill of Muletas, with its woodlands, which is in the Ambitrebatia *pagus* of the territory of Veleia, delimited by [the properties of] M. Mommeius Persicus, Satrius Severus, and the people, valued at 108,000 sesterces; he will receive 8692 sesterces and give this farm as security.

[AD 109–112. Veleia. Rubric and first registration from the city's alimentary scheme, as recorded on two large bronze tablets. The rubric specifies number and size of payments, and the rest of the text lists the properties given as security and the amount loaned on them. The full list amounts to 300 properties, owned by 48 separate landowners. Unlike the private benefactions covered in Chapter 9, this was part of the imperial scheme and operated on a much larger scale.]

223. SHA, *Life of Antoninus Pius* 8–9

[Antoninus] arranged support payments for girls, known as the Faustinianae, in honour of Faustina. Of his public works, these survive: in Rome, the temple of Hadrian, which was dedicated in honour of his father, the Greek stadium, which was restored after a fire, and the amphitheatre, which was repaired, the tomb of Hadrian, the temple of Agrippa, the Sublician bridge and the restored lighthouse. Also, the harbour of Caieta, the harbour of Tarracina, which was restored, the baths at Ostia, the aqueduct at Antium and the temples at Lanuvium. He also helped many cities with money, either to build new buildings or to rebuild old ones. He also gave financial help to magistrates and senators to help them carry out their duties.

Honouring the emperor

224. Augustus, *Res Gestae* 25.2

The whole of Italy swore allegiance to me of its own free will, and demanded me as leader in the war which I won at Actium.

225. Suetonius, *Life of Augustus* 59

Some Italian cities made the date of his first visit to them into their New Year.

226. Augustus, *Res Gestae* 10.2

After a number of years, and after the death of the man who had taken the opportunity of civil disturbance to take possession of it, I received this priesthood in the consulship of P. Sulpicius and C. Valgus, and such a multitude flowed in from all of Italy to my election assembly as had never previously been recorded at Rome.

[13 BC. Lepidus, who was *Pontifex Maximus*, died and was succeeded in office by Augustus.]

227. Augustus, *Res Gestae* 9.2

And all the citizens together have unanimously and unceasingly prayed for my health at all the *pulvinaria*, both as individuals and as citizens of *municipia*.

[Prayers for the emperor's health are here linked with the *pulvinaria*, traditional ceremonies at which images of the gods were displayed on a couch (*pulvinar*).]

228. *ILS* 157

To perpetual Augustan peace and the public freedom of the Roman people. To the *genius* of the *municipium* in the 704th year from the founding of Interamna to the consulship of Cn. Domitius Ahenobarbus and L. Arruntius Camillus Scribonianus. To the providence of Tiberius Caesar Augustus, born for the continuation of the Roman name, on the occasion of the removal of a most dangerous enemy of the Roman people. Faustus Titius Liberalis, *Sevir Augustalis* for the second time, had this [monument] made at his own expense.

[AD 32. Interamna Nahars. Dedication by an *Augustalis* to the *genius* of the city of Interamna and to the emperor, to commemorate the fall of Sejanus. The name of Arruntius is partially erased because of *damnatio memoriae* after his revolt in AD 42. The duality of loyalty in Italy, divided between the home city and Rome, is amply demonstrated here, where the dedication is jointly to the emperor and Rome and to the *genius* of Interamna.]

229. *ILS* 233

To the deified Poppaea Augusta, wife of the emperor Nero Caesar Augustus. Set up by L. Titinius L. F. Gal. Glaucus Lucretianus, *flamen* of Roma and Augustus, *duovir* for the fourth time, patron of the colony, *sevir* of the *Equites Romani, Curio, Praefectus Fabrum* under a consul, military tribune of the Legion XXII Primigenia, prefect of the Balearics instead of a *Legatus*, military tribune of the Legion VI Victrix, in fulfilment of a vow for the safety of the emperor Nero, which he made whilst in the Balearics in the consulship of A. Licinius Nerva, and the duovirate of L. Sufeius Vegetus and Q. Aburius Nepos. When he wished to build this, his prayer having been granted, he set it up to Jupiter, Juno, Minerva, Roman Felicitia, and the deified Augustus.

To the emperor Nero Claudius Caesar Augustus Germanicus, son of the deified Claudius, grandson of Germanicus Caesar, great-grandson of the deified Augustus, *pontifex maximus*, holder of tribunician power for the 13th time, *imperator* 11 times, consul four times. Set up by L. Titinius L. F. Gal. Glaucus Lucretianus, *Flamen* of Roma and Augustus, *duovir* for the fourth time, patron of the colony, *sevir* of the *Equites Romani, Curio, Praefectus Fabrum* under a consul, military tribune of the Legion XXII Primigenia, prefect of the Balearics instead of a Legatus, military tribune of the Legion VI Victrix, in fulfilment of a vow for the safety of the emperor Nero, which he made whilst in the Balearics in the consulship of A. Licinius Nerva, and the duovirate of L. Sufeius Vegetus and Q. Aburius Nepos. When he wished to build this, his prayer having been granted, he set it up to Jupiter, Juno, Minerva, Roman Felicitas, and the deified Augustus.

[AD 66–67. Luna. Dedication in honour of Poppaea and Nero. Unusually, Poppaea is mentioned as the main subject of the text although Nero's safety is the subject of the original vow. Like No. 228, this relates to a conspiracy against the emperor, in this case the Pisonian conspiracy of AD 65. The name of the second consul for that year, M. Vestinius Atticus, who was executed as part of the conspiracy, is omitted.[23]]

230. *Fasti Praenestini*

. . . February 5th: a holiday, by senatorial decree, because on that day, Imperator Caesar Augustus, *pontifex maximus*, holding tribunician power for the twenty-first year, and consul 13 times, was named father of his country by the senate and people of Rome.

[Excerpt from the *Fasti Praenestini*, an example of the official calendars of public holidays and festivals which have been found in several parts of Italy [cf. No. 318]. Many of the holidays included are connected with birthdays or other anniversaries of the imperial family.[24]]

231. Dio 55.10.9

These were all done in honour of Mars, but sacred games were voted in honour of Augustus himself at Naples in Campania, ostensibly because he had restored it when it was demolished by an earthquake and a fire, but actually because the Neapolitans, alone of all the Campanians, tried to copy the customs of the Greeks . . .

232. Suetonius, *Life of Nero* 25

Coming back from Greece, Nero entered Naples, the city in which he had made his first appearance as an artist, on a white horse, through a dismantled part of the walls, as is the custom for victors in the sacred games; he entered Antium, then Albanum, then Rome in the same manner; but at Rome, he used the chariot in which Augustus had once ridden in his triumphs, and he was dressed in a purple *chlamys* decorated with gold stars, wearing the Olympic crown on his head and carrying the Pythian crown in his right hand . . .

[Nero was notably philhellenic in his sympathies, and was a frequent participant in Greek games in both Greece and Italy. He was particularly fond of the Greek colony of Naples, which he visited often, and which was the scene of many of his performances. His return to Italy in AD 67 was marked by the honours granted in the Greek world to victors of one of the four sacred games (Olympic, Pythian, Isthmian and Nemean) and underlined by his adaptation of the forms of a Roman triumph, substituting the triumphal dress and crown of a Roman general for the Greek robe (*chlamys*) and the crowns of an Olympic and Pythian victor.]

233. Gasperini (1971), *3° Misc. Greca e Romana*

In honour of Imperator Caesar Trajanus Augustus Germanicus Dacicus, son of the deified Nerva, *Pontifex Maximus*, holder of tribunician power 14 times, awarded six triumphs, consul five times, *pater patriae*, set up by the people of Tarentum.

[AD 109–10. Tarentum. Commemoration of Trajan's departure for Parthia.]

234. SHA, *Life of Hadrian* 19.1

He held the praetorship in Etruria while he was emperor. In Latin cities he was *dictator* and *aedile* and *duumvir*, at Naples he was *demarchos*, in his own city [Italica, in Spain], he was *quinquennalis*, and similarly, *quinquennalis* at Hatria – his other home town, so to speak – and *archon* at Athens.

[The holding of municipal magistracies by emperors and their relatives was a recognized phenomenon, usually because of a grant by a city wishing to honour the *princeps*. Hadrian's reputation as a municipal benefactor clearly attracted many of these honours. The reason why Hatria is cited as Hadrian's place of origin is that there was a tradition that he was descended from Italians from Hatria who migrated to Italica.]

CHAPTER SIX

The Italian economy

Any attempt to write a history of the economy of Italy comes up against a formidable variety of methodological problems. The evidence of ancient writers on economic subjects clashes on several important points with the picture revealed by archaeological survey and excavation, while the undoubted importance of agriculture to the ancient economy tends to overshadow the roles played by trade, taxation and finance.

Even at the highest theoretical level, the notion of the ancient city as a consumer city – a parasite on its territory – first promulgated by Sombart and Weber, and later developed by Finley – is the source of some dissatisfaction amongst historians but has not been successfully challenged.[1] Attempts by Leveau and Engels[2] to characterize the ancient city as, respectively, an administrative centre and a provider of services do not fully explain the relationship between the city and its territory. What is certain is that this relationship was both closely-knit and complex. Throughout Roman history there was a close connection between the population, even the urban population, and the land. The existence of small farms and market gardens even within the walls of cities[3] attests to the interaction between urban and rural economies, something which is also stressed in Roman literature [No. 258].

Ultimately, the starting-point for any examination of the Italian economy has to be agriculture. Italy was rich in natural resources and some regions, notably Campania, were extremely fertile [Nos 235–9]. Cultivation of the territory was central to the economy of any individual city and, in addition, land was a privileged form of wealth in Roman law. The census rating of a citizen, and hence his military duties, were defined by his wealth in land and income from it, and senators were required to draw a substantial portion of their wealth from Italian land [No. 202]. At the same time, it is important not to lose sight of the fact that there were other important spheres of economic activity – trade, banking and money-lending, investment in urban property.

Nevertheless, the economic bottom line for Italian states was that each controlled a certain amount of territory owned by the citizens and worked, to a greater or lesser extent, with a view to providing the basic food supply. Deficits could be made good or items not locally available imported from elsewhere, and surpluses or manufactured goods could be exported, but the core economy was based on the territory. To a large extent, this remained true until the second century BC when major structural changes in the economy of Italy took place as a result of Rome's conquest of an overseas empire and the rapid growth of the city of Rome itself. The concentration of elite activity in Rome from the first century BC onwards, and the sheer size of the city, profoundly distorted the economy of Italy. In effect, Latium, southern Etruria and northern Campania became a greatly enlarged *suburbium* for Rome – a hinterland whose economy was geared to supplying the markets of the city with luxury foods or perishable commodities, such as fruit, flowers and vegetables, which could not travel far. Even outside this area, the impact was profound. In the second and first centuries BC, Rome was the major market for Italian goods, and Roman activity was significant in generating others. The conquest of the Mediterranean necessitated the maintenance of a large army, which required clothing, equipment and supplies, many of which came from Italy in the first instance, although standing armies in the provinces were later supplied locally.[4]

One of the basic problems is that the few ancient sources extant are all written from the viewpoint of the Roman elite, and therefore give a highly partial account of economic activity, reflecting elite preoccupations rather than economic realities.[5] The moral and intellectual assumptions which lie behind ancient comments on agriculture deeply colour what is written and how. Senators such as Varro were keen to stress the aspects of villa agriculture which were appropriate to a class which placed great emphasis on urbanity, *otium* and social appropriateness. Wine production, particularly of fine wines, was an activity which was thought to be appropriate for an aristocrat, as well as a good investment, and thus features prominently in the ancient literature.[6] The same is true of some of the more exotic luxury products, although those who were too obviously dilettante in their approach to their estates were frowned upon. As Purcell has stressed,[7] the emphasis of upper class writers was on creating a pastoral idyll, not on portraying a grittily realistic picture of the villa and its products. A similar process is at work in sources relating specifically to the second century BC and the situation in the Gracchan period. Intellectually and emotionally, there was a tension, which increased as Italy became more urbanized and as conspicuous consumption increased among the elite, between the ideal of the simple rustic life of the peasant farmer and the reality of the rural economy. The Gracchan programme was based on a very conservative agenda looking back to a mythical golden age in which the independent Italian peasant was the moral and political backbone of the state.

The evolution of the agrarian economy from small-scale farming to villa agriculture was a complex process which had a profound effect on the Italian countryside, but it was by no means the destructive and crisis-ridden occurrence portrayed in the writings of some historians, both ancient and modern. The traditional view, as enunciated by Toynbee and refined and modified by Brunt and Hopkins,[8] is that the devastation of the Hannibalic war and the changes caused by Rome's acquisition of an overseas empire generated a series of disastrous developments. The ever-increasing demand for military manpower made serious inroads on the Italian peasantry, taking farmers away from the land for long periods. At the same time the increased wealth from war booty and rich trading opportunities with the Greek world, together with the great increase in cheap slave labour, enabled the elite to buy up land and accumulate *ager publicus*, thus acquiring large estates run by slaves and dedicated to specialized cash crops. The supposed depopulation of the land and consequent increase in rural poverty and decline in military manpower was the inspiration for the Gracchan land reforms of the second century BC, and later the source of another crisis in the first century AD.

This gloomy picture is not, however, borne out by the evidence. The development of villa agriculture was not a specifically second century phenomenon. A large-scale land survey in the territory of Metapontum shows development of substantial estates there in the third century BC[9] and the recently discovered villa at Gravina is of similarly early date.[10] The second century was undoubtedly the beginning of the principal shift from subsistence to estate-based agriculture, but this did not become widespread until the first century in many regions. Appian leaves in no doubt that a certain amount of violence and coercion took place during the second century, centred around the issue of who owned and farmed tracts of land (see Chapter 3), but nevertheless, the case for devastation and demographic collapse in the Italian countryside seems overstated.

Despite the increasing importance (and supply) of slave labour, there is evidence that tenancy by free farmers on large estates was very important. Tenancy is nearly impossible to identify in the archaeological record,[11] but it is well represented in the literary sources. Cicero makes reference to the purchase of land by *municipia* which was then rented out to provide an income [No. 252], something which later became both central to many municipal economies and a highly uncertain form of income. Columella, writing in the second century AD, also has a strong preference for tenanted farms rather than a slave workforce [No. 243]. Pliny's letters contain numerous references to his trials and tribulations with the tenants on his estates, for whom debt seems to have been an endemic problem [Nos 250–51]. Small farms also seem to have been given to members of his household as pensions, the idea being that they rented these out to tenants and lived off the income produced [No. 249].

The size of the estates which were developing at this date is also a matter of contention. Although Pliny the elder says that much of the land in Italy was concentrated into huge estates (*latifundia*), which he considered to have been the ruination of the Italian economy, there is a considerable body of evidence to the contrary. The picture which emerges from both archaeological and historical evidence is of the increasing concentration of land into the hands of the elite, but as a large number of medium-sized estates, not as huge monolithic blocks of property.

Cicero's accounts of his journeys around Italy and the provinces imply that he and his friends all had a substantial number of villas scattered throughout Italy, which could be used as staging posts on journeys or lent to friends for the same purpose, although only those situated in Latium or Campania were regularly used for longer stays. Even within a particular region, similar patterns of physically dispersed estates owned by the same person are found. The Etruscan magnate Sextus Roscius owned a sizeable estate near his native Ameria, but this was comprised of 13 separate farms in the Tiber valley [No. 248]. By the end of the first century AD, it seems to have been recognized good practice not to concentrate estates in a single area. One of Pliny's letters describes his dilemma over an estate adjoining one of his own which came onto the market. In the end, although he fully acknowledges the sound economic arguments against concentrating one's property, he was unable to resist the purchase, mainly for non-economic reasons such as the pleasantness of the location and the convenience of having adjoining estates [No. 250].

The archaeological evidence also supports the arguments against the development of large estates at an early date. Surveys of the Volturnus valley, the *Ager Falernus* and other areas show that farms and villas of medium size were the norm until the end of the second century AD.[12] Even in northern Campania, the region most closely associated with specialist wine production and therefore with the development of elite-owned and fairly specialized villas, the patterns of land ownership are not consolidated before the end of the second century AD.[13] In the late republic and early principate, such evidence as is available from amphora stamps, and other inscriptions points to a concentration of land into the hands of a relatively small number of people, but not as large consolidated blocks of territory. The development of very large villas and the consolidation of land holdings was very much a phenomenon of the late empire in this region. A similar pattern emerges in Samnium, where surveys around Ligures Baebiani, and examination of the land ownership details included in the alimentary list found there, indicate the existence of a flourishing Oscan elite whose wealth was based on medium-sized estates in the second century BC, and a gradual concentration of resources into fewer hands, with a consequent decline in rural population, during the first century AD.[14] Clearly, there is some measure of regional variation in this process, but overall, the evidence does not point to a total collapse of rural populations or an agrarian crisis in either the second century BC or the first century AD. Excavations of villas at Francolise and Posta Crusta[15] indicate that far from being *latifundia* of the type described by Pliny, they were estates which would have fitted comfortably within the Gracchan limit of 1,000 *iugera*.

Nevertheless, this is not to deny that the second century BC was a time of profound economic change. Archaeological surveys in regions as various as South Etruria, Northern Campania and Lucania[16] reveal a similar pattern of decline in numbers of small rural sites and individual farms in favour of growth of urban centres and villas during this period. Surveys of the Bussento valley in Lucania also illustrate changes in land use as a result of colonization. A third century BC settlement pattern, an even scatter of sites up the valley between the small Greek city of Pyxus on the coast and the Lucanian city at Roccagloriosa in the hinterland, is disrupted by the foundation of the colony of Buxentum on the site of Pyxus. As a result, Roccagloriosa declines and disappears over the course of the second century BC, and rural settlement is concentrated at the lower end of the valley, around the Roman colony.[17] In Magna Graecia, an extensive survey of the territory of Metapontum[18] indicates a very sharp decline in rural settlement at this date, giving some support to the notion of agrarian crisis, but the local nature of this is revealed by similar studies of the territory of Croton,[19] where a less marked decline is followed by a period of recovery.

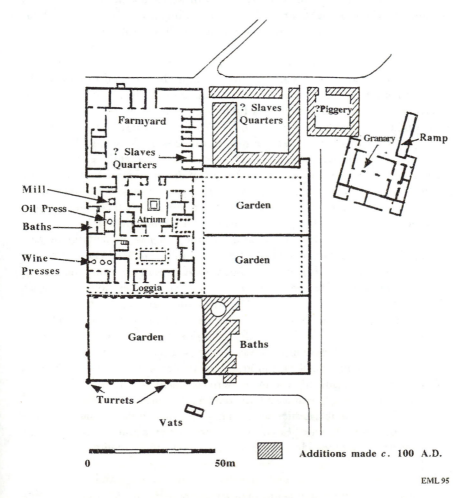

7. *Settefinestre: plan of the Roman villa*

The notion that villa agriculture was a specialized form of land exploitation is also open to question. Despite Finley's assertions, it is unlikely that the Roman and Italian elites were not interested in profit. After all, most of their wealth came from their estates, and substantial wealth was an absolute prerequisite for a public career. This does not, however, necessarily imply specialization of agriculture or the raising of "cash-crops" on estates, and the extent to which they actively sought to maximize profit is open to question. Roman works on agriculture all described villas with mixed economies, growing grain, vines, olives and fruit as well as raising livestock and sometimes luxury goods such as exotic fish and gamebirds. This is very largely backed up by excavations of villa sites, where the tendency is towards medium-sized estates with a mixed economy, of the type described by Cato[20] rather than the *latifundia* of Pliny [No. 241]. Even the huge villa-complex at Settefinestre is not specialized, but has facilities for producing a range of crops.

The notion of an agrarian crisis in the first century AD is based in part on a decree of Domitian, who sought to curb wine production and to enforce the growing of grain [No. 201]. However, this is not necessarily a clear case of over-specialization leading to disaster. As Patterson[21] points out, the production of wine was largely an elite occupation, and if Domitian was restricting this, he was effectively restricting elite (and more specifically senatorial) wealth. The decree can therefore be seen as an attack on the senatorial order rather than a response to economic crisis. It may also have related much more to economic activity in the provinces than to Italy. In at least one area of Italy, Samnium, the pattern in the first century is not one of sudden crisis, but of a more gradual concentration of agrarian resources and consequent decline in the rural population.

Wine, in particular, has a high profile in the study of ancient agriculture, because there is a substantial body of literature relating to the production of, and trade in, fine wines, and because the high survival rate of transport and storage amphorae, including a reasonable number stamped with the producer's name, allows study of the source of the wine and its trade. However, there is evidence that even here, winemaking was a lucrative and high-profile, but not exclusive, activity on many villas. The dangers of overemphasizing agrarian specialization are demonstrated by Jongman's analysis of the agrarian economy of Pompeii,[22] which makes the point that if wine production by villas in the territory of Pompeii had run at the level assumed by some modern commentators, the populace of the city would have starved, or at least been reduced to a lifetime of liquid lunches. Clearly a city must be able to subsist, and a model which posits complete domination of resources by an elite geared to wine production cannot be tenable. The point is further underlined by Pliny's reference to the poor quality of Pompeian wine.[23]

The rearing of livestock and large-scale transhumance and pasturage is another phenomenon which is unduly blamed by the sources for dispossessing the Italian peasantry. In point of fact, pasturage was traditionally a major part of the economy of Appennine Italy. It was by no means a new introduction in the second century, although the scale of transhumance may have increased during the late republic and early empire, and some Roman authors stress the high rates of return on stockrearing [No. 268]. Much of Samnium and Apulia was criss-crossed by drove roads, enabling flocks to be moved between summer and winter pastures, or driven from grazing-grounds to the market. This process undoubt-edly caused much friction. The dividing line between herding and banditry was recognized to be a fine one, and herdsmen were one of the least controllable groups of people in ancient society. A letter from the imperial secretariat to the magistrates of Saepinum ordered them to stop impeding the passage of imperial flocks through the city and imposed a settlement of ongoing grievances between the herdsmen and the townsfolk [No. 270]. Despite these incidents and the apparent increase in size of flocks in the early empire, there is no reason to as-sume that they were occupying otherwise arable land in large quantities, or that they represented a move away from traditional forms of land use.

Although agriculture was a major part of the ancient economy, it was by no means the only element. Other aspects which must be considered are taxation and finance, trade, manufacturing, and the relation of Italy to the wider economy of the empire as a whole. In terms of taxation, Italy escaped very lightly. Direct taxation for Roman citizens was suspended in 187 BC, and permanently abol-ished in 167, on the strength of the income from the conquest of Macedon. When the rest of Italy was enfranchised in 90–89 BC, this exemption was extended to cover the whole country. The only taxes which remained in place were indirect ones, such as sales taxes, manumission taxes on freed slaves and the levy to pay for the public post. In practice, even this small tax base declines, as a number of taxes were abolished by imperial decree and tax remissions became commonplace (cf. Chapter 5). In this sense, Italy was parasitic on the provinces of the empire, whose exports and taxes went to underwrite the economy of Italian cities, and more specifically, of Rome.

The level of trade and manufacturing in Italy, and the nature of the urban, as opposed to the rural, economy is notoriously difficult to pin down. Because Roman law privileged land ownership over everything else as a source of wealth, making it a condition for holding high rank and office and also the basis of census ratings and assessments for military service, our view of Roman attitudes to other forms of wealth and economic activity are deeply distorted. Cicero [No. 262] explicitly says that trade and finance was not a fit occupation for a gentleman unless conducted on an international scale, and one of the most memorable fig-ures of Roman literature is the horribly vulgar and *nouveau riche* Trimalchio, a freedman who made his money in trade.[24]

To set against this, however, there is also a strong financial and mercantile ele-ment in Italian history. The vast amount of trade with the eastern empire in the second and first centuries BC was conducted by both Italians and Romans. Unlike Trimalchio, these men were not freedmen, but came from leading Italian families, up to and including Roman senators, although they were forced to oper-ate through agents due to legal restrictions on senatorial involvement in trade.

Two close friends of Cicero were Cluvius and Vestorius, Puteolan aristocrats with a wide network of financial contacts and dealings in the provinces.[25] Other *negotiatores* known from inscriptions also seem to have been free men, and many of the names are those of aristocratic Campanian families – Heii, Statii, Blossii, etc.[26] It is possible that the social position of *negotiatores* changed somewhat during the first century AD, brought about by a combination of great social stigma and increasing presence of freedmen in trade, but the view that trade and profit making was somehow frowned upon by the ancient elite is over-simplified. The mere fact that access to land and sea routes and ease of transport were stressed as an asset, both for villas [No. 253] and for cities [No. 255], indicates that trade was more important than usually allowed.

In the middle of the first century BC, a notorious case of extortion recorded by Cicero [No. 134] concerned a loan made by Brutus to the city of Salamis on Cyprus, at an extremely high rate of interest. Cicero became involved while governing Cilicia, when Brutus' agent demanded a squadron of cavalry to harass the city for its arrears. Cicero's refusal to comply caused considerable surprise and ill feeling. Another feature of the Ciceronian period was that many of the aristocratic families of municipal Italy were of equestrian status, and it was this group who were most actively involved in finance, and particularly in tax collection. It seems, therefore, that whatever happened during the principate, the Ciceronian period was one where there was much elite activity in trade and financial dealings, at least on a large scale. A century later, Claudius made active efforts to tempt wealthy men and women into trade, offering privileges in return for the fitting out of ships to import grain into Italy [No. 208]. This may reflect a greater reluctance to become involved and the consequent need to provide incentives, but it also suggests that the social stigma was not strong enough to be insurmountable.

Even within a locality, the prevalence of market days, and inscriptions announcing them, indicate that local networks of trade and exchange were important in the economic life of Italy right down the social scale. The furore caused by the holding of a market on a villa rather than in the nearby city of Vicetia suggests that this undercutting of the markets in the city was perceived as a threat to the urban economy [No. 261]. The exchanges which took place at these local markets would be very different from the sort of large-scale trade discussed above, but it was clearly of vital economic importance for a locality. The gulf between the two is emphasized in the contrast drawn by Pseudo-Vergil [No. 259] whose peasant takes his produce to market in the city, but returns having bought nothing from the *macellum* there. The produce sold by the peasant is the surplus from his farm, but the goods sold in the covered urban market were not daily necessities but luxury produce, which he could not, or would not, afford.

Unfortunately, it is difficult to reconstruct the level of imports and exports from ancient Italy and the ways in which trade was structured. What does seem certain, however, was that Italy, while exporting luxury items such as fine wines and textiles, was also becoming increasing dependent on the provinces. Taxes and goods from an inner group of pacified, demilitarized, provinces were becoming increasingly crucial, both for supplying the army on the frontiers and in supplying Italy and the city of Rome.[27] Tacitus and Pliny [Nos. 240–1] fulminated against Italy's growing economic dependence on food from overseas, and the problems of supplying grain for the city of Rome was a constant anxiety. At the beginning of Rome's imperial expansion, the need to feed, clothe and equip large armies may well have been a factor which triggered economic growth in Italy.[28] Contracts to supply the necessary goods were lucrative and required increased artisan production to meet demand. Later, however, the task of supplying the army shifted elsewhere and Italy became rather less economically productive.

What little is known about how manufactured goods were produced and how artisans operated comes mostly from inscriptions. Pompeii and Herculaneum, and to a lesser extent Ostia, are rich in texts which cast light on how goods were produced, although there are still many gaps in the record. At Pompeii, where textile production is well attested,[29] artisans mostly worked in small units, some (such as fullers) housed in specialist workshops and others in more general *tabernae*. Inscriptions show that there was a high degree of craft organization, with *collegia* of fullers, dyers, weavers, carders, etc. A noticeable absence is any reference to spinners, but this may have been regarded as a female occupation, undertaken in the home and unsuitable for a formal craft guild. Clearly, the work was separated into a number of distinct processes performed by individual specialists. Attempts to construct a model of a municipal elite drawing its wealth from manufacturing have, however, come to grief.[30] No connections can be made between the economic activities of the *collegia* and any elite families. The civic benefactress Eumachia was probably patron of the *collegium* of fullers, but there is no other provable connection between her family and the wool trade, and no certain evidence that the grand building opening onto the forum which she paid for was either a cloth market or the headquarters of this *collegium*, as has been suggested. The entrepreneur Caecilius Iucundus rented a fullery from the city of Pompeii in AD 58, but this is an isolated instance in a large business empire, and in any case, Iucundus, although undoubtedly wealthy, was not demonstrably a member of the elite.

Another feature of the urban economy which is amply documented at Pompeii and Herculaneum is the thriving market in urban property. Advertisements for properties to rent are found at Pompeii, and concern about the activities of property speculators is demonstrated by a decree found at Herculaneum which regulated such activities. The Iucundus archive is also full of items recording loans, securities, sale and rental of small properties and warehouse space, all of which attest to a thriving amount of financial and commercial activity going on amongst the ordinary population of the city.

The Italian economy, then, is a highly complex organism, which underwent profound changes during the period under examination, but remains resistant to the more apocalyptic theories of crisis and desolation. Agriculture was a vital part of this economy, but Italy was becoming increasingly reliant on the provinces despite having impressive natural resources. Its privileged tax status and high density of increasingly urbanized population meant that it could no longer be self-supporting. Nevertheless, both trade and finance flourished, on the international as well as the local level. The overall trend is of increasing concentration of resources into the hands of a small number of people, and an increasing dependence on resources from the provinces, but archaeological evidence suggests that this was much more gradual and less dramatic than the literary sources imply.

Natural resources of Italy

235. Strabo, *Geographies* 5.1.12

As for the excellence of the region [Gallia Cisalpina], it is proved by the good reserves of manpower, the size of their cities and their wealth, in all of which the Romans there have surpassed the rest of Italy. For not only does the cultivated land yield produce in large amounts and of all kinds, but the forests have such quantities of acorns that Rome is fed principally on the herds of pigs from the region. The yield of millet is also outstanding, since the earth is well watered; millet is the greatest preventer of famine, since it stands against all adverse weather and can never fail, even when there is scarcity of all other grain. The region also has good pitch production; with regard to the wine, the amount is shown by the amphorae, for the wooden ones are larger than houses; the excellent supply of pitch helps towards the good coating the amphorae receive. With regard to wool, the soft type is produced by the area around Mutina and the River Scoltenna (which is the finest of all); the coarse wool is produced by Liguria and the territory of the Symbrians, from which most of the households in Italy are clothed; the medium grade is produced by the area around Patavium, from which is made expensive carpets and coverings and all things of this kind which are woolly on either both sides or only one. With regard to the mines, currently they are not being worked in this region as much as previously, perhaps because of the fact that those in Gallia Transalpina and in Spain are more profitable.

236. Polybios 3.91

The plains around Capua are unsurpassed in Italy for their fertility and beauty and their accessibility by sea; the harbours of the area are the destination for those who travel by sea to Italy from virtually all parts of the civilized world. The cities are the finest and most famous of the peninsula – Sinuessa, Cumae and Dikaiarchia, Naples beyond those, and lastly the people of Nuceria who control the coast, while the inland area belongs to Cales and Teanum to the north, and Nola and the Daunians to the south. The centre of the plains is Capua, which was once the most fortunate and best-developed city of them all . . . Also, the region is protected because it is very difficult of access; . . .

237. Pliny, *Natural history* 3.60

. . . the land of fierce competition between the gods of wine and corn. Moving from the territories of Setia and Caecubum, we come to the Ager Falernus and the territory of Cales; the mountains rise around – Massicus, Gaurus and the hills of the Surrentum peninsula. The wide expanse of the *Campi Leborini* is here, whose harvest of garlic delights gourmets. These shores run with the water of hot springs and surpass all other coasts in the fame of their shellfish and other seafood. Nowhere produces richer olive oil, the other commodity whose different types compete to give pleasure to mankind. It has been ruled by Oscans, Greeks, Umbrians, Etruscans and Campanians.

238. Cicero, *De lege agraria* 2.80

Have you forgotten what huge armies you maintained on the produce of the *Ager Campanus* during the Italian war, when all other sources of income were lost?

239. Diodorus 5.13.1–2

Off that city of Etruria called Populonia there is an island which people call Aethalia [Elba]. It is about 100 *stades* away from the coast and gained the name it is called by from the smoke which lies so thickly around it. The island possesses a great quantity of iron ore, which they quarry so as to smelt and cast it and so produce iron, and they have a great abundance of this. . . . These [the iron pigs] are bought by traders in exchange for goods and taken to Puteoli or other *entrepôts*, where there are men who buy cargoes of this type and with the help of many metalworkers whom they have gathered together, they work it again and manufacture iron objects of all kinds.

Dependence on provinces

240. Tacitus, *Annals* 3.54

So why did frugality once prevail? Because people could control themselves, and because we were citizens of a single city; nor did domination of Italy excite us. Overseas conquest taught us to consume the wealth of others, and the civil wars taught us to spend our own. . . . But nobody makes any proposal about the fact that Italy depends on supplies from overseas, and the life of the Roman people is daily tossed at the mercy of the sea and the wind. And if the harvests of the provinces ever fail to come to the assistance of our masters, slaves and fields, then our own estates and villas will not sustain us.

[AD 22. Tiberian letter to the Senate.]

Villas in Italy

241. Pliny, *Natural history* 18.4

When Roman customs were of this kind, Italy not only had enough for its requirements without relying on any of the provinces for its food, but also the price of food was unbelievably cheap . . . This cheapness did not have its origin in the *latifundia* of individuals encroaching continually on their neighbours, because the landed property of each person was limited to 500 *iugera* by the law of Licinius Stolo (he was himself convicted under his own law of possessing more than this amount, by registering some in the name of his son). This was the size of estates when the state was growing rapidly. The comment made by M' Curius, after his triumphs had added an enormous amount of land to Roman rule, is also well known – "any man for whom seven *iugera* of land are insufficient must be looked upon as a dangerous citizen" – because this was the amount of land which was allotted to the people after the expulsion of the kings. Then what was the cause of this great fertility? The fact that at that time the land was farmed by the hands of the generals themselves, and the soil rejoiced beneath a ploughshare crowned with laurel wreaths and guided by a farmer honoured with triumphs . . . Today, these same fields are cultivated by slaves whose legs are chained, by the hands of criminals and men with branded faces.

[Pliny's analysis of the rise of the landed estate is one of the few in ancient literature to actually employ the word *latifundia* with references to large estates. In this passage, he seems to use it to mean any land holding of 500 *iugera* or more, but elsewhere [No. 242], he links it to use mass slave labour and ranching and pasturage rather than arable farming. The theme of this passage is, like the ideology behind the Gracchan land reforms, deeply conservative. It exploits the theme of an uncorrupted "golden age" in which a greater level of social and economic simplicity prevailed, contrasting with (and providing the moral basis for) Rome's growing power. Pliny locates the age of farmer-soldiers not in the early days of the republic, but in the period of the conquest of Italy. M' Curius Dentatus, referred to in the text, was consul in 290 BC. The *Lex Licinia* is usually dated to 367 BC. Pliny, however, misquotes it as limiting all landholdings to a maximum of 500 *iugera* per person, while Gracchus' attempts to revive and enforce it make it clear that this only applied to holdings of *ager publicus*, not to *ager privatus*.]

242. Pliny, *Natural history* 18.35

The men of earlier times believed that beyond all else, moderation should be practised in land holding, for they judged that it was better to sow less and plough more intensively. I see that Vergil agreed with this as well. To tell the truth, *latifundia* have ruined Italy, and will soon ruin the provinces too.

[This passage is central to the debate about land holdings and *latifundia* in Italy, and to the nature of the imperial economy. Pliny's gloomy view (backed up by the statistic that half of the province of Africa was owned by only six men at the time when Nero had these six executed) chimes with the equally doom-laden prognoses of authors who describe the background to the Gracchan land law (cf. Chapter 3), but rather less well with the results of archaeological surveys. Villas of the late republic and the first century AD are not, with some exceptions, the huge estates which Pliny identifies as the cause of ruination, but are mostly medium-sized holdings. The clue to the problem lies in the pattern of land tenure rather than size of single estates. Pliny is particularly outraged by the concentration of a large amount of property in the hands of a very small number of people. Archaeological survey to some extent supports this, in that individuals or families could own large quantities of land in a region without this land necessarily forming a single estate. The *Ager Falernus*, for instance, shows precisely this pattern of disparate land holdings. *Latifundia* in the modern sense of huge monolithic blocks of land do not appear until the third century AD.]

243. Columella, *De re rustica* 1.6–9

The size of the villa and the sum of its parts should be proportional to the entire enclosed area, which should be divided into three parts: the *villa urbana*, the *villa rustica*, and the *villa fructuaria* . . .

Enough has been said about the location of the *villa rustica* and its various components. Next, the *villa rustica* must have these things close to it: an oven and a mill, of whatever size may be needed for the number of tenants; at least two ponds, one for geese and cattle, and the other to soak lupins, elm sticks, twigs and other things appropriate to our needs. . . .

When all these things have been acquired or made, the master should, amongst other matters, give close attention to labourers; these can either be tenants or slaves (unchained or chained). He should be polite in his dealings with tenants and show himself to be friendly, and should be more demanding of work than of payments [of rent], since this gives less offence, but is usually more profitable. When land is carefully farmed, it usually makes a profit, and never makes a loss unless it is assailed by exceptionally bad weather or by brigands; and so the tenant does not dare ask for a reduction of rent. But the master should not demand his rights on every point to which he has bound his tenant, such as the exact day of payment for money, or in demanding firewood, or other trivial exactions. . . . I remember hearing P. Volusius, an old man, of consular rank and very wealthy, say that the estate which had natives of the region as tenants, and which kept them because of long association even from birth, as if born on their own father's property, was the most fortunate. It is my definite opinion that constant reletting of a farm is bad, but that a tenant who lives in the city, and prefers to farm the land by means of slaves rather than by his own hand, is worse. Saserna said that the return from this sort of person was usually a legal case, not an income, so because of this, we should take care to retain tenants who are of rural origin and are conscientious farmers, if we are unable to farm the land ourselves and cannot do so with our own household. Even so, this does not happen except in areas which are laid waste by the severity of the climate and the sterility of the land. But when the climate is reasonably salubrious and the land reasonably good, personal attention always gives a larger profit from the land than does that of a tenant. Even reliance on an overseer gives a greater return, except in case of great negligence of greed on the part of this slave. Both of these offences are, without doubt, usually committed or encouraged by the fault of the master, seeing that he has the power to stop such a man being placed in charge of his business, or to see that he is removed if he is in such a position. However, on distant estates, which are difficult for the owner to visit, it is better for all types of land to be under free farmers than slave overseers, but this is especially true in the case of land growing grain. A tenant cannot do much damage to this type of land, in the way that he can to vineyards and trees, while slaves can do a lot of harm.

[Saserna = Hostilius Saserna, a late republican writer on agriculture.]

244. Columella, *De re rustica* 3.3

. . . the principle that we should first carefully weigh up and inquire whether growing vines will enrich the landowner . . .

People dedicated to the study of agriculture must be told one thing first, namely that there are very rich profits from vineyards . . . We can barely remember a time when cereal crops, throughout most of Italy at least, gave a yield of 4:1. Then why is vine growing frowned upon? Certainly not through any fault of its own, . . . In fact, most people seek the richest possible return as soon as possible; they make no provision for the future, but as if living for the day, they make such demands of their vines and overload them with young shoots in such a way as to give no thought to future generations. After doing all, or at least the majority, of these things, they would sooner do anything than admit their culpability. but they complain that their vineyards – which they have ruined themselves by greed, ignorance or neglect – do not make a profit. But anyone who combines great care with systematic knowledge, even if they get not 40 amphorae per *iugerum* but 30, by my estimate, or even 20, using a minimum estimate as does Graecinus, will easily surpass those who stick to their hay and vegetables in the profits from their ancestral estates.

[Graecinus = Julius Graecinus, a senator who published works on viticulture early in the first century AD.]

245. Livy 38.52.1

This was the last day of glory to illuminate P. Scipio [Africanus]. Since, after this, he saw envy and quarrels with the tribunes in prospect, he secured a longer adjournment and retired to his property at Liternum with the firm intention of not being present to speak for himself.

[187 BC. Prosecution of Africanus for corruption and immoral behaviour while on active service in Sicily. His villa at Liternum is one of the earliest owned by a Roman in the area of the Bay of Naples.]

246. Cicero, *De officiis* 2.87

With regard to property, it is a duty to make money, but only in ways in which there is no disgrace, and to increase it by diligence and thrift. . . .

247. Varro, *De re rustica* 1.4.1–2

Prepared with this knowledge, the farmer should aim at two goals, profit and pleasure; the object of the first is material returns, and that of the second, enjoyment. The profitable aspect plays a more important role than the pleasurable, but for the most part, the methods of farming which improve the appearance of the land, such as the planting of fruit or olive trees in rows, make it not just greater in profit but also easier to sell, and add to the value of the estate. . . . .

248. Cicero, *Pro Roscio Amerino* 20–22

The size of his fortune was proven; the excellence of his estate (for he left 13 farms, all of which bordered the Tiber), and the helplessness and isolation of [Roscius the younger] were noted; they showed that, since the father of this Sextus Roscius, a man of such standing and popularity, had been killed without trouble, it would be easy to remove this man, who was unsuspecting and rustic and unknown in Rome. They [T. Roscius Capito and T. Roscius Magnus, from another branch of the same *gens*] promised themselves to this. . . . the name of Sex. Roscius, a man most committed to the nobility, was entered in the proscription lists; Chrysogonus was the buyer. Three estates, the best-known, were handed over to Capito, who possesses them today; this T. Roscius seized the rest of the property in the name of Chrysogonus, as he says himself. These goods worth 6,000,000 sesterces were sold off for 2,000.

[Sextus Roscius the Elder was a typical example of a municipal magnate of the first century BC. Elsewhere, Cicero stresses that he was a man of importance both at Ameria and in the region as a whole, and had an extensive network of contacts and interests at Rome. As such he illustrates the extent to which wealthy Italians of equestrian rank rose to importance during the generation after the Social War. Although Cicero hints at business interests in Rome, the core of his wealth is clearly the substantial estate amassed in the Tiber valley. Chrysogonus was a freedman of Sulla and the background to the case is the Sullan proscription.]

Tenancy

249. Pliny, *Letters* 6.3 (to Verus)

Thank you for taking over the running of the small farm which I gave to my nurse. It was, when I gave it to her, worth 100,000 sesterces; since then, its value has declined, the returns having diminished, but now that you are looking after it, it will recover. But remember that I have entrusted to you not so much the trees and land, although these are included, but my little gift; for it is of as much interest the farm should be as productive as possible to me, the donor, as to her, the recipient.

250. Pliny, *Letters* 3.19

As usual, I turn to you for advice in connection with my property. An estate which adjoins my own lands, and mingles with them, is for sale. There are many things which urge this purchase on me, but others no less important which deter me. Firstly, the attractiveness of the joint property prompts me [to buy], then the utility as well as pleasure of being able to visit both in one trip, to have both tended by the same bailiff and almost by the same foremen, as well as only maintaining and furnishing one house . . . On the other hand, I fear that it might be risky to place such a large property under the same risk of storms and other disasters. It seems safer to guard against an uncertain fate by having scattered estates. It is also pleasurable to exchange location and views and to travel between estates. Now, the crux of the matter is that the land is fertile, rich and well-irrigated and the estate consists of fields, vineyards and woods, the timber from which yields a modest but stable return. But this fertile land has been exhausted by stupid cultivation. The previous owner would frequently sell the tenants' possessions and, while he reduced their debts at the time, he drained their resources for the future, and so their debts grew again. So they will have to be provided with good slaves, which increases the expense. I do not use chain-gangs, and nor does anyone else around here.

[Like Columella, Pliny clearly envisages an estate as farmed by tenants under direction from the overseers and owner, with slaves providing the heavy labour. The comment about slaves in the locality suggests that patterns of labour may have been regional. The letter goes on to discuss the price of the estate (three million sesterces) and the need to call in loans and investments and take out further loans to raise the money.]

251. Pliny, *Letters* 9.37

. . . especially since I have to stay here in order to lease out my farms on a long-term basis, for which I am having to adopt a new method. During the last five years, the tenants' arrears have increased, although I granted considerable remission [of rent]. Many of them do not care about reducing these debts because they despair of ever paying them off; they even seize and consume the things which are produced, because they see no gain for themselves in keeping it. Therefore I must face this growing problem and find a solution. The only measure for improving this would be to lease not for money but for a proportion of the produce and appoint some of my staff to keep watch on the harvest.

252. Cicero, *Letters to his friends* 13.7

. . . I spoke to you about the rented land, which is situated in Gaul, belonging to the *municipium* of Atella and demonstrated the extent of my concern for the city. After your departure, I thought I should write to you more fully, since you hold me in high esteem, and since it concerns important affairs of a most respected city and one closely connected with myself, and an important obligation on my part. However, I am not ignorant of the situation at this time and your powers, and I well understand that C. Caesar has given you business to transact, not judgement to exercise. I am asking only as much as I think you can do, and will willingly do for me. Firstly, I ask you to believe (as is the case) that the finances of this city depend entirely on this rent, and that in these times, this city is struggling under heavy burdens and great difficulties. Many others seem to share these problems, but I believe that unusually severe setbacks have happened to this city; I will not recall them, so as not to implicate men whom I do not wish to offend in complaining of the distress of my associates. And so, if I did not have a good hope of proving the city's case to C. Caesar, there would be no reason to bother you at this time; but I am confidently persuaded that he will bear in mind the status of the city, the equity of this matter, and its goodwill [towards him], so I have no doubts about advising you to leave the case open for him. I would ask no less of you if I had not heard that you had done so in another case, but I became more hopeful after it was mentioned to me that you had conceded this to the people of Rhegium; although they have connections with you, your affection for me compels me to hope that you will do for my connections what you do for your own, especially since I ask only on behalf of one city, although I have connections with more cities with similar problems. I do not think you will consider that I have acted without cause or that I am moved to approach you by frivolous attention-seeking, I want you to believe me when I affirm that I am under a great obligation to this city; there was never a time, either in my achievements or my troubles, in which this city did not give me outstanding support.

[45 BC. Letter to C. Cluvius, who was a commissioner in charge of land distribution in Gaul. Since Cluvius was clearly sent as an administrator, Cicero asks that the case of the land owned by Atella should be referred to Caesar. The gist of the problem was that cities were coming increasingly to draw revenue from purchasing and renting out land in the provinces, and that confiscation and redistribution of this land by the Caesarian commissioners would have left the finances of the city severely impoverished. Cicero is also keen to stress the social factor of his role as patron of Atella, which continued to support him during his exile, but to avoid the charge that he was currying favour with the municipalities for political popularity.]

Markets and transport of goods

253. Pliny, *Letters* 2.17

You wonder that I am so attached to my Laurentine villa (or, if you prefer, my "Laurens"). But you will cease to be surprised when you know about the delights of the villa, the convenience of its location, and the prospect of the coast. It is 17 miles from Rome, so that having done whatever you are doing, you can stay at Laurentum after having completed the day. There is not just one road to it; for you can go via both Laurentum or Ostia – from the Laurentum road, you turn off at the 14th milestone, but from the Ostian road, at the 11th.

[Despite Pliny's insistence here that one of the great advantages of this villa is its accessibility and good transport, elsewhere (5.6) he stresses the joys of another villa precisely for its remoteness.]

254. *CIL* 4.5380

Market days: In Pompeii, Saturday; In Nuceria, Sunday; in Atella, Monday; in Nola, Tuesday; in Cumae, Wednesday; in Puteoli, Thursday; in Rome, Friday.

[Pompeii. List of *nundinae*, or market days.]

255. Strabo 5.4.8

Pompeii, on the river Sarnus, was the seaport for Nola, Nuceria and Acerrae (which has the same name as a settlement near Cremona), and it both receives and dispatches cargoes.

256. Cicero, *In Pisonem* 67

He has no baker in his house, and no storeroom; he gets his bread and wine from a shopkeeper . . .

[Cicero emphasizes that the reliance on shops and markets for supplies, rather than producing his own bread and wine, is a mark of Piso's frugality. The contrast is with the more usual late republican villa-owner, who produces his own food and has bakers, etc. as part of his own household.]

257. Juvenal, *Satires* 10.100–02

Would you rather be a magistrate at Fidenae or Gabii and give judgements about measures, or a ragged aedile at deserted Ulubrae, breaking an undersized jar?

[A satirical comment on the duties of an aedile, which included supervision of the markets and checking the accuracy of weights and measures. This was an activity which was taken seriously by the authorities. There is evidence from Pompeii that the Oscan weights and measures (stamped with names of Oscan magistrates) were recalibrated when the city became a Roman colony.[31]]

City and countryside

258. Pliny, *Natural history* 19.51

In any case, in Rome, a garden was in itself the farm of a poor man.

[The importance of gardens and other arable land inside city walls is well documented in municipal Italy, particularly at Pompeii.[32] This form of land use, with its blurring of the divisions between urban and rural, is also found in many pre-Roman cities. Many cities include a proportion of cultivated land within their walls.[33]]

259. Pseudo-Vergil, *Moretum* 78–81

On the ninth day [the *nundinae* or market day], he carried bundles of goods into the city on his shoulder, returning from there with a lighter neck but heavier purse since he hardly ever brought any purchases with him from the *macellum* of the city.

[This stresses the one-way flow of produce from territory to city,[34] but also the different levels of markets and marketing. The subject of the poem is a countryman, taking produce from his farm to sell at the periodic market. The *macellum*, however, is the market held in a permanent market building and was associated with high-status luxury goods, not basic farm produce. What is stressed is the countryman's frugality and the cultural gulf between town and country, in that he does not need/ cannot afford/does not want the luxury goods of the *macellum*.]

260. Pliny, *Letters* 2.17

The neighbouring woods give a supply of fuel; all other goods can be supplied by the colony of Ostia. For a frugal man even the next village, from which only one villa separates it is enough. In this place, there are as many as three public baths, which is very convenient if either the suddenness of my arrival or the shortness of my stay makes it impossible to heat up the baths at my house.

[Pliny's Laurentine villa and its relation to its neighbourhood.]

261. Pliny, *Letters* 5.4

A small thing, but with consequences which are not small, has happened. Sollers, a man of praetorian rank, has petitioned the senate to allow him to hold a market on his estate; the representatives of the people of Vicetia [modern Vicenza] spoke against this; Tuscilius Nominatus was present [as counsel for Vicetia]; the case was postponed. At another meeting of the senate, the Vicentini came in without their advocate and said that they had been deceived, but who knows whether they were speaking in the heat of the moment or whether they really thought this. They were asked by Nepos, the praetor, whom they had instructed, and they replied, the same man as before. Asked whether he had appeared for them for free, they replied, for 6,000 sesterces; and for the second appearance, they said they had given him 1,000 *denarii*. Nepos proposed that Nominatus should be ordered to attend the meeting.

[This passage illustrates the difficulties for municipalities who wished to pursue a petition or complaint in front of the senate. It also emphasizes the extent of senatorial control over many aspects of Italian life, in that a periodic market could not be established without formal permission. The reason for the objection by Vicentia is not stated, but an out-of-town *nundinae* held at Sollers' villa would probably undercut the markets held in the city and threaten to remove a focus of economic activity from Vicetia. The result of Nominatus' behaviour and Nepos' inquiry into it is the subject of a later letter.[35]]

Trade and taxation

262. Cicero, *De officiis* 1.150–151

First of all, those occupations are unsuitable which incur the odium of other people, such as tax-collecting and money-lending. Also unsuitable and vulgar are the occupations of all those who work for hire, who are paid for their labour rather than for their skills; for their very wage is a sign of their servitude. The people who buy [goods] from merchants for immediate sale must also be considered vulgar; they would not make any profit without lying to some extent; and there is nothing as disgraceful as misrepresentation. And all craftsmen are engaged in a vulgar trade; for no workshop is in any way worthy of a free man. And the least respectable trades of all are those which minister to pleasure . . . However, those skills which either need greater knowledge or which are of no small utility, such as medicine or architecture, or teaching of decent subjects, these are honourable for those to whose status they are appropriate. Trade is to be considered vulgar, if it is on a small scale; if it is on a large scale and in quantity, importing in bulk from all regions and distributing to many people without dishonesty, it is not to be condemned, and it even seems to deserve the highest regard if the men who are engaged in it, satiated, or perhaps I should say satisfied, with the fortunes they have made, make their way from the ports to farmlands and country estates, as they have often made it from the sea into the harbour. But, of all the occupations by which gains are made, none is better than agriculture, none more profitable, none more delightful, none more fitting for a free man.

263. Juvenal, *Satires* 14.200–05

You should produce some commodities which you can sell for more than 50 per cent profit, nor should you be overwhelmed with disgust at any goods which have to be relegated to the far side of the Tiber (i.e. tanned goods), nor believe that there is any distinction between perfume and hides: the odour of profit is good, no matter what things it comes from.

264. Cicero, *In Verrem* 2.5.154

The whole of Puteoli is here; a great crowd of businessmen has come to this trial, men of substance and good reputation, some of whom say that their associates, others their freedmen, yet others their fellow-freedmen, have been robbed and thrown into prison, some of them dying in prison, and others being executed.

[This passage emphasizes both trade with Sicily and the important role in Roman trade played by Puteoli and its citizens. The context is Cicero's prosecution of Verres for extortion, which involved many witnesses to his malpractice from the Italians trading with the province.]

265. Plutarch, *Life of Aemilius Paullus* 38.1

The almost unlimited popularity of Aemilius with the people can be ascribed to his achievements in Macedon, as so much money was then brought to the public treasury that the people did not need to pay direct taxes any longer, until the time of Hirtius and Pansa, who were consuls during the first war between Antony and Caesar (Octavian).

[Abolition of direct taxation for Roman citizens in 187 BC. In point of fact, this seems to have been introduced as a 20-year remission of taxation, but the spoils from the conquest of the eastern Mediterranean were such that it was never re-introduced.[36]]

266. Tacitus, *Annals* 4.6

Indirect taxes in grain and cash, and other revenues, were collected by associations of Roman *equites*. The emperor entrusted his own property to carefully chosen men, some of whom were unknown to him except by repute, and once appointed, they held their jobs without limit, and many of them grew old in post. The people suffered from high grain prices, but no blame for this attached to the emperor. He combated both infertile territory and rough seas with as much money and diligence as he could.

[Extent of imperial estates and management of taxation system and personal property, *c.* AD 23. The use of equestrian tax-farmers is also a feature of the Ciceronian era, when they were very poorly regulated and well hated in the provinces for their extortions (cf. Chapter 4).]

Pastoralism

267. Tacitus, *Annals* 4.27

That same summer, chance delivered Italy from the beginnings of a slave war. The author of the disturbance was T. Curtisius, once a soldier in the praetorian guard, who, by secret meetings at Brundisium and neighbouring towns, soon followed by openly published pamphlets, called on the fierce slaves of the distant forests to break free, just as, by a gift of the gods, three biremes used for protecting free passage in those waters put into harbour. The quaestor Cutius Lupus, whose province (an ancient one) was control of the pasturage, was in the region. Having organized the crews into a force, he suppressed the rising in its early stages. Staius, a tribune sent rapidly by the emperor with a strong force, took the leader himself and his most daring associates back to Rome, where there was now great alarm, owing to the mass of slaves which had grown immensely, in contrast to the decline of free people.

[AD 24. Slave rebellion, again in Apulia. The reason why Apulia was so restless may lie in the fact that the slaves there were primarily herdsmen, and being a mobile population, were more difficult to control. The quaestorian post of overseer of the drove roads and pasturage (abolished in the reign of Claudius) was probably intended to monitor this type of problem, as well as sorting out disputes over drove roads and rights of way.]

268. Cicero, *De officiis* 2.89

. . . external factors may be compared, so that glory is preferred to wealth, and urban rents to rural ones. The comparison of Cato the elder belongs to this type: when he was asked what was the best way to make profit from an estate, he replied "Raise cattle well"; and the second best way? "Raise cattle moderately well"; and the third? "Raise cattle badly"; and the fourth? "Grow crops"; the man who was questioning him then said "what do you think about money-lending?" Cato replied "what do you think about killing a man?"

[This passage provides a contrast to Cato's own work on agriculture, which clearly advocates villas with a mixed economy, and also with Columella's strictures on the subject. Although this aphorism of Cato's was much quoted by ancient authors (Columella also cites it), it is possible that it was intended to be satirical rather than a serious opinion.]

269. Cicero, *Pro Cluentio* 161

You have said that the bailiff of this man [Cluentius Habitus] committed assault and battery on the herdsmen of Ancharius and Pacenus. When a dispute broke out between herdsmen on the pastures, as often happens, Habitus' bailiffs defended their master's property and private rights of occupation. When a complaint was lodged, this was explained to them [Ancharius and Pacenus] and they left without taking the case to court.

270. *CIL* 9.2438

From Bassaeus Rufus and Macrinius Vindex to the magistrates of Saepinum, greetings. We have attached a copy of the letter sent to us by Cosmus, imperial freedman and financial secretary, along with the one which was added to his, and we warn you to stop threatening the men who lease the flocks of sheep, to the serious harm to the imperial treasury, in case it becomes necessary to investigate and punish these actions, if the facts are as stated.

Letter of Cosmus, imperial freedman and financial secretary, to Bassaeus Rufus and Macrinius Vindex, most eminent men, praetorian prefects: I have attached a copy of a letter sent to me by Septimianus, my assistant and fellow freedman, and I ask that you will be good enough to write to the magistrates of Saepinum and Bovianum to stop abusing those who lease the flocks who are under my supervision, so that the imperial treasury may be protected against loss by your kindness.

Letter to Cosmus, written by Septimianus: Since the lessees of the flocks of sheep, who are under your supervision, are repeatedly complaining to me that they often suffer injury along the drove roads of the mountain pastures from the *stationarii* and the magistrates of Saepinum and Bovianum, in so far as they arrest their hired slaves and draught animals while in transit, saying that they are runaways, with stolen animals (and by this means even the emperor's sheep are lost to them during these disturbances), and we thought it necessary to write to them again and to instruct them to act more moderately, so that there should be no loss to imperial property. Since they persist in this same insolence, saying that they will ignore my letters and that it will be useless even if you write to them, I ask you, sir, that if you think fit, you will tell Bassaeus Rufus and Macrinius Vindex, praetorian prefects and most eminent men, to write to these magistrates and *stationarii* . . .

[AD 169–72. Saepinum. Latin inscription set above the city gates, recording attempts to resolve a dispute between the contractors in charge of flocks on imperial estates and the cities through which they passed on their seasonal transhumance. The *stationarii* were small detachments of troops manning guard posts and customs posts throughout Italy.]

Loans, rentals and purchases

271. *AE* 1973, No. 138

Consulship of Cn. Acceronius Proculus and C. Petronius Pontius, three days before the Kalends of July (28 June). I, G. Novius Eunus, have recorded that I have received a loan *in absentia* from Euenus Primianus, freedman of the Emperor Tiberius, through the agency of his slave Hesychus, and owe him 10,000 sesterces, which I will repay to him on demand; and Hesychus, slave of Euenus Primianus, freedman of the emperor Tiberius, asked assurance that the aforementioned 10,000 sesterces are correctly and legally given and I, C. Novius Eunus gave assurance, and in return for the 10,000 sesterces, gave as security 7,000 *modii*, or thereabouts, of wheat from Alexandria, and 4,000 *modii*, or thereabouts, of chickpeas, pulses and lentils in 200 bags, all of which are in my possession, deposited in my possession in the public Bassian warehouse at Puteoli, and which I declare to be free from all damage at my own risk.

[28 June, AD 37. Pompeii. Record of a loan made by an imperial freedman, found inscribed on a wax tablet.]

272. *AE* 1969–70, No. 100

In the consulship of C. Caesar Germanicus Augustus and Ti. Claudius Nero Germanicus, six days before the Nones of July (2 July). I, Diognetus, slave of C. Novius Cypaerus, have recorded, on the instructions, and in the presence, of my master, Cypaerus, that I have let to Hesychus, slave of Ti. Julius Euenus, imperial freedman, Space Twelve in the central block of the public Bassian warehouse at Puteoli, in which has been placed the wheat from Alexandria which he received today from C. Novius Eunus as a security; similarly he has deposited 200 bags of pulses which he received as security from this same Eunus in the lower block of the same warehouse, between the pillars. From the Kalends of July (1 July) at a rent of one *nummus* per month, in cash. [Agreement] made at Puteoli.

[2 July, AD 37. Contract for storage of the goods provided as security by C. Novius Eunus in relation to the loan described in No. 270. 1 nummus = 1,000 sesterces. cf. Crook (1978), 234–6.]

273. *AE* 1973, No. 140

In the fifth consulship of Ti. Claudius Caesar, and the consulship of L. Calventius Vetus, two days before the Ides of October (5 October), a notice was posted in the forum at Puteoli on the rectangular column in the portico of Augustus built by Sextius, on which this was written: The man Felix, the man Carus, the man Januarius, the woman Primigenia, the woman Primigenia the Younger, and the boy Ampliatus, goods which M. Egnatius Suavis was said to have given to C. Sulpicius Cinnamus by mancipation for 1 sesterce on transaction of fiducia for a debt of 23 sesterces, will be offered for sale the day before the Ides of October (14th) in the forum at Puteoli in front of the portico of Caesonius; the security was forfeit from the fifteenth day before the Ides of October (15 September).

[5 October, AD 51. Pompeii. Wax tablet recording sale of slaves offered as security for a loan on which Egnatius Suavis has defaulted.]

274. *FIRA* 3.128a

For the sale of a mule to M. Pomponius M. L. Nico, 520 sesterces, a sum which M. Cerrinius M. L. Euphrates is sworn to have made the object of a stipulatory contract with L. Caecilius Felix. M. Cerrinius M. L. Euphrates swore that he received the whole of the sum specified above from Philadelphus, slave of Caecilius Felix. Transaction took place four days before the Ides of June (28 May) at Pompeii, in the consulship of Drusus Caesar and C. Norbanus Flaccus.

[AD 15. Pompeii. Record of transfer of the proceeds from a sale.]

275. *FIRA* 3.128c

For the sale of a box plantation belonging to C. Julius Onesimos, on the Ides (15th) of July, 1,985 sesterces, less fee, a sum which was under a stipulatory contract with L. Caecilius Iucundus. C. Julius Onesimos swore that he received this from M. Fabius Agathinus on behalf of L. Caecilius Iucundus. Transaction took place five days before the Ides of May (10 May) at Pompeii, in the consulship of M' Acilius Aviola and M. Asinius Marcellus.

[AD 54. Pompeii. Part of the archive of Caecilius Iucundus, a moneylender and auctioneer.]

Property rentals

276. *CIL* 4.138

Shops with stalls, good-quality second floor flats, and a house, to rent from next Ides (15th) of July in the Insula of Arrius Pollio, owned by Cn. Alleius Nigidius Maius. Prospective tenants may apply to Primus, the slave of Cn. Alleius Nigidius Maius.

[Graffito. Pompeii. Urban property was regarded as a good investment in Roman Italy, although direct evidence such as this advertisement of domestic and commercial premises to rent are confined to a small number of sites. The shops usually occupied the street frontages of an *insula*, some being merely a single room, while others have a second room or a mezzanine to serve as living quarters for the shopkeeper and his family. Most *tabernae* were entirely open on the street side, and were closed with shutters at night. Apartments were situated behind and above. The house may be a larger and grander living unit within the *insula*.]

277. *CIL* 4.1136

The high-class Venus Baths, shops, stalls and second floor flats, on property owned by Julia Sp. F. Felix, to let from the Ides of August (13th) to the following Ides of August, or for five years continuously. Anyone interested may apply to the landlord in this matter.

[Pompeii. Graffito advertising property to rent.]

278. *CIL* 10.1401

In the consulship of Cn. Hosidius Geta and L. Vagellius, ten days before the Kalends of October (22 September). Decree of the senate. Because the foresight of our most excellent emperor has also made provision for the permanence of the buildings of our city and of the whole of Italy, which he himself has benefited not only by his most august precept but also by his own example, and since protection to both public and private buildings is fitting and appropriate to the happiness of the approaching age, and since everyone should desist from the most vicious type of speculation and not cause an appearance most incompatible with peace by demolition of houses and villas; the senate decrees that if anyone purchases any building as a speculation, so that by pulling it down he shall obtain a greater price than that for which he bought it, then he shall pay to the treasury double the amount for which he bought this property, and despite this, the matter will be brought before the senate. Since a sale involving such a bad precedent is not more admissible than such a purchase, so that the vendors who sell contrary to this expressed decision of the senate, knowingly and with criminal intent, can also be restrained, the senate decrees that sales of this type shall be invalid. But, the senate confirms that this [decree] shall not in any way affect owners who transfer parts from one property to another with the intention of remaining in possession of their properties, provided that this is not done for purposes of speculation. Accepted. Present in the senate: 383 [senators].

[AD 45–6 and AD 56. Herculaneum. Bronze tablet with Latin inscription recording a decree of the senate from the reign of Claudius. The reference to the approach of a new era is a reference to the Saecular Games, which had been introduced by Augustus to celebrate peace and renewal. The purpose of the decree is to restrict the activities of property speculators in the cities of Italy by making it illegal to demolish standing buildings or to benefit from a speculatory transaction. This is a preoccupation which resurfaces again and again in Roman law and edicts. The first century BC charter of Tarentum [No. 323] and several other municipal charters prohibit the demolition of houses unless replaced by a building of equivalent or greater size and value, as well as limiting the property transactions of the decurial order by requiring each member to maintain a house of specified minimum size in the city. This decree is more specifically directed towards speculators and reflects the popularity of urban property as an investment.]

CHAPTER SEVEN

Cults, sanctuaries and priesthoods in Roman Italy

Religious cults and their associated acts of worship were central to the culture of ancient Italy in a way that is hard to grasp in a predominantly secular modern world. For the Romans, everything fell under the protection of a god, from the great decisions of state which took place under the aegis of the Olympian deities to mundane acts such as opening a door, which were governed by a host of minor tutelary spirits or *numina*. All of these had to be honoured and placated by performance of the appropriate sacrifices and offerings, couched in the correct ritual. The rituals and festivals of each city were also highly public occasions. Religious acts and observances were not so much an act of faith or private belief as a political act and a statement of social status and cultural identity. The choice of cult and forms of worship, either by a city or an individual, symbolized political loyalties as much as religious conviction. The ancient city was also entirely polytheistic until the fourth century AD, and cults were by no means exclusive affairs. Archaic cults involving non-personalized (and sometimes very obscure) *numina* coexisted quite happily with the Olympian pantheon which formed the basis of state religion, with pre-Roman Italic cults, with a multiplicity of imports from all parts of the empire, and with cults established for a very specific purpose, such as the imperial cult.

In order to study such a diverse selection of elements, and in order to remove the intellectual presuppositions created by the dominance of the Judaeo-Christian tradition, we must first of all abandon both the most obviously "religious" approach – an attempt to elucidate what exactly the Romans believed and whether they did so sincerely – and the traditional ethnographic approach, which attempts to relate historically attested practices and beliefs to ancient mythology. As a general point, cults and ritual behaviour in a society are widely recognized as a powerful indicator of its social and cultural structure, if a somewhat conservative one, which changes only slowly.[1] As such, we can best approach the religious life of

165

Roman Italy by examining it for what it can tell us about the way in which this society operated. This chapter will attempt to treat religious cults and their attendant ceremonies, buildings and personnel as cultural and social artefacts, and demonstrate some ways in which study of these artefacts can contribute to our understanding of Roman Italy. We need to examine, not the specific detail of individual cults and rituals, but their significance for the society which generated them.

As already noted, the most ancient of all forms of religious belief attested in Italy is the animist tradition of *numina*, the tutelary spirits possessed by every object and occurrence, which had to be placated as a routine part of daily life.[2] These gave rise to a large number of rituals in the religious calendar of the city of Rome, and probably other states as well, which may seem rather bizarre to modern eyes, and whose roots in the traditions of an archaic peasant society sit uneasily with the urban sophistication of imperial Rome. Examples of the appeasement of a particular *numen* are the *Robigalia*, at which a red dog was sacrificed to banish Robigus, the *numen* of crop rust, from the year's crops, and the offerings made to Vaticanus, the tutelary *numen* who presided over the first cry of a new-born baby. It is the juxtaposition of these archaic-seeming elements, often rendered even more odd by the calendrical shifts which progressively removed seasonal festivals from their correct times of year, with a sophisticated urban culture which causes such difficulties of comprehension for modern students of the subject. In fact, the conflict is not as great as it may initially seem. The essence of Roman religion was that it was both deeply conservative, in the sense that great importance was placed on carrying out the traditional rituals at the same time, and in the same manner, as had always been the case, and experimental, in the sense that it was always able to accommodate new developments and extra cults as the situation demanded. There was a deep taboo against changing existing rites, but nothing that prevented addition of new elements.[3] The other factor which must not be forgotten is that the Romans were perfectly capable of abstraction. The fact that the vagaries of the calendar could remove seasonally specific rituals such as the gathering of the first corn by the Vestal Virgins from the spring to the depths of winter did not necessarily undermine their symbolic value.[4] Literal belief in these was not required and lack of it did not in any way undermine the importance of ritual and festivals as instruments of social cohesion.[5]

Rome itself is the best-documented city in Italy in terms of details of religious ritual, but the pattern of religious behaviour seems to be broadly similar elsewhere in Italy. Indigenous cults are based around natural phenomena, but many show signs of increasing anthropomorphism. For instance, the cult of Mephitis, widely disseminated in southern and central Italy, is in essence a cult dedicated to placating the spirit of earthquakes and volcanic activity. However, this cult rapidly comes to revolve around an anthropomorphic deity who is presumed to govern seismic behaviour. The status of the goddess as an equal of any in the Graeco-Roman pantheon is illustrated by the inscriptions from the sanctuary of Mefitis Utiana at Rossano di Vaglio in Lucania, which not only address her in equivalent terms to Jove, the other god honoured at Rossano, but in many cases give her precedence.[6] The same process of anthropomorphism and syncretism can be seen in the numerous cults of nymphs and river gods in Magna Graecia, in which native water spirits have been personalized and subsumed into a Hellenized structure by the Greek colonists. The cults of the sirens Leucothea and Parthenope at Velia and Naples, and the sea god Taras at Tarentum illustrate this.[7] Many of the localized cults (some of them of more than local appeal), seem to have originated in like manner. It would also be a mistake to assume that such cults were merely archaic survivals which died out or diminished in importance at a later date. Mephitis remained a prominent deity in earthquake-prone southern Italy, and Pliny's description of the Umbrian sanctuary of Clitumnus [No. 307], another river god, indicates that it was flourishing in the early second century AD. The Roman cults of the Lares and Compitales gained a new lease of life under Augustus, and an important role in his religious reforms because they were both archaic and characteristically Roman, and also because they could be adapted to give a central role to Augustus himself.[8]

The other principal focus of interest is on the Graeco-Roman pantheon based on the Olympian deities which formed the basis of state religion, along with a small number of later additions. In this, the religious history of Roman Italy bears a superficial resemblance to that of the Greek world, but there are in fact many important differences, although it is true to say that there was no fundamental incompatibility between the Olympian cults in Greece and in Italy. The similarity is reinforced by the tendency for Roman/Italian gods to become equated with their Greek counterparts and to take on many of their attributes and legends as Italy became progressively more Hellenized. For instance, the Italic god of war, variously known as Mars (Latin), Mavors (Umbrian) and Mamers (Oscan) could be equated with his Greek equivalent, Ares, and take on some of his legends and attributes, but this did not undermine the cult's essentially Italic nature.

The most striking distinction between Greek and Roman cults perhaps lies in the tripartite nature of most Roman cults, which is physically represented in the temple structures. This grouping of gods into triads is found most strikingly in Etruria, the source of many of Rome's religious customs, but is also found in Latium and elsewhere in Italy. The central state cult of Rome, the Capitoline cult, is not just a cult of Jupiter Capitolinus, as the name implies, but also of Juno and Minerva. Even when Greek rites were specially established for reason of their Greekness, a certain restructuring was required. Cicero and Dionysios of Halicarnassus describe the establishment of a Greek cult of Demeter [No. 301] in 496 BC in precisely these terms. The priestesses of the cult were Greeks from Naples and Velia (where the cult of Demeter Thesmophoros is attested as late as the second century AD) and this was still the case in Cicero's day, but they were given Roman citizenship on appointment to this office so that they could perform their duties in a suitably Roman frame of mind, and the cult itself was a tripartite one in the Italian style, dedicated to Ceres, Liber and Libera.

The degree of similarity between cults and ritual at Rome and less well-attested areas of Italy is uncertain in the period before the second century BC, but it seems very likely that there was a broadly similar framework of cults with some local variation. Cults of Jove/Jupiter, Mars, Venus, Juno, Diana, Minerva and Hercules are attested all over Italy, other than in Magna Graecia, where Greek cults remained dominant until after the Roman conquest, except in those cities that were overrun by Oscans at the end of the fifth century. Perhaps another exception to this is Etruria, which had a somewhat different, if rather obscure pantheon.[9] Having said this, it is also true that the Etruscans had a notably high influence on the way in which Roman ritual developed. Apart from the tripartite temple, with a *cella* divided into three transepts, and a number of other features of temple architecture, the Etruscans were noted as the originators, and most skilled practitioners, of a number of divinatory skills which came to play an important role in public life. Both augury and the taking of the auspices, rites which were performed before many public actions or decisions, were conducted according to Etruscan practice. Nor was their importance confined to Rome. *Auguracula*, or augural enclosures, are found at a number of other locations in Italy. These were square enclosures with specially marked boundary stones giving a precise orientation in which the augur stood to observe the heavens and take the auspices. One example has been found in the forum of Minturnae and another at Bantia, in Lucania.[10] Given that augury was an important part of the rite for founding and orienting a new colony, it is possible that most cities founded (or resettled) by Rome involved constructing such an enclosure.

The role of the gods in the Roman city was central to the life of the community. Apart from affording divine protection, they had the role almost of a "super-citizen", in that their physical presence was important and their identification with the city was total. In particular, each community seems to have had one cult to which it looked for protection above all others. At Praeneste, this role was fulfilled by Fortuna Primigenia, at Veii by Juno, at Alba Fucens by Hercules Curinus and at Rome by the Capitoline cult. If the gods withdrew their presence, either literally or metaphorically, this could have disastrous consequences. During the conquest of Italy, this was something which was actively used as part of the Roman war effort, and for which there were recognized prayers and invocations. Macrobius [No. 279] describes two methods used to undercut the divine support of Rome's enemies – *evocatio* and *devotio*. The first of these drew forth the protecting deity of the enemy and won it over to Rome, the other invited the gods of the underworld to take possession of the now defenceless city. Livy attests a number of occasions when Rome lured away enemy gods by promising temples dedicated in Rome, and later backed this up by physically removing the relevant cult statues.[11] Before the capture of Veii in 392 BC, the Roman general Camillus called upon Juno to desert Veii and assist the Romans, promising a new temple at Rome.[12] An alternative approach, adopted by Fabius Maximus after his reconquest of Tarentum in 209 BC was to forbid the removal of cult statues from the city on the grounds that, as a faithless ally, their own gods might be disposed to punish the Tarentines.[13]

The vital role played in any community by ritual is underlined by the strenuous measures undertaken by Rome to control cults and their rites. The Bacchana-lian scandal of 186 BC, which is discussed in more detail below, is an early exam-ple of the imposition of senatorial authority on Italy in such a matter. Having deemed the cult of Bacchus to be destabilizing and potentially treasonable, strin-gent restrictions were imposed by the senate on Bacchic sects and their ability to meet, with the explicit proviso that these were to be applicable to all Rome's allies in Italy and that the text of the *senatusconsultum* setting out this decision was to be published in all allied communities [Nos 68–72]. After the Social War, this form of control became much easier as the whole of Italy was bound by Roman law. According to Tacitus [No. 309], the ability of the Roman senate to take religious decisions affecting the whole of Italy was well established, allowing it to take decisions about setting up a dedication in a temple at Antium without any con-sultation. Laws passed by Caesar and Augustus regulating *collegia* also had reper-cussions, in that *collegia* now had to have explicit permission from the emperor or senate to exist legally. There were similar laws regulating priesthoods, such that any new priestly appointments had to be ratified by the board of *Quindecemviri Sacris Faciundis* in Rome [No. 308].

Although one of the notable features of ancient religion was its pluralism and tolerance, this was by no means unlimited. During the empire, it was not at all unknown for adherents of cults thought to be unsuitable to be ejected from Italy by imperial edict or senatorial decree. Tiberius deported a group of Jews and Egyptians to Sardinia on religious grounds, and used them as forced labour [No. 302]. Nor is this by any means an isolated incident. Given the pervasiveness of religious ritual in civic life, such defensiveness is perhaps not surprising. Choice of cult and form of ritual were deeply bound up with a sense of communal identity. The prominence of Capitoline temples in Italian cities, particularly those which were Roman colonies, was deeply symbolic of loyalty and attachment to Rome. In the same way, prominent pre-Roman cults could be used to affirm a continuing independent identity. At Rhegium, a series of inscriptions recording sacrifices to Apollo and Artemis, cults dating to at least the fifth century BC, has been found. These texts probably date to the first century AD, well after the Roman conquest of the region, but they are written in Greek and describe a Greek state cult [No. 312]. At Velia, an archaic Greek priesthood, the office of *pholarchos*, appears as part of the political structure of the Roman city, and at Naples a festival in honour of Augustus was instituted in 2 BC in the form of Greek games.[14] In each of these three instances, cities of Greek origin were asserting their continued (or revived) Greek identity through emphasis on Greek cults and festivals. Perhaps the most complex case study of this phenomenon is Augustus, who instituted a whole ideo-logical programme through manipulation of religious imagery and cult prac-tice.[15] Temples damaged during the civil war were rebuilt either in classicizing Greek style or in the form of archaizing "Tuscan" temples. Antony and his sup-porters were identified with the contemporary orientalized culture of the Hellen-istic East, which was decried as un-Roman and which became a symbol of subversion and disloyalty. Apollo was adopted as the tutelary deity of the

Augustan regime, with all his attendant attributes of order and rationality, as opposed to Antony's association with Dionysos. This exploitation of cults and religious imagery is reflected in art and literature, but occurs most graphically in Augustus' rebuilding of the temple of Apollo on the Palatine as part of his own house.

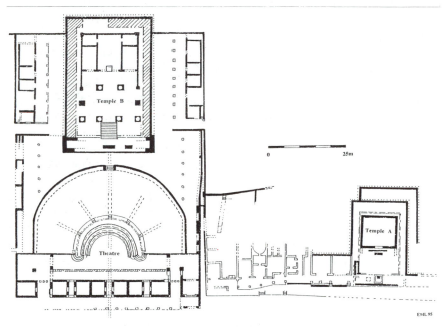

8. Pietrabbondante: plan of the sanctuary

Cult places in Roman Italy had a range of functions other than the purely religious. Many of the earliest and most important sanctuaries are not located in cities but at significant locations in their territories. Some, such as Nemi and Lucus Feroniae in Latium, were sacred groves, others, such as Aqua Ferentina, also in Latium, were the sites of sacred springs, and many more were liminal sanctuaries, marking the boundaries of a city. River mouths and promontories were also frequent sites of temples and cult places – for instance the sanctuary of Hera Lacinia on Cape Lacinium in the territory of Croton, the Heraion at Foce del Sele near Paestum, and the sanctuary of Marica near Sinuessa.[16] Despite the rural setting, these were major centres of religious and political activity. Aqua Ferentina and Cape Lacinium were the regular meeting places of the Latin League and Italiote League respectively until the fourth century BC, when the Latin League was dissolved by Rome and the Italiote League transferred its headquarters to Heraklea. In non-urbanized Samnium, most of the political, legal and administrative activity which would otherwise have taken place in the city was carried out at sanctuaries. Each *pagus* seems to have had its own cult centre, as did each *touto*.[17] The grandest of all the Samnite sanctuaries, at Pietrabbondante (Illus. 8), was probably the meeting place of the council of the Samnite League. During the second century BC, the economic resources which were poured into creating monumental buildings and spaces in cities in other regions of Italy were used in Samnium to monumentalize the sanctuaries [Nos 285–7, 291–5]. At Pietrabbondante, a grand new temple, a theatre, a series of terraces, porticoes, and a water supply were built, and inscriptions attest to public works paid for both by magistrates and private individuals. The close association between these cult places and non-Roman culture and forms of government is demonstrated by their later history. After the Social War and the final suppression of the Samnites by Rome, Pietrabbondante underwent a rapid decline.[18] The sanctuary buildings fell into disuse and although the site was not entirely abandoned, its main function was now as the burial place of a leading family from nearby Terventum, the Socellii. Traces of small-scale activity at Temple B persists until the fourth century AD, but it was clearly a site of only minor importance. The background to this is the breakup of the indigenous Samnite states and the imposition of a Romanized system of *municipia*. The loss of political and social significance of the sanctuaries in Samnium can be documented throughout the region.[19] During the generation after the Social War, and particularly during the Augustan period, elite families in Samnium began to consolidate their influence locally and in Rome. This was matched by an increasing concentration of resources into fewer hands, and by a marked shift in the focus of elite activity. The beneficiaries of aristocratic munificence were no longer the indigenous sanctuaries but the Roman cities. A similar process is visible at Rossano di Vaglio in Lucania. The Lucanian sanctuary of Mefitis and Jove continued in use but at a much reduced level, as the neighbouring Lucanian city of Serra di Vaglio was abandoned and political and social activity came to focus on the Roman colony of Potentia, a short distance away.[20]

Apart from being central to the political life of the Oscan regions of Italy, and having a deep cultural significance, sanctuaries played an important economic role. The sacred nature of such sites made them useful places for trade and economic exchange as well as social contact and political or diplomatic exchanges. In a turbulent world where warfare was endemic, sanctuaries, particularly during festivals, allowed interaction of all kinds under the protection of a sacred truce. In south-east Italy, where interstate interaction was dominated by short-lived and constantly changing alliances and conflicts between different groups of Greeks and Italians, temples and sanctuaries acted as *emporia* where goods could be traded in safety.[21] A description of Lucus Feroniae makes it clear that this was an important point of contact and exchange for the Latins [Nos 281–2]. Sanctuaries also controlled considerable economic power in their own right. Important ones built up wealth through expensive gifts and votives, and many also housed state funds, either because the sanctuary itself was politically important, as in Samnium, or to afford the treasury the protection of the gods. In fact, robbing temples was a well-recognized, if somewhat risky, source of wealth for indigent rulers. Pyrrhus of Epirus raided the treasury of the sanctuary of Proserpina at Locri in 276 BC to pay for continued campaigns in Italy and Sicily, but was swiftly visited by retribution for his impiety, as his fleet was struck by a storm in the Straits of Messina and many of his troops were lost [No. 283].

One of the principal trends discernible in Italic religion during the period in question is a shift from rural pre-Roman cults to Romanized urban ones. This is perhaps most easily traceable in patterns of temple-building and in the use of sanctuaries. As noted above, many of the extra-urban sanctuaries of republican Italy were major centres of political and economic activity. After the Social War, the decline of these centres was symbolic of increasing Romanization. Emphasis shifted towards temples and shrines in the growing (and Romanized) cities. All cities in Italy were equipped with a substantial number of temples and religious buildings, many of them constructed, embellished and repaired at the expense of private individuals.[22] However, the pattern of construction of temples and sanctuaries was not entirely random or dependent on individual whim. As Vitruvius [No. 284] notes, there are certain restrictions and taboos on the siting of some temples, and there are others which were routinely given prominent locations. Temples could be (and were) used to make a very emphatic political point. In Roman colonies, but also in many other Italian cities, the temple which enjoyed highest status was the *capitolium*, the temple of Jupiter, Juno and Minerva. It was a visible symbol of loyalty to Rome and of Roman power, and as such, frequently occupied either the highest point in the city or the most prominent position in the forum (figures 8 and 9). At Pompeii, the point was underlined by there being a temple of Jove already under construction in the forum at the time of the Sullan colonization. This was promptly rededicated as a *capitolium*, thus providing a physical reminder of the new power in the city. Later, temples of the imperial cult played a similar role as a focus of loyalty to the new regime.[23] New temples and sanctuaries, or changes to the forms of existing ones, could be an important symbol of cultural change.

Emphasis on urban cults and the decline of the extra-urban sanctuaries does not, however, imply the total disappearance of rural cults. Nor does the non-urban location of some cult places, either before or after the Social War, mean that these were cults of merely local importance or of significance primarily to rural populations. The economic and political role of the great republican sanctuaries of central Italy and the high level of elite activity taking place there indicates that this was not the case. Even after these centres declined in prominence, a significant number of rural shrines continued to be important. Pliny describes the sanctuary of Clitumnus, a sacred grove and stream dotted with shrines and temples and with a sizeable body of inscribed sacred texts and votives. His condescending tone cannot disguise the fact that this is a busy cult place with a steady flow of visitors, sufficient to warrant the construction of special guest-houses to accommodate them. This was not just a local shrine, but one which could expect to attract worshippers from a much wider area. The same phenomenon is archaeologically attested. Some rural sanctuaries which housed healing cults have deposits of votives – usually terracotta models of human limbs – of a size which indicates a wide catchment area.[24] Even the most obviously "rustic" cult, that of Silvanus, proves to be no such thing. Although Silvanus [No. 304] looks like an archetypal primitive rustic deity – a god of the woodland – his cult is a relatively late development which does not gather momentum until the first century AD, and was at least as popular amongst the urban population as it was in the countryside.[25] Cato's description [No. 305] of rites and sacrifices for use on the farm show that there was a level of rural religious activity in Italy, but most of the other evidence, even that which is found outside the city, points to domination of religious activity by the social and political elite, even when this activity physically takes place outside the urban environment. The impact of the shift of elite activity away from extra-urban sanctuaries is not to create a division between urban and rural cults as such, but to emphasize increasing Romanization and a move away from pre-Roman customs to city based Roman ones.

Cult personnel also played an important role in the life of an Italian community. In Roman Italy, the status of priests varied according to the prestige of their cult, but those of the major state cults wielded considerable power. The extent to which religion was integrated with the political process is emphasized by the fact that many priesthoods were part of a public career, and were held in conjunction with state magistracies. This is typified by the way in which the emperor came to hold not just consular and tribunician powers, but was also *pontifex maximus*, the chief priest of the Roman state. Unlike Greek priests, Roman ones were not repositories of specialist religious knowledge or mediators between gods and men. This role belonged to the senate.[26] The *onus* on the officiating priest at a ceremony was to protect the state by performing the prescribed rituals with scrupulous correctness, even repeating them if necessary. The expectation was that magistracies would involve performance of some religious duties and that the higher priesthoods would be held by men pursuing a public career. This overlap between religious and political is found throughout Italy, not just in Rome. Even in instances where a particular priest or priestess does not necessarily hold any other public position, many of those involved in state cults are clearly drawn from the political classes.

Further down the social scale, there are also examples of religious posts which confer enhanced social status. The celebrants of the imperial cult were often wealthy freedmen, who were not eligible for secular office, but whose aspirations were channelled into membership of the *Ordo Augustalis*. Other cult associations, usually local in origin and scope, are found in the cities of Italy which gave slaves or freedmen a role in civic life. Cicero mentions the case of the *Martiales* at Larinum, slave priests of Mars who were regarded as members of the household of the god, and therefore not as proper members of the community [No. 314], and there is a large group of inscriptions at Minturnae[27] which were set up in connection with dedications to various gods by associations of slave or freedman *magistri* or *ministri* [No. 313]. Most of the members of the various cult associations involved in celebrating festivals of the *Magna Mater* were also slaves or freedmen. Apart from the obvious religious function of these groups, they played an important social role in giving otherwise disenfranchised or marginalized social groups a role in the life of the state.

In addition to the state pantheon there were also many foreign cults. Roman religion was, by definition, polytheistic and open to external influences, but was by no means indiscriminate.[28] The range of external cults represented in Italy by the second century AD can all too easily give the impression that the Romans (and Italians) were unconcerned at religious activity provided the demands of the state cults were satisfied, but this was far from the case. In fact, the senate exercised careful control over the establishment of new cults in Rome, and later in Italy. Although numerous cults from the eastern empire later established themselves as part of the process of immigration into Italy, there was a distinct hierarchy which differentiated those which were officially welcomed, through those which were merely tolerated, to those which were unacceptable at the higher levels of society. There was also a distinction of social role and acceptability between those cults which were accepted as part of the fabric of public life – including some foreign cults such as that of the Magna Mater – and which had a role defined by the state, and others, such as those of Isis, Serapis, Mithras, etc. – which were not involved in the public life of a community and which were largely a matter of private initiation and belief. By and large, these were tolerated by the state as long as they did not cause unrest or public outcry, and the cult of Mithras is notable for the extent to which it was eventually accepted by the state as a cult prominent in the legions.

Having said this, there is absolutely no doubt that religious beliefs and actions, particularly in Italy, came under close senatorial scrutiny. The basic difference between external cults which were acceptable and those which were not was drawn at an early date as being a difference between those which were established in Rome at the behest of (and under control of) the senate, and those which were not. Imports from Greece and Asia, such as the cult of Asklepios in 293 BC and that of the Magna Mater in 205, were the subject of formal legislation by the senate, which despatched envoys to escort the cult images to Rome and installed these in purpose-built temples [Nos 296–301]. In contrast, the Bacchanalian cult which was suppressed by order of the senate in 186 BC was not authorized by the senate, but was a spontaneous development which originated outside Rome. Although there was a long tradition of importing cults from the Greek world, the unsanctioned nature of this example provoked the wrath of Rome, and provided a precedent for the eventual extension of senatorial authority on religious matters to the whole of Italy. Matters were not helped by the fact that the cult took hold in some of the areas which Rome regarded as highly troublesome – Campania, Etruria and southern Italy – and that the devotees met in secret, thus raising the suspicion of conspiracy. Roman suppression of the cult was not, however, a sign of growing rejection of foreign religions, but of a reassertion of senatorial control, and the extension of this to Rome's Italian allies.[29]

During the principate, this ability to absorb, or even invent, new cults was very valuable. Within the framework of senatorial and imperial supervision most of the cults and religious practices of the empire could be accommodated, although occasionally a religious sect would have its activities curtailed, or even be ejected from Italy. One very important attribute of this tolerance and of the increasing influence of Hellenistic customs was the creation of the imperial cult. Ruler worship was a well-established practice in the eastern empire, and it was natural that there should be some demand for the right to honour Augustus in this manner. He, however, was initially very cautious, as his entire ideology was based on a rejection of the Hellenistic culture which had been espoused by Antony. In order to deflect possible criticism, cults of Augustus were permitted only in those parts of the empire where Hellenistic ruler worship already existed, and wherever possible, his cult was established as a joint sanctuary of Roma and Augustus. In the western empire, where this was not the case, temples to Julius Caesar and to Roma were permitted, but not to Augustus himself, thus sidestepping the issue of whether it was un-Roman to honour a living ruler while still allowing honours to the regime as a whole [Nos 315–21]. Apart from temples, regular games and festivals were also dedicated in honour of the emperor, and it is notable that the taboo against honouring an emperor during his own lifetime soon broke down. By the middle of the first century AD, the imperial cult was an important feature of civic life all over the empire. Temples dedicated to the emperor usually occupied prominent locations within cities, and the various festivals and sacrifices to mark the birthdays of the members of the imperial family, or other significant anniversaries, added up to a substantial calendar of annual celebrations [No. 318]. Socially, the cult personnel were mostly wealthy freedmen, whose duties gave them an important role in the life of the city, the nature of which is discussed further in Chapter 9. The impact of the cult was to bring overt and personalized symbols of loyalty to the ruling regime into the very heart of civic life.

To sum up, the religious culture of Roman Italy was both highly conservative and surprisingly flexible, and it permeated all aspects of public and private life. Religion was inextricably intertwined with politics, economic activity and social interaction, as well as being a powerful indicator of cultural identities and political allegiances. The forms of expression changed significantly, with a decline in the status of the great non-urban cult centres of pre-Roman Italy and an increasing emphasis on Romanized urban cults as the core of the state religion, but it remained central to the life of the state and the individual. It both reflects and reinforces the social and political changes which took place during the transition from republic to principate and was also a powerful agent of Romanization. For all the apparent religious tolerance and flexibility of the Roman world, cults were closely linked with the establishment and exercise of Roman power.

The gods as protectors of the city

279. Macrobius, *Saturnalia* 3.9

It is well known that all cities are under the protection of a god, and it was a clan-destine practice of the Romans, unbeknown to many people, that when they were besieging a city belonging to an enemy and had come to the point where they were sure it could be captured, they called forth the tutelary deities by a certain ritual. Otherwise, they believed that either the city could not be captured, or in the event that it could, it would be sacrilege to take the gods captive. This is why the Romans themselves wished to keep secret both the god under whose protec-tion Rome falls and the Latin name of the city . . .

[Macrobius goes on to give the text of the formula used for calling forth the gods of an enemy city, with particular reference to its use at Carthage. This was by no means the earliest example of this ritual. Livy makes frequent reference to this in the wars against the Falisci and Etruscans in the fifth and fourth centuries BC, adding the detail that the cult statues were usually taken to Rome and installed in their own temples there, marking a symbolic transfer of divine power and protec-tion from the conquered city to Rome.]

280. Livy 6.29.8–10

T. Quinctius, who had won one battle, captured two camps and nine cities, and received the surrender of Praeneste, returned to Rome and bore the statue of Jupi-ter Imperator, which he had taken from Praeneste, in triumph to the Capitol. It was dedicated between the shrines of Jupiter and Minerva and a tablet was set up beneath it, as a commemoration of his deeds, with an inscription as follows: "Jupiter and all the gods granted this, that T. Quinctius, the dictator, should cap-ture nine cities."

[380 BC. Capture of Praeneste.]

Temples and sanctuaries: form, function and upkeep

281. Dionysios of Halicarnassus, *Roman antiquities* 32.1

Many went into this temple [at Lucus Feroniae] from the surrounding cities at the appointed festivals, who offered prayers and sacrifices to the goddess, and also many merchants, craftsmen and farmers [who were] making money out of this festival, and the markets there became the most famous in the whole of Italy.

282. Dionysios of Halicarnassus, *Roman antiquities* 4.49

As a way of ensuring that the treaties made with those cities might last forever,

Tarquinius decided to assign a temple for the joint use of the Romans, Latins, Hernicians, and those of the Volscians who had entered into the alliance, so that by gathering together each year at the appointed place, they might celebrate a common festival, feast together and share in joint sacrifices. Since this proposal was gladly accepted by them all, he nominated as the place of assembly a high mountain located almost in the centre of these peoples, and commanding the city of the Albani; he enacted a law that an annual festival should be celebrated upon this mountain, during which they should all refrain from acts of war against all the others, and should make joint sacrifices to Jupiter Latiaris, as he is named, and should feast together, and he laid down the share which each city was to contribute to these sacrifices, and the share that each was to receive. The cities which shared in this festival and these sacrifices numbered 47. The Romans celebrate these festivals and sacrifices to this day, and call them Latin festivals; some of the cities which take part bring lambs, some cheeses, and others a certain quantity of milk, and others offerings of similar kind. One bull is sacrificed jointly by all of them, with each city receiving its designated share of meat. The sacrifices which they offer are on behalf of all cities, and the Romans oversee them.

[Sixth century BC. Foundation of the Latin League, using religious festivals as common ground between the Latin cities and a sanctuary as a common meeting place. The interweaving of religious ceremonies and cult places with political activity is well documented in the ancient world. Tarquinius Superbus offered treaty rights to all the Volscians, as well as to the Latins and Hernici, but only Antium and Ecetra elected to join the League. This league formed the basis for Rome's gradual domination of central Italy, but was dissolved in the aftermath of the Latin War, in 388 BC, although the festivals continued under Roman supervision.]

283. Dionysios of Halicarnassus, *Roman antiquities* 20.9–10

Seeing that Pyrrhus was looking for money from all possible sources, the worst and most corrupt of his friends, Euegoros, son of Theodoros, Balakros, son of Nikander and Deinarchos, son of Nikias, followers of godless and accursed beliefs, suggested an impious way of raising money – to open up the sacred treasures of Proserpina. For there was a sacred temple in that city [Locri] which contained great wealth, guarded and untouched from earliest times; amongst this was an uncounted quantity of gold, buried underground out of sight of the masses. Misled by these flatterers and under a necessity stronger than any scruple, Pyrrhus used the men who had made the suggestion as his henchmen in sacrilege; loading the gold plundered from the temple into ships, he sent it to Tarentum, together with his other funds, and was now filled with great optimism. But a just Providence showed its power. For although the ships, having left the harbour, found a land breeze and made headway, a contrary wind blew up and, holding throughout the night, sank some of them, drove others into the Straits of

Messina, and in the case of those transporting the offerings and the gold yielded by them, drove them ashore on the beach at Locri.

[There was a strong connection between religious sanctuaries and both economic and diplomatic activity. Many such sanctuaries were located outside cities, often quite deliberately, as liminal cults were a powerful way of marking boundaries, and acted as centres where people from a number of different cities could meet. The sacred nature of these places, and the fact that festivals might involve a sacred truce, provided a guarantee of neutrality which would allow even warring states to meet to negotiate or to trade. For the same reason, many were chosen as the meeting places and treasuries of pre-Roman leagues – e.g. the sanctuary of Hera Lacinia at Croton (Italiote League), Aqua Ferentina (Latin League), Pietrabbondante (Samnite League, or part of it).]

284. Vitruvius, *De architectura* 1.7

Those [temples] which are dedicated to gods who protect the city, and those sacred to Jupiter, Juno and Minerva should be on the very highest point, commanding a vista of the greater part of the city walls. The temple of Mercury should be close to the forum, or in the market, like those of Isis and Serapis; those of Apollo and Bacchus should be near the theatre; that of Hercules should be near the circus, if there is no gymnasium; the temple of Mars should be outside the city, near the military practice field, and that of Venus outside the city close to the harbour. The writings of the Etruscan *haruspices* also say that sanctuaries of Venus, Mars and Vulcan should be located outside the city, so that youths and married women do not become used to the pleasures of the flesh.

285. Poccetti, *Nuove documenti Italici* No. 175

In the suffect censorship of L. Puccidius, son of Va[. . .], Herennius Pomponius, son of Herennius, ordered the construction and setting up of bronze statues of the kings, according to the decision of the senate, and provided 450 *nummis* for them.

[Third century BC. Rossano di Vaglio, Lucania. Oscan inscription commemorating the construction and setting up of a number of bronze statues in the sanctuary. There are a number of problems in interpretation, notably centring on the identity of the *reges* or kings and the nature of the censorship. Poccetti suggests that the censor's title may be *quinquennalis*, but Lejeune reads it as *suffectus*.[30] The identity of the *reges* is a mystery. It is possible that they may be dictators or war leaders,[31] but they may also be dedicatory statues of the rulers of the sanctuary, i.e. Mefitis and Jove. Unlike the dedications of Stennius Titidius and Cn. Acerronius, this is not a purely personal initiative, but is undertaken by decision of the senate.]

286. M. Lejeune, "Inscriptions de Rossano di Vaglio"
RAL 8.30 (1975), 319–39

[Cn.] Acerr[onius . . . .] F., consul, constructed this building in honour of Mefitis Utiana.

[*c.*AD 25–50. Rossano di Vaglio, Lucania. Latin building inscription. The Latin describes the construction as an *aedes*, or temple, but the inscription was found in association with a *stoa*. The name of the dedicator is fragmentary, but can be reconstructed as Acerronius fairly securely. The Acerronii are a prominent *gens* in Lucania, and appear in many inscriptions from Potentia and the surrounding region. It is possible that this particular Acerronius may be Cn. Acerronius Proculus, who was consul in AD 37, and who is known to have family connections in Lucania.[32]]

287. Poccetti, *Nuove documenti Italici* No. 14

Paccius Staius, L. F., *Meddix tuticus*, canalized the water and . . . undertook the construction of this and paid for the same.

[Pietrabbondante, Samnium. One of a series of three Oscan inscriptions from a cylindrical cistern. All refer to the provision of a water supply to the sanctuary, although all but this example are fragmentary.]

288. *CIL* 10.16

To Jupiter Optimus Maximus, and the immortal gods and goddesses and Roma the everlasting, from the people of Locri.

[Locri. Dedication to Jupiter Optimus Maximus, the main deity of Rome, and to Roma, the personification of Rome.]

289. *CIL* 10.39

Q. Vibullius Q. F. Q. N. and C. Cincius C. F. Paul[us] *quattuorviri iure dicundo.* oversaw the repair and erection of a statue of Proserpina and rebuilding of an altar, undertaken by a decree of the senate . . .

[Vibo Valentia. Repair of the sanctuary of Proserpina.]

290. *CIL* 10.1613

L. Calpurnius, L. F. built the temple of Augustus, with its decoration, at his own expense.

[Undated. Puteoli.]

Italic cults

291. Poccetti, *Nuove documenti Italici* No. 164

Stenius Titidius, son of Orcius, offers this to Mefitis Utiana, in thanks.

[Rossano di Vaglio, Lucania. Oscan dedicatory inscription to the Oscan goddess Mefitis. The epithet Utiana is a common one, which is also found in Latin inscriptions at Rossano and elsewhere in Lucania.]

292. Poccetti, *Nuove documenti Italici* No. 167

L. Nanonius, son of Spellius, quaestor, on the instructions of the senate. To Jove.

[Second century BC. Rossano di Vaglio, Lucania. Oscan dedicatory inscription to Jove. It was, however, found in the sanctuary of Mefitis, which may have housed other cults. Poccetti No.177, also from Rossano, is a dual dedication to Mamers, the Oscan war god, and Mefitis. Like most of the Oscan inscriptions from Rossano, it is written in the Greek alphabet.]

293. Poccetti, *Nuove documenti Italici* No. 16

Maras Staius, son of Bantius, and Lucius Decitius, son of Maras, gave this gift to Victory.

[Early first century BC. Pietrabbondante, Samnium. Bronze tablet with Oscan inscription, found in the forum, close to Temple B. The nature of the dedication is not clear, but given that it is dated to the period of the Social War, it is clearly an offering for victory against Rome.]

294. Vetter No. 147

The sacrifices which must take place in the sanctuary of Ceres: to [Vezkei], on the appointed day; to Euclus on the appointed day; to Ceres on the appointed day; to the daughter of Ceres on the appointed day; to Inter Stita on the appointed day; to the mother of Ceres on the appointed day; to the Lymphae on the appointed day; to [Liganakdix Intera] on the appointed day; to Imbres on the appointed day; to Matae on the appointed day; to Jove Juventus on the appointed day; to Jove Rigator on the appointed day; to Hercules Cerealis on the appointed day; to Patana Pistia on the appointed day; to Diva Genitia on the appointed day.

The sacred [*tefurum*] will be sacrificed on the fiery altar every two years.

During the festival of Flora, sacrifices will be made near the sanctuary to: Perna Cerealis, Amma Cerealis, Flora Cerealis, Euclus Pater.

There are altars in the sanctuary to: [followed by a list of the gods named in the first paragraph and a repeat of the second paragraph].

[Third or second century BC. Agnone, Molise. Bronze tablet inscribed on both sides in Oscan. It lists the deities to be worshipped in the sanctuary of Ceres, a sacred grove containing a number of altars. The gods entitled to be worshipped within the sanctuary are specified, as are those whose rites take place outside the precinct. Many of the named deities have Roman equivalents or translations (given above, wherever possible; undeciphered Oscan text is enclosed in square brackets), but some do not. The Lymphae were Italic water-goddesses, Matae may be equivalent to the Mater Matuta, and Euclus may be identified with Mercury. The main festival was celebrated biennially by sacrifice (or possibly consecration) of a sacred object, the *tefurum*, the nature of which is not known. There were also 15 annual sacrifices to named deities, and four, which took place during the Floralia, to deities worshipped outside the sacred precinct.]

295. Vetter, No. 108

Gifts given to Jupiter Flagius, on behalf of youth.

[Third or second century BC. Cumae. Oscan inscription from the temple of Apollo. The Oscan cult of Jupiter Flagius (also known as Jupiter Flazzus) was widespread in Campania, and equates broadly with the Latin cult of Jupiter Fulgurator. Dedications made *pru vereiiad* (Lat. *pro iuventute*), known as Iovilae, are found in large numbers at Capua, and clearly relate to a festival celebrating youth. They may have been offered as part of coming-of-age ceremonies or have related to an Oscan adaption of the Greek *ephebeia*.]

Foreign cults

296. Dionysios of Halicarnassus, *Roman antiquities* 4.62

In short, there is no other possession of the Romans, either sacred or secular, that they guard as carefully as they do the Sybilline oracles. They consult them on the instruction of the senate, when the state is in the grip of instability or a great disaster has befallen them in war, or if there have been some important prodigies or apparitions which are difficult to interpret, as have frequently occurred. Until the time of the Marsic war, so-called, these oracles were kept in a chest, underground and guarded by ten men. But when the temple was burned, after the end of the 173rd Olympiad (either on purpose, as some people think, or accidentally) these oracles, together with all the offerings dedicated to the god were destroyed by the fire. Those oracles which still survive were gathered together from many places – some from cities in Italy, others from Erythrai in Asia . . .

[The Sybilline oracles, acquired, according to legend, by Tarquinius Superbus from the Cumaean sybil, were kept in the temple of Jupiter Optimus Maximus on the Capitol. It was destroyed by fire in 83 BC.]

297. De viris illustribus 22.1–3

Because of an epidemic, the Romans, on the instructions of the Sybilline books, sent ten ambassadors under the leadership of Q. Ogulnius to bring Asklepios from Epidauros. When they had arrived and were marvelling at the enormous statue of the god, a snake, which was an object of veneration rather than revulsion, slid from the temple; to everyone's astonishment, it moved through the centre of the city to the Roman ship and coiled itself up in the tent of Ogulnius. The ambassadors sailed to Antium carrying the god, where the snake made its way through a calm sea to a nearby temple of Asklepios, and returned to the ship after a few days. When the ship was sailing up the Tiber, the snake leapt onto an island close by, where a temple to him [Asklepios] was founded.

[293 BC. Epidauros was an important sanctuary from the fourth century onwards. Shrines of Asklepios such as those of Kos or Epidauros had extensive diplomatic networks, maintaining systems for exchanging honours and privileges with cities and individuals throughout the Greek world. Cults of Asklepios were already established in Italy, at Greek cities such as Naples and Velia. The connection with Antium may be anachronism on the part of Livy, as there is no archaeological evidence for a temple of Asklepios there earlier than the second century BC.]

298. Livy 5.13.4–5

The severe winter was followed, either as a result of the sudden change from such inclement weather to the opposite extreme, or for some other reason, by a summer which was poisonous and harmful to all living things. Since they were not able to discover the causes of the incurable damage of this plague, or put a stop to them, the senate voted to consult the Sybilline books. The *duumviri sacris faciundis* then celebrated the first Lectisternium to be held in Rome, and for a period of eight days made sacrifices to Apollo, Latona and Diana, to Hercules, Mercury and Neptune, spreading couches for them with all the magnificence then available. They also observed the ceremony in their homes. It is reported that throughout the city, doors stood wide open, all sorts of food were spread out for general consumption, all visitors were welcomed, whether known or not . . .

[399 BC. The *lectisternium* involved the display of images of the Olympian gods on sacred couches, sacrifices in their honour, and a general amnesty during which prisoners were temporarily released, lawsuits were suspended and private quarrels ended. It was originally a Greek rite, and was an important stage in the process of assimilation between the Greek Olympic pantheon and native Roman religion.]

299. Livy 29.10–11

A prophecy was found that if a foreign enemy should ever invade Italy, he could be beaten if Cybele, the Idaean mother of the gods, were brought from Pessinus to Rome. . . . So they began to seriously deliberate the best way of transferring the image of the goddess to Rome, so as to enjoy victory as soon as possible. . . . So believing that Attalus would assist them if possible, they decided to send envoys to him.

300. Livy 29.14

As well as this, there were discussions about the reception of the Idaean Mother at Rome; M. Valerius, one of the envoys, had hurried back ahead of the others to report that she would arrive in Italy at any moment, and another, more recent, report arrived saying that she had reached Tarracina. . . . P. Cornelius, together with the married women of Rome was ordered to meet the goddess at Ostia; he was to receive her from the ship, carry her ashore, and hand her over to the matrons. After the ship had reached the mouth of the Tiber, just as he had been ordered, his ship sailed out to sea, received the goddess from the priests, and carried her to land. The leading matrons of the city, amongst whom the name of one Claudia Quinta is noted, received her. . . . The goddess came into the city of Rome, passed from hand to hand by the matrons, one after another, with all the city crowding to meet her, placing censers before the doorways along her route and praying that she came willingly and propitiously, and was placed in the temple of Victory on the Palatine on the day before the Ides of April; that day was a feast day. The people, crowding, took gifts for the goddess to the Palatine, there was a *lectisternium*, and games were held, called the Megalensia.

[204 BC. Arrival of the image of the Magna Mater in Rome. The cult image originally came from Asia Minor, and the mediation of Attalus of Pergamum was required to negotiate its removal. P. Cornelius Scipio, who received the image, was the nephew of Scipio Africanus and was chosen for his youth and good character, according to Livy, although it is likely that his high connections also helped.]

301. Cicero, *Pro Balbo* 55

Our ancestors, gentlemen of the jury, wanted the worship of Ceres to be carried out with the greatest reverence and ceremony; since the rites were introduced from Greece, they were always looked after by Greek priestesses and everything was enumerated in Greek. But although the priestess, who could demonstrate and perform the Greek rites, was chosen from Greece, nevertheless they wanted a citizen to perform these rites on behalf of citizens, so that she could pray to the immortal gods with skill which was foreign and derived from outside, but in a spirit which was domestic and civic. I see that these priestesses were mostly from Naples and Velia, which I have no doubt were allied cities.

183

[Cicero follows this up by expounding the technicalities of enfranchising Greek priestesses. The cult of Demeter, Dionysos and Kore was introduced in 496 BC, at a time of famine, and dedicated under the Roman names of Ceres, Liber and Libera in 493.[33]]

302. Tacitus, *Annals* 2.85

Consideration was given to the expulsion of Egyptian and Jewish rites, and a decision was taken by the senate that 4,000 freedmen of adult age who were infected by these superstitions should be sent to the island of Sardinia to suppress brigands there; and if the bad climate killed them off, it would be little loss; the others must leave Italy unless they gave up their profane rituals before a fixed date.

[AD 19. Senatorial ruling on Egyptian and Jewish religion. It is uncertain from this passage who "the others" are, unless the reference to the transportation of adults only implies that the remainder included children.]

303. *CIL* 10.1

Sacred to Isis and Serapis. Sacred objects paid for by Q. Fabius Ingenuus, freedman of Titianus, *sevir augustalis*, and by Fabia Candida.

[Early fourth century AD. Rhegium. The Fabii Titiani were a prominent family in Sicily, and the patron of Fabius Ingenuus may have been the Q. Fabius Titianus who was consul in 337 AD.]

Rustic cults

304. G. Pani, *6° Misc. Greca e Romana* (1976)

To the sacred spirit of Silvanus Sanctus . . . Ti. Claudius Priscus gives as a gift to the *collegium* at his own expense an image of the emperor Caesar Hadrian Augustus of one pound of silver, with a bronze base for the gift. Enacted on the fifth day before the Kalends of June (25 May), in the consulship of Q. Gargilius Antiquus and Q. Vibius Gallus.

[AD 116–17 or AD 118–19. Latin inscription recording dedication to Silvanus. Found near the catacombs of S. Callixtus on the Via Appia, several miles south of Rome. There may have been a *collegium* dedicated to Silvanus in the area, which possibly had its own *schola*, or meeting house. The formal presentation of the inscription, complete with date and consular year, is typical of collegial inscriptions. The votive is designed to demonstrate loyalty to the regime. The epithet Sanctus is often applied to Silvanus, causing major confusion among later Christians, who misread the texts as commemorations of the blessed Silvanus and assumed that he was an early Christian martyr.]

305. Cato, *De agri cultura* 83

Make an offering in this manner for your work oxen, to keep them healthy. Make an offering to Mars Silvanus in the wood during the daytime for each head of work oxen. Three pounds of spelt, four and a half pounds of lard, four and a half pounds of meat and three *sextiarii* of wine. You may place the dry ingredients together in one dish, and likewise the wine. Either a slave or a freedman can offer this sacrifice. When it has been offered, eat it immediately in the same place [as the offering ceremony]. No woman should be present at this sacrifice or see how the offering is made.

306. Gasperini, L. *11° Misc. Greca e Romana*

Sacred to Bona Dea and Valetudus. A dedication from Cn. Pacilius Marna, a *sevir* at Sutri and an *Augustalis* at Falerii. Sacred to Bona Dea Castrensis, dedicated by Pacilia Primitiva.

[Late first century/early second century AD. Dedication of a votive offering from a sanctuary of the Bona Dea and Valetudus, located on the border of the territories of Falerii and Sutri. This shrine is probably an example of syncretism between Roman and pre-Roman chthonic deities. In this case, the Bona Dea is a Romanization of the Etruscan cult of Suri, a chthonic goddess. The epithet Castrensis is regularly found in names of cults and sanctuaries, and often indicates that the cult site is a liminal one, on the edge of a city's territory, or in the territory of another city altogether. The proximity of Sutri and Falerii is reflected in the fact that Pacilius Marna was a member of the *Ordo Augustalis* at both cities, and held the office of *Sevir* at Sutri. This shows that he was almost certainly a freedman, but his name is unusual. Instead of the more frequent servile cognomina, he has the cognomen Marna, an Etruscan name, and a further indication of the fusion of Roman and Etruscan populations in this area.]

307. Pliny, *Letters* 8.8

The river banks [of the river Clitumnus, in Umbria] are clothed in many ash trees and poplars whose green reflections can be clearly seen in the river, as if they were immersed in it. The river is as cold and as pale as snow. Nearby is an ancient and sacred temple. There stands Clitumnus himself, clothed in the *toga praetexta*. The *sortes* there demonstrate the presence, and even the oracular power, of the deity. Scattered around this are a number of small shrines, each with its own deity. Each of these has its own name and its own cult, and some even their own [sacred] spring. For besides that which is the parent stream, there are several lesser ones, each with a separate source, but which flow into the river, which is spanned by a bridge. This marks the boundary between the sacred and secular areas [of the stream]. Only boats may sail above the bridge, but swimming is also allowed downstream from it. A swimming area is maintained at public expense by the citizens of Hispellum, to whom the deified Augustus gave this place, and they also provide a guest-house. Nor is there any lack of villas, which occupy the most beautiful sites along the river bank.

In short, there is nothing there in which you will not take pleasure. You will even find something to study; for many inscriptions, by many people, are written on every column and wall, which honour the sacred spring and its god. You will admire many, but you will laugh at a few of them; although in fact you will not laugh at any, because of your good nature.

[In this passage, Pliny describes an archaic rural shrine sacred to Clitumnus, the guardian deity of the Umbrian river of the same name. By this date, it was in the territory of Hispellum, although it only became so by decree of Augustus, probably as part of a reorganization of territory during the foundation of a colony, or as a reward for support by Hispellum during the civil wars. Although it is clearly an Italic rural sanctuary of considerable antiquity, it is also a focus for patronage by the municipality of Hispellum, which built a bathing place and hostel for visitors to the sanctuary. Despite the condescending reference to the inscriptions, this is obviously not just a rustic backwater. The reference to villas lining the most scenic parts of the river points to the presence of the local elite, and the necessity for a guest-house for visitors demonstrates that it was of more than just local significance. There is also a hint that it may have been an oracular cult. Perhaps the most significant element of this passage is the reference to the copious number of inscriptions which honour the god and which record "*leges*" – possibly oracles and religious laws governing the sanctuary. Writing and a body of written documents were clearly important to the cult.[34]]

Cults and Roman control

308. *CIL* 10.3698

Passed in the consulship of M. Magrius Bassus and L. Ragonius Quintianus, on the Kalends of June, in the temple of the deified Vespasian at Cumae, at a meeting of the decurions which was called by the praetors M. Mallonius Undanus and Q. Claudius Acilianus. The decree and election were witnessed by Caelius Pannychus, Curtius Votivos and Considius Felicianus. The praetor having referred the election of the priest of the Mother of the Gods at Baiae in place of Restitutus, the deceased priest, it was unanimously decided that Licinius Secundus should become priest.

From the *Quindecemviri Sacris Faciundis Populi Romani* to the magistrates of Cumae, greetings. When we learned from your letter that Licinius Secundus had been elected priest of the Mother of the Gods by you to replace the deceased Claudius Restitutus we willingly confirmed this . . .

[AD 289. Baiae. A decree arranging the replacement for the priest of the Mother of the Gods, who had recently died. Baiae was not an independent *municipium* but was part of the *colonia* of Cumae, hence the fact that the business was dealt with by the senate of Cumae. The second part of the text is a letter from the *Quindecemviri Sacris Faciundis* at Rome, who supervised all such appointments and who had to ratify this appointment.]

309. Tacitus, *Annals* 3.71

Then there was religious business concerning the temple in which the Equites should place the gift vowed by them to Fortuna Equestris for Augustus' recovery from illness. There were many shrines to the goddess in Rome, but none with this title. A temple with this name was discovered at Antium, and since all rites, temples and statues of gods in Italian towns were under the control and legal supervision of Rome, the dedication was therefore set up at Antium.

[AD 22. Religious business in the senate concerning a dedication for the health of Augustus. Since this must pre-date his death in AD 14, this demonstrates the length of time taken to implement some religious vows and dedications. It also highlights the degree of central control by Rome over all aspects of civic religion in Italy.]

Priests and cult personnel

310. *IG* 14.760

Decree in honour of Tettia Casta, priestess for life of [. . .] *oikos* of the women. In the consulship of Domitian Caesar, son of Augustus, and C. Valerius Festus, on the 14th of Lenaia. The motion was proposed by Lucius Frugi, Cornelius Cerialis, and Junius [. . .]. Concerning the proposal which the *archon*, Tranquillius Rufus placed before the *proskletos*, the following decision was taken. It was agreed by a unanimous decision that there should be public mourning at the untimely death of Tettia Casta, a woman who loved honour and who showed universal piety and goodwill towards the city, and that a silver statue should be set up to the gods for her generous benefactions to the city, and that Tettia Casta should be honoured by a statue and inscribed shields and that the cost of her funeral should be at public expense, but be the responsibility of her family, it being difficult to give comfort by [. . .] and that a place should be given for a tomb and these things paid for.

In the consulship of Domitian Caesar, son of Augustus, and C. Valerius Festus, on the [. . .] of July, Granius Rufus, Lucius Pudes and Poppaeus Severus were present. Concerning the proposal which the *archon*, Fulvius Probus, placed before the *proskletos*, the following decision was taken. The statue at public expense which the *boule* had decreed to Tettia Casta out of sympathy, is approved. It is good, and worthy of praise and should be crowned with a gold crown, giving testimony to her life with public praise . . .

In the consulship of L. Flavius Fimbria and Attilius Barbarus [. . .], Ariston, son of Bukkos, Avillius Appianus and Verius Liberalis were present. Concerning the proposal which the *archon*, Julius Laevinus, referred to the *proskletos*, the following decision was taken. A place for burial was decreed to Tettia [. . . fragmentary passage detailing the size and position of the tomb and stele], and no one else shall be granted permission to be buried in this place. [. . . fragmentary passage referring to Tettia's son, Domitius Lepidus and her husband, L. Domitius.]

[AD 71. Naples. Greek decree of the Senate and assembly of Naples, granting honours to the priestess Tettia Casta and expressing sorrow at her death. This is the longest and most elaborate example of a genre which occurs several times at Naples in the Flavian period. Greek constitutional terminology is used throughout, although Naples was by this date a Roman *municipium*. The *boule* and *eskletos* almost certainly correspond to the *senatus* and *comitia*. The role of the *archon* and *antarchon* is less certain. The terms may be used here as equivalents of *duumvir*. The language used, stressing Tettia's moral qualities and role as public benefactor, is strongly reminiscent of that of Greek honorific decrees from the eastern empire. The cult of which she was priestess is uncertain, due to the fragmentary state of part of the text, but the reference to the "*oikos* of the women" suggest that it was the cult of Demeter, which was both prominent and prestigious at Naples.[35]]

311. *ILS* 6286

To Q. Decius Q. F. M. N. Saturninus, *pontifex minor* at Rome, flute-player at the public ceremonies of the Roman people, the Quirites, *praefectus fabrum* to a consul for three years, *curator* of the Via Latina and Via Labicana, military tribune, *praefectus fabrum* for the administration of justice and selection of jurors by lot in Asia, *quattuorvir iure dicundo* at Verona, quaestor for two years, *duovir iure dicundo* and *duovir quinquennalis*, *praefectus quinquennalis* of Tiberius Caesar, and then of Drusus Caesar, Ti. F., and for a third time, of Nero Caesar, son of Germanicus, priest, *flamen* of Roma and the deified Augustus in perpetuity by the authority of Ti. Caesar Augustus and chosen patron of the colony with his permission. [Set up] at public expense, by decree of the decurions.

[First century AD. Aquinum.]

312. *IG* 14.617

Prytanis at his own expense, and *archon* for a term of five years: Sex. Numonius Sex. F. Maturus; *Synprytaneis*: C. Hortorius C. F. Balbillus, M. Pemponius M. F. Pulcher, M. Cornelius M. F. Martialis; *Hieroskopoi*: M. Cornelius Verus, C. Antonius Thytes; *Hierosalpistes*: C. Julius Reginus; *Hierokeryx*: C. Calpurnius Verus; *Hieroparektes*: C. Caecilius Reginus; *Tamias*: Meliphongos, son of Maturus; *Spondaules*: Natalis; *Kapnauges*: Helikon, son of Maturus, M. Apros Zosimos.

[First century AD. Rhegium. Greek inscription recording sacrifices to Apollo and Artemis, in the presence of the magistrates (given under their Greek titles of *Prytanis* and *Synprytaneis*), priests and their attendants.[36] Despite the trappings of Hellenism, the elite participants are all Roman/Italian, as shown by the names. Only the slave or freedman attendants are Greek. The cults of Apollo and Artemis were prominent at Rhegium, originating from the Greek phase of the city's history, and had a choral festival associated with them.]

313. Johnson, *Excavations at Minturnae I* No. 25

In the duovirate of P. Hirrius M. F. and P. Stahius P. F., these *magistri* gave this gift to Mercury Felix: Eros, slave of C. Calidius; A. Mustius A. L. Straton; M. Raecius M. L. Barnaeus; Philinus, slave of C. Cod[. . .]; Dama, slave of C. Lusius; Papias, slave of M. Novius; Theuphilus, slave of P. Staius; Antiochus, slave of L. Cae[. . .]; Leonidas, slave of M. Epidius.

[Mid-first century BC. Minturnae. One of a group of 29 inscriptions set up in or near the forum at Minturnae by *magistri* of various religious cults, including those of Mercury Felix, Venus and Ceres. All are identical in form and inscribed on *cippi* of local tufa (which are the gifts referred to at the beginning of the inscription). These may have acted as altars for libations and ceremonies connected with these cults, none of which are known to have had a temple at Minturnae. The vast majority of the lists have 12 names placed in three groups, possibly reflecting a geographical distribution between three regions of the city. Like most other colleges of *magistri* found in Italy, the lists are composed mainly of slaves and freedmen. As well as privately owned slaves, there are also a small number of slaves owned by trade associations, notably the *socii salinatores* (association of salt manufacturers) and the *socii picarii* (associations of pitch makers). Johnson's analysis of the onomastic patterns gives a total of 190 individual slave owners and 121 families who owned slaves, but some names (notably that of M. Epidius) occur with extreme frequency, suggesting large households or workforces, and therefore substantial wealth.]

314. Cicero, *Pro Cluentio* 43

At Larinum, there were people called *Martiales*, public priests of Mars and dedicated to the god by ancient regulations and religious customs of Larinum; they were great in number, and as is the case with the many priests of Venus in Sicily, so these priests at Larinum were counted as belonging to the household of Mars; suddenly Oppianicus began to claim that they were free men and Roman citizens. This was a great blow to the decurions and citizens of Larinum. So they asked Habitus to take up the case and defend it in the public interest.

[The case of the *Martiales* of Larinum illustrates the numerous grey areas in the law governing citizenship. Most of the *Martiales* are likely to have been slaves or freedmen, but it was not unusual in ancient religion to regard the priest as some sort of dependent of the god. Oppianicus' motive seems to have been to increase his own standing and *clientela* by making himself responsible for enrolling large numbers of new citizens (cf. *Cluent.* 41, where he is caught altering the census records). The case was ultimately referred to Rome, where Habitus was murdered by associates of Oppianicus before a decision was reached.]

The imperial cult

315. Tacitus, *Annals* 1.54

In the same year, new ceremonies were introduced, in the creation of a new association of the priests of Augustus, just as Titus Tatius had once instituted the association of Titius, in order to maintain the Sabine rites. Having cast lots, 21 members were chosen from leading men of the state: Tiberius, Claudius, Drusus and Germanicus were added. The Games of Augustus, which were first introduced then, were disrupted by strife between certain actors.

[AD 15. Development of the structure of the imperial cult.]

316. Dio 51.20.6–8

[Augustus] ordered the Romans living in these cities [Ephesus and Nicaea] to give honours to these deities [Roma and the deified Caesar], but he allowed non-Romans, whom he called Hellenes, to consecrate certain shrines to himself – at Pergamum by the Asians and at Nicomedia by the Bithynians. This practice, which began under Augustus, has continued under other emperors, not just among the Greek peoples, but also among all others under Roman rule. In Rome itself and the rest of Italy, however, no emperor has dared to do this, no matter how deserving of fame; but even there, divine honours are granted posthumously to those emperors who have ruled honestly, and in fact, sanctuaries are built to them.

[29 BC. Establishment of the imperial cult in the East, as a cult of Roma and Caesar.]

317. *ILS* 154

In the consulship of Tiberius Caesar, for the third time, and Germanicus Caesar, for the second time, the duovirs being Cn. Acceius Cn. F. Arn. Rufus Lutatius and T. Petillius, P. F. Quir., it was decreed that:
 The shrine, these statues, and a victim for the dedication [were voted]. For the birthday of Augustus eight days before the Kalends of October (24 September), two victims, usually sacrificed in perpetuity at the altar of the divinity of Augustus, should be sacrificed on the ninth and eighth days before the Kalends of

October. Similarly, the decurions and people should, in perpetuity, banquet on the birthday of Tiberius Caesar – the expense of which Q. Cascellius Labeo promises to pay in perpetuity, in order that he should be thanked for his generosity – and a calf should be sacrificed each year on this same birthday. On the birthdays of Augustus and Tiberius, before the decurions begin to dine, the *genii* of Augustus and Tiberius should be invited to feast at the altar of the *numen* of Augustus, with wine and incense. We have had an altar of the *numen* of Augustus built at our own expense, and we have supervised games held for six days from the Ides of August (13th) at our own expense. On the birthday of the Augusta, we gave wine and cakes to the women of the city for the Bona Dea at our own expense. Similarly, we gave wine and cakes to the decurions and people at our own expense at the dedication of the statues of the Caesars and the Augusta, and vowed that we would always give them on the anniversary of the dedication. So that day may be better attended every year, we will keep it six days before the Ides of March (10th), the day on which Tiberius Caesar was most happily made *pontifex maximus*.

[AD 18. Civic decree from Forum Clodii, Etruria. It describes in detail the provisions made by Forum Clodii for celebrating the imperial cult by providing altars, statues and sacrifices, and designating days for festivals marked by distributions of food and wine. It also demonstrates how the imperial cult can be linked to other festivals, in this case by the connection between the birthday of Livia and the festival of the Bona Dea. Like many aspects of civic religion, the festivals are paid for by a combination of private munificence and obligations *ob honorem*.]

318. *CIL* 10.8375

Fourteenth day before the Kalends of September [19 August]. Day on which Caesar took up his first consulship. Thanksgiving.

[4 or 22 September]. Day on which Lepidus' army surrendered to Caesar. Thanksgiving.

Eighth day before the Kalends of October [23 and 24 September]. Caesar's birthday. Sacrifice of animal to Caesar. Thanksgiving.

Nones of October [7th]. Birthday of Drusus Caesar. Thanksgiving to Vesta.

Fifteenth day before the Kalends of November [18 or 19 October]. Day on which Caesar assumed the *toga virilis*. Thanksgiving to Spes and Iuventus.

Sixteenth day before the Kalends of December [16 November]. Birthday of Tiberius Caesar. Thanksgiving to Vesta.

Eighteenth day before the Kalends of January [15 December]. Day on which the altar of Fortuna Redux, who brought Caesar back from overseas provinces, was dedicated. Thanksgiving to Fortuna Redux.

Seventh day before the Ides of January [7 January]. Day on which Caesar first assumed the *fasces*. Thanksgiving to Jupiter [. . .]

Third day before the Kalends of February [16 January]. Day on which Caesar was named Augustus. Thanksgiving to the *numen* of Augustus.

[30 January]. Day on which the Ara Pacis was dedicated. Thanksgiving to the rule of Caesar Augustus, protector of Roman citizens and the world. Day before the Nones of March [6 March]. Day on which Caesar was elected Pontifex Maximus. Thanksgiving to Vesta and the public Lares of the Roman People, the Quirites.

[*c.* AD 4. Cumae. Excerpt from a fragmentary Latin inscription of the *Feriale Cumanum*, the official calendar of holidays and celebrations observed by the city of Cumae, mostly in conjunction with the anniversaries of Augustus and his family. It was common practice for Italian cities to take the date of Augustus' first visit to them as their New Year, which may explain why Cumae had a calendar beginning in August.]

319. Tacitus, *Annals* 3.70

The emperor forbade the prosecution of L. Ennius, a Roman of equestrian rank, who was charged with treason because he had melted down a silver statue of the emperor in order to turn it into silver plate.

[AD 22. Tiberian restrictions on the application of the *maiestas* laws to images associated with the imperial cult.]

320. Saladino, V. *ZPE* 39 (1980), No. 24

[Made] in fulfilment of a vow for the safety and return and British victory of Ti. Claudius Caesar Augustus Germanicus, *pontifex maximus*, holding tribunician power for the fifth time, *imperator* ten times, *Pater Patriae*, consul designate for the fourth time; Aulus Vicirius Proculus, priest of Augustus, military tribune, made good his vow for the British victory.

[AD 45. Rusellae. Inscription from the base of a statue of Victory.]

321. Pliny, *Letters* 10.8

When your deified father, sir, had encouraged all citizens to be munificent, in his fine speeches and estimable example, I asked his permission to transfer to the city some statues of former emperors which had been kept on my distant estate, just as they had been handed down to me through several bequests, and to add his statue to them. Since he gave permission with full approval, I immediately wrote to the decurions so that they could allot a site on which to build a temple at my own expense; in honour of my plan, they offered me the choice of site. But first of all my own illness, then that of your father, and finally the duties of the post which you gave me, have held me back, but it now seems convenient for me to go there. My duty month ends on the Kalends of September and there are several holidays in the following month. Therefore, I ask you to let me decorate the temple I am going to build with your statue, along with the rest, and then, so as to do this as soon as possible, to grant me leave of absence.

[c. AD 99. Pliny's request for leave of absence from Rome involves constructing a temple to the imperial cult and donation of a family collection of statues, but also, as the remainder of the letter makes clear, to attend to his estates. This probably refers to the property at Tifernum inherited from his uncle.]

CHAPTER EIGHT

Municipal Italy 1:
constitutions and political life of the city

One of the most striking features about Italy during the Roman period was the high density of urban settlement. Approximately 400 sites are known from pre-Roman and Roman Italy which have a good claim to be regarded as cities. Many of these were very small by modern standards – estimates vary, but it is likely that something in the region of 60 per cent had a population of no more than 10,000 and the vast majority of the remainder fell into the range 10,000–40,000. Only a very small number of cities anywhere in the empire approached anything like the size of even a small modern city. Nevertheless, this level of urbanization was unequalled in western Europe until the eighteenth century. It is also quite clear from ancient literature than cities occupied a pre-eminent place in political and social thought, for both the Romans and the Greeks. There was a powerful equation between civilization and the city; only barbarians lived in non-urban settlements.[1] In addition, the Romans made an equally strong connection between their forms of urban life and *Romanitas* itself.[2] Where cities did not exist, their formation was encouraged, if not actually imposed by Rome, and the colonies actively founded by the Romans provided a pattern of what a Roman city, and by implication, Romanized life, was expected to be. In essence, then, study of the socio-political structure and history of Roman Italy is the study of the city and how it functioned. Although it is very difficult to separate social and political aspects of the ancient city, particularly in the context of elite behaviour, this chapter will focus primarily on the formal constitutional structures of Italian cities, their administration, and their political life, while Chapter 9 will examine social relations and how they worked.

Before the Social War, cities and non-urban states which were independent allies of Rome rather than colonies had their own forms of government, often peculiar to their region or ethnic background. After the war and the subsequent enfranchisement of all Italians, forms of government became largely, although not entirely, standardized along Roman lines. Surviving municipal charters, or portions of them, give some idea of what this framework of government included. The most important of the Italian documents, the charter of Tarentum and the Latin Table of Heraklea [Nos 323–4], preserve a fragment of the municipal charter of Tarentum and a document which is now thought to be a digest of excerpts from Roman municipal legislation (the notion that it is a *Lex Julia Municipalis* passed by Caesar is no longer widely accepted).[3] Although incomplete, these give a flavour of what was expected of civic magistrates. The surviving fragment from Tarentum covers rules restricting elite mobility, to ensure that wealthy families did not leave the city permanently, but most of it is devoted to rules for monitoring public finances and sanctions against misuse of municipal funds. The inscription from Heraklea covers the duties of the aediles and other officers in respect of upkeep of the urban amenities. Comparison with similar documents from the rest of the empire (e.g. the charter of Urso in Spain[4]) shows that these were fairly typical of city charters in general. What is striking, however, is that this type of Romanized constitution was already being copied in Italy well before the Social War even amongst allied states. An Oscan inscription from Bantia in Lucania is a section from a city constitution dating to 150–100 BC which, although drafted by an independent allied city, adheres closely to Roman models [No. 322]. The actual magistracies named are Oscan, although the title of the *meddix* is Latinized as *praetor* (cf. No. 325) but otherwise the structure of the official career pattern and the judicial arrangements has a distinctly Roman flavour.

If Romanization of structures of government began well before the Social War in some regions, it is equally true that pre-Roman elements were preserved for a considerable period afterwards. There were many anomalies in the century after the Social War, not least in the distribution of *quattuorviri* and *duoviri* as chief magistrates, as discussed in Chapter 4. Some states actively retained pre-Roman magistracies, such as Arpinum, Formiae and Fundi, which were governed by boards of three aediles [No. 326] and Caere, which was governed by a dictator [No. 419] and provision is made for irregular magistracies in the Table of Heraklea [No. 324]. The Greek cities of Velia, Naples and Rhegium have some Greek elements embedded in otherwise Romanized constitutions as late as the second century AD [Nos 310, 312], although gaps in the evidence and the context of the inscriptions concerned suggest that these may be renewals of ancient tradition rather than genuine survivals.[5]

The other area of government in which pre-Roman structures remained important is in the substructures of civic organization – the *pagi* and the *vici*. *Vicus* was the generic term for a village, but it also came to be applied to subdivisions within a city or its territory.[6] However, it seems to have been a largely Roman institution, whereas the *pagus*, which fulfilled much the same function, was an Italian institution, which does not exist in pre-Social War Roman law.[7] As late as the Augustan period, the *pagus* was being used as a basic building block to construct and dismantle cities. At Arpinum, the *pagus* of Cereatae was split off to form the independent city of Cereatae Marianae, while at Capua, *pagi* were central to the reuniting of the cities of Calatia, Casilinum and Urbana.[8] Even in states where such drastic changes did not take place, *pagi* played an important part in urban and rural government and social relations. Ulpian [No. 337] cites the *pagus* as integral to the census formula for describing geographical location, and Jongman argues that they were vital agents of ideological control, playing an important part in elite domination of the electoral process.[9] They seem to have elected their own magistrates – termed *magistri* or *ministri* – whose duties included celebrating festivals and looking after cults in the *pagus* and maintaining (in some cases constructing) public buildings [Nos 334–9]. It is clear from the numerous references to building activity and to dedication of statues and monuments that the *pagi* must have had their own funds, and that they were used as a forum for acts of munificence on the part of patrons or members of the elite, even in rural *pagi* such as those of Sinuessa.[10] At Capua, the day-to-day running of the community may have devolved on the *magistri campani* after the dismantling of the structures of civic government by Rome in 211 BC [Nos 334–5]. The social status of these *magistri* is unclear, but is not likely to have been as exalted as that of the main city magistrates. The single largest (and earliest) body of evidence, the inscriptions of the *magistri campani*, shows an apparent shift from participation by free citizens of Capua in the earliest texts to a majority of freedmen by 90 BC.[11]

In contrast, the political life of the *municipium* was dominated by the social and economic elite. The principal deliberative body in the Italian city was composed of men drawn from the *ordo decurionum*, analogous to the senatorial order at Rome, membership of which required free birth and a property qualification of 100,000 sesterces per year. The size of this ruling order in any given city varied considerably in accordance with prosperity and distribution of economic resources. The *ordo* of Canusium, as listed on a large and detailed inscription dating to AD 223[12] was 123 strong, drawn from *c.* 63 families, whereas at Petelia, only 20 elite families are known.[13] The norm probably lay somewhere between these two extremes, although there is little reliable data, and iteration of magistracies, as in No. 341 and No. 345, suggests that there were cases in which either power became concentrated into the hands of very few people, or there was only a small pool of men eligible to take on civic office.[14]

There is a perceptible chronological variation in who constituted the municipal elite in any given city. Cicero[15] gives us several detailed snapshots of local elites in the generation after the Social War. At this period, they were clearly highly competitive bodies with a strong local identity which was in no way undermined by growing connections with Rome. Many of the men who feature in his municipal law cases were of equestrian rank, and most seem to have had interests outside their own region. Plancius was of an equestrian family whose wealth came from tax-farming; Sextus Roscius was an eminent man in both Ameria, the surrounding region, and Rome, with estates in his native region and business interests elsewhere [Nos 401, 413–15]. Most of Cicero's Italian clients were able to call on large numbers of eminent fellow-citizens to support them during their careers at Rome, and turn up to impress the courts with the strength of their following [Nos 177–8, 401]. The turbulence of the civil wars was felt in Italy as well as Rome, as individuals and cities were forced to choose sides and suffered the consequences accordingly. The *Pro Roscio* and *Pro Cluentio* give vivid portrayals of the way in which Sullan partisans rose to power in Italy and used their new influence to settle personal scores. The *Pro Sulla* examines a process which has gone one step further. The founders of the Sullan colony at Pompeii may have made an attempt to exclude the indigenous population from the political process,[16] although this is not certain. Cicero denies that this was the case, but epigraphic evidence shows that the names of the pre-Sullan elite rapidly disappear from the record during the first century, to be replaced by those of Roman incomers.[17] Whatever the details of the issue, there were grievances centring both on changes to the physical structure of the city and on the application of the constitution which were profound enough to cause deep divisions within the citizen body [No. 349].

Later colonizations caused less dramatic, but no less profound, changes. The settlement of a group of veterans in a community, as became routine during the principate, could transform membership of the local elite. The discharge payment made to men of the rank of centurion upwards was enough to give them the decurial census, and the tendency to settle colonists according to their army unit gave a ready-made support base for electoral purposes. A significant number of elite commemorative inscriptions show that retired soldiers could (and did) go on to hold municipal office [Nos 342, 344, 408–10]. As new families entered the municipal elite, many of the more established elite families of Italy moved onto a wider stage, and the gulf between senatorial and municipal elites grew wider. As noted in Chapter 5, Augustus made considerable use of Italian supporters, and an increasing number of Italian senators emerge during the first century AD. By the second century, Rome is firmly established as the centre of interest for anyone of serious ambition. Grandees such as Pliny clearly feel a strong attachment to their native cities (cf. Chapter 9), maintaining connections within the locality and offering benefactions, but the active local participation of the Ciceronian era has gone. These local sentiments must also be offset against the evidence of Juvenal, who habitually stresses the emptiness and peripheral nature of Italian cities. The small-town magistrate whose primary duty is checking measures in the market is a symbol of futility [No. 257].

The little epigraphic evidence for municipal politics concerns Pompeii, where some of the electoral graffiti have survived. This is, however, notoriously difficult to interpret. Jongman suggests a long chronology for the surviving documents, which would imply that offices were contested but not very vigorously, with only a small number of candidates standing at each election.[18] Mouritsen takes the opposite view, arguing that most of the surviving posters are likely to date to AD 79 or to only a few years earlier.[19] Given that wall-space was routinely used to advertise elections, games and other events, it seems highly likely that electoral *programmata* would have only a short lifespan before being painted over. This compresses the number of known candidates into a much shorter chronology and creates a much livelier impression of political life, with a larger number of candidates for each post and a particularly intense interest in the office of *quinquennalis*, as one would expect. The election notices record expressions of support for candidates, often from groups of people, but sometimes from individuals. Candidates are not judged on specific policies or programmes but on their status, their moral qualities, and on their record of benefactions to the community – a factor which is entirely consistent with the emphasis on euergetism, as will be discussed in the following chapter. It also illustrates the symbiotic relationship between political and social behaviour in the ancient world, and the lack of clear distinction in the Roman mind between the two spheres of activity.

The other problem which must be faced, however, is that of the typicality, or otherwise, of Pompeii. Given that evidence from Pompeii in almost all areas of civic life is far more abundant than that from most other cities, it is not surprising that there is a tendency to treat this as a "type site" and extrapolate from conclusions based on Pompeian data to create general models of the ancient city. However, Italy was (and still is) a highly regionalized country, and for this reason, caution must be exercised in extending patterns observable in one city to the remainder of Italy. This is particularly underlined in the context of Pompeian politics. A recent study of political behaviour by the elite of Herculaneum reveals a quite different pattern, with a much lesser degree of competition for office.[20] Even within this limited area on the Bay of Naples, there are two quite different patterns of behaviour, and on this basis it must be assumed that although the Pompeian evidence gives an interesting insight into a possible political scenario, it must be borne in mind that this was not automatically repeated elsewhere.

The scope of the civic magistrates was in theory wide, within the confines of the city, but in practice it became increasingly circumscribed by imperial and senatorial edicts and by Roman law. As far as we can tell from the surviving municipal charters and from inscriptions detailing their activity, the main role of the chief magistrates – *quattuorviri*, *duoviri* or their equivalents – was to hear lawsuits, oversee the financial affairs of the community, conduct business in the local council, and undertake a variety of euergetic actions, both in buildings and upkeep of the fabric of the city, and in games and public entertainments, which were required as a condition of holding office [Nos 322–4]. The epigraphic record may, however, be distorted by the fact that routine activity was unlikely to be recorded, whereas more spectacular events, such as major benefactions, were commemorated with inscriptions. The possibility that civic magistracies became increasingly ceremonial rather than executive in function is, however, raised by the fact that age limits for the holding of office were disregarded in some cities, and there are cases where magistrates or decurions were in fact children or adolescent sons of important families. In these cases, the emphasis is clearly on honouring a family rather than choosing an active participant in running the city [Nos 340, 348]. Aediles were in general placed in charge of the day-to-day functioning of the city, with responsibility for such matters as monitoring weights and measures, supervising markets and fairs, and undertaking mundane construction tasks such as road repairs. Our understanding of the role of the local councils is also beset by the problem that it tends to be the honorific decrees rewarding prominent citizens which survive, and there is little way of telling whether this type of exchange of honours was the staple of decurial business or the exception.

The level of autonomy for the Italian city was relatively high until the second century AD. Although acceptance of Roman law and the direct authority of the emperor and senate was a prerequisite of the acceptance of Roman citizenship, Italian cities were self-governing entities. However, there was a tendency for both legal control and administrative authority to encroach, particularly in the second century AD. The gradual extension of Roman supervision in Italy, often using the need to maintain public order as an excuse, which took place in the second century BC, has already been discussed.[21] During the principate, Italian cities were nominally under the supervision of the senate, although the emperor could, and did, intervene. During the reign of Trajan, however, supervision of civic activity in Italy and the provinces became more routine. *Ad hoc* appointments of agents with the title *curator rei publicae*, whose duty was to supervise municipal finances and the conduct of public affairs, became increasingly common. These were often men who had close connections with the cities which they oversaw. Many were drawn from the local elite of the city or region for which they were responsible, or were already patrons of the city to which they were assigned [No. 330]. Eventually, the majority of cities seem to have been under the supervision of these curators, but only by a process of piecemeal appointments. Hadrian and Marcus Aurelius consolidated this process by creating a number of consular *iuridici* to oversee civil law cases [Nos 183–4], and during the third century AD, the administrative centralization of Italy was completed by the division of the country into a number of regions, mostly comprising two of the Augustan *regiones*, which were each administered by a *corrector* of consular rank. The region around Rome was more closely supervised than the rest of Italy from an earlier date, falling under the authority of the *praetor urbanus* [No. 331]. Certain areas of civic life were also controlled by Rome directly. There is a substantial body of law governing benefactions and bequests [Nos 386–90];[22] all associations and *collegia* were under senatorial supervision [No. 432]; appointments of patrons had to be formally ratified by the senate [Nos 391–2];[23] all religious activity was under control of the senate, which was allowed to act in matters concerning temples and their personnel anywhere in Italy without any further consultation [No. 309]. Altogether, although the cities of Italy were nominally self-governing states, there was an increasing tendency in the second century AD towards central supervision which was the culmination of a creeping process dating back to the pre-Social War period.

Politically and administratively, therefore, the history of Italy is characterized by slow but perceptible centralization and the growth of Roman control. In the first generation after the Social War, there are frequent signs of pre-Roman survivals in the political structures of Italian cities, but these gradually decline, although some persist into the second century AD. Municipal constitutions, even some of those which pre-date the Social War, follow Roman patterns in the essentials despite these differences in detail, and both the senate and the emperor were able to supervise the behaviour of Italian states. By the end of the second century AD, the local autonomy of the Italian city was being progressively eroded in favour of more centralized systems of control.

How cities were constituted: municipal charters

322. *FIRA* I.16

. . . he must swear the oath with the agreement of a majority of the senate, so long as no fewer than 40 people are present when the matter is under consideration.

If anyone prevents the assembly by right of intercession, before doing so he must swear that he vetoes the meeting knowingly and in good faith, and for the public good, rather than from partiality or ill will towards anyone, and that he does this in accordance with the judgment of the senate. A presiding magistrate whose assembly is obstructed in this manner shall not hold an assembly on this day.

From now on, any magistrate who holds an assembly about a case involving a capital penalty or a fine shall make the people pass judgment after swearing that they will give whatever judgment on these issues as they believe to be in the greatest public interest, and he shall prevent anyone from swearing in this matter with deliberate ill will. If anyone acts, or holds an assembly, contrary to this [provision] the fine shall be 2,000 sesterces. If any magistrate prefers to fix [the sum of] this fine, he may do so, so long as it is for [a sum] less that half the property of the guilty person.

If any magistrate has set a day for another [magistrate] in a case involving the death penalty or a fine, he must not hold the assembly until he has made the accusation four times in the presence of the people, knowingly and in good faith, and the people have been informed of the fourth day. He can argue the case with the defendant four times, but not more than five, before he pronounces the summons, and when he has argued it for the final time with the defendant, he must not hold the assembly for 30 days from then. If anyone contravenes this, if any magistrate prefers to fix [the sum of] this fine, he may do so, so long as it is for [a sum] less that half the property of the guilty person.

When the censors take the census of the Bantians, anyone who is a citizen of Bantia shall be assessed, both himself and his property, according the rules that the censors have drawn up for the taking of the census. If anyone fraudulently fails to attend the census, and is convicted of doing so, he shall be flogged in the assembly, under the supervision of the praetor and in the presence of the people, and the rest of his household and all his unregistered property shall become public property without any recompense to him.

If anyone wishes to go to law with another person or wishes to make a forcible seizure [of property] as if judgment had been given in the issues which are addressed in these laws, the praetor, or the *praefectus*, if one happens to be at Bantia after this [decree], shall not impede them for ten successive days. If anyone causes an impediment contrary to this [law], the fine shall be 1,000 sesterces. And if any magistrate prefers to fix [the sum of] this fine, he may do so, so long as it is for [a sum] less that half the property of the guilty person.

Nobody shall be praetor or censor of Bantia unless he has already been quaestor, and nobody shall be censor unless he has already been praetor. And if anyone is praetor and [. . .] he shall not become a tribune of the people afterwards. If anyone is made tribune of the people contrary to this, he is appointed wrongly.

[*c.*150–100 BC. Bantia, Lucania. Oscan inscription containing part of the municipal charter of Bantia. It probably comprises about a sixth of the full document and contains details of safeguards for trials of capital crimes, and processes for bringing cases before the magistrates, for holding the popular assembly, for conducting the census and penalizing avoidance or false declarations. The final clause lays down the form of the *cursus honorum*, the sequence of public offices and the order in which they were to be held. Bantia was a Lucanian city, and as such, was Oscan in language and culture, but this text indicates the influence of Rome on the machinery of government elsewhere in Italy. For instance, the basic structure for lawsuits is similar to that of the Roman law courts – a number of preliminary hearings, followed by a interval of several weeks, before the actual trial – but the details differ. Similarly, the cursus is very similar to that of Rome, with junior magistrates and the principal executive magistrate elected annually, and the censor as the most senior post. The importance of the census, the basis of all military recruitment as well as a record of wealth, is echoed by the severity of the penalties for non-attendance. The use of the Oscan language despite the Romanized content of the text is significant. Another inscription was found on the reverse of this, which is considerably earlier, dating to the third century BC, and which is written not in Oscan but in archaic Latin. This seems to represent a reversion from Latin back to Oscan as the language of the political class and is a probable indication of a disaffection from Rome and reaffirmation of Oscan identity during the period leading up to the Social War.]

323. *CIL* 1^2.590

. . . and nobody shall take by fraud or steal any money which belongs, or will belong, to this *municipium*, whether public or sacred or used for sacred purposes, or do anything to assist the occurrence of such a fraud or theft; nor shall he deliberately damage public property by fraud or maladministration of public accounts. Anyone who acts in this way will incur a fine of four times the amount involved, and will be condemned to pay this money to the *municipium*, and can be sued or prosecuted for this amount by any magistrate of the *municipium*.

With regard to the *quattuorviri* and *aediles* first created by this charter, whichever of them have come to Tarentum must, after the promulgation of this charter, take steps, within the 20 days following their arrival in Tarentum, whereby he will stand as surety for himself; and he must provide sufficient safeguards and securities before the *quattuorviri* as a guarantee that any money belonging to this *municipium*, whether public, sacred, or used for sacred purposes, which passes into his hands during his magistracy will be secured correctly to the *municipium* of Tarentum, and that he will submit an account of this in whatever manner the senate shall decide. And this *quattuorvir* to whom such guarantees shall be given, shall accept these and see that the matter is entered in the public accounts. Moreover, anyone who holds an assembly for the election of *duoviri* or aediles shall, before any candidate at this assembly is declared to be elected by a majority of the *curiae*, accept satisfactory securities from this candidate, as a guarantee that any money belonging to this *municipium*, whether public, sacred, or used for sacred purposes, which passes into his hands during his magistracy will be secured correctly to the *municipium* of Tarentum, and that he will submit an account of this in whatever manner the senate shall decide and that he will also see that the matter is entered in the public accounts. With regard to anyone to whom any business in the *municipium* has been publicly assigned by senatorial decree, or who has undertaken any public business, or who has spent or received any public money, it will be the duty of the person to whom such business has been given, or who has publicly transacted such business or who has spent or received public money, to give and submit an account of this to the senate in good faith within the ten days following the decree issued by the senate of this *municipium*.

Everyone who is, or will be, a decurion of the *municipium* of Tarentum, or who has declared his vote in the senate of this *municipium*, will in good faith own a house of his own roofed with no less than 1,500 tiles, in the city of Tarentum or within the territory of this *municipium*. Any of these men who does not possess his own house, or who has bought such a house or received one by formal transfer in order to fraudulently evade this law, will be liable to pay the sum of 5,000 sesterces to the *municipium* of Tarentum for each year of the offence.

Nobody shall unroof or demolish or destroy any house within the *municipium* of Tarentum without a decree of the senate, unless he intends to restore such a house to its previous state. Anyone acting contrary to this regulation shall be liable to pay to the *municipium* a sum of money equal to the value of the house and may be sued for that sum by any person who wishes. The magistrate who collects such fines will pay one half into the public treasury; he may spend the other half on the public games he will give during his magistracy, or if he wishes to spend it on a public monument to himself, it will be legal for him to do so without risk of incurring a punishment.

If any *quattuorvir*, *duumvir* or aedile wishes, for the public good of the *municipium* and within the territory belonging to the municipium, to make, lay out, alter, build or pave any roads, gutters or sewers, it will be legal for them to do this provided that no injury is done to private persons.

Anyone who owes money to the *municipium* of Tarentum and is a citizen of the *municipium* but has not been *duumvir* or aedile during the previous six years shall be allowed to move away from the municipium of Tarentum without risk of personal punishment.

[*c.*88–62 BC. Tarentum. Inscription on a bronze tablet (originally the ninth in a long series) containing part of the municipal charter of Tarentum. This was the formal constitution drawn up for the city as part of the process of municipalization of Italy after the Social War. It replaced the institutions of both the Greek city and the Gracchan colony founded there in 123 BC. This section of the code is principally concerned with safeguards for conduct of the city's financial affairs and penalties for fraud and peculation by public officials.]

324. *CIL* I².593

Nobody in *municipia*, colonies, *praefecturae* or *fora* or *conciliabula* of Roman citizens who is a *duumvir* or *quattuorvir* or holds a magistracy or powers under any other name by the vote of those who belong to any *municipium*, colony, *praefectura* or *forum* or *conciliabulum*, is to enrol anyone in that *municipium*, colony, *praefectura* or *forum* or *conciliabulum* in the senate or decurions or *conscripti* or enrol in replacement or co-opt or see that they are read out, except in place of somebody who has died or been condemned or has confessed that it is not legal under this law for him to be a senator or decurion or *conscriptus* there. . . .

No one who is, or will be, less than 30 years of age after the next Kalends of January but one, is to stand for, or accept, or hold, the office of *duovir* or *quattuorvir* or any other magistracy in a *municipium* or colony or *praefectura*, unless he has served three campaigns on horseback in a legion or six on foot in a legion and he has served those campaigns in camp or in a province for the greater part of each of these years, or two campaigns of six months in each year which it may be appropriate to count for him instead of each yearly one . . . or unless he has exemption from military duty by statute or plebiscite or treaty, in which case it may not be appropriate for him to serve against his will; nor must anyone who practises the trade of crier or usher or undertaker stand for, or accept, or hold, the office of *duovir* or *quattuorvir* or any other magistracy in a *municipium* or colony or *praefectura* while he practises any of these, nor is he to be a senator or decurion or *conscriptus* there, nor is he to offer his opinion; anyone of those who are listed above who has acted contrary to these rules, is to be condemned to pay 50,000 sesterces to the people, and there is to be a lawsuit for that amount by anyone who wishes. . . .

In any *municipia*, colonies or *praefecturae* of Roman citizens which are, or will be, in Italy, anyone in these *municipia*, colonies or *praefecturae* who holds the highest magistracy or highest office at the time when a censor or any other magistrate holds a census of the people at Rome, within the following 60 days of his knowing that a census is being held at Rome, he will hold a census of all his fellow *municipes*, colonists or people who live in the *praefectura*; and he is to receive under oath from them their *nomina*, their *praenomina*, their fathers or patrons, their tribes, their *cognomina*, how many years old each of them is, and a list of their property, according to the schedule of the census which has been published at Rome by whoever is about to hold the census of the people; and he must ensure that this is all entered into the public records of the *municipium*; and he must send these books by envoys, whom the majority of the decurions or *conscripti* have decided should be despatched and sent for this purpose at the time when the matter was discussed, to those who hold the census in Rome; and he is to ensure that when there are more than 60 days left before the day on which the person holding the census at Rome ends the census of the people, [the envoys] should approach him and present the books of the *municipium*, colony or *praefectura*; and the censor, or any other magistrate who is conducting the census of the people, must, within five days of being approached by the envoys of the *municipium*, colony or *praefectura*, accept the books of the census which the envoys have given him without any wrongful deceit; and he must ensure that the things which have been written down there are entered from these books into the public records, and that those records are stored in the same place as the other public records in which the census of the people is written down. . . .

[First century BC. Heraklea. Extracts from the Table of Heraklea, a digest of extracts from Roman municipal legislation. There is no agreed date for the inscription, and some of the clauses appear to be of different dates. All are probably later than 89 BC, and many appear to be of Caesarian date.[24]]

Roman magistrates and pre-Roman survivals

325. *ILLRP* 576

M. Marius, M. F. Praetor by the decision of the senate.

[First century BC. Cumae. Funerary inscription, which apparently shows that the chief magistracy of Cumae was the praetorship, instead of the duovirate, which became current by the first century AD. There is much debate over the provenance and significance of this text, but if correct, this would represent a Latinized survival of the Oscan/Campanian office of *meddix*.[25]]

326. *CIL* 10.6105

L. Cemoleius L. F., L. Statius L. F. and Q. Paccius M. F., the aediles, undertook the construction of the city gates by the decision of the senate, and paid for them.

[Early first century BC. Formiae.]

327. *ILLRP* 675

L. Mummius L. F. and C. Manlius C. F. praetors and *duoviri* for the games undertook the construction of two towers on the decision of the senate.

[First century BC. Telesia.]

Roman control: *praefecti,* curators and senatorial supervision

328. *ILS* 910

M. Herrenius M. F. Rufus, of the tribe Maecia, *Praefectus Capuam Cumas*

[First century BC. Alsium, Etruria. This represents the only epigraphic occurrence of the office of *Praefectus Capuam Cumas*, who supervised the cities of Roman Campania.]

329. *CIL* 14.2922

To T. Flavius Germanus, T. F.: overseer of the most fortunate second triumph against the Germans of the Emperor Caesar Lucius Aurelius Commodus Augustus; honoured by the same emperor with the most illustrious priesthood of *pontifex minor*; procurator of the 5 per cent inheritance tax; procurator of the imperial estate office; procurator of the Great Games; procurator of the Morning Games; procurator of the *vici*, with additional responsibility for paving streets in two regions of the city; procurator for the inheritance tax in Umbria, Etruria, Picenum and Campania; *curator alimentarum* in Lucania, Bruttium, Calabria and Apulia; curator of public works and religious buildings in good repair; aedile; *duovir*; *flamen* of the deified Augustus; *duovir quinquennalis*; patron of the colony. [Dedicated to] an incomparable patron by Cerdo, his freedman, together with Flavius Maximinus, Germanus and Rufinus, his sons, who are honoured with equestrian status.

[Late second century AD. Praeneste. Epitaph with details of equestrian career, which included a number of high level procuratorships as well as municipal offices. Germanus was also chosen as patron of Praeneste.]

330. *CIL* 10.482

To M. Tullius M. F. Cicero, of the tribe Maecia, *Eques Romanus*, member of the Laurentes and Lavinates, Patron of the Colony, *Curator* of the cities of Volcei, Atina, Accerentum, Velia, Buxentum and Tegianum, a man of the highest integrity. . . .

[Third century AD. Paestum. Epitaph of M. Tullius Cicero. Despite the name, the Paestan *Tullii Cicerones* were not directly descended from the orator, but possibly from one of his freedmen. The order of *Laurens Lavinas* was a priesthood at Rome.]

331. *Digest* 1.12.1

According to a rescript of the deified emperor Severus addressed to Fabius Cilo, the *Praetor Urbanus*, the *Praetor Urbanus* has control over all crimes, not only

those committed within the city, but also those committed outside the city in Italy.
. . . Therefore any crime committed within the city is considered to be under the
jurisdiction of the *Praetor Urbanus*; likewise, any crime committed within 100
miles is considered to be under the jurisdiction of the *Praetor Urbanus*; any crime
committed beyond the 100th milestone is outside the jurisdiction of the *Praetor
Urbanus* . . .

332. Tacitus, *Annals* 1.78–9

On the ½ per cent auction tax which was introduced after the civil wars and
which was disliked by the people, Tiberius decreed that the military treasury
needed these revenues. . . . Next, a discussion was brought forward in the senate
by Arruntius and Ateius about whether the flooding of the Tiber should be mod-
erated by diverting the streams and lakes which fed into it. Representations from
municipia and *coloniae* were heard, the Florentines pleading that Clanis should
not be diverted from its usual route into the Arnus, something which would be of
great detriment to them. The case of the Interamnates was similar: the most fertile land in Italy would be ruined if the river Nar (as was proposed) was spread
out in small channels. Nor were the Reatini quiet about Lake Velinus, which if
obstructed at its entry into the Nar, would flood the surrounding area. . . .
Whether because of the petitions of the *coloniae* or the difficulties of the work, or
superstition, a proposal by Piso was carried by the senate that nothing should be
changed.

[AD 15. Senatorial and imperial administration of Italy. The passage implies that
financial questions were of more interest to the emperor than routine public
works. It also illustrates the working relationship between Rome and the Italian
municipia and *coloniae*. The individuals concerned are Cn. Ateius Capito, L.
Arruntius and Cn. Calpurnius Piso.]

333. Tacitus, *Annals* 3.31

The same Corbulo, complaining that many roads in Italy were broken and im-
passable because of fraudulent contractors or negligent magistrates, willingly
offered to undertake the prosecution of the matter; this produced less benefit to
the public than damage to many reputations and fortunes by the many convic-
tions and forced sales.

[AD 21. Concern for failure of the infrastructure of communications in Italy. This
surfaces at regular intervals in the sources for imperial Italy. Roads were clearly a
source of imperial anxiety and required both supervision and central finance to
guarantee an adequate state of repair. Augustus (Nos 213, 360) encouraged the
Roman elite to invest in road repairs, but this seems to have fallen on deaf ears.]

Divisions within the city: Pagi and Vici

334. *ILLRP* 715 (= *CIL* 1.678, *CIL* 10.3778, *ILS* 3397)

T. Iunius N. F., C. Numoleius Cn. F., M. Fisius M. F., M. Fufius L. F., C. Tittius C. F., Q. Monnius N. F., D. Roscius Q. L. Lintio, D. Iteius Cn. L., M. Valerius M. L., Q. Fulvius Fulviae L., P. Pactumeius C. L., L. Pomponius C. L. These magistrates of Castor and Pollux built a wall and *pluteum* and held games, in the consulship of Q. Servilius and C. Atilius.

[106 BC. Capua.]

335. *ILLRP* 719 (= *CIL* 1.628, 10.3772, *ILS* 6302).

The Pagus Herculaneus decided, ten days before the festival of *Terminalia*, that the *magistri* of Jove Compagus should build a portico for the *pagus* at their own expense, according to the law of the *pagus* arbitrated by Cn. Laetorius C. F., the *magister* of the *pagus*, and that the *magistri* of Jove Compagus should have a [reserved] seat in the theatre, provided that they have given games.

    L. Aufustius L. L. Strato, C. Antonius M. L. Nico, Cn. Avius Cn. L. Agathocles, C. Blossi M. L. Protemus, M. Ramnius P. L. Diopantus, T. Sulpicius P. Q.Pu. L., Q. Novius Q. L. Protemus., M. Paccius M. L. Philemus., M. Licculeius M. L. Philinus, Cn. Hordeionius Cn. L. Euphemio, A. Pollius P. L. Alexander, N. Munnius N. L. Antiochus.

    In the consulship of C. Coelius C. F. Caldus and [L.] Domitius Cn. F. Ahenobarbus.

[94 BC. Capua. Both these inscriptions belong to a series from Capua, set up by boards of magistrates known collectively as the Magistri Campani, who took over the day to day running of Capua after its civic administration was dismantled in 200 BC. Most of them refer to the building of temples and public buildings and to the provision of public entertainment. The boards are equally composed of free men and freedmen, many of whose names suggest they were slaves of eminent Capuan families. The second of the two examples seems to tie the boards of *magistri* to specific *pagi*, of which only the Pagus Herculaneus is attested.[26]]

336. *CIL* 11.3040

P. Sergius P. F. Rufus and T. Braetius T. F. Rufus, magistrates, for the second time, of the Pagus Stellatinus, undertook the construction of a temple and statues at their own expense.

[Augustan. From territory of Velletri.]

337. Ulpian, *Digest* 50.15.4

The censorial formula warns that the lands should be registered in the census in this manner: the name of the farm and its owner: in what city and what *pagus* it is located: and what are the nearest neighbours.

338. *CIL* 10.1283

Sacred to Augustus. The cult association of the Laurinienses restored this at their own expense.

[First century AD. Nola. Altar set up by the *cultores* of the Pagus Lauriniensis.]

339. *CIL* 10.924

. . . the *ministri* of the Pagus Augusta Felix Suburbanus first set this up, in the consulship of Ti. Claudius Nero and C. Calpurnius Piso.

[4 BC. Pompeii. Dedication of a monument, possibly a statue, by the *ministri* of the *pagus*.]

Municipal career structures and the political process

340. *CIL* 10.479

Q. Ceppius Q. F. Maec. Longinus, . . . *duumvir* designate, who lived 20 years. Set up by Q. Ceppius Callimachus, his father, and Aviana, his mother.

[Probably first century AD. Paestum. Latin epitaph of a man who had been elected *duumvir* but not yet taken up office. The age of Ceppius illustrates the extent to which the normal age qualifications for holding municipal office could be waived, either to accommodate the sons of powerful families or to compensate for a declining number of the decurial class or a dearth of suitable candidates. In some cities, offices were held more than once, for similar reasons [No. 341].]

341. Mingazzini, *ASMG* 1 (1954)

Cornelius L. F. Rom. Gemellus, *duovir* twice, quaestor, *quattuorvir iure dicundo* twice, *gymnasiarchos*, *quattuorvir iure dicundo* for a third time.

[Late first century BC. Velia. Commemorative inscription for a magistrate who had held multiple offices, including the Greek post of *gymnasiarchos*.]

342. *ILS* 2688

To Sex. Aulienus Sex. F. An., *primuspilus* twice, military tribune, *praefectus armatorum*, *praefectus castrum* of the emperor Caesar Augustus and Tiberius Caesar Augustus, prefect of the fleet, *praefectus fabrum*, *duovir* at Venafrum and Forum Julii, *Flamen of* Augustus; [set up by] Nedymus and Ganymede, his freedmen.

[Mid-first century AD. Venafrum.]

343. *ILS* 5531

Cn. Satrius Cn. F. Rufus, *quattuorvir iure dicundo*, added panelled ceilings to the basilicas, added iron to the rafters, faced them in stone and enclosed them with a faced step: For the duovirate: 6,000 sesterces; For the supply of the legions: 3,450 sesterces; for the rebuilding of the temple of Diana: 6,200 sesterces; for the victory games of Augustus Caesar: 7,750 sesterces.

[Early first century AD. Iguvium. Accounts for building activities by a magistrate and allowances for specified purposes.]

344. *ILS* 2243

M. Billienus M. F. Rom. Actiacus, of the 11th legion, was settled in the colony after the end of the naval battle, and chosen as a decurion by his unit . . .

[Augustan. Ateste. This gives some insight into how a veteran colony could operate. It makes it clear that the troops were settled according to their military units, keeping the same units together, and that they had a significant group vote in local politics, at least to the extent of being able to adlect their own decurions.]

345. *ILS* 6361b

To M. Holoconius M. F. Rufus, military tribune chosen by the people, *duovir iure dicundo* for five years, *duovir quinquennalis* twice, priest of Augustus Caesar, patron of the colony.

346. *ILS* 6362

To M. Holoconius Celer, *duovir iure dicundo*, *quinquennalis* designate, priest of Augustus.

[First century AD. Pompeii. Two of a group of three inscriptions from the theatre extolling the Holoconii brothers, who paid for the construction of the building (cf. Chapter 9).]

347. *CIL* 10.793

A. Clodius A. F. Flaccus and Numerius Arcaeus Num. F. Arellianus Celadus, *duoviri iure dicundo*, on the calibration of measures, by decree of the decurions.

[Augustan. Pompeii. Inscription on a *mensa ponderaria*, a device for calibrating weights and measures. It was a flat surface with five cavities for checking the size of weights. It is of particular interest as it was originally inscribed with the names of Oscan measures, which had been partially erased, and the size of the cavities have been altered.]

348. *CIL* 10.846

N. Popidius N. F. Celsinus restored the temple of Isis, which had collapsed due to an earthquake, from its foundations at his own expense. On account of this generosity, the decurions gratefully enrolled him, in his sixth year, in their order.

[First century AD. Pompeii. Inscription from the Temple of Isis. The very young age of Celsinus points to the likelihood that he was merely a "front" for the honour, and the benefaction which occasioned it. His father, Popidius Ampliatus, is known from other inscriptions[27] and was almost certainly a wealthy freedman who could not join the *Ordo* in his own right.]

349. Cicero, *Pro Sulla* 60–62

Now, with reference to this charge that Sulla compelled the Pompeians to join that conspiracy and nefarious crime, I cannot understand what this means. Does it seem to you that the Pompeians conspired? Who ever said this, or was there even the smallest suspicion of such a thing? He says "Sulla divided them [the Pompeians] from the colonists, so that having caused this dissension and discord, he could get the town into his power through the Pompeians." First of all, the whole disagreement between the Pompeians and the colonists was revealed to the patrons when it had already become endemic and been so for many years; secondly, when the matter was looked into by the patrons, the others did not differ in any respect from the opinions of Sulla; lastly, the colonists themselves knew that Sulla was not defending the Pompeians more than he was defending them. And this, gentlemen of the jury, you can understand from this great crowd of colonists, most honourable men, who are present on behalf of this patron, the defender and guardian of the colony, who, if they are unable to keep him unharmed in wealth and reputation, wish to help and preserve him, through you, in this misfortune by which he is afflicted. The Pompeians, who have also been summoned by [the prosecutors] to stand trial, are present with equal enthusiasm; although they differ about *ambulatio* and voting, they agree about the safety of the community. Nor does it seem to me that we should pass in silence over this achievement of P. Sulla, because, though he himself founded the colony and although the needs of the state came between the interests of the colonists and those of the Pompeians, he is so popular and well thought of by both sides that he is seen not as dispossessing one group but as establishing both.

[The interpretation of this passage hinges on the meaning of *ambulatio*, apparently a covered structure similar to a portico, the first example of which was constructed by the Sullan colonists on land which may have been misappropriated, and which thus became an issue of controversy at Pompeii.[28]]

350. *CIL* 1².1640

L. Aquitius, a good man: colonists, I ask you to elect him as *duovir*.

[First century BC. Pompeii. Electoral graffito. The colonists called on here are Sullan veterans.]

351. *CIL* 4.768

I ask you to elect M. Epidius Sabinus as *duovir iure dicundo*. He is worthy. Vote for the defender of the *colonia* on the decision of the sacred judge, Suedius Clemens, and the consent of the decurial order, because of his merits and his probity, and because he is worthy to the community. Sabinus the *dissignator* does so with applause.

[Pompeii. Electoral graffito, dating to AD 70–79. This text is somewhat later and more detailed than No. 350, and has a more specific historical context. T. Suedius Clemens was an agent of tribunician rank sent by Vespasian to adjudicate in a property dispute between the *colonia* of Pompeii and a number of private individuals.[29] In this case, and several others,[30] he clearly involved himself in the elections. Epidius' role in the dispute, if any, is not known, but the phrase *defensor coloniae* might conceivably indicate that he represented the interests of the city on that occasion. His supporter, Sabinus, is a *dissignator*, a theatre usher, whose job was to supervise seating arrangements according to social rank.]

352. Cicero, *Letters to his friends* 13.11

. . . I do not doubt that you know not only which *municipium* I come from but also how diligently I look after my fellow citizens of Arpinum. All their income and resources, from which they maintain their sacred rites and the upkeep of buildings and sacred places, lie in rents from property which they own in Gaul. To collect the rents owing from the tenants and oversee and administer the entire business, we have sent out as envoys the Roman knights Q. Fufidius, Q. F., M. Faucius, M. F., and Q. Mamercius, Q. F. I ask you, on account of our friendship, to take care of the matter and see that the business of the *municipium* is transacted as smoothly and quickly as possible with your help, and to treat the men whose names I have written with the greatest courtesy and consideration, as is your nature. You will add some worthy men to your friendship and your benefaction will bind to you a most grateful city, and I shall be even more grateful because although I am always accustomed to care for my fellow citizens, this year I have a particular care and duty. For I wanted my son, my nephew and M. Caesius, a man who is a great friend of mine, to be elected aediles this year, to order the affairs of the city; For in our city, it is the custom to appoint this magistracy and no other.

[46 BC. Plea to Brutus by Cicero on behalf of Arpinum to expedite the collection of rents from municipal properties in Cisalpine Gaul.]

CHAPTER NINE

Municipal Italy 2:
the social structure of the city

In many respects, the social structure of the Roman city and the way in which it functioned is indivisible from its political nature. Amongst the elite, it is very difficult to draw a distinction between the political aspects of their behaviour and purely social forms of interaction. Friendship (*amicitia*) involved political and economic obligation just as much as it implied moral and emotional bonds; similarly, *inimicitia* was not simply a case of falling out but entailed a highly ritualized and public set of actions which affected all areas of life – as in the case of Oppianicus [No. 402] in which public disapproval manifested itself by excluding him from all forms of social and economic activity including the daily round of salutations and perambulations by which inhabitants of the Roman city visibly signalled their position in society. Basic forms of vertical social contact and interaction, such as euergetism or patronage, make this integration of social and political, private and public, still more obvious. Patronage was a social bond of which one aspect was a requirement to give political support, while public munificence was expected (and sometimes vocally insisted on) by the populace as a basic form of social exchange, but one in which the political implications were also recognized.

The social structure of the Roman city was also notable for its relative flexibility. There was a strict legal division between Roman citizens and non-citizens, but even this could be breached by manumission of slaves and absorption, after one generation, of the families of freedmen. Within the citizen body, status was based on wealth and birth, but a family could very easily fluctuate in status over several generations. An economic misfortune or the necessity of dividing an estate between a large number of surviving offspring could send even a family of equestrian or decurial rank below the census level for their class, as could political disgrace or certain types of criminal conviction. Relative status of families within the senatorial or decurial orders depended on success in maintaining a steady grip on high office within the *municipium* or at Rome over several generations. Similarly, unexpected economic gain, sometimes with a helping hand from a patron, could elevate a family to a higher rank, and the phenomenon of the upwardly mobile freedman, who gains wealth, establishes his own status through the *ordo augustalis* and sets his descendants on the road to membership of the decurial order, is well known. Broadly, this system of limited but perceptible mobility held good until the middle of the second century AD, when the distinctions between the *honestiores* – the elite – and the *humiliores* – everyone else – became more crystallized and restricted social movement.[1]

The other feature which will be immediately obvious about Roman society is that full legal rights and all political participation were restricted to men. Women were by no means intended to be invisible or anonymous, as they were in Athens. Greek authors regarded Italian (and particularly Etruscan) women as almost scandalously liberated. Roman history has a strong tradition of powerful and influential women, but these were the exception rather than the rule, and were virtually all the wives, mothers or daughters of important men, as were most of the female benefactors included in this chapter. Women could participate at the very highest level of civic life, but only in certain well-defined spheres, and mostly as part of a family effort, not as independent initiators.[2] Because of the restrictions of space, women and their role in society will inevitably play only a small part in this discussion of Italian society, although recent research on literary and epigraphic evidence, as well as on iconography and the spatial dynamics of the ancient city are beginning to open up interesting new perspectives on Roman women.

One of the features of the generation immediately after the enfranchisement of Italy was the emergence of men of Italian origin as members of the Roman elite. Although very few reached the nobility (Cicero being a notable exception), more became senators, and a very large number attained equestrian rank. Both literary sources and epigraphic evidence from the great trading centres of the eastern empire attest to the prominent role of Italians in trade and finance, and their widespread involvement as *publicani*. At this stage, there was a clear tension between local and Roman identity for many Italians, clearly demonstrated both in Cicero's own sentiments and in the backgrounds of the Italians whom he defended in the law courts. By the Augustan period, however, members of the Italian nobility were becoming much better integrated into the senatorial order, their position secured by the centrality of Italy to the ideology of the regime and by the weakening of the old republican *gentes*, in both numbers and influence. During the first century AD, the position of the Italian elite was secure, and the issue now was the increasing number of provincial senators.

This gradual incorporation of a proportion of municipal families into the senatorial elite had important implications for their native municipalities. Although the intensity of debate about identity which is perceptible in Cicero's works is no longer there, it is clear that senators still felt a high degree of attachment to their native cities, and that a local family made good could ensure protection for the interests of a city and a steady flow of gifts and patronage. Many commemorative inscriptions attest to prestigious careers in the senate or as imperial administrators carved out by Italians during the first and second centuries AD, and many also allude to the role these men played as benefactors or patrons of their cities [Nos 393–4]. More detailed evidence is available from the letters of Pliny, who maintained a strong sense of attachment to his native city of Comum, and who makes frequent reference to his benefactions to the town and to his role in assisting fellow-citizens in their careers and private lives. His benefactions to individuals included gifts or loans of money to secure the equestrian census for friends, assistance in finding husbands for the daughters of friends, and gifts of tenanted farms, made as a form of pension, to retired members of his household. Gifts to the community were many and various, including the purchase of a Corinthian bronze as a gift for the temple of Jupiter, the endowment of a library and a school, and the establishment of an alimentary scheme. It is abundantly clear that local identities were still important to the elite of Roman Italy, and that even highly placed individuals such as Pliny, who had property throughout Italy and patronal obligations to many cities, were deeply attached to their places of origin.

The extent to which senators relied on a local power base, and the extent to which their aspiration shaped the development of communities is illustrated by research carried out in Samnium.[3] Here, there is a marked shift in the first century BC from elite activity centred on sanctuaries to elite activity centred on cities, reflecting a general trend to prioritize the new Romanized settlements over the indigenous ones. Epigraphic and archaeological evidence points to the construction of Roman building types – fora, temples, baths, theatres, amphitheatres, aqueducts, etc. – funded by elite families, either as private benefactions or as the munificence expected of a magistrate. This coincides with changes in patterns of land distribution which indicate an increasing tendency for land ownership to be concentrated in the hands of a smaller number of people, and with the emergence of Roman senators of Samnite origin. These three phenomena, together with onomastic evidence for senatorial families in Samnium, point to a close relationship between concentration of economic resources, munificence, and the emergence of a group of senatorial families. It is not altogether clear whether the munificence was part of the process of social enhancement or the result of activity by people who had already reached senatorial rank and, like Pliny, were concerned for the status of their home cities, but what is clear is that this phenomenon was important in the Romanization of the region and the related process of urbanization. Given the great social and economic differences between regions, it is unclear how far this model can be used more generally as a pattern for connections between elite behaviour and Romanization. The emergence of senators of municipal origin was, in itself, a highly regional phenomenon. By far the greatest number come from Augustan *Regio* I – Latium and Campania – with a moderate number from Etruria and Samnium, and very few from anywhere south of Campania. The chronological distribution is similar, with the vast majority of Italian senators of the first century BC coming from Latium and a gradual broadening of geographical origin during the first century AD.[4] However, there does seem to be a broad correlation between levels of urbanization and Romanization in a region, and the number of senatorial families which it produced.[5]

Patronage and euergetism, no matter what their source, are vital concepts to our understanding of how a Roman city functioned. At most levels of Roman society, possession of a patron was essential, while possession of clients was an indication of one's status – the greater their number and the more important they were as individuals, the more greatly the status of the patron was enhanced. The role of a patron and the duties of a client could vary considerably according to context, but the root of the relationship was that the patron had an obligation to protect the interests of the client while the client was obliged to support those of the patron. Freed slaves were obliged to take their former owner as patron and were under a number of legally specified obligations which did not apply to clients of free birth. At a higher social level, the inequalities of such a relationship were disguised by the language of *amicitia*, but obligations were present, nevertheless. Pliny, for instance, drops broad hints to Romatius Firmus that he should bear in mind that he owes his equestrian rank to Pliny, and behave accordingly [No. 399]. The role of patron of a *municipium* or of a *colonia* was similar but rather more specific. The duty of the patron nominated by a city was to protect its interests at Rome, and to represent the community in any legal disputes, but it was also expected that he would give gifts and benefactions to the community in return for honours and tokens of gratitude voted to him. There were quite specific restrictions on who could be appointed as a patron. The *Lex Ursonensis* explicitly excludes anyone who holds *imperium* or a magistracy at Rome at the time of appointment and specifies that appointment can only be made if there is a majority of three-quarters of the decurions in favour.[6] An appointment of a municipal patron had to be ratified by the Roman senate, and was usually recorded on a bronze *tabula patronatus*, which would be displayed in the house of the patron [Nos 391–2]. Within these limitations, designed to prevent officeholders from abusing their power to amass a large *clientela*, cities were free to nominate whoever they pleased, although patronage of some cities was hereditary and passed down through the same families. The majority of patrons were men, for the obvious reason that only men could represent the city in the public arena, but some women of high status, often priestesses and always with highly connected male relatives, were chosen [No. 392]. Most patrons were of senatorial rank, or were prominent members of the regional elite, since it was vital to choose someone with influential connections. Local connections were also a prerequisite, although the patron did not necessarily have to come from the city itself. Pliny was patron of Tifernum Tiberinum, an office which went with the estates in the area which he inherited from his uncle in AD 79. In return for the public expressions of honour and support offered by the city, he was obliged to provide some benefit for the community, in this case a temple which he paid for and attended the dedication of [No. 393]. Other duties could involve representing the legal interests of a city, and a patron could also require expressions of support from his clients in his own court cases [Nos 413–7]. The fact that high-ranking patrons could be a valuable source of both protection and munificence made them much sought-after, hence the need for restrictions on over-ambitious senators and the occasional need for attempts to restrain the enthusiasm of potential clients. During his governorship of Cilicia, Cicero actively discouraged cities from honouring him, on the basis that competitive honours, in the form of statues, inscriptions and hero-shrines, were a waste of financial resources [No. 355].

Euergetism is a much more intangible concept, which is easy to recognize but difficult to define, not being codified in Roman law as patronage was. As the Greek terminology suggests, it had its roots in the Hellenistic city, in which the exchange of formal expressions of honour and benefactions to the community became accepted tools of interaction within cities and in international diplomacy. Paul Veyne[7] defines it as "private munificence for the public benefit", and it became an essential means of harnessing elite wealth to provide public amenities and other benefits to the city in a world where there was little in the way of civic bureaucracy to undertake these things on behalf of the state. At the same time, given that elite society in the Hellenistic and Roman worlds was driven by competition for power, honours and status, competitive generosity became an important part of civic life. Games and festivals paid for, or buildings erected, embellished or repaired, could secure enhanced status for oneself or one's family, which could be visibly represented in honorific statues and inscriptions, or in honours and votes of thanks granted by the municipal council. The process involved not just the elite of a particular city, but also important men within the wider region or from elsewhere and as such, was also an instrument of diplomatic relations and of relations with the dominant power, whether this be the Roman senate, the emperor, or a Hellenistic monarch. Some activity of this type was undertaken *ob honorem*, in other words, as part of the specified duties of a magistrate, although this was still at private expense, but much was done as an expression of voluntary generosity on the part of private individuals.[8] Euergetism could also be retrospective, designed to secure the memory of oneself or add to the status of one's family. Testamentary bequests to construct buildings or to provide for a public feast or distribution of food or money to commemorate one's birthday or the anniversary of one's death were very common, so much so that there was a substantial body of law on testamentary bequests to cities and what could be done with them [Nos 385–90].

The status of benefactors varied tremendously, as did the types of benefactions. A chronological and geographical breakdown shows that there are clear differences in forms of euergetism and types of benefactor. During the republic, the evidence available points to a higher level of euergetism *ob honorem* than of private benefactions, and of an emphasis on particular types of building, notably temples and fortifications.[9] As already noted, the late Republic saw a shift in the focus of euergetic activity, away from pre-Roman sites and towards cities, with an emphasis on creating a Romanized urban environment. From the Augustan period onwards, private euergetism became more prevalent than euergetism *ob honorem*, and patterns of building shifted away from provision of temples and city walls to construction of places of public entertainment – baths, theatres and amphitheatres – and the monumentalization of the forum and its associated structures. It is significant that there are extensive regulations governing who could build what and where, controlling speculation and preventing indiscriminate demolition of buildings. It is also true that outsiders regarded the level of building activity in Italy, and particularly in Rome, as worthy of comment [No. 366]. Provision of entirely non-functional items such as statues of prominent individuals, or small hero-shrines, also became prevalent, sometimes as a means of recording an act of generosity such as the provision of games or a public banquet. By the second century AD, the emphasis had shifted away from construction of new structures and towards repair or embellishment of existing ones and more markedly, towards endowment of public banquets and *sportulae*, or of less obvious benefits such as paying for free heating or oil supplies for baths, or even, in one instance, provision of a municipal cemetery [No. 378]. Games and wild beast shows were popular throughout the history of Roman Italy, and a certain level of expenditure on games was often legally required of civic magistrates [No. 323], but these occasions could also be paid for by private benefaction. Frustratingly, much of the evidence for civic benefactors comes from epitaphs or commemorative inscriptions, most of which set out in some detail the honours given by a grateful populace in the way of commemorative statues, conspicuous tombs and funerals at public expense, and sometimes commemorative dinners or *sportulae* endowed by the heirs, but very little about the benefactions themselves. Most of our evidence for acts of munificence comes from individual building inscriptions and records of dinners and *sportulae*, but this does not enable us to piece together the pattern of munificence over an entire career. The rare exceptions to this are honorific decrees by city councils, which sometimes give details of the generosity in return for which thanks is being expressed or honours awarded.

There were some attempts to work out a morality of munificence. Cicero inveighs against the profligacy of those who spend their money on ephemera such as games and feasts which are designed only for their own selfish ends, and draws up a list of activities which can be termed genuinely munificent rather than merely extravagant [No. 353]. These include provision of dowries for daughters of indigent friends, payment of friends' debts and ransoming of captives. On a similar note, Pliny congratulates himself on being a better class of benefactor for Comum because he has endowed a library, a school and an alimentary scheme rather than spent the money on games [No. 356]. Other views of the process were more basic. A Greek horoscope [No. 354] explicitly points out the nexus between wealth, munificence and power, something that the rationalizations of Pliny and Cicero conveniently gloss over. There was also a high degree of social pressure and expectation which ensured that adequate levels of munificence were maintained. On one occasion when the family of a wealthy centurion was not sufficiently liberal with funeral games, the citizens of Pollentia, his *municipium*, confiscated the corpse and refused to allow the funeral to proceed until the relatives had done what was expected of them in the way of public entertainment [No. 192].

Benefactors came in all shapes and sizes, and the *ethos* of competitive munificence percolated well down the social scale, but the principal source of euergetism was the municipal elite or the patrons of the city. A rich patron or a prominent senator with local roots could be a valuable source of munificence, but then decurions and their families who were competing for status within a single community were also very active. Naturally, most patrons were male, but a number of high status females also turn up. Sextia Kana of Cumae was honoured by donation of a tomb at public expense in recognition of her (unspecified) benefactions to the community [No. 381], and one of the most prominent benefactors at Pompeii was the priestess Eumachia [Nos 364–5]. It is, however, significant that the vast majority of these women were not acting independently but in conjunction with, and for the political benefit of, their male relatives.[10] Surprisingly, perhaps the most obvious source of benefactions, the emperor and his family, does not feature as highly as one might expect. As noted in Chapter 6, imperial munificence tended to be directed towards disaster relief, projects which would benefit the city of Rome and the overall infrastructure of Italy, or to large constructions such as aqueducts which might fall outside the administrative and financial scope of a single community. One of the largest and most systematic imperial schemes in Italy was the *alimenta* set up by Trajan, but this was not an imperial benefaction as such. It was a scheme with a certain amount of imperial capital to initiate it, which was designed to stimulate investment from within the communities in which these foundations were based, and encourage emulation by private donors. Whatever the original intention, the result seemed to be a child-support scheme which focused not on the poorer and lowest populated regions of Italy, where such an initiative was most needed, but on those areas with the strongest, richest and most active urban elite.[11] There were exceptions to this, particularly if the emperor or a member of his family had a specific connection with a particular city, but this was broadly the trend.[12]

What is very noticeable within a given city is that the *ethos* of competitive munificence percolates a considerable way down the social scale. Organizations within the overall civic body, such as the *pagi* or *vici*, the *Augustales* or any of the *collegia*, show much the same sort of process. *Augustales* are regularly mentioned in inscriptions as having given a gift to the community, in the form of a building or money for a public celebration, or as having made a gift of some sort to the *Augustales* as a body, and conversely, as being the recipients of decrees of thanks or of civic honours voted by the city council.

The structure of urban society in Roman Italy was both deeply hierarchical and, to some extent, flexible. Political, social and economic power was concentrated in the hands of an elite, often a relatively small one, namely the decurial class, which was defined by law as requiring qualifications of birth (free) and wealth (an annual income of 100,000 sesterces). Other members of society were linked to this group by reciprocal ties of patronage or bonds of slavery and legal dependence.[13] Contacts within the group were maintained through kinship – e.g.

intermarriage or adoption – or through bonds of ritualized hospitality or friend-ship, which implied certain well defined roles and mutual obligations. Infringe-ment of the accepted norms of social conduct could result in total exclusion within the peer group, such as that experienced by Oppianicus at Larinum [No. 402], who was no longer invited to take part in the activities which symbolized social bonds, including witnessing of wills, guardianship proceedings, dinners, etc. Some of the sanctions used against him are obviously motivated by the need to exclude someone untrustworthy from financial transactions, but others, such as the refusal to dine with him or to greet him in public, belong purely to the sphere of social interaction. Roman life was lived very largely in public and for a member of the urban elite, the details of the daily round – of who called upon whom; who was invited to dinner, with whom and in what order of seating and service; who strolled around the forum with whom; how many clients, and of what rank, one was seen with in public, and who deferred to one in public greet-ings – were a highly visible means of demonstrating one's position in the local pecking order. Being treated with affection and familiarity by someone important in public was a sign of social advancement; isolation of the sort inflicted on Oppianicus was a public and humiliating sign of disgrace.

Although municipal society in Italy was flexible to some extent, it was very far from being open. The basis of one's rank was still free birth, Roman citizenship (either by birth or acquisition), and one's census rating. Romans were by no means as polarized as Greeks in their views of outsiders, but they had a healthy sense of their own Roman and Italian identity and its superiority. Other ethnic groups are frequently reduced to crude stereotypes in literature – Gauls were drunkards but courageous, Greeks were clever but verbose and impractical, Orientals were lascivious and untrustworthy, and so on.[14] By the principate, both Rome and the larger cities of Italy had a sizeable population of non-Italians, some of whom had migrated voluntarily for various reasons, and many who had been transported as slaves. These were, by and large, tolerated with more or less good-will, although some were easier to assimilate than others. There are periodic signs of imperial distaste for certain groups who were thought to be particularly turbu-lent or disruptive in their behaviour and customs, as when Tiberius deported a group of Jews and Egyptians from Italy [No. 301], but no systematic rejection of aliens. In any case, those who arrived as slaves could be absorbed into the citizen body. Manumission by a Roman citizen conferred citizenship, although with some strings attached. The freedman or freedwoman was still legally bound to his or her patron in a number of ways, but full, unrestricted, membership of the citi-zen body was available to any children born after manumission.

The foundation of a veteran colony also placed the *onus* on a city to absorb a large group of incomers, some of non-Italian origin, although all would have been substantially Romanized. This created the added difficulty of coming to terms with the profound demographic changes and shifts in balance of power within the community which such a foundation entailed. As described in the pre-vious chapter, veterans, particularly those at or above the rank of centurion, frequently had the means to qualify for the decurial census and thus brought about a change in the composition of the elite.

One of the problems raised by this relatively large pool of freedmen and freed-women with limited citizen rights was how to integrate them into mainstream municipal society without fully admitting them to social and political equality. This was particularly pressing in the case of those who had set up in business, either alone or on behalf of their patron, and gained considerable wealth, as this type of mismatch between economic power and social status could, understand-ably, cause grievances. A number of bodies grew up which could provide a sense of community and a role which conferred status within society for freedmen and even slaves. The most prestigious of these was the *ordo augustalis*, which was composed mainly, although not exclusively, of freedmen.[15] Members were required to be wealthy, and their status is reflected in the fact that in any hierar-chical list of social groups, they are found immediately below the decurions and above the rest of the adult male population [No. 375]. The principal function of the *Magistri*, or *Seviri Augustales*, boards elected from members of the *ordo*, was to administer the imperial cult and its attendant buildings and festivals, but the importance of the *Augustales* ran far beyond this. Like members of the elite, they were expected to indulge in munificence, directed either at the population as a whole or at their own *ordo*. Membership gave not just a stake in society to those without access to political influence but considerable status.

There could be a surprising degree of gradation in the status and role of freed-men in municipal society. At the top of the scale was the imperial freedman, who could wield enormous power and influence, and was often an influential figure and municipal benefactor [No. 419]. As already indicated, *augustales* were also high on the social scale, but there were many other organizations which could confer status and give a stake in society to freedmen of less exalted status. The *magistri* and *ministri* who ran numerous minor cults and organized the activities of the *pagi* were usually freedmen [Nos 313–14, 334–5] or slaves, as were the majority of those involved in the cult of the Magna Mater. All of these associations seem to have been organized on similar lines, often with their own meeting houses, statutes, elected officers and communal gatherings.

The *collegium* was also important to the poorer free born inhabitants of a city. Numerous crafts and trades had their own guilds, run on the lines described above, which provided both a form of social cohesion and some essential services, given that the Roman city was without any of the amenities taken for granted in modern ones. By the second century AD, for instance, it was becoming increas-ingly common for the *collegia fabrorum*, the guilds of builders, to double as the local fire brigade. There was also a growth during the principate of general-purpose *collegia*, the main function of which was to act as social clubs and mutual benevolent societies, granting benefits to subscribing members who needed them. Given the Roman preoccupation with personal commemoration and proper burial, many of them existed ostensibly as funeral societies, which would organize and pay for the burial and commemoration of their subscribers, although they also acted as a social focus for members during their lifetime. Where names of members are listed, the onomastic patterns suggest that the majority of members were freedmen (and sometimes women), with an admixture of slaves and free citizens [Nos 430–32].

Inevitably any introductory study of the social structure of the Italian city can only provide an outline of the most important features of civic life, and the balance of evidence makes it very difficult to do other than concentrate on the male elite. Nevertheless, recent research on Roman society has opened up interesting new perspectives. There is now greater sensitivity to the cultural constraints which dictated patterns of epigraphic evidence and understanding of how to interpret who was recording what, why, and in what manner. There is equally a much greater use of archaeological and iconographic evidence to try to reconstruct the lives of those largely or wholly ignored by the literary sources – women, slaves, the non-elite or rural population, foreigners or conquered groups – and of the techniques of urban geography and town planning to understand urban space and how it shaped society. The principal works giving insight into new techniques for studying ancient society have been included in the bibliography.

Euergetism and the idea of munificence

353. Cicero, *De officiis* 2.55–7

In general, there are two sorts of those people who give on a large scale: one type is extravagant, the other one is generous. The extravagant are those who squander their money on public dinners, handouts of meat amongst the people, gladiatorial games, magnificent spectacles and wild beast shows – vanities of which only a fleeting memory will remain, or none at all – but the generous will use their means to ransom captives from bandits or undertake friends' debts, or help to provide dowries for their daughters, or help them to acquire or augment their property. And I am amazed at what was in Theophrastus' mind in that book which he wrote on wealth; in it there are many fine things but on this he is absurd: for there are many things in praise of magnificence and the appurtenances of popular games and he thinks that the greatest privilege of wealth is the support of such outlay.

354. Neugebauer, O. and Hoesen, H. B. (1959) *Greek horoscopes* No. 97

... later, having gained a legacy and improved his fortunes by careful investments, he became ambitious, dominating and munificent ...

[Although not a specifically Italian example, this extract from a Greek horoscope expresses the confluence of civic munificence with social and political power which was central to the social history of imperial Italy.]

355. Cicero, *Letters to Atticus* 5.21

In return for these favours, by which they [the people of Cyprus and Cilicia] are amazed, I allow no honours to be decreed to me except verbal ones, and I prohibit statues, shrines, chariots, nor do I burden the cities in any other way . . .

[50 BC. Cicero illustrates conflicting views on public honours. Here, he expresses concern for the financial burden on the cities of his province, and asserts the right to refuse honours. The *beneficia* to which he refers are the attempts he has made to curb official corruption and financial impositions by his staff.]

356. Pliny, *Letters* 1.8 (to Pompeius Saturninus)

For I am going to ask you to examine again the speech which I made to my fellow citizens when I dedicated the library at Comum. . . . This will increase my modesty, even if the style itself is slight and simple, because I was impelled to discuss the munificence of my parents as well as my own. . . . From this exercise arose a certain contempt for money. For, while all men seem to be constrained to guard their money by nature, a long and carefully considered love of liberality freed me from the general chains of avarice, and my munificence seemed to be more praiseworthy, because I drew it not from any sudden impulse but from reflection. There was also the consideration that I was not promising games or gladiators but the annual expense of feeding free-born children.

Building and munificence

357. Tacitus, *Annals* 3.72

Around the same time, Lepidus petitioned the senate for permission to reinforce and decorate the basilica of Paulius, a monument of the Aemilii, at his own expense. At that time, public munificence was the custom; Augustus had forbidden neither Taurus, nor Philippus, nor Balbus to use war booty or great wealth to adorn the city for the glory of posterity. Although of only modest wealth, Lepidus followed their example in rebuilding the monument of his ancestors. But when the theatre of Pompey burned down, the emperor promised to rebuild it himself because no one from that family [i.e. the Pompeii] had enough money to restore it, but he retained the name of Pompeius.

[AD 22. There was a continuing presumption in Rome, even after the civil wars, that members of senatorial families would retain responsibility for the upkeep, repair and decoration of the public buildings constructed by their ancestors. However, a contrast is implied between Augustus, who retained the republican practice of allowing grandees to use private wealth or spoils of war for building projects (the first stone theatre, reconstruction of the temple of Hercules Musarum and first stone amphitheatre in Rome, respectively), and the practice of

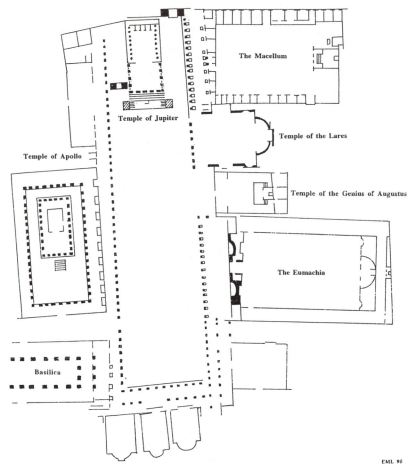

The Macellum

Temple of Jupiter

Temple of the Lares

Temple of Apollo

Temple of the Genius of Augustus

The Eumachia

Basilica

EML 95

9. Pompeii: the forum [c. AD100]

Tacitus' own day. Lepidus apparently had a recognized duty to look after the fabric and decoration of the Basilica Aemilia (constructed by the consul of 50 BC, the grandfather of this particular Lepidus) despite his moderate funds, whereas similar costs to the Pompeii were remitted by Augustus, and by implication, public munificence fell out of fashion entirely at a later date.]

358. Suetonius, *Life of Tiberius* 31

In a similar decision, in which he [Tiberius] allowed the people of Trebia to transfer money left to them for building a new theatre to [pay for] paving the roads, he could not prevent the wishes of the testator from being ratified.

[Suetonius cites several cases of Tiberius being overruled by the senate. Here, he supports the Trebians in their wish to use a legacy for road-building, but is voted down in favour of ratification of the will, which specified the building of a theatre. The passage also illustrates the extent to which Rome, in the form of an imperial decision or *senatusconsultum*, could interfere in the minutiae of civic life.]

359. *CIL* 11.368

The emperor Caesar Domitianus Augustus Germanicus, son of the deified Vespasian, *Pontifex Maximus*, holder of tribunician power for the twelfth time, *imperator* for the twenty-second time, consul 16 times, censor in perpetuity, father of the nation, undertook the construction of this [building].

[AD 93. Latin inscription from Ariminum, from a portico which forms part of a larger public building, apparently paid for by the emperor Domitian.]

360. *ILS* 84

By the senate and people of Rome, in honour of the emperor Caesar Augustus, son of the deified Caesar, *pontifex maximus*, *imperator* seven times, consul seven times and consul designate for an eighth, the Via Flaminia and the other busiest roads in Italy having been built at his behest and at his own expense.

[27 BC. Ariminum. Inscription on an arch over the Via Flaminia. On Augustus' own claims to road building, cf. No. 213.]

361. *CIL* 10.103

Imperator Caesar T. Aelius Hadrianus Antoninus Augustus Pius, *pontifex maximus*, holder of tribunician power for the sixth time, consul for the third time, *pater patriae*, triumphing for the second time, gave water to Colonia Minerva Nervia Augusta Scolacium.

[Second century AD. Scolacium (Calabria). Imperial grant to build an aqueduct for the colony of Scolacium, by Antoninus Pius.]

362. *CIL* 10.123

P. Magius P. F. Iunc[. . .] and Q. Minucius L. F. oversaw the construction of a basilica, by decree of the senate.

Late Republican. Thurii. Building of a basilica by the magistrates and senate.

363. *CIL* 10. 3685

Cn. Lucceius and Cn. Lucceius, father and son, holders of the praetorship, restored the sanctuary of Demeter. Lucceia Cn. F. Polla, who . . . and Lucceia Cn. F. Tertulla . . . restored the temple of Demeter and the buildings and porticoes around the temple from their own money.

[First century AD. Cumae. The Lucceii were a prominent family in the region.[16]]

364. *CIL* 10.810

Eumachia, L. F., public priestess, built this porch, passage and covered portico in honour of Concordia Augusta and to Pietas, at her own expense, in her own name and that of her son M. Numistrius Fronto.

[First century AD. Pompeii.]

365. *CIL* 10.813

In honour of Eumachia, L. F., public priestess, by the [guild of] fullers.

[First century AD. Pompeii.]

366. Strabo, *Geography* 5.3.7

They build continuously, because of building collapses, fires and repeated sales, which also go on continuously. In fact, the repeated sales are intentional collapses, one may say, since they pull down some buildings and put up others in their place. . . .

[Building habits in Rome. Strabo's comments reflect the hazards of urban property, which was notoriously prone to fire and collapse due to poor building techniques, as confirmed by many other authors. The frenetic building activity which he seems to find so strange may be a reflection of the period in which he was writing, which was a period of intense urban renewal at Rome, and in many other cities. Some of this was to repair the damage caused by the civil wars, but other projects were additions to urban amenities or remodelling of existing features.]

367. *ILS* 5759

To M. Volcius M. F. Sabinus, military tribune, for bringing the Aqua Julia to this place at his own expense. By the citizens of Rufrae.

[First century AD. Rufrae.]

368. *ILS* 5638

The Marci Holoconii, Rufus and Celer, built the arcade, platforms and theatre at their own expense.

[First century AD. Pompeii. From a group of three inscriptions from the theatre, relating to its construction by the Holoconii brothers. For the other inscriptions, cf. Chapter 8.]

369. Ehrenburg and Jones, No. 236

M. Vecilius M. F. L. N. Campus, *praefectus fabrum*, military tribune, *duovir iure dicundo*, *pontifex*, built the amphitheatre and its surrounding precinct on his private land and at his own expense in honour of the emperor Caesar Augustus and the colony of Luceria.

[Early first century AD. Luceria. Inscription relating to the building of the amphitheatre as an act of private munificence. Despite the private context, however, it is explicitly linked with the founding of the Augustan colony and expression of loyalty to the emperor.]

"Bread and circuses": Games and *sportulae*

370. Pliny, *Letters* 7.19 (to Caninius Rufus)

You ask my advice about how to ensure that the money, which you have given to our fellow citizens for feasts, is safe after your death. It is an honourable question, but there is no easy answer. Should you pay the money to the city? There is a danger of it being wasted. Should you donate lands? They may be neglected, as public lands often are. Nothing better occurs to me than that which I did myself. Since I had promised to give 500,000 sesterces for the upkeep of free-born boys and girls, I sold some of my land (which was worth more than this) to the municipal agent; I then received it back again to be charged with an annual rent of 30,000 sesterces. By these means, the capital is secured for the city, the interest is ensured, and the land itself will always find a tenant, as its value exceeds the rent by a long way . . .

371. Cicero, *Pro Plancio* 63

He gave games at Praeneste. So what? Have other quaestors not done so? In Cyrene, he was generous to the *publicani* and just to the companies. Who can deny it? But so much happens in Rome that it is scarcely possible to listen to the things that happen in the provinces.

[54 BC. Cicero's defence of Plancius relates to a challenge to the validity of his election as aedile by Juventius Laterensis, one of the unsuccessful candidates. The main thrust of Cicero's argument, here and in other writings, stresses the strong local ties and importance of municipal support for the elite, and the very fact that Laterensis took the trouble to give games outside Rome and cultivate the equestrian order suggests that, contrary to the interpretation offered, these were important.]

372. *CIL* 9.976

M. Mindius M. F. Maximus, of the tribe Galeria set up a statue of Mercury as his obligation as *quinquennalis* and at the dedication of this, he distributed one *denarius* per head to the people. The site was given by decree of the decurions.

[First century AD. Compsa. Latin inscription, commemorating the dedication of a statue by a member of the city's elite. This is a dedication *ob honorem*, in other words a statutory obligation on the part of a magistrate. As an example of *honoraria*, this is on a fairly modest scale. The Mindii are a prominent family at Compsa and appear in a number of other inscriptions concerning public office or public works.]

373. *CIL* 10.5654

In honour of [.] Fla[vius] C. F. Proculeianus, *quinquennalis* of the *municipium* of Fabrateria Vetus, *curator kalendarii novi*, curator of Formiae, who undertook all the obligations [required by] the *municipium*, in whose name his grandfather C. Mollius Fl[avius] Proculeianus, patron of the *municipium*, gave 25,000 sesterces to the *ordo decurionum* and the people, so that a *sportula* could be shared every year on his birthday, the 12th day before the Kalends of January. On account of his worthiness the devotees of the goddess Ceres have set up a statue to their patron, . . . and he has given 4,000 sesterces to the above-mentioned devotees so that from the interest, they can distribute a *sportula* every year on his birthday, the 12th day before the Kalends of January. If a distribution is not made on the day specified above, then that sum shall become the property of the state. By public decree of the council.

[Fabrateria Vetus. Latin inscription of imperial date (name forms suggest second century AD or later). This records, in more detail than usual, the arrangements for a *sportula* in honour of Flavius Proculeianus.]

374. Susini, No. 93

To Sextus Silettius Sex. F. Cam. Maximus, *quattuorvir iure dicundo*, by decree of the senate. Sextus Silettius Epitynchanus and Vipstania Helice, his parents, having accepted this honour, remit the expense and on the occasion of its dedication grant 12 sesterces to decurions and also 4 sesterces to citizens and *incolae*.

[Imperial date. Lupiae. Large white marble statue base, found close to the amphitheatre. The text records a statue voted to Sextus Silettius and the decision of his parents to remit the expense to the city and to fund a cash donation to the decurions and citizens on the occasion of the monument's dedication. The phrase *municipes et incolae*, rare in other inscriptions, occurs several times in this region. The *incolae* are probably inhabitants of the territory around Lupiae, and may include people who were not full citizens of the *municipium*.[17]]

375. *CIL* 10.109

To Julia C. F. Prepis and C. Julius C. F. Glago, the most dutiful daughter and the grandson of Septimia Prepusa, who in celebration of the dedication of their statue, gave eight sesterces each to the decurions and their children, six sesterces each to the *augustales* and their children, four sesterces each to the rest of the people and two sesterces each to women. C. Julius Anthus, . . . freedman of Prepusa . . . The land was given by decree of the senate.

[Croton. Imperial date.]

376. *CIL* 10.107 (= *ILS* 6466)

To Futia C. F. Lolliana, the most dutiful daughter of C. Futius Onirus, *duumvir* for the second time, who gave the following: ten sesterces to the decurions so that, from the interest on this, they can gather together on the 7th day before the Ides of April, my daughter's birthday, for a feast, and 400 sesterces for a communal gathering and 200 sesterces for a distribution. This money cannot be diverted to any other use. The land was given by decree of the senate.

[Croton. Imperial date.]

377. *CIL* 10.5056

In honour of T. Helvius T. F. Basila, aedile, praetor and proconsular legate to Augustus Caesar, who left 400,000 sesterces to the people of Atina in order that the interest could provide their children with grain until they came of age and afterwards provide 1,000 sesterces. Set up by Procula, his daughter.

[First century AD. Atina, Latium. Inscription in honour of a local notable who pursued a senatorial career at Rome. Its occasion is a testamentary bequest to set up an alimentary scheme. The monument is set up by his daughter, unlike many commemorations of benefactors, which are paid for by the state.]

378. *CIL* 12.2123

Horatius [.]. F. Balbus gave a burial place, at his own expense, to this city and its residents, apart from those who had hired themselves out as gladiators, hanged themselves as their own doing, or had pursued a polluted craft for profit, each site, per person, having 10 feet frontage and 10 feet depth, between the bridge over the river Sapis and the topmost monument which is on the boundary of the Fangonian estate. Anyone who so wishes may build a tomb before he dies on plots where nobody is buried. On plots where someone has been buried, it is permissible only to build a memorial to that person and to his descendants.

[Sarsina, Umbria. Donation of cemetery to citizens, with exemptions for suicides, gladiators or anyone else whose profession involved pollution.]

379. *CIL* 4.3884

Twenty pairs of gladiators belonging to Decimus Lucretius Satrius Valens, *flamen* in perpetuity of Nero, son of Caesar Augustus, and ten pairs of gladiators belonging to his son, Decimus Lucretius Valens, will fight at Pompeii on 8th, 9th, 10th, 11th and 12th of April. There will be a full programme of wild beast fights, and awnings [will be provided]. Aemilius Celer [painted this] by moonlight, alone.

[First century AD. Pompeii. Advertisement for games, painted on a wall.]

380. *ILS* 5053

Clodia, A. F., public priestess of Ceres, by decree of the decurions.

Lassia, M. F., public priestess of Ceres, by decree of the decurions.

A. Clodius, A. F. Pal., secretary, *Magister* of the Vicus Augustus Felix Suburbanus.

A. Clodius A. F. Flaccus, *duovir iure dicundo* three times, *quinquennalis*, military tribune by the wish of the people. At the festival of Apollo, during his [i.e. Clodius Flaccus'] first duovirate, he put on, in the forum, a procession, bulls, bullfighters, runners, three pairs of platform fighters, groups of boxers and Greek boxers, spectacles of every type and with all sorts of pantomimes, and Pylades, and 10,000 sesterces donated to the city for the duovirate. At the festival of Apollo, during his second duovirate, he put on, in the forum, a procession, bulls, bullfighters, runners and groups of boxers; on the next day, he put on at the games 30 pairs of athletes and five pairs of gladiators by himself, and 35 pairs of gladiators and beast-hunts, bulls, bullfights, boars, bears and other kinds of beast hunt with his colleague. In his third duovirate, he provided a show with the first theatre company, with other acts added by his colleague. Clodia, A. F., set up this monument for herself and her family, at her own expense.

[Augustan. Pompeii. The second duovirate of A. Clodius Flaccus is thought to have been in AD 2.]

Commemorations and honorific inscriptions

381. *CIL* 10.3703

To Sextia L. F. Kana, a monument at public expense was set up by decree of the decurions of Colonia Julia, in recognition of her munificence to the colony.

[First century AD. Cumae. From a circular funerary monument near Lago Fusaro. There is some debate about the date at which Cumae gained colonial status but a small group of inscriptions, of which this is one, seem to point to an Augustan colony which conferred the title of Colonia Julia on the city.]

382. G. Forni, *Kokalos* 3–4 (1957–8), 61–70

The senate and people of Velia, to C. Julius Naso, in recognition of his distinction and excellence.

[First century AD. Velia. Inscribed base, probably of a statue, dedicated to C. Julius Naso. The inscription is bilingual in Greek and Latin, in which the Greek version uses many of the conventions of a Hellenistic proxeny decree.]

383. *CIL* 10.3903

Since [. . .] the *duoviri* stated that [. . . .] it was right to decorate the most worthy of men with every honour, both private and public; having been asked for their opinion on this, this decree has been passed:

Since L. Antistius Campanus, after a full military career, having won the admiration of the deified Caesar and the deified Augustus, and having been settled by Augustus in our colony, has been munificent both in private and in public so that he has virtually shared his estate with the city by bearing many different expenses in person, and always seemed more willing to spend his money on the public than in the interests of himself and his family, and grew old in accumulating leading civic offices, so that even now he is concerned with our most important business; and since he has now given way in his labours, which were valuable to the city but burdensome to his age, the conscript fathers have decided that the memory of a most worthy and valuable citizen [. . .] should be adorned with these honours: that he should be carried from the forum to his pyre in a funeral contracted [. . .] and sanctioned by one or both of the *duoviri*, and that the day set for the funeral can be postponed, so that nothing may stop as many as possible of the people attending the funeral of the most virtuous and munificent of men, and that a gilded statue should be set up to him at public expense, with this [. . .] decree of the decurions inscribed on it, in whatever place Antistius Campanus, the most worthy of sons and heir to his service and munificence, should select [. . .] also with the other statues, shields and gifts which he received [. . .] to his death, and the honours granted to him posthumously, and that a site should be given at public expense which L. Antistius Campanus should select [. . .]

[First century AD. Capua. Decree of public mourning in honour of the Augustan colonist and benefactor L. Antistius Campanus.]

384. *CIL* 10.5835

To A. Quinctilius A. F. Pal. Priscus, *quattuorvir aedilicia potestate*, *quattuorvir iure dicundo*, *quattuorvir quinquennalis*, chosen in accordance with the decree of the senate, *pontifex*, *praefectus fabrum*. On account of his exceptional generosity to his fellow citizens, the senate ordered a statue of him to be publicly placed in the forum, wherever he wishes. Having accepted this honour, he remitted the expense. By arrangement with the senate, he bought, for 70,000 sesterces, the

Ceponian, Roianan and Mamianan farms and the Exosco meadow from the city and gave them back to the city for its perpetual ownership, and from the annual return of 4,200 sesterces on this, there should be given on his birthday, six days before the Ides of May, in perpetuity to the citizens, and other residents and married women who are present one pound of cakes and one *hemina* of *mulsum* per person; and to the decurions, around dining couches, cakes and *mulsum* and a distribution of ten sesterces per person, and the same to their sons, who will be added to the senate; and to the *seviri Augustales* and those who are to dine with them, cakes, *mulsum* and eight sesterces each; and in addition to this, at my own dining couch, one sesterce per person; and for the upkeep of my own statue and *imagines*, let the city spend 30 sesterces in perpetuity at the discretion of the *quattuorviri*, and under the supervision of the aediles. It is acceptable if they [the senate] provide the sons of the people, without discrimination as to freedom, with a scattering of 30 *modii* of nuts and the distribution of drinks from six jars of wine, in a manner appropriate to the next generation.

[Early second century AD. Ferentinum. Rock-cut inscription. The text is surrounded by a sculpted framework resembling a temple frontage. Cf. *CIL* 10.5852 for the statue base mentioned in the text. The switch from third to first person in the course of the text indicates that the foundation was established during the lifetime of Priscus.]

Euergetism and the law

385. *Digest* 35.1.39.1

When it has been written into a will that "a structure should be built in the forum" and it has not been specified which forum, Labeo says that if the testator's wishes are unclear, it should be built in the forum of the city in which the testator had his principal home.

386. Ulpian, *Epit.* 24.28

All cities which are under the rule of the Roman people can inherit: this was introduced by Nerva and afterwards was most carefully established by Hadrian, on the authority of the senate.

[There are a number of ambiguities in this statute governing the abilities of cities to accept communal bequests. Although it specifies that all cities under Roman rule have the right to accept legacies left to the city, it then goes on to imply that this was not a universal right until reforms introduced by Nerva and subsequently confirmed by Hadrian and by the Senate.]

387. *Digest* 33.2.17

(Scaevola) Someone leaves property to the state, from the interest on which he wants annual games to be held, and adds: "I petition and request, decurions, that you decide to convert that which I have bequeathed to another form or another purpose." The state cannot give games for four consecutive years: I asked whether the interest, which the state receives for four years, should be returned to the heirs or whether they should be compensated by some other form of bequest from the same will.

388. *Digest* 33.1.23

(Marcianus) When someone wishes to give a distribution to the decurions on his birthday, the deified Severus and Antoninus decreed that it is not to be judged a bequest for one year, but a perpetual legacy.

389. *Digest* 31.30

I make a bequest to the state of the Graviscans for the upkeep and rebuilding of the roads within the colony "as far as the Via Aurelia": It is asked whether this legacy is valid.

390. *Digest* 32.35.3

(Scaevola) "Most dear fellow citizens of Tibur, you know that the Julian baths, adjoining my house, are willingly offered free for public use by my heirs for ten months of the year." He was asked whether the heirs must undertake the necessary repairs.

Municipal patrons: appointment, status and activities

391. *ILS* 6106

In the consulship of L. Arruntius Stella and L. Julius Marinus, 14 days before the Kalends of November. M' Acilius Placidus and L. Petronius Fronto, *quattuorviri i(ure) d(icundo)* consulted the senate of the Ferentini who were assembled in the temple of Mars. Q. Segiarius Maecianus and T. Munnius Nomantinus were present to witness the record. This was unanimously decided: That T. Pomponius Bassus, a *vir clarissimus*, in accordance with the policy of the most indulgent emperor Nerva Trajan Augustus Germanicus, was performing the task given to him by [the emperor], whereby the emperor has provided for the eternal duration of Italy so that each generation should be grateful for [Bassus'] administration, and that a man of such virtue must be of assistance to our city. That which they wished to do about this matter was decided thus: "That the senators are pleased to send delegates from this order to T. Pomponius Bassus, *vir clarissimus*, to persuade him to be so gracious as to receive our city into the patronage of his great household and to allow himself to be co-opted as patron and to permit a record of guest-friendship inscribed with this decree to be placed in his house." It was decided. Despatched as envoy: A. Caecilius A. F. Quirinalis and Quirinalis [son of A. Caecilius Quirinalis].

[Rome, AD 101. Bronze tablet with Latin inscription. The text is a *tabula patronatus*, a legal ratification of the appointment of T. Pomponius Bassus as *patronus* by the *municipium* of Ferentium. The formal appointment of a municipal patron was a strict legal procedure, involving an initial decision by the municipal senate according to terms and procedures specified in their colonial or municipal charter, followed by referral to Rome for ratification by the senate and emperor. The appointment was recorded in an inscribed *tabula patronatus*, and the patron could adopt the title *patronus municipium* (or *colonia*). The title and obligations of patronage were hereditary.]

392. *ILS* 6110

In the consulship of C. Vettius Atticus and C. Asinius Praetextatus. The day before the Ides of April. The senate of the Vestini of Peltuinum being assembled in the *curia* of Augustus, T. Avidiaccius Restitutus and T. Blaesius Natalis, the quinquennial aediles, were present to witness the record. This was passed unanimously: that Nummia Varia, C. F., priestess of Venus Felix, . . . on account of her customary benevolence, deserves, just as her parents did, by universal consensus, to become the patron of our *praefectura*, an honour which is the highest amongst us, . . . so that we can be safe and protected in all things. That which they wished to do about this matter was decided about thus: "It unanimously pleases the senators to offer the patronship of our *praefectura* to Nummia Varia, C. F., the priestess of Venus Felix, for the enhancement of her status, and to request from her clear and distinguished goodwill that she willingly and with favourable mind accept this honour offered to her by us, and condescend to receive us, individually and collectively, and our state, into the clientship of her household, and . . . she will, by interceding with her authority and status, guarantee safety and protection; and that a bronze tablet containing the text of our decree be offered to her by Avidiaccus Restitutus and Blaesius Natalis the *quinquennales* and also by Numisenius Crescens and Flavius Priscus the leading men of our order." It was decided.

[Rome. Bronze tablet with Latin inscription. *Tabula patronatus* conferring rank of patron of Peltuinum on Nummia Varia, a priestess of the cult of Venus Felix. Female civic patrons, as well as public benefactors below the rank of patronus/a, are attested from elsewhere in Italy, but they are, unsurprisingly, much rarer than male ones.]

393. Pliny, *Letters* 4.1.3–4

There is a town close to my estate (named Tifernum Tiberinum) which, when I was still almost a youth, co-opted me as patron, showing as much excess enthusiasm as small amount of judgement. It celebrates my arrival, bemoans my departure, and rejoices in my honours. So that I may return their good wishes, I have built a temple there at my own expense (for it is most disgraceful to be outdone in love), whose dedication, since it is complete, it would be impious to delay any longer. Therefore, we will be there on the day of the dedication, which I have decided to celebrate with a feast.

[Letter to the grandfather of Pliny's wife. The appointment of Pliny as *patronus* of Tifernum Tiberinum clearly occurred at an unusually young age, probably while in his late teens. The context may have been the death of Pliny the Elder in AD 79. The younger Pliny inherited estates in the area of Tifernum from his uncle and may have inherited the position of patron along with them.]

394. *CIL* 9.5074

Q. Poppaeus Q. F., the patron of the *municipium* and *colonia* gives to the citizens, colonists and *incolae* and visitors to the city free bathing in perpetuity at his own expense.

Interamnia, Umbria. Latin inscription of imperial date. Q. Poppaeus, a patron of the city pays for perpetual free access to the baths for the citizens and visitors. Although all free inhabitants are included, the different categories of population are carefully enumerated. The *incoles* appear as a separate category in a number of inscriptions in Roman Italy and their exact identity is uncertain. They may in this case be the inhabitants of the outlying farms and villages in the territory of Interamnia.]

395. *CIL* 10.483

To Digitia L. F. Rufina, on account of her uncommon degree of chastity and modesty. M. Tullius M. F. Cicero, of the tribe *Maecia*, *Eques Romanus*, priest of the Laurentes and Lavinates, and patron of the colony, buried his wife, having remitted the cost to the public. The burial place was given by decree of the senate.

[Third century AD. Paestum. Epitaph of Digitia Rufina, wife of M. Tullius Cicero. The *Tullii Cicerones*, probably descended from a freedman of the orator rather than directly from his family, were prominent among the elite of Paestum, held equestrian status, and intermarried with other leading families, notably the *Digitii* and the *Venneianii*. The *Laurentes Lavinatesque* were a Roman priesthood.]

396. *CIL* 10.110

To L. Lollius L. F. L. N. L. Pro. N. Marcianus, of the tribe *Cornelia*, who was awarded the *equus publicus*, was patron of the colony and undertook everything with honour. Futia C. F. Longina, the mother of a most dutiful son, in commemoration of the dedication of his statue, gave a dinner to the decurions and *augustales* and an individual distribution to the people. The land was provided by decree of the senate.

[Imperial date. Croton. Dedication of a commemorative statue in honour of L. Lollius Marcianus, a patron of Croton, who held equestrian rank (the *equus publicus* was a specific grade of this). This inscription also records the intermarriage of two of the leading families of Croton, the *Futii* and the *Lollii Marciani*.]

397. *CIL* 11.5211

Dedicated with thanks to our excellent patron Cn. Domitius [. . . .] Curvius Tullus, Sex. F.; consul; proconsul of Africa; fetial; *praefectus* of all auxiliaries against the Germans; when he was praetor designate as candidate of the emperor, he was sent as praetorian legate to the army in Africa by the Emperor Vespasian Augustus, and was promoted to praetorian status in his absence; he was decorated with the mural crown, rampart crown and golden crown by the emperor Vespasian Augustus and Titus Caesar, and also with three spears and three standards; enrolled as a patrician; tribune of the plebs; quaestor of Caesar Augustus; military tribune of the Legion V Alauda; *decemvir stlitibus iudicandis*.

[Second century AD. Fulginiae, Umbria. Dedication to a civic patron, listing details of his career, which was mainly military. The crowns, spears and standards are military decorations.]

Social rules and attitudes

398. Pliny, *Letters* 1.14 (to Junius Mauricus)

You ask me to look for a husband for your brother's daughter; . . . His [Minicius Acilianus, Pliny's choice for Mauricius' niece] home town is Brixia, of our area of Italy, which retains and preserves much straightforwardness, frugality and even old-fashioned rusticity. His father is Minicius Macrinus, a leading member of the equestrian order, because he wanted nothing higher; he would have been admitted to praetorian rank by the deified Vespasian, but he preferred honest obscurity to our status, or should I say most continuous ambition. He has as a maternal grandmother Serrana Procula, from the *municipium* of Patavium. You know the customs of the place; however, Serrana is an example of propriety even among the Patavians. His uncle, Publius Acilius, is exceptional in his gravity, prudence and integrity. In all, you will find nothing in the entire household which would not please you in your own. Indeed, Acilianus himself has great energy and industry, although also the highest modesty. He has held the quaestorship, tribunate and praetorship with the highest distinction, so you will be spared the necessity of campaigning on his behalf. . . . I do not know whether I should add that his father has ample means. For when I imagine you, and the person for whom we are seeking a son-in-law, I think I should remain silent about wealth; but when I consider the customs of the age and even the laws of the city of Rome, which consider a man's census rating to be of the first importance, it seems that this matter should not be passed over. And in thinking of children and future generations resulting from the marriage, this consideration must be given due weight . . .

399. Pliny, *Letters* 1.19 (to Romatius Firmus)

You are a fellow-citizen [of Comum] of mine, a school contemporary and companion from an early age, your father was a friend of my mother and uncle, and of me, in as far as it was the difference in age allowed; there are many and serious reasons why I owe it to you to support you and increase your status. The census of 100,000 sesterces which you hold is enough to indicate that amongst us in Comum, you are a decurion. Therefore, so that I may enjoy seeing you not only as a decurion, but also as a Roman *eques*, I offer you 300,000 sesterces to bring you up to the equestrian qualification. The length of our friendship guarantees that you will remember this gift . . .

400. Velleius Paterculus 2.14

When Drusus was having a house built on the Palatine, his architect promised to make it entirely private and free from being overlooked by anybody. But Drusus said "No. I wish you to use all your expertise to build me a house in which everybody can see whatever I am doing.'

[This comment by Livius Drusus (tribune 92 BC) does not merely reflect exhibitionism on his part, but typifies the face-to-face nature of public life in the Roman city, in which it was regarded as right that most aspects of public (and also private) life took place in full view of the rest of the citizens. Conversely, the Romans were deeply suspicious of an undue wish for privacy, equating it with the need to hide illegal or disreputable behaviour.]

401. Cicero, *Pro Roscio Amerino* 15–16

Sextus Roscius, the father of this man here, was a citizen of Ameria, and by birth, rank and wealth was easily the leading citizen not only of his city but also of the entire region, flourishing in his good relations and connections of hospitality with men of the highest rank. For he not only had reciprocal hospitality with the *Metelli, Servilii* and Scipios, who, as is right, I name with the respect due to their high character and rank, but also private contact and familiarity with them. But of all these advantages he left only this one to his son: for his inheritance is possessed by brigands from within the family, taken by force, and the reputation and life of this innocent are defended by guests and friends of his father. Since he was a supporter of the nobility at all times, especially during the recent disturbances, when the status and safety of all nobles came under threat, he defended their party and cause more than anyone else in the region, with deeds, enthusiasm and influence. He thought it was right to fight for the honour of those on account of whom he was numbered amongst the most honourable men. After victory had been established and we had laid down arms, when men had been proscribed and those who were thought to have belonged to the opposition were arrested in all regions, he was often in Rome, and showed himself in the forum every day, before the eyes of all, seeming rather to exult in the victory of the nobles than to fear that disaster would strike him.

402. Cicero, *Pro Cluentio* 41

It was Oppianicus whom the decurions of Larinum unanimously judged to have corrupted the public records of the censors. Nobody would have any financial dealings, or any other sort of dealings, with him; nobody amongst all his relatives and associates would appoint him guardian to his children; nobody thought it right to visit him, meet him, talk with him, or dine with him; everyone spurned him, everyone hated him, everyone fled from him as a savage and dangerous beast . . .

Municipal senators

403. *CIL* 9.2845

P. Paquius Scaeva, son of Scaeva and Flavia, grandson of Consus and Didia, great grandson of Barbus and Dirutia: quaestor; member of the *decemviri stlitibus iudicandis*, after his quaestorship, by *senatusconsultum*; member of the *quattuorvir* for capital cases, after his quaestorship and decemvirate, in accordance with a *senatusconsultum*; tribune of the plebs; curule aedile; judge in the criminal court; praetor in charge of the treasury; he governed the province of Cyprus as proconsul; curator of the roads outside the city of Rome for a period of five years, by *senatusconsultum*; extraordinary proconsul for a second time by the authority of Augustus Caesar, and sent to restore order in the rest of the province of Cyprus by *senatusconsultum*; fetial; cousin and husband of Flavia, the daughter of Consus, granddaughter of Scapula, great-granddaughter of Barbus, buried together with her.

[Augustan. Histonium. Funerary inscription from large tomb. The text includes details of a senatorial career and also indicates the extent to which families intermarried within local elites. Flavia and Paquius were apparently cousins, although a number of different reconstructions of their family tree are possible. It is one of a matched pair (the other is the epitaph of Flavia herself) which is, unusually, inscribed on the inside of their sarcophagus, and was therefore not intended as a public document.]

404. *ILS* 932

In honour of Q. Varius Q. F. Geminus, legate of the deified Augustus for two years, proconsul, praetor, tribune of the people, quaestor, inquiry judge, *praefectus frumenti dandi*, *decemvir stlitibus iudicandis*, curator for the supervision of sacred buildings and public monuments. He was the first of all the Paelignians to become a senator and hold these offices. [Set up by] the people of Superaequum to their patron, at public expense.

[First century AD. Superaequum.]

405. *ILS* 937

In honour of M'. Vibius M'. F. Vel. Balbinus, military tribune, *praefectus fabrum*, *praefectus equitum*, quaestor, plebeian aedile, praetor of the *aerarium*, legate of the deified Augustus and of Tiberius Caesar Augustus, proconsul of the province of Narbonensis.

[First century AD. Treia, Picenum]

406. *CIL* 5.5262

C. Plinius L. F. Ouf. Caecilius Secundus, consul, augur, praetorian legate in the province of Pontus and Bithynia, sent to that province with consular authority with a decree of the senate by the emperor Caesar Nerva Traianus Augustus Germanicus Dacicus, *pater patriae*, commissioner for the Tiber riverbed and banks, and for the sewers of Rome, *praefectus* of the *aerarium* of Saturn, *praefectus* of the military *aerarium*, praetor, tribune of the people, quaestor of the emperor, *sevir* of the *equites romani*, military tribune of the legion III Gallica, *decemvir stlitibus iudicandis*, left . . . sesterces in his will for building baths, with an additional 300,000 sesterces for decoration and an additional 200,000 sesterces for upkeep, and for the upkeep of his freedmen, 100 men, he left 1,866,666 sesterces to the state, the income from which he wished, afterwards [i.e. after the freedmen had died] to provide an annual dinner for the people. While he was still living, he gave 500,000 sesterces for the upkeep of boys and girls of the people of the city and 100,000 sesterces for a library and its upkeep.

[Second century AD. Comum. Inscription commemorating Pliny the younger and his benefactions.]

Equestrian careers

407. *CIL* 9.1556

P. Vedius P. F. Pollio built the shrine of [Julius] Caesar for the emperor Caesar Augustus and the colony of Beneventum.

[Augustan. Beneventum.]

408. *ILS* 9007

Q. Octavius L. F., C. N., L. ProN. Ser. Sagitta, *duovir quinquennalis* three times, *praefectus fabrum*, *praefectus equitum*, military tribune chosen by the people, procurator of Caesar Augustus among the Vindelici and Raeti and in the Poenine valley for four years and in the province of Spain for ten years and in Syria for two years.

[First century AD. Superaequuum.]

409. Ehrenburg and Jones, No. 225

To Ti. Caesar Augustus, son of the deified Augustus, *pontifex maximus*, holding tribunician power for the 38th time, consul five times, by the terms of the will of M. Pulfennius Sex. F. Arn., centurion of the Legion VI Ferrata. C. Herennius T. F. Arn. Capito military tribune for three years, *praefectus equitum*, *praefectus veteranorum*, procurator of Julia Augusta, procurator of Tiberius Caesar Augustus, procurator of C. Caesar Augustus Germanicus. Ten pounds of silver.

[Early first century AD. Teate Marrucinorum. Inscription on a silver bust of Tiberius, made of ten pounds of silver under the provision of the will of the veteran M. Pulfennius.]

Veterans in Italy

410. *ILS* 2689

To Sex. Pedius Sex. F. An. Lusianus Hirrutus, *primuspilus* of the 21st Legion, prefect of the Vindelici and Raeti of the Poenine valley and light-armed troops, *quattuorvir iure dicundo*, judicial prefect of Germanicus Caesar, by decree of the senate, for five years, and for a second five-year term. He built the amphitheatre at his own expense. [Set up by] M. Dullius M. F. Gallus.

[Mid-first century AD. Paelignian.]

411. *ILS* 2231

To C. Edusius Sex. F. Clust., from Mevania, centurion of the 41st legion of Augustus and centurion of the fleet, under the terms of his will.

[First century AD. Tuder. Unlike the example above, in which colonists are allocated according to their unit, not their place of origin, Edusius returned to his native Umbria, and may not have been a colonist.]

412. *ILS* 2819

Julia Cleopatra, also known as Lezbia, daughter of C. Julius Menoetes of Syrian Antioch, [set up] by Daphne, wife of Malchio, trierarch of Caesar in the trireme Triptolemos.

[Julio-Claudian. Brundisium.]

Local patriotism

413. Cicero, *Pro Caelio* 5

With reference to your objection that this young man [Caelius] was disapproved of by his fellow citizens, none of the Praetuttiani ever had higher honours conferred on them while living there than M. Caelius has had *in absentia*; while he was absent, he was co-opted into the highest rank of society, and he was offered, without having sought them, honours which many who actively seek them are denied; and they also sent a delegation of most eminent men from our order and the equestrian order to this trial who gave a most weighty and eloquent testimony on his behalf. . . . For you would not consider this man to be highly enough recommended to you, if he was disapproved of not only by such a father but also by such a distinguished and important city.

[M. Caelius Rufus, the defendant in this case was a citizen of Interamna Praetuttiorum and a member of the decurial order of the city as well as being of a Roman senatorial family. The honours conferred on him by his native city are not specified, but they may have included the status of *patronus municipium*. Despite the fact that the family now lived in Rome, this passage illustrates the continuing importance of local ties, something that Cicero, himself a *novus homo* from Arpinum, was at pains to stress.]

414. Cicero, *Pro Plancio* 22–4

Everything I say about Plancius, I say from my own experience. We [the Arpinates] are neighbours of the people of Atina. Local patriotism is to be praised and even loved, keeping the ancient custom of duty and untainted by ill-will, not accustomed to lies, pretension, hypocrisy, not educated in the dissimulations of the suburbs or even the city. No one at Arpinum did not support Plancius, nor at Sora, Casinum, nor Aquinum. The whole of the celebrated districts of Venafrum and Allifae, all of our rough countryside, both mountainous and loyal, simple and faithful, considered his honour a distinction and his status an increase of standing. Roman knights have come from these *municipia* to give testimony: their anxiety for him now is as great as their support for him then. . . . Let us join to this, if you wish, that Plancius' father was a *publicanus*, which you think is a disgrace to him: who does not know how much that order helps in seeking office? For the flower of the Roman knights, the ornament of the city, the foundation of the state, are found among the ranks of the *publicani*.

415. Cicero, *De Legibus* 2.3

To tell the truth, this is the home city of myself and my brother; we are descendants of a very ancient family of the area, here are our sacred rites, our family, and memorials of our ancestors. What more? You see this villa, as it is now, the building extended by the interest of our father, who spent most of his time in study here, being an invalid. I was born in this place, during my grandfather's lifetime, when the villa was small, according to ancient tradition, just like that of Curius in the Sabine territory.

416. Pliny, *Letters* 3.6 (to Annius Severus)

I bought it [a small Corinthian bronze], however, not so as to have it at home (for I do not have any Corinthian bronzes at home yet), but in order to place it in a prominent place in my home city, preferably in the temple of Jupiter; for it seems a worthy gift for a temple and a worthy gift for a god. Therefore, take this task, as you always do everything which is asked of you by me, and order a base to be made immediately, of whatever marble you wish, on which my name is to be inscribed, and my honours, if you think they should be added.

417. Pliny, *Letters* 6.18 (to Statius Sabinus)

I will take up the interests of the people of Firmum, as you asked me, although I have a large amount of business on my hands. For I wish to oblige such a distinguished *colonia* by my professional services and yourself by a most acceptable favour. For, since our friendship, as you always say, was sought as a support and distinction to you, there is nothing I could refuse you, especially when asked on behalf of your home city. For what prayers can be as honourable as those of a loyal man or what as effective as those of a friend? You can give my word, then, to your, or rather our, people of Firmum; their high reputation is enough of a guarantee that they are deserving of my efforts and attention . . .

418. Smallwood 48

Good luck to the people of Puteoli. Good luck to all the people of Nuceria. And the hook for the Pompeians and Pithecusans.

[Mid-first century AD. Pompeii. This graffito, written in two separate hands, illustrates a degree of municipal rivalry around the Bay of Naples. The "hook" referred to may be the fork used to drag dead gladiators out of the arena.]

Augustales

419. *CIL* 11.3614

Vesbinus, a freedman of the emperor, having received a location from the municipium of Caere, gave a *phretrium* [a meeting house for the *Augustales*], with all its embellishments, to the *Augustales* as a gift at his own expense. This document was copied and certified in the porch of the temple of Mars, from notes which Cuperius Hostilianus ordered to be offered by T. Rustius Lysiponus, the scribe, in which was written that which is written below: In the consulship of L. Publilius Celsus (for the second time) and C. Clodius Crispinus, on the Ides of April, M. Pontius Celsus being *dictator* and C. Suetonius Claudianus *aedilis iure dicundo* and prefect of the *aerarium*. From the daily record book of the *municipium* of Caere, page XXVII section VI:

M. Pontius Celsus, the *dictator*, and C. Suetonius Claudianus convened the decurions in the temple of the gods, where Vesbinus, an imperial freedman, requested that a site might be given to him by the community below the portico of the *Basilica Sulpiciana*, so that he could build a *phretrium* for the *Augustales* in that place, and at which, by the decision of the decurions, the site which he asked for was granted and it was unanimously decided that a letter should be sent to Curiatus Cosanus, the curator, about this matter. Present at the meeting were Pontius Celsus, the *dictator*, Suetonius Claudianus, *aedilis iure dicundo*, M. Lepidus Nepos, aedile in charge of the *annona*, Pollius Blandus, Pescennius Natalis, Pollius Callimus, Petronius Innocens and Sergius Proculus.

On the next page, section I: Magistrates and decurions of Caere to Curiatius Cosanus, greetings. Ides of August. Since Ulpius Vesbinus wished to petition us, we called a meeting of the decurions, from which he requested that a site in the corner of the porticus of the basilica should be given to him by the community, on which he promised to build a public *phretrium* for the *Augustales* which would enhance the status of the community. These proposals were unanimously welcomed and it was decided to write to you, so that you would also be consulted on this matter. This location is not used by the city and cannot produce any revenue. Page VIII, section I: Curiatus Cosanus to the magistrates and decurions of Caere, greetings. I not only consent to your proposals but congratulate you on them, if they will enhance the status of the city. I accede to your decisions not only as curator but also as one of your decurial order, when such honest actions cause such an honorific enhancement. Dispatched the day before the Ides of September. Ameria.

Passed on the Ides of June, in the consulship of Q. Ninnius Hasta and P. Manilius Vopiscus. Dedicated on the Kalends of August in the same consular year.

[Early second century AD. Caere. Decree by the senate of Caere with reference to the proposal (accepted) by Vesbinus, a freedman of Trajan, that the city should give him a plot of unused land for the purpose of constructing a meeting house for the *Augustales* of Caere. The text also preserves the correspondence between the curator for the district and the municipality of Caere. This document underlines a number of points about municipal administration and euergetism. It is extracted from the day book of public proceedings, indicating detailed recording and archive procedures for documenting and storing public business. It also indicates the levels of external bureaucracy involved in civic administration, since it is clearly thought advisable, if not actually obligatory, to refer the decision to the curator for ratification. It is also notable that the curator, apparently a citizen of Caere, regards such a building as not just desirable but also a significant addition which would increase the status of Caere.]

420. *ILS* 5373

In honour of Imperator Caesar Augustus, son of the deified Julius, *pontifex maximus*, father of his country and of the *municipium*. The *Magistri Augustales* C. Egnatius M. L. Glyco, C. Egnatius C. L. Musicus, C. Julius Aug. L. Isochrysus and Q. Floronius Q. L. Princeps paved the Via Augusta, for the games, from outside the city gate to the temple of Ceres using stone from the Via Annia, at their own expense.

[Augustan. Falerii.]

421. *ILS* 1945

M. Caelius M. L. Phileros, orderly of T. Sextius, commander in Africa, aedile at Carthage, *praefectus iure dicundo* for selling the quinquennial tax in 83 towns, built the temple of Tellus at his own expense. He was duovir twice at Clupea; He was an *Augustalis* at Formiae and decorated the temple of Neptune at his own expense, with variegated stonework. To Fresidia Num. L. Flora, his most obedient wife. To Octavius Antimachus, freedman of Gaia, a dear friend.

[First century AD. Territory of Formiae.]

Slaves and freedmen

422. *ILS* 2818

Ti. Julius Diogenes, freedman of Augustus and the Augusta, trierarch, on behalf of himself and his wife, Nigidia Eutychia, and his family. Nigidia Eutychia, on behalf of her friend Staberia Margarita, freedwoman of C. Staberius. This monument does not pass to the heir.

[Julio-Claudian. Naples. A combination of military and imperial careers, as an imperial freedman from the households of both Augustus and Livia who went on to command a ship in the fleet. Both Diogenes and his wife are of Greek origin, as indicated by the names, and his rank is given in Greek as *trierarch(os)*.]

423. *ILS* 1847

Ti. Julius Latinus, son of [.] Julius Leonidas, tutor of the Caesars, military tribune in the Legion IV Scythica, who lived 37 years.

[First century AD. Urbinum. Epitaph of the son of an imperial freedman, probably of Tiberius.]

424. *CIL* 10.486

D(is) M(anibus) To Bennia Ephesia, wife of Primus, the treasurer of the colony.

[Second or third century AD. Paestum. Primus, the public treasurer or accountant would probably have been a slave.]

425. *CIL* 10.495

D(is) M(anibus). To Quintilia, who lived 19 years and 7 months, from Primigenius, her fellow-slave. She was well-deserving.

[Second or third century AD. Paestum. Epitaph.]

426. Turano (1963), Klearchos 5, 76–82

To C. Julius Celos, freedman of Julia, daughter of the deified Augustus, on behalf of himself and his father, C. Julius Thiasos, freedman of Julia, daughter of the deified Augustus, who was one of the *Seviri Augustales*, and his mother Julia, a freedwoman of the deified Augusta, set up by the terms of his will.

[First century AD. Rhegium. Testamentary epitaph of two imperial freedmen, members of the households of Julia, and a freedwoman of Livia. Julia lived in exile at Rhegium after her original banishment to Pandateria was commuted.[18] Like many imperial freedmen, these enjoyed high status in the community reflected in the office of *Sevir Augustalis* held by Julius Thiasos.]

427. Gasperini (1971), 3° *Misc. Greca e Romana*

Camulus, slave of Crispinilla, herdsman, who lived 35 years, lies here.

[Territory of Tarentum. Epitaph of shepherd, providing epigraphic evidence of sheeprearing in the *Ager Tarentinus*.]

428. *ILS* 6579

The Council of 100 of the *municipium* of Veii Augusta, meeting at the temple of Venus Genetrix in Rome, decided unanimously, to be allowed by unanimous authority until the decree is drafted, that the most appropriate honour is to be granted to C. Julius Celos, freedman of the deified Augustus, who has not only helped the *municipium* of Veii on all possible occasions by his care and favour, but also sought to enhance it by his expenditure, and through his son: he is to be numbered amongst the *Augustales*, as if he had actually held the office, and allowed to sit amongst the *Augustales* on his own double seat at all shows in the city, and to participate amongst the 100 at all public dinners; and it is also decreed that no tax of the *municipium* of Veii Augusta should be levied on him or his descendants.

Those present were: C. Scaevius Curiatus and L. Peperna Priscus, duovirs; M. Flavius Rufus, quaestor; T. Vettius Rufus, quaestor; M. Tarquitius Saturninus, L. Maecilius Scrupus, L. Favonius Lucanus, Cn. Octavius Sabinus, T. Sempronius Gracchus, P. Accuvius, P. F. Tro.; C. Veianus Maximus, T. Tarquitius Rufus, C. Julius Merula. In the consulship of Gaetulicus and Calvisius Sabinus.

[AD 26. Veii. Municipal decree in honour of C. Julius Celos, an imperial freedman. Another Julius Celos, also an imperial freedman is known from Rhegium Julium, but it is not certain that he was the same person.]

Collegia and their activities

429. *Digest* 47.22.1–3

Provincial governors are instructed by imperial edict not to allow political societies to exist and not to permit soldiers to form *collegia* in camp. The *humiliores* are, nevertheless, permitted to make monthly contributions so long as they meet only once a month, so that no illegal *collegium* can meet under this kind of pretext. The deified Severus also said in a rescript that these stipulations were valid not only in the city of Rome, but also in Italy and the provinces. They are not forbidden to gather for the purpose of religion as long as nothing is done by these means against the decree of the senate by which illegal *collegia* are outlawed. Nobody can be a member of more than one lawful *collegium*, as was decreed by the deified brothers. It was stated in this rescript that if anyone is a member of two, he must choose the one which he prefers to stay in and is to receive from the one which he leaves whatever is owed to him as his share of the communal fund.

430. *CIL* 14.2112

This was voted unanimously: That whoever wishes to join this *collegium* shall pay an initiation fee of 100 sesterces and an amphora of good-quality wine, and a monthly subscription of five *asses*. Furthermore, that if anyone does not pay the subscription for six months consecutively, his claim to burial will not be considered, even if he has provided for [payment] in his will. That on the death of a member of our number who has paid, 300 sesterces will be due to him from the treasury from which a funeral fee of 50 sesterces will be deducted, for distribution at the pyre; the funeral will be conducted on foot.

That if a member dies more that 20 miles from the city and the *collegium* is informed, three men selected from our number will have to go there to make arrangements for his funeral; they must give an account to the members in good faith, and if they are found to be guilty of fraud, they must pay a quadruple fine; they will be given money for the cost of the funeral and a travel grant, there and back, of 20 sesterces per person. [. . .] If a member dies intestate, the form of his burial will be decided by the *quinquennalis* and the members.

That if a member of this *collegium* who is a slave dies, and his master or mistress refuses without reason to hand over the body for burial, and he has not left written instructions, a token funeral ceremony will be held.

That if any member kills himself, whatever the reason, his claim to burial will not be allowed.

That if any member who is a slave becomes free, he must donate an amphora of good-quality wine [. . .]

Masters of the feast in the order of the list of members, appointed in turn in groups of four, must each provide an amphora of good-quality wine, and for as many members as the *collegium* has, bread costing two *asses*, four sardines, a table setting, and warm water with service [. . .]

That any member who becomes *quinquennalis* in this *collegium* shall be exempt from these obligations for the time when he is *quinquennalis*, and he will receive a double share of all distributions.

That any member who has conducted the office of *quinquennalis* creditably shall receive one and a half shares of everything as a mark of honour, so that other *quinquennales* will hope for the same thing by undertaking their duties properly.

That if any member wishes to make a complaint or raise any matter, he is to raise it at a business meeting, so that we can feast peacefully and cheerfully on feast days.

It was voted that any member who moves from one place to another so as to cause a disturbance shall be fined four sesterces. Any member who speaks abusively about another or causes a disturbance shall be fined 12 sesterces. Any member who uses abusive or insulting language to a *quinquennalis* at a banquet shall be fined 20 sesterces.

That on the festival days during his term of office, each *quinquennalis* is to conduct worship with incense and wine and is to perform his other duties dressed in white, and on the birthdays of Diana and Antinoüs he is to provide oil for the collegium at the public baths before they dine.

[AD 136. Lanuvium. Regulations of the *collegium* of Diana and Antinoüs for burials and mutual assistance. The text is prefaced by an extract from a senatorial decree restricting the *collegium* to one meeting per month and to collection of contributions for funerals.]

431. Gasperini (1971), *3° Misc. Greca e Romana*

D(is) M(anibus) the well-deserving *collegium* of the *viatores* built this.

[Tarentum. Inscription from a communal tomb. The *Collegium* of the *Viatores* was probably a burial association, offering a cheap burial in one of its tombs to subscribing members.]

432. *CIL* 11.5748

In the second consulship of P. Cornelius Saecularis and the second consulship of Junius Donatus, on the Kalends of July, at Sentinum, at a meeting of the full membership of the *Collegium Fabrum* of Sentinum in their meeting-house, C. Junius Martialis and C. Casidius Rufinus, the *quinquennales*, presiding, it was stated that: a great effort has always been made by our most splendid members in the past to show respect to those individuals who are worthy, and most of all to the honour and status of Memmia Victoria, a woman of illustrious memory, "mother" of our members, and the name of her family has been consistently and wholeheartedly upheld, so that all of her relatives shall be called patrons of our *collegium* amongst our membership, and it is hoped that all should seem universally unharmed within our membership, and since the most noble Coretius Fuscus should be moved by the example of the piety of his parents and the honourableness of his mother, therefore it was unanimously agreed that a bronze tablet should be offered to him, and on this matter, the following was decided: that the report of our two good men, *quinquennales* of our *collegium*, was excellent and therefore, since Coretius Fuscus is of noble birth, so that he may better understand our means of honouring him, it is our decision that an inscribed bronze tablet should be offered to him and that he should be asked to be gracious enough to accept our offering with good will, and that delegates should be chosen for this purpose who will pursue the matter in a suitable manner: Titratius, Ampliatius, Orfius Veritas, Aemilius Victor, Bebidius Justus, Casidius Martialis, Julius Martialis, Casidius Rufus, Bebidius Januarius, Aetrius Romanus, Casidius Clementinus, Aetrius Verna, Vassidenus Favor, Casidius Justissimus, Satrius Verecundus, Statius Velox, Veturius Celerinus.

[AD 260. Sentinum. Bronze tablet inscribed with the record of a meeting of a *collegium fabrum* – either a guild of builders or of the city's firemen. Although clearly originating at Sentinum, it was found in Rome. The *collegii fabrorum* were initially guilds of builders, but during the second century AD they increasingly took on the duties of firefighting as well. Coretius Fuscus was a decurion of Sentinum and was patron of all three of its main *collegia* (cf. *CIL* 11.5749). The list of names at the end are presumably those of the delegates appointed. Most of the *cognomina* point to their owners being slaves or freedmen.]

Notes

Introduction

1. The best discussion, although not directly related to the ancient world, is F. Braudel (trans. S. Reynolds) *The Mediterranean and the Mediterranean world in the age of Philip II* (London, 1972).
2. E. Pulgram, *The tongues of Italy* (Cambridge, Mass., 1958), pp. 210–16; M. Nava, "Greek and Adriatic influences in Daunia in the early Iron Age", in J-P. Descoeudres (ed.), *Greek colonists and native populations* (Oxford and Canberra, 1990).
3. E. T. Salmon, *Samnium and the Samnites* (Cambridge, 1965), pp.14–27.
4. Salmon, *Samnium and the Samnites*, pp. 33–186.
5. M. W. Frederiksen, "Changes in patterns of settlement" in *Hellenismus in MittelItalien*, P. Zanker (ed.) (Göttingen, 1976), pp. 341–55; J. R. Patterson, "City, settlement and elite in Samnium and Lycia", in J. Rich and A. Wallace-Hadrill (eds), *City and country in the ancient world* (London, 1990), pp.146–68.
6. M. Pallottino, *A history of earliest Italy* (London, 1991).
7. Pallottino, *A history of earliest Italy*, pp. 99–110.
8. p. 39. See also Salmon, *Samnium and the Samnites*, pp. 77–100; T. J. Cornell, "The conquest of Italy", in *Cambridge Ancient History* VII.2 (Cambridge 1989), pp. 351–9.
9. M. Pallottino, *The Etruscans* (Harmondsworth, 1976); Pallottino, *A history of earliest Italy*.
10. M. W. Frederiksen, *Campania* (London, British School at Rome, 1984), pp. 117–33.
11. K. Lomas, *Rome and the western Greeks. Conquest and acculturation in Southern Italy* (London, 1993), pp. 39–57.
12. E. Gabba, "Urbanizzazione e rinnovamenti urbanistici nell'Italia centro-meridionale del I sec. a. C." *Studi classici e orientali* 21, (1972), pp. 73–112; Frederiksen, "Changes in patterns of settlement", pp. 341–55; Patterson, "City, settlement and elite".
13. For a full discussion of Augustan symbolism, see P. Zanker, *The power of images in the age of Augustus* (Ann Arbor, 1988).
14. A. Woodman and D. West (eds), *Poetry and politics in the age of Augustus* (Cambridge, 1984); C. A. Powell (ed.), *Roman poetry and propaganda in the age of Augustus* (Bristol, 1992).

15. F. G. B. Millar, "Italy and the Roman Empire. Augustus to Constantine", *Phoenix* **40** (1986).
16. Gabba, "Urbannizzazione e rinnovamenti"; Patterson, "City, settlement and elite".
17. G. W. Bowersock, *Augustus and the Greek World* (Oxford, 1965), pp. 81–4; Lomas, *Rome and the western Greeks*, pp. 174–85.
18. F. Brown, *Cosa: The making of a Roman town* (Ann Arbor, 1980), pp. 1–13 .
19. Gabba, "Urbanizzazione e rinnovamenti".
20. Full lists of buildings, with maps and statistics, are given by H. Jouffroy, *La construction publique en Italie et dans l'Afrique Romaine* (Strasbourg, 1986). For discussion see P. Gros, *Architecture et société à Rome et en Italie centro-méridionale aux deux derniers siècles de la République* (Brussels, 1978).
21. C. Renfrew and J. Cherry (eds), *Peer polity interaction and socio-political change* (Cambridge, 1986), pp.1–18.
22. Patterson, "City, settlement and elite".
23. E. D. Rawson, *Intellectual life in the late Roman Republic* (London, 1985), pp.19–37.

Chapter One

1. E. T. Salmon, *Samnium and the Samnites* (Cambridge, 1965), pp. 28–186.
2. M. Pallottino, *A history of earliest Italy* (London, 1991), pp. 97–125; K. Lomas, *Rome and the western Greeks. Conquest and Acculturation in southern Italy* (London, 1993), pp. 34–37.
3. M. W. Frederiksen, *Campania* (London, 1984), pp. 117–33.
4. Salmon, *Samnium and the Samnites*, pp. 187–95.
5. Salmon, *Samnium and the Samnites*, pp. 188–213; T. J. Cornell "The conquest of Italy", pp. 359–62.
6. Frederiksen, *Campania*, pp. 207–12.
7. Salmon, *Samnium and the Samnites*, pp. 214–54, Cornell; "The conquest of Italy", pp. 368–91.
8. For example, Livy 9.32.1, 41.8; 10.3.6, 9.1–9,14.1–9.
9. Sora (303 BC), Alba Fucens (303 BC), Carseoli (298 BC), Narnia (299 BC).
10. P. Leveque, *Pyrrhos* (Paris, 1957); P. R. Franke, "Pyrrhus". *Cambridge Ancient History* 2nd edn VII.2, pp. 456–68; Lomas, *Rome and the western Greeks*, pp. 47–57.
11. Salmon, *Samnium and the Samnites*, pp. 288–92.
12. Salmon, *Samnium and the Samnites*, pp. 340–97; A. Keaveney, *Rome and the unification of Italy* (London, 1987), pp. 117–30.
13. P. A. Brunt, *Italian manpower* (Oxford, 1971).
14. Livy 27.10, 29.15.
15. E. Gruen, *The Hellenistic world and the coming of Rome*, (Berkeley and Los Angeles, 1984), pp. 145–57; Lomas, *Rome and the western Greeks*, pp. 62–4.
16. Livy 24.1.1–3.15, 25.8.3–13.10,25.15.2–5; Pol. 8.24.7.
17. Lomas, *Rome and the western Greeks*, pp. 68–70.
18. Livy 21.48.
19. For a full account of the Capuan secession, see Livy 23.1–11.
20. Livy 27.25.
21. Livy 29.21.8.

Chapter Two

1. A. N. Sherwin-White, *The Roman citizenship*. 2nd edn (Oxford, 1973), pp. 38–58.
2. M. Humbert, *Municipium et civitas sine suffragio* (Rome, 1978).
3. Sherwin-White, *The Roman citizenship*, pp. 35–58.
4. A. Keaveney, *Rome and the unification of Italy* (London, 1987), pp. 3–39 .
5. Dion. Hal. 4.24, T. J. Cornell, "Rome: the history of an anachronism", in A. Molho, K. Raaflaub and J. Emlen (eds), *City-states in classical antiquity and medieval Italy* (Ann Arbor,1994), pp. 53–70.
6. Sherwin-White, *The Roman citizenship*, pp. 35–6.
7. Sherwin-White, *The Roman citizenship*, p. 121.
8. Sherwin-White, *The Roman citizenship*, p. 154.
9. E. T. Salmon, *Roman colonisation under the Republic* (London, 1969).
10. Salmon, *Roman colonisation*.
11. Livy 34.45.4–5, 53.2; Vell. Pat. 1.14.7.
12. Livy 39.23.3–4.
13. Sherwin-White, *The Roman citizenship*, pp. 98–118.
14. e.g. Livy 39.20.1, 38.10; 42.31.1–9, 35.4–7.
15. P. A. Brunt, *Italian manpower* (Oxford, 1971) pp. 85–7, 278–84.
16. Livy *Per.* 14; Vell. Pat. 1.14.7.
17. J. Pedley, *Paestum* (London 1990), pp. 113–14.
18. F. Brown, *Cosa: The making of a Roman town* (Ann Arbor, 1980).
19. For instance, the city of Fundi, which had alliances with both Rome and Privernum. Livy 8.19.4–13.
20. *ILLRP* II, 516 (Callatis); *IGRR* IV. 1028 (Astypalaia); R. Sherk, *Roman documents from the Greek east* (Baltimore, 1969), no. 26d (Mytilene).
21. Cic. *Balb.* 53.
22. *ILLRP* II, 516; *IGRR* IV. 1028; Sherk, *Roman documents from the Greek east*, no. 26d.
23. W. V. Harris, *War and imperialism in Republican Rome, 327–70* BC (Oxford, 1979).
24. A. J. Toynbee, *Hannibal's legacy* (Oxford, 1965), I. pp. 424–6; Brunt *Italian manpower*, pp. 545–8.
25. Livy 39.20.1, 38.10; 42.31.1–9, 35.4–7.
26. Sherwin-White, *The Roman citizenship*, pp. 120–5; E. S. Gruen, *The Hellenistic world and the coming of Rome* (Berkeley and Los Angeles, 1984), pp.14–16.
27. Cic. *Balb.* 46, 50, *Arch.* 6; Gruen, *The Hellenistic world and the coming of Rome*, p.14.
28. W. V. Harris, *Rome in Etruria and Umbria* (Oxford, 1971).
29. *CIL* 1².158; Plin. *NH* 5.36, 7.136.
30. See also no. 139.
31. Sherwin-White, *The Roman citizenship*, pp. 120–5.
32. Livy 8.26.6.

Chapter Three

1. Livy 30.43–5.
2. Livy 33.48–9.

3. See Chapter 1.
4. Livy 31.29.9–10, 38.42.5–6, 39.39.8–10.
5. P. A. Brunt, *Italian manpower, 225 BC–AD 14* (Oxford, 1971), pp.168–70.
6. A. J. Toynbee, *Hannibal's legacy* (Oxford, 1965); Brunt, *Italian manpower*, pp. 269–77; K. Hopkins, *Conquerors and slaves* (Cambridge, 1978), pp. 1–74.
7. Brunt, *Italian manpower*, pp. 269–77.
8. Brunt, *Italian manpower*, pp. 168–70.
9. S. L. Dyson, *Community and society in Roman Italy* (Baltimore and London, 1991), pp. 50–55.
10. Pol. 30.20.7, 31.10.
11. J. Hatzfeld, "Les Italiens résident à Delos", *BCH* 36 (1912), 1–202 and *Les trafiquants Italiens dans l'orient Héllenique* (Paris, 1919) provides lists of examples.
12. A. J. N. Wilson, *Emigration from Italy in the Republican age of Rome* (Manchester, 1966); L. Moretti "Problemi di storia Tarentina", *Taranto nella civiltà della Magna Grecia. Atti di 10 Convegno sulla studi di Magna Grecia* (1971), pp. 57–66.
13. E. Rawson, *Intellectual life in the late Roman Republic* (London, 1985), pp. 1–18.
14. A. G. Gossage, "The comparative chronology of inscriptions relating to the Boeotian festivals in the first half of the first century BC", *ABSA* **70** (1975), pp. 115–34.
15. Wilson, *Emigration from Italy*, pp. 13–18.
16. Plin. *NH*. 34.34, 34.40.
17. Brunt, *Italian manpower*, pp. 278–84.
18. Y. Sochat, "The lex agraria of 133 BC and the Italian allies", *Athenaeum* **48** (1970), pp. 25–45; D. Stockton, *The Gracchi* (Oxford, 1979).
19. Livy 44.17; A. Keaveney, *Rome and the unification of Italy* (London, 1987), pp. 48–50.
20. J. S. Richardson, "The ownership of Roman land. Tiberius Gracchus and the Italians", *JRS* **70** (1980), pp.1–11.
21. G. P. Verbrugghe, "The *elogium* from Polla and the First Slave War", *Class. Phil.* **68** (1970), pp. 23–35; B. Nagle "The failure of the Roman political process in 133 BC", *Athenaeum* **48** (1970), pp. 111–28; M. W. Frederiksen, "The Contribution of archaeology to the agrarian problem of the Gracchan period", *DdA* **4/5** (1971), pp. 330–57.
22. E. Greco, *Magna Grecia* (Bari, 1981), pp. 163–7.
23. L. Keppie, *Colonisation and veteran settlement in Italy, 47–14 BC* (London, 1983), pp. 143–7.
24. M. H. Crawford, *Roman statutes* (London, 1995).
25. F. de Polignac and M. Gualtieri, "A rural landscape in western Lucania", in G. Barker and J. A. Lloyd (eds), *Roman landscapes. Archaeological survey in the Mediterranean region* (London, 1991), pp. 194–203.
26. E. S. Gruen, *Studies in Greek culture and Roman policy* (Leiden, 1990), pp. 37–88.
27. Livy 39.17.6.
28. Livy 39.18.8–9.
29. Livy 40.43.7.
30. Plut. *Aem*. 38; Plin. *NH* 33.56.
31. Dyson, *Community and society*, pp. 44–6.
32. Cic. *Rep*. 1.31, 3.41; Richardson, "The ownership of Roman land".
33. T. P. Wiseman, "Roman republican road building", *PBSR* 28 (1970), pp. 122–35.

Chapter Four

1. Livy 39.3.4–5.
2. E. T. Salmon, "The cause of the Social War", *Phoenix* 16 (1962), pp. 107–19.
3. P. A. Brunt, "Italian aims at the time of the Social War", *JRS* 55 (1965), pp. 90–109.
4. A. Keaveney, *Rome and the unification of Italy* (London, 1987), pp. 53–5.
5. G. Tibiletti, "La politica delle colonie e città Latine nella guerra sociale", *RIL* 86 (1953), pp. 45–63.
6. Brunt, "Italian Aims", pp. 90–91.
7. P. A. Brunt, *Italian manpower* (Oxford,1971), pp. 425–34.
8. Livy 27.9–10.
9. Livy 29.15–16.
10. Keaveney, *Rome and the unification of Italy*, p. 15.
11. Sall. *Jug.* 59.4; App. *Num.* fr.3; Plut. *Marius* 8.
12. Keaveney, *Rome and the unification of Italy*, 53–55.
13. E. Badian, "Roman politics and the Italians 131–91 BC", *DdA* 4/5 (1970/71), pp. 385–91; Brunt, "Italian Aims".
14. Keaveney, *Rome and the unification of Italy*, pp. 81–7.
15. Keaveney, *Rome and the unification of Italy*, pp. 87–92.
16. E. T. Salmon, *Samnium and the Samnites* (Cambridge, 1965), pp. 340–5; Keaveney, *Rome and the unification of Italy*, pp. 118–22.
17. K. Lomas, *Rome and the western Greeks. Conquest and acculturation in southern Italy* (London, 1993), pp. 92–4.
18. E. A. Sydenham, *The coinage of the Roman Republic* (London 1952), nos. 619–21, 628, 640–41.
19. Diod. 37.2.4; Keaveney, *Rome and the unification of Italy*, pp. 122–3.
20. For an outline of the events of the war, see Salmon, *Samnium and the Samnites*, pp. 354–87; Keaveney, *Rome and the unification of Italy*, pp. 131–93.
21. Cic. *Arch.* 8.
22. U. Laffi, "Sull'organizzazione amministrativa dell'Italia dopo la guerra sociale", *Akten des IV Internationalen Kongresses für Griechisches und Lateinisches Epigraphik* (Munich 1972), pp. 37–53; W. Eck, *Die Staatliche Organisation Italiens in der hoher Kaiserzeit* (Munich 1979).
23. Lomas, *Rome and the western Greeks*, pp. 174–85.
24. P. Castren, *Ordo Populusque Pompeianus. Polity and society in Roman Pompeii* (Rome, 1975); Cic. *Sull.* 60–62.
25. M. H. Crawford, *Roman statutes* (London, 1995).
26. Cic. *Rep.* 1.31, 3.41.
27. J. S. Richardson, "The ownership of Roman land: Tiberius Gracchus and the Italians", *JRS* 70 (1980), pp. 1–11; Keaveney, *Rome and the unification of Italy*, pp. 48–50.
28. Plut. *G. Gracch.* 10.
29. Badian, "Roman Politics and the Italians", pp. 385–91.
30. Val. Max. 9.2.
31. Cic. *Att.* 6.1.
32. Cic. *Att.* 6.1, 6.2.
33. Badian, "Roman Politics and the Italians", pp. 385–91; Keaveney, *Rome and the unification of Italy*, pp. 61–70.

34. cf. Sen. *ad Marc.* 16.4.

35. Cic. *Leg.* 2.31, 2.41, *Dom. Suo* 41, 50; Diod. 37.10.

36. App. BC 1.37; Val. Max. 8.6.4; Cic. *Brut.* 304.

37. Vell. Pat. 2.20.2; Keaveney, *Rome and the unification of Italy*, pp. 170–1.

38. A fragment of Sisenna (fr. 17P) makes an obscure reference to the creation of two new tribes by L. Calpurnius Piso, a tribune of 89 BC.

39. Gaius, *Inst.* 2.274.

40. Cic. *Fam.* 13.30.

Chapter Five

1. F. G. B. Millar, "Italy and the Roman Empire. From Augustus to Constantine", *Phoenix* **40** (1986).

2. Dio 48.33.1; Cic. *Brut.* 1.17.4; R. Syme, *The Roman Revolution* (Oxford, 1939), pp. 129–30.

3. Cf pp. 81–4.

4. Suet. *Aug.* 5–7.

5. A. Woodman and D. West (eds), *Poetry and politics in the age of Augustus* (Cambridge, 1984); C. A. Powell (ed.), *Roman poetry and propaganda in the age of Augustus* (Bristol, 1992).

6. P. Zanker, *The power of images in the age of Augustus* (Ann Arbor, 1988).

7. L. Keppie, *Colonisation and veteran settlement in Italy, 47–14 BC* (London, 1983), pp. 114–22.

8. K. Lomas, "The idea of a city. Elite ideology and the evolution of urban form in Italy, 200 BC – AD 200", in H. Parkin (ed.), *Beyond the consumer city*. (forthcoming).

9. J. R. Patterson, "Crisis: what crisis? Rural change and urban development in imperial Apennine Italy", *PBSR* **55** (1987), pp. 115–46.

10. pp. 221.

11. Suet. *Aug.* 64.

12. M. Corbier, "Fiscus and patrimonium: The Saepinum inscription and transhumance in the Abruzzi", *JRS* **73** (1983), pp. 126–31.

13. No.86; Plut. *Aem.* 38; Plin. *NH* 33.56.

14. Keppie, *Colonisation and veteran settlement*, pp. 114–22

15. G. Woolf, "Food, poverty and patronage. The significance of the Roman alimentary inscriptions in the epigraphy of early imperial Italy", *PBSR* **59** (1990).

16. SHA *Vit Had.* 6.7, *Vit Ant.* 3.1.

17. cf. Dio 71.32.2.

18. N. Purcell, "Wine and wealth in ancient Italy", *JRS* **75** (1985), pp. 1–19.

19. Patterson, *JRS* (1987), pp. 115–46; P. Arthur, *Romans in northern Campania* (London, 1991), pp. 81–7.

20. cf. No. 360

21. Suet. *Tib.* 48; Tac. *Ann.* 2.33, 3.55.

22. Woolf, "Food, poverty and patronage".

23. Tac. *Ann.* 15.68–9

24. For Augustus as *pater patriae*, cf. RG 35.1; Suet. *Aug.* 58.2.

Chapter Six

1. M. Weber (trans. D. Martindale and G. Neuwirth), *The city* (New York and London, 1958), M. I. Finley, *The ancient economy* (London, 1985), C. R. Whittaker, "Do theories of the ancient city matter?", in T. J. Cornell and K. Lomas (eds), *Urban society in Roman Italy* (London, 1995), pp.11–19.
2. P. Leveau, "La ville antique et l'organisation de l'espace rurale: villa, ville, village", *Annales ESC* 4 (1983), pp. 920–42; D. Engels, *Roman Corinth* (Chicago, 1990).
3. W. F. Jaschemski, *The gardens of Pompeii* (New York, 1979).
4. T. J. Cornell, "Warfare and urbanization in Roman Italy", in Cornell and Lomas, *Urban society*, pp. 121–35.
5. N. Purcell, "Wine and wealth in Ancient Italy" *JRS* 75 (1985), pp. 1–19; "The Roman *villa* and the Landscape of Production", in Cornell and Lomas, *Urban society*, pp. 151–80.
6. Purcell, "Wine and wealth", pp. 1–19.
7. Purcell, "The Roman villa and the landscape of production", pp. 151–80.
8. A. J. Toynbee, *Hannibal's legacy* (Oxford, 1965); P. A. Brunt, *Italian manpower* (Oxford, 1971); K. Hopkins, *Conquerors and slaves* (Cambridge, 1978).
9. J. C. Carter, "Rural settlement at Metaponto", in G. Barker and R. Hodges (eds), *Archaeology and Italian society* (Oxford, 1981), vol.2, pp.167–78.
10. A. Small, *Gravina. An Iron Age settlement in south-east Italy* (London, 1991).
11. P. De Neeve, *Colonus* (Leiden, 1984); S. L. Dyson, *Community and Society in Roman Italy* (Baltimore and London, 1991); P. Arthur, *Romans in northern Campania* (London, 1991).
12. J. R. Patterson, "Crisis: what crisis? Rural change and development in Imperial Appennine Italy", *PBSR* 55, 115–46; "Settlement, city and elite in Samnium and Lycia", in J. Rich and A. Wallace-Hadrill (eds), *City and country in the ancient world* (London,1991), pp. 147–68; Arthur, *Romans in northern Campania*, pp. 81–7.
13. Arthur, *Romans in northern Campania*, pp. 81–7.
14. Patterson, "Crisis: what crisis?".
15. M. A. Cotton, *The late Republican villa at Posto, Francolise* (London, 1979); G. deBoe "Villa romana in località Posta Crusta", *NSc* (1976), 516–30.
16. T. W. Potter, *The changing landscape of South Etruria* (London 1979); Arthur, *Romans in northern Campania*, pp. 63–7; F. De Polignac and M. Gualtieri, "A rural landscape in western Lucania", in G. Barker and J. A. Lloyd (eds), *Roman landscapes. Archaeological survey in the Mediterranean region* (London, 1991), pp. 194–203.
17. De Polignac and Gualtieri, "A rural landscape in western Lucania", pp. 194–203.
18. J. C. Carter, "Rural settlement at Metaponto", pp.167–78.
19. D. Ridgway, "Archaeology in Sardinia and southern Italy", *Archaeological Reports*, 1989, 130–47; J. C. Carter, "Crotone", in *Crotone. Atti di 23o convegno sulla studi di Magna Grecia* (Naples 1984), pp. 169–77.
20. Cato, *Agr. passim.*
21. Patterson, "Crisis: what crisis?"; see also Patterson, "Settlement, city and elite" and Purcell, 'Wine and wealth".
22. W. Jongman, *The economy and society of Pompeii* (Amsterdam 1988), pp. 97–154.
23. Plin. *NH.* 14.70.
24. Petr. *Sat.* 28–79; J. H. D'Arms, *Commerce and social standing in ancient Rome* (Cambridge, Mass. 1981), pp. 97–120.
25. J. Andreau, "A propos de la vie financière à Pouzzoles: Cluvius et Vestorius", in M.

Cèbelliac-Gervasioni (ed.), *Les bourgeoisies municipales Italiennes aux IIe et Ier siècles av. J.-C.* (Paris and Naples 1983), pp. 9–20.

26. J. Hatzfeld, "Les Italiens résident à Delos", *BCH* **36** (1912), pp. 2–218, *Trafiquants Italiens dans l'orient Hellenique* (Paris 1919).

27. K. Hopkins, "Taxes and trade in the Roman Empire (200 BC – AD 400)", *JRS* **70** (1980), 101–25.

28. Cornell, "Warfare and urbanization", pp. 127–32.

29. Jongman, *Economy and society of Pompeii*; W. O. Moeller, *The wool trade of ancient Pompeii* (Leiden, 1976).

30. Jongman, *Economy and society of Pompeii*, pp. 155–86; Moeller, *The wool trade of ancient Pompeii*.

31. J. M. Frayn, *Markets and fairs in Roman Italy* (Cambridge 1993), p. 111.

32. Jaschemski, *The gardens of Pompeii*.

33. P. Arthur, "Problems of the urbanization of Pompeii: excavations 1980–81", *Antiquities Journal* **66** (1986), 29–44; K. Lomas, "The city in south-east Italy. Ancient topography and the evolution of urban settlement, 600–300 BC", *Accordia Research Papers* **4** (1993).

34. Frayn, *Markets and fairs*, pp. 61–4.

35. Plin. *Epist.* 5.13.

36. cf. Cic. *Offic.* 2.76.

Chapter Seven

1. C. Geertz, *The interpretation of cultures* (New York, 1973), pp. 87–125; J. A. North, "Conservatism and change in Roman Religion", *PBSR* **44** (1976), pp. 1–12.

2. H. H. Scullard, *Festivals and ceremonies of the Roman Republic* (London, 1961); R. M. Ogilvie, *The Romans and their gods* (London, 1986), pp. 10–12.

3. North, "Conservatism and change", pp. 1–12.

4. M. Beard, "A complex of times. No more sheep on Romulus' birthday" *PCPS* **213** (1987), pp. 1–15.

5. cf. R. Gordon, "From Republic to Principate: priesthood, religion and ideology", in M. Beard and J. A. North (eds), *Pagan priests* (London 1990), pp. 179–98 for the suggestion that the very obscurity of ancient rites may have strengthened the position of the elite and the *status quo* by reinforcing popular perception of priests as having access to knowledge denied to the rest of the population.

6. E. Greco, *Magna Grecia* (Bari, 1981), 171–2.

7. G. Giannelli, *Culti e miti della Magna Grecia* (Florence,1960); K. Lomas, *Rome and the western Greeks. Conquest and acculturation in southern Italy* (London 1993), pp. 130–31.

8. Dio 55.8.

9. M. Pallottino (trans. J. Cremona), *The Etruscans* (London, 1976), pp. 138–52. On methodological approaches, see N. Spivey and S. Stoddart, *Etruscan Italy* (London 1990), pp. 110–26.

10. M. Torelli, "Un *templum augurale* d'età repubblicana a Bantia", *RAL* **21** (1966), pp. 293–315; F. Coarelli, *Lazio* (Bari, 1982), pp. 370–7.

11. E. S. Gruen, *Culture and national identity in Republican Rome* (London 1993), pp. 86–8.

12. Livy 5.20–21.

13. Livy 27.16.8; Plut. *Marc.* 21.3–4, *Fab.* 22.6; Gruen, *Culture and national identity*, pp. 101–3.
14. Lomas, *Rome and the western Greeks*, pp. 134–41.
15. P. Zanker, *The power of images in the age of Augustus* (Ann Arbor, 1988).
16. I. E. M. Edlund, *The gods and the place* (Stockholm, 1987).
17. E. T. Salmon, *Samnium and the Samnites* (Cambridge, 1965), pp. 94–101.
18. M. J. Strazzulla and B. de Marco, *Il santuario sannitico di Pietrabbondante* (Rome, 1982); F. Coarelli and A. La Regina, *Abruzzo Molise* (Bari, 1984), pp. 230–57.
19. J. R. Patterson, "Settlement, city and elite", in J. Rich and A. Wallace-Hadrill (eds), *City and country in the ancient world* (London, 1990).
20. E. Greco, *Magna Grecia* (Bari 1980), pp. 171–2.
21. R. Whitehouse and J. Wilkins, "Greeks and natives in south-east Italy: Approaches to the archaeological evidence", in T. C. Champion (ed.), *Centre and periphery. Comparative studies in archaeology* (London, 1989).
22. H. Jouffroy, *La construction publique en Italie et dans l'Afrique romaine* (Strasbourg 1986).
23. A. and M. de Vos, *Pompeii, Ercolano, Stabia* (Bari, 1982).
24. A. Comella "Complessi votive in Italia in epoca medio–e tardo-repubblicana", *MEFRA* 93 (1981), pp. 717–803; J. A. North, "Religion and rusticity", in T. J. Cornell and K. Lomas (eds), *Urban society in Roman Italy* (London 1995), pp. 135–50.
25. P. F. Dorcey, *The cult of Silvanus. A study in Roman folk-religion* (New York, 1992); North, "Religion and rusticity", pp.142–3.
26. M. Beard, "Priesthood in the Roman Republic", in Beard and North, *Pagan Priests* (London 1990), pp. 18–48.
27. J. Johnson, *Inscriptions at Minturnae I. The Republican magistri* (New York, 1933).
28. For discussion of these cults, see R. Lane Fox, *Pagans and Christians* (London, 1987), pp. 64–101.
29. E. S. Gruen, *Studies in Greek culture and Roman policy* (Leiden 1990), pp. 34–77.
30. P. Poccetti, *Nuove documenti Italici* (Pisa, 1979), No. 175; M. Lejeune, "Inscriptions de Rossano di Vaglio", *RAL* **8.26** (1971), 663–84.
31. cf. Strab. 6.254 on Lucanian dictators.
32. Tac. *Ann.* 14.5–6; *CIL* 10.6638.
33. Dion. Hal. 6.17.2.
34. M. Beard, "Ancient literacy and the function of the written word in Roman religion" in J. H. Humphreys (ed.), *Literacy in the Roman world* (*JRA* supp. 3, 1991), pp. 35–58.
35. Lomas, *Rome and the western Greeks*, pp. 172–82.
36. For other examples, cf. *IG* 14.618–621 and *SEG* 29. 987–9.

Chapter Eight

1. Tac. *Germ.* 16.
2. In Tac. *Hist.* 4.64, the Germans define their Roman cities as symbols of slavery.
3. M. H. Crawford (ed.), *Roman statutes* (London, 1995).
4. *FIRA* 28.
5. K. Lomas, *Rome and the western Greeks. Conquest and acculturation in southern Italy* (London, 1993), pp. 170–86.
6. M. W. Frederiksen, "Changes in patterns of settlement", in P. Zanker (ed.), *Hellenismus in*

MittelItalien (Göttingen, 1976), pp. 341–55; P. Arthur, *Romans in northern Campania* (London, 1991), pp. 44–5, 58–62.

7. Frederiksen, "Changes in patterns of settlement".

8. F. Coarelli, *Lazio* (Bari, 1984), p. 238; Frederiksen, "Changes in patterns of Settlement".

9. W. Jongman, *The economy and society of Pompeii* (Amsterdam, 1988), pp. 292–301.

10. Arthur, *Romans in northern Campania*, pp. 61–2.

11. M. W. Frederiksen (ed. N. Purcell), *Campania* (London, 1984), pp. 264–84.

12. *CIL* 9.338.

13. S. L. Dyson, *Community and society in Roman Italy* (Baltimore and London, 1991), pp. 204–5; P. Garnsey, "Aspects of the decline of the urban aristocracy in the empire", *ANRW* **2.1** (1974), 229–52.

14. Garnsey, "Aspects of the decline of the urban aristocracy"; F. Jacques, *Le privilège de liberté: politique imperiale et autonomie municipale dans les cités de l'Occident romain* (Rome, 1984).

15. The principal texts are *Pro Plancio, Pro Roscio Amerino, Pro Cluentio* and *Pro Sulla*. For discussion, see Dyson, *Community and society*, pp. 56–88.

16. R. M. Laurence, *Roman Pompeii: space and society* (London, 1994), p. 23.

17. P. Castrèn, *Ordo populusque Pompeianus: polity and society in Roman Pompeii* (Rome, 1975).

18. Jongman, *Economy and society of Pompeii*, pp. 289–329.

19. H. Mouritsen, *Elections, magistrates and municipal elite. Studies in Pompeian epigraphy* (Rome, 1988); "A Note on Pompeian epigraphy and social structure", *Classica et Medievalia* **61** (1990), pp. 131–49.

20. H. Mouritsen, "Municipal elites in Pompeii and Herculaneum", in H. Parkin (ed.), *The Roman city: New approaches* (forthcoming).

21. See Chapter 4.

22. D. Johnson, "Munificence and *Municipia*. Bequests to towns in classical Roman law", *JRS* **75** (1985), pp. 105–25.

23. J. Nichols, "Pliny and the patronage of communities", *Hermes* **108** (1980), pp. 365–85.

24. Crawford, *Roman statutes*.

25. F. Sartori, *Problemi di storia costituzionale Italiota* (Rome, 1953), pp. 39–41.

26. Frederiksen, *Campania*, pp. 264–7.

27. *CIL* 10. 847–8.

28. T. P. Wiseman, "Cicero *Pro Sulla* 61–2"; *LCM* **2** (1977); 61–2, Laurence, *Roman Pompeii*, p. 23.

29. cf. *CIL* 10.1018, R. Duncan-Jones, "Age rounding, illiteracy and social differentiation in the Roman Empire", *Chiron* **7** (1977), pp. 333–53, Castren, *Ordo populusque Pompeianus* p.117, and Jongman, *Economy and society of Pompeii*, pp. 287–8.

30. *CIL* 4.791, 1059.

Chapter Nine

1. G. Alföldy, *The social history of Rome* (New Jersey, 1975), pp. 106–15.

2. M. Lefkowitz, "Influential women", in A. Cameron and A. T. L. Kuhrt, *Images of women in antiquity* (London, 1983), pp. 49–64; R. van Bremen "Women and wealth" *ibid.*, pp. 223–42.

3. J. R. Patterson, "Crisis: what crisis? Rural change and urban development in imperial Appennine Italy", *PBSR* **55** (1987), pp. 115–46; J. R. Patterson, "City, settlement and elite in Samnium and Lycia", in J. Rich and A. Wallace-Hadrill (eds), *City and country in the ancient world*, (London, 1990), pp. 146–68.

4. G. Camodeca, "Ascesa al senato e rapporti con i territori d'origine Italia", *Epigrafia e ordine senatorio* (Rome, 1982).

5. G. Woolf, "Food, poverty and patronage. The significance of the Roman alimentary inscriptions in the epigraphy of early imperial Italy", *PBSR* **59** (1990), pp. 197–228.

6. *FIRA* **28**, 130.

7. P. Veyne (trans. B. Pearce), *Bread and circuses. Historical sociology and political pluralism* (London, 1990), p. 10.

8. Veyne, *Bread and circuses*, pp. 10–11.

9. H. Jouffroy, *La construction publique en Italie et dans l'Afrique Romaine*. (Strasbourg, 1986); P. Gros, *Architecture et société à Rome et en Italie centro-méridionale aux deux derniers siècles de la République*, (Brussels, 1978).

10. Lefkowitz, "Influential women", pp. 58–62; van Bremen, "Women and wealth", pp. 223–42.

11. Woolf, "Food, poverty and patronage".

12. F. G. B. Millar, "Italy and the Roman Empire. Augustus to Constantine", *Phoenix* **40** (1986); J. R. Patterson, "The Emperor and the cities of Italy", in T. J. Cornell and K. Lomas (eds), *Euergetism and municipal patronage in Roman Italy* (forthcoming, 1996).

13. Alföldy, *The social history of Rome*, pp. 146–56.

14. Juv. *Sat.* 3 is the most exaggerated example, but cf. J. P. V. D. Balsdon, *Romans and aliens*, (London, 1979), pp. 30–71 for a survey of the evidence.

15. R. Duthoy, "La fonction sociale de l'augustalité", *Epigraphica* **36** (1974), pp. 134–54.

16. *CIL* **10**. 3686–8.

17. Susini, No. 117 (Lupiae), *EE* 8.57 (Tarentum); S. L. Dyson, *Community and society in Roman Italy* (Baltimore and London) 1992, p. 164.

18. Dio 55.13; Suet. *Aug.* 65.20.

Bibliography

Andreau, J. 1974. *Les affaires de Monsieur Jucundus*. Rome.

—1977. Fondations privées et rapports sociaux en Italie romaine (Ier–IIe s. ap. J. C.). *Ktema* **2**, pp. 157–209.

Arthur, P. 1986. Problems of the urbanization of Pompeii: excavations 1980–81. *Antiquities Journal* **66**, pp. 29–44.

—1991. *Romans in northern Campania*. London.

Badian, E. 1971. Roman politics and the Italians (133–91 BC). *DdA* **4–5**, pp. 373–409.

—1972. Tiberius Gracchus and the beginning of the Roman revolution. *ANRW* **1**.1, pp. 668–731.

Barker, G. 1977. The archaeology of Samnite settlement in Molise. *Antiquity* **51**, pp. 20–24.

Barker, G. & J. A. Lloyd (eds) 1991. *Roman landscapes. Archaeological survey in the Mediterranean region*. London.

Beard, M. 1987. A complex of times. No more sheep on Romulus' birthday. *PCPS* **213**, pp. 1–15.

Beard, M. & J. A. North (eds) 1990. *Pagan priests*. London.

Boatwright, M. T. 1989. Hadrian and Italian cities. *Chiron* **19**, pp. 235–70.

Bodei-Giglioni, G. B. 1977. *Pecunia fanatica*: L'incidenza economica dei templi Laziali. *Rivista Storica Italiana* **89**, pp. 33–76.

Bourne, F. C. 1960. The Roman alimentary programme and Italian agriculture. *TAPA* **91**, pp. 47–75.

Braudel, F. (trans. S. Reynolds) 1972. *The Mediterranean and the Mediterranean world in the age of Philip II*. London.

Brown, F. 1980. *Cosa: the making of a Roman town*. Ann Arbor.

Brunt, P. A. 1965. Italian aims at the time of the Social War. *JRS* **55**, pp. 90–109.

—1971. *Italian manpower, 225 BC–AD 14*. Oxford.

Burton, G. P. 1979. The curator rei publicae. Towards a reappraisal. *Chiron* **9**, pp. 464–87.

Carandini, A. 1985. *Settefinestre: una villa schiavistica nell'Etruria romana*. Bari.

Carter, J. C. 1981. Rural settlement at Metaponto. In G. Barker & R. Hodges (eds), *Archaeology and Italian society*. Vol.2, pp. 167–78. Oxford.

Castren, P. 1975. *Ordo populusque Pompeianus. Polity and society in Roman Pompeii*. Rome.

Cébeillac-Gervasioni, M. (ed.) 1983. *Les 'bourgeoisies' municipales italiennes aux II^{ieme} e Ire siècles av. J.-C.* Paris.

Clarke, J. R. 1991. *The houses of Roman Italy, 100 BC–AD 250*. Berkeley and Los Angeles.

Clementi, G. 1972. Il patronato nei collegia dell'impero romano. *SCO* 21, pp. 142–29.

Coarelli, F. 1982. *Lazio*. Bari.

Corbier, M. 1983. Fiscus and patrimonium: The Saepinum inscription and transhumance in the Abruzzi. *JRS* 73, pp. 126–31.

Cornell, T. J. 1994. Rome: The history of an anachronism. In A. Molho, K. Raaflaub & J. Emlen (eds), *City-states in classical antiquity and medieval Italy*, pp. 53–70. Ann Arbor.

Cornell, T. J. & K. Lomas (eds) 1995. *Urban society in Roman Italy*. London.

—(forthcoming) *Euergetism and municipal patronage in Italy*.

Crawford. M. H. 1995. *Roman statutes*. London.

D'Arms, J. H. 1970. *The Romans on the Bay of Naples*. Cambridge, Mass.

—1974. Puteoli in the second century. *JRS* 65, pp. 104–24.

—1981. *Commerce and social standing in ancient Rome*. Cambridge, Mass.

—1984. Upper class attitudes towards *viri municipales* and their towns in the early Roman empire. *Athenaeum* 62, pp. 440–67.

de Neeve, P. W. 1984. *Colonus*. Amsterdam.

de Ruyt, C. 1983. *Macellum. Marché alimentaire des Romains*. Louvain-la-Neuve.

de Vos, A. & M. de Vos 1982. *Pompeii, Ercolano, Stabia*. Bari.

Dixon, S. 1983. A family business: women's role in patronage and politics at Rome, 80–44 BC. *Classica et Medievalia* 34, pp. 91–112.

Dobson, B. 1970. The centurionate and social mobility during the principate. In C. Nicolet and C. Leroy (eds), *Recherches sur le structures sociales dans l'antiquité classique*. pp. 99–116. Paris.

Duncan-Jones, R. 1977. Age rounding, illiteracy and social differentiation in the Roman Empire. *Chiron* 7, pp. 333–53.

—1982. *The economy of the Roman empire*, 2nd edn. Cambridge.

Duthoy, R. 1979. "Curatores rei publicae" en occident durant le principat. *Ancient Society* 10, pp. 171–238.

—1984–6. Le profil social des patrons municipaux en Italie sous le haut-empire. *Ancient Society*, 15–17, pp. 121–54.

Dyson, S. L. 1991. *Community and society in Roman Italy*. Baltimore and London.

—1978. Settlement patterns in the Ager Cosanus: the Wesleyan University Survey 1974–76. *Journal of Field Archaeology* 5, pp. 251–68.

Eck, W. 1979. *Die Staatliche Organisation Italiens in der hoher Kaiserzeit*. Munich.

Edlund, I. E. M. 1987. *The gods and the place*. Stockholm.

Engels, D. 1990. *Roman Corinth*. Chicago.

Evans, J. C. 1980. Plebs rustica: The peasantry of classical Italy. *AJAH* 5, pp. 19–47, 134–73.

Finley, M. I. 1977. The ancient city: from Fustel de Coulanges to Max Weber and beyond. *CSHS* 18, pp. 305–27.

—1985. *The ancient economy*, 2nd edn. London.

Forbis, E. P. 1990. Women's public image in Italian honorary inscriptions. *AJP* 111, pp. 493–512.

Fracchia, H. & M. Gualtieri 1989. The social context of cult-practices in pre-Roman Lucania. *AJA* 93, pp. 217–32.

Franke, P. R. 1990. "Pyrrhus". *Cambridge Ancient History*, 2nd edn. VII.2, pp. 456–68.

Frayn, J. M. 1993. *Markets and fairs in Roman Italy*. Oxford.

Frederiksen, M. W. 1971. The contribution of archaeology to the agrarian problem of the

Gracchan period. *DdA* **4/5**, pp. 330–57.

—1976. Changes in patterns of settlement. In P. Zanker (ed.), *Hellenismus in Mittelitalien*. Göttingen, pp. 341–55.

—1984. *Campania*. N. Purcell (ed.). London.

Gabba, E. 1972. Urbanizzazione e rinnovamenti urbanistici nell'Italia centro-meridionale del I sec. a. C. *SCO* **21**, pp. 73–112.

Gabba, E. & S. Pasquinucci 1979. *Strutture agrarie e allevamento transumante nell'Italia romana (III–I a. C.)* Pisa.

Garnsey, P. 1970. *Social status and legal privilege in the Roman Empire*. Oxford.

—1979. Where did Italian peasants live. *PCPS* **25**, pp. 1–25.

—1981. Independent freedmen and the economy of Roman Italy under the Principate. *Klio* **63**, pp. 359–71.

Geertz, C. 1973. *The interpretation of cultures*. New York.

Giannelli, G. 1960. *Culti e miti della Magna Grecia*. Florence.

Giardiana, A. & A. Schiavone (eds) 1981. *Società romana e produzione schiavistica*. Rome and Bari.

Gossage, A. G. 1975. The comparative chronology of inscriptions relating to the Boeotian festivals in the first half of the first century BC. *ABSA* **70**, pp. 115–34.

Greco, E. 1981. *Magna Grecia*. Bari.

Gros, P. 1978. *Architecture et société à Rome et en Italie centro-méridionale aux deux derniers siècles de la République*. Brussels.

Gruen, E. S. 1984. *The Hellenistic world and the coming of Rome*. Berkeley and Los Angeles.

—1990. *Studies in Greek culture and Roman policy*. Leiden.

—1993. *Culture and national identity in Republican Rome*. London.

Harris, W. V. 1971. *Rome in Etruria and Umbria*. Oxford.

—1979. *War and imperialism in Republican Rome, 327–70 BC*. Oxford.

Hatzfeld, J. 1912. Les Italiens résident à Delos. *BCH* **36**, pp. 1–202.

—1919. *Les trafiquants Italiens dans l'orient Héllenique*. Paris.

Hermansen, G. 1981. *Ostia. Aspects of city life*. Edmonton.

Hopkins, K. 1978. *Conquerors and slaves*. Cambridge.

—1980. Taxes and trade in the Roman Empire (200 BC–AD 400). *JRS* **70**, pp. 101–25.

Humbert, M. 1978. *Municipium et civitas sine suffragio*. Rome.

Jacques, F. 1984. *Le privilège de liberté: politique impériale et autonomie municipale dans les cités de l'Occident romain*. Rome.

Jaschemski, W. 1979. *The gardens of Pompeii*. New York.

Johnson, D. 1985. Munificence and *municipia*. Bequests to towns in classical Roman law. *JRS* **75**, pp. 105–25.

Jongman, W. 1988. *The economy and society of Pompeii*. Amsterdam.

Jouffroy, H. 1986. *La construction publique en Italie et dans l'Afrique romaine*. Strasbourg.

Kampen, N. 1981. *Image and status: Roman working women in Ostia*. Berlin.

Keaveney, A. 1987. *Rome and the unification of Italy*. London.

Kehoe, D. 1988. Allocation of risk and investment on the estates of Pliny the Younger. *Chiron* **18**, pp. 15–42.

Keppie, L. 1983. *Colonisation and veteran settlement in Italy, 47–14 BC*. London.

Kertzer, D. I. & R.P. Saller (eds) 1991. *The family in Italy from antiquity to the present*. New Haven.

Laffi, U. 1972. Sull'organizzazione amministrative dell'Italia dopo la guerra sociale. *Akten des IV Internationalen Kongresses für Griechisches und Lateinisches Epigraphik* (Munich), pp.

37–53.

Laurence, R. M. 1991. The urban *vicus*: the spatial organisation of power in the Roman city. In E. Herring, R. Whitehouse & J. Wilkins (eds), *The archaeology of power.* vol I. London.

—1994. *Roman Pompeii. Space and society.* London.

Leveau, P. 1983. La ville antique et l'organisation de l'espace rurale: villa, ville, village. *Annales ESC* 4, pp. 920–42.

Leveque, P. 1957. *Pyrrhos.* Paris.

Lomas, K. 1993. *Rome and the western Greeks. Conquest and acculturation in southern Italy.* London.

—(forthcoming). The idea of a city. Elite ideology and the evolution of urban form in Italy, 200 BC–AD 200. In H. Parkin (ed.) *The Roman city: New approaches.*

Meiggs, R. 1973. *Roman Ostia.* 2nd edn. Oxford.

Millar, F. G. B. 1986. Italy and the Roman Empire. From Augustus to Constantine. *Phoenix* 40, pp. 295–318.

Moeller, O. 1976. *The wool trade of ancient Pompeii.* Leiden.

Moretti, L. 1971. Problemi di storia Tarentina. *Taranto nella civiltà della Magna Grecia. Atti di 10 Convegno sulla studi di Magna Grecia,* pp. 57–66.

Mouritsen, H. 1988. *Elections, magistrates and municipal elite. Studies in Pompeian epigraphy.* Rome.

—1990. A note on Pompeian epigraphy and social structure. *Classica et Medievalia* 61, pp. 131–49.

—(forthcoming). Municipal elites in Pompeii and Herculaneum. In H. Parkin (ed.), *The Roman city: New approaches.*

Mrozek, S. 1972. Crustulum et mulsum dans les villes Italiennes. *Athenaeum* 50, pp. 294–300.

Nagle, B. 1970. The failure of the Roman political process in 133 BC. *Athenaeum* 48, pp. 111–28.

—1973. An allied view of the Social War. *Athenaeum* 77, pp. 367–78.

Nichols, J. 1980. Pliny and the patronage of communities. *Hermes* 108, pp. 365–85.

North, J. A. 1976. Conservatism and change in Roman religion. *PBSR* 44, pp. 1–12.

Ogilvie, R. M. 1986. *The Romans and their gods.* London.

Ostrow, S. 1985. Augustales along the Bay of Naples. A case for their early growth. *Historia* 34, pp. 64–101.

Owens, E. J. 1991. *The city in the Greek and Roman world.* London.

Painter, K. (ed.) 1980. *Roman villas in Italy.* London.

Pallottino, M. 1976. *The Etruscans.* Harmondsworth.

—1991. *A History of earliest Italy.* London.

Patterson, J. R. 1987. Crisis: what crisis? Rural change and urban development in imperial Apennine Italy. *PBSR* 55, pp. 115–46.

Pedley, J. 1990. *Paestum.* London.

Poccetti, P. 1979. *Nuove documenti Italici.* Pisa.

Potter, T. W. 1979. *The changing landscape of South Etruria.* London.

—1987. *Roman Italy.* London.

Purcell, N. 1985. Wine and wealth in ancient Italy. *JRS* 75, pp. 1–19.

Rathbone, D. 1983. The slave mode of production in Italy. *JRS* 73, pp. 160–68.

Rawson, E. D. 1985. *Intellectual life in the late Roman Republic.* London.

Rich, J. & A. Wallace-Hadrill (eds) 1991. *City and country in the ancient world.* London.

Richardson, L. 1988. *Pompeii: an architectural history.* Baltimore.

Richardson, J. S. 1980. The ownership of Roman land. Tiberius Gracchus and the Italians. *JRS* 70, pp. 1–11.

Ruoff-Väänän, E. 1978. *Studies on the Italian fora*. Helsinki.

Salmon, E. T. 1962. The cause of the Social War. *Phoenix* **16**, pp. 107–19.

—1965. *Samnium and the Samnites*. Cambridge.

—1969. *Roman colonisation under the Republic*. London.

Sartori, F. 1953. *Problemi di storia costituzionale Italiota*. Rome.

Schmidt-Pantel, P. (ed.) 1992. *A history of women. From ancient goddess to Christian saints*. Cambridge, Mass. and London.

Scullard, H. H. 1961. *Festivals and ceremonies of the Roman Republic*. London.

Shenk, R. 1969. *Roman documents from the Greek East*. Baltimore.

Sherwin-White, A. N. 1973. *The Roman citizenship*, 2nd edn. Oxford.

Skydsgaard, J. E. 1974. Transhumance in ancient Italy. *ARID* **7**, pp. 7–36.

—1980. Non-slave labour in rural Italy during the late Republic. In P. Garnsey (ed.), *Labour in the Graeco-Roman world*. Cambridge.

Small, A. 1991. *Gravina. An Iron Age settlement in south-east Italy*. London.

Sochat, Y. 1970. The lex agraria of 133 BC and the Italian allies. *Athenaeum* **48**, pp. 25–45.

Spivey, N. & S. Stoddart 1990. *Etruscan Italy*. London.

Spurr, S. 1986. *Arable cultivation in Roman Italy*. London.

Strazzulla, M. J. & B. de Marco 1982. *Il santuario sannitico di Pietrabbondante*. Rome.

Sydenham, E. A. 1952. *The coinage of the Roman Republic*. London.

Syme, R. 1939. *The Roman revolution*. Oxford.

Tchernia, A. 1988. *Le vin d'Italie romaine*. Paris.

Tibiletti, G. 1953. La politica delle colonie e città latine nella guerra sociale. *RIL* **86**, pp. 45–63.

Todd, M. 1985. Forum and capitolium in the early Empire. In F. Grew & B. Hobley (eds), *Roman urban topography in Britain and the Western Empire*. London.

Torelli, M. 1966. Un *templum augurale* d'età repubblicana a Bantia. *RAL* **21**, pp. 293–315.

Toynbee, A. J. 1965. *Hannibal's legacy*. Oxford.

Verbrugghe, G. P. 1970. The *elogium* from Polla and the First Slave War. *Class. Phil.* **68**, pp. 23–35.

Veyne, P. 1990. *Bread and circuses*. London.

Wallace-Hadrill, A. (ed.) 1988. *Patronage in ancient society*. London.

Wallace-Hadrill, A. 1994. *Houses and society in Pompeii and Herculaneum*. Princeton.

Weber, M. (trans. D. Martindale & G. Neuwirth) 1958. *The city*. New York and London.

Whitehouse, R. & J. Wilkins 1989. Greeks and natives in south-east Italy: Approaches to the archaeological evidence. In T. C. Champion (ed.), *Centre and periphery. Comparative studies in archaeology*. London.

Whittaker, C. R. 1990. The consumer city re-visited: The *vicus* and the city. *JRA* **3**, pp. 110–18.

Wilson, A. J. N. 1966. *Emigration from Italy in the Republican age of Rome*. Manchester.

Wiseman, T. P. 1970. Roman republican road building. *PBSR* **28**, pp. 122–35.

—1971. *New men in the Roman Senate, 139 BC–AD 14*. Oxford.

—1977. Cicero *Pro Sulla* 61–2. *LCM* **2**, pp. 21–2.

Woodman, A. & D. West (eds) 1984. *Poetry and politics in the age of Augustus*. Cambridge.

Woolf, G. 1990. Food, poverty and patronage. The significance of the Roman alimentary inscriptions in the epigraphy of early imperial Italy. *PBSR* **59**, pp. 197–228.

Zanker, P. 1988. *The power of images in the age of Augustus*. Ann Arbor.

Index

271